Family Matters:
Family Breakdown and its Consequences

Family Matters:
Family Breakdown and its Consequences

Patricia Morgan

New Zealand Business Roundtable
Wellington, New Zealand

First published in 2004 by the New Zealand Business Roundtable,
PO Box 10–147, The Terrace, Wellington, New Zealand
http://www.nzbr.org.nz

National Library of New Zealand Cataloguing-in-Publication Data

Morgan, Patricia.
Family matters : family breakdown and its consequences /
Patricia Morgan.
ISBN 1-877148-83-0
1. Family—New Zealand. 2.Marriage—New Zealand. I. New
Zealand Business Roundtable. II. Title.
306.80993—dc 22

ISBN 1–877148–83–0

Typeset by Civitas, London
Printed and bound by Astra Print Ltd, Wellington
Cover design by Richard Gyde, Creative Services, Wellington

Contents

Author

Patricia Morgan, Senior Research Fellow at Civitas: Institute for the Study of Civil Society, is a sociologist specialising in criminology and family policy. Her books include *Delinquent Fantasies*, 1978; *Facing Up to Family Income,* 1989; *Families in Dreamland*, 1992; *Farewell to the Family?*, 1995; *Are Families Affordable?*, 1996; *Who Needs Parents?*, 1996; *Adoption and The Care of Children*, 1998; *Adoption: The Continuing Debate*, 1999; *Marriage Lite*, 2000 and *Children as Trophies*, 2002. She has contributed chapters to *Full Circle, Family Portraits, The Loss of Virtue, Tried But Untested, Liberating Women from Modern Feminism, Just a Piece of Paper?* and *The Fragmenting Family,* as well as articles for periodicals and national newspapers.

Acknowledgments

Thanks are due to all those who provided helpful information and comments on the text of this book, especially Bill Atkin, George Barker, Peter Bushnell, Paul Callister, Sylvia Dixon, Greg Dwyer, Lesley Hall, Ross Judge, Alison Laurie, Barry Maley, Muriel Newman, Jan Pryor, Peter Saunders, Patricia Schnauer, Robert Stephens, Charles Waldegrave, Robert Whelan and Bryce Wilkinson. I am also indebted to John McNeil and the staff of the Maxim Institute for supplying statistics. Special thanks are due to Roger Kerr and his staff at the New Zealand Business Roundtable for their unstinting support and patience during the genesis of this book. Needless to say, any remaining errors are my own.

Foreword

The New Zealand Business Roundtable takes an interest in social policy because it is important for the well-being of all New Zealanders. In 1996 it published *From Welfare State to Civil Society: Towards Welfare that Works in New Zealand* by David Green who was at that time director of the Health and Welfare Unit at the Institute of Economic Affairs in London.[1]

Among other matters, David Green's book examined the rise in family breakdown, out-of-wedlock births and sole parenthood in New Zealand. It found that trends in New Zealand were similar to those of comparable countries and noted some of their origins and consequences:

> Because our eyes have been fixed on 'the economy' we have not been alert to mistaken doctrines which have caused family breakdowns and turned voluntary associations—once sources of that strength of character which insulates nations from tyranny—directly or indirectly into instruments of the state.[2]

This follow-up study, *Family Matters: Family Breakdown and its Consequences*, was commissioned to investigate family issues in greater depth and to contribute to public debate on policies affecting the family in New Zealand. The decision by the government to establish a Families Commission reflects community concern about the state of the family and signals a heightened interest in family policy. On the other hand, the government's Working for Families package in the 2004 Budget, which was announced after this study was completed, was more focused on income levels than on the state of the family.

The author of the study, Patricia Morgan, is a Senior Research Fellow at Civitas: The Institute for the Study of Civil Society in London. She is a sociologist who has written extensively on family policy.

There is a substantial international literature on family breakdown and its social consequences which is drawn on to assess the state of the family in New Zealand. The findings of this investigation are worrying. Patricia Morgan reports that:

> Using all of the standard indicators, the family is now in a worse state in New Zealand than almost anywhere else. The situation of Maori is a particular cause for concern. It is comparable to that of American blacks, amongst whom, in large areas, the family based on marriage has virtually disappeared (p. 3).

Some people have celebrated the decline of the traditional family and view marriage as an oppressive institution or an aberration. However, Patricia Morgan writes:

> ... the married couple and their dependent children living together in their own home ... has been the normative child-rearing institution in Western society, in terms of both prevalence and ideal (pp. 4-5).

vii

She cites a large body of research that finds that the traditional family is generally best for children, parents and society.

This view was recently challenged by the Hon. Steve Maharey, minister of social development and employment, who was reported as stating: 'I know of no social science that says a nuclear family is more successful than other kinds'.[3] No one who reads *Family Matters* will be able to make such a claim in future.

The point is not that children brought up in nuclear families always do better than, say, children brought up by sole parents. Many sole parents do a fine job. Rather, the point is that, on average, two-parent families fare better, and this is what matters for social policy. As a Nobel laureate in economics, George Stigler, pointed out: 'We must base public policy not upon signal triumphs or scandalous failures but upon the regular, average performance of the policy'.[4] Not all smokers die of lung cancer, but most health policy practitioners now agree that smoking is typically bad for health. Similarly, in matters of family policy the evidence in favour of two-parent families suggests it is unwise to bet against the odds. This finding is not a criticism of sole parents.

Some may still contest the conclusions of researchers like Patricia Morgan on family outcomes. The 1992 comment by David Popenoe, Professor of Sociology at Rutgers University in the United States, in *Controversial Truth: Two Parents Are Better*, is relevant in evaluating any such criticisms:

> Social science research is almost never conclusive. There are always methodological difficulties and stones left unturned. Yet in three decades of work as a social scientist, I know of few other bodies of data in which the weight of evidence is so decisively on one side of the issue: on the whole, for children, two-parent families are preferable ... If our prevailing views on family structure hinge solely on scholarly evidence, the current debate would never have arisen in the first place.[5]

More recently, Popenoe has written that, internationally, the tide has turned in response to the weight of evidence:

> In the last decade, even once-hostile academics and media people have reached a consensus about the importance of strengthening married two-parent families; but the change didn't come easily.[6]

The rise in family breakdown in many countries, including New Zealand, since the 1960s didn't happen by accident. People's behaviour is influenced by incentives. Patricia Morgan attributes the New Zealand trends in large part to changed incentives arising from changes in such areas as welfare policies (especially the Domestic Purposes Benefit), taxation and family law, as well as to changes in social attitudes, particularly those influenced by some versions of feminism. The good news, however, is that incentives can be reshaped by better policies and ideas. This is the challenge to social policy makers trying to go forward.

Family Matters: Family Breakdown and its Consequences documents family policy changes and their impact on the institution of the family in New Zealand, and calls for greater support for public policies which signal that family stability is important for children and society as a whole. While not necessarily endorsing all of its findings, the Business Roundtable believes the book is a thorough and thought-provoking study and is pleased to publish it as a contribution to debate on a vital topic.

Roger Kerr
Executive Director, New Zealand Business Roundtable

Section A

The Family in New Zealand
From Boom to Bust

1

The Fission in the Nucleus of the Family

Summary: All Western nations have witnessed a decline in the institution of the family based on marriage. Indicators of this decline are falling marriage rates and rising divorce rates, linked with falling overall fertility, accompanied by rising numbers of out-of-wedlock births. In New Zealand these trends have been remarkable in their intensity. In the period following the second world war, the family was particularly strong and popular. Using all of the standard indicators, the family is now in a worse state in New Zealand than almost anywhere else. The situation of Maori is a particular cause for concern. It is comparable to that of American blacks, amongst whom, in large areas, the family based on marriage has virtually disappeared. The 'fission in the nucleus of the family' which is occurring is of a different order to previous cultural shifts, like the move away from extended families or towards smaller families.

In the short span of time since organised European settlement began in the mid-nineteenth century, New Zealand has shown the most extreme manifestations of family trends which, while observable in other—particularly English speaking—societies, have occurred at a pace and on a scale that are unrivalled elsewhere.

In the post-war world, dominant opinion was emphatic that the family was *not* declining:

> [A] higher proportion of the adult population than ever before is married; an increasing number of young men and women marry before their majority; the shortening of time between marriage and the first child is a measured fact; more people than ever before are married for a longer period of their life span'.[1]

The rise in fertility was sharper in New Zealand than anywhere else, and it lasted much longer; with the peak not coming until the mid-1960s. The women born around 1940 had an average of 3.5 children each, while their mothers had had 2.5.[2] All of this applied as much or more to ethnic minorities as it did to the European population:

> Reckoned by age groups, the proportion of Maori adults who are married is consistently higher than that of non-Maori, the proportion of the never-married population lower. In 1961, of those aged between 16 and 21, eight per cent of the

3

males and 22 per cent of the females were married, compared with 2.1 per cent and 13 per cent for non-Maori males and females respectively. Maori marriages are broken by death earlier and more often than those of non-Maori ... On the other hand, fewer Maori are legally separated or divorced. [3]

By the 1970s these trends were all in reverse. The key features of family decline and fragmentation, which this book will explore, are a decrease in two-parent households and an increase in sole parents, a big rise in the number of children born ex-nuptially, a decline in marriage and an overall fall in births.

Figure 1:1
Percentage of dependent children in sole-parent households

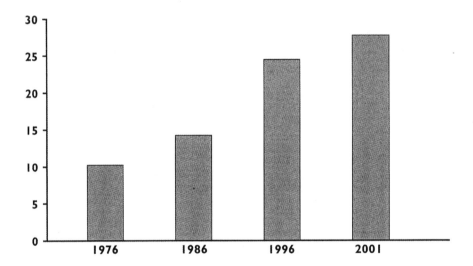

Source: Statistics New Zealand

This now begs a question, which hardly arose in the past, of how to define or characterise a family, or the family. Minimally, when we speak of family we are referring to a group of people connected by blood, marriage or legal adoption. In this sense, all or most of us have, or have had, family relationships or family ties, and we may live with family members in a two- or even three-generational unit. Marriage brings what are initially non-kin relationships—but ones vital to the creation and maintenance of further kin relationships—into their orbit, although a childless couple have, by themselves, rarely been construed as 'a family', but as a married couple. Through marital relationships, as the core of the family system, children are affiliated to adult males as well as females. The married couple and their dependent children living together in their own home, providing support and care for each other, has been the normative child-rearing institution in Western society, in terms of both prevalence and ideal. With the latter, the 'family' is precisely a morally loaded concept embodying an ideal image or model of relationships, to be striven for independently of the numbers approximating to it.

The 'problem of definition' emerged when the family became the focus of attention as something problematic, optional and disposable. It then became one among many, even an 'infinite diversity of families', often as the least among equals, and certainly the one destined to die out. With derogatory intent, it is described as the 'bourgeois' (i.e. oppressive) family, the 'nuclear' (residual and suffocating) family, the 'traditional' (reactionary) family or the 'patriarchal' (enslaving) family.

By 2001, an estimated 27 per cent of New Zealand children under 16 lived in households headed by a sole parent—nearly three times the proportion in 1976 (see Figure 1:1). Forty-four per cent of Maori children were with sole parents, as were 31 per cent of Pacific Island children and 20 per cent of European children.[4] Thirty-one per cent of New Zealand families with dependent children were headed by a sole parent. Sole-parent families trebled as a proportion of all families with dependent children between 1976 and 2001 (see Figure 1:2).

Figure 1:2
Families headed by sole parents as a percentage of all families with dependent children, New Zealand, 1976 - 2001

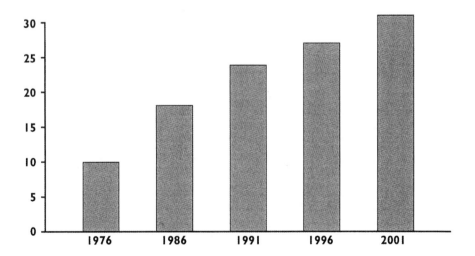

Source: Statistics New Zealand

The rate of increase has been most rapid for Pacific Island people, amongst whom sole mothers increased from 21 per cent to 30 per cent of all mothers in the decade 1986-1996. Amongst Maori, they increased from 31 per cent to 43 per cent.[5]

A study of the dynamics of family formation and dissolution in New Zealand suggested in 1987 that possibly 40 per cent of all children who start life in two-parent families may end up with a sole parent by 16 years of age.[6] When those born to sole parents were included, the number of children who would spend time with a sole parent increased to a half. While the prospects of a child who experienced family breakdown re-entering a two-parent family were relatively high (nearly three-quarters, or 71 per cent in five years), these unions are particularly unstable.[7] Thus:

> ... the hope that entry into a two-parent family will resolve the problems of single parent families proves to be vain. ... many children are likely to encounter multiple family situations arising from successive family formation and breakdown. For this cohort, by the age of nine years in the region of 27 per cent had experienced at least two family situations and 18 per cent had encountered three or more family situations; the maximum family changes recorded was 25 during a nine year period.[8]

Where Sole Parents Come From:
Broken Marriages to No Marriages

The proportion of children with widowed parents has dropped significantly, so that the growth of lone parenthood partly reflects the sharp rise in divorce in recent decades, with a higher-than-average rate of marriage breakdown among Maori. Until 1961, the level of divorce in New Zealand was around three divorces per thousand married women. This increased to just over seven in 1976. After the Family Proceedings Act 1980, which came into effect in 1981, rates shot up, and then settled to between 12 or 13 per thousand in the 1990s (see Figure 1:3, p. 7). Divorce rates for New Zealand and Australia are now virtually identical and somewhat below those for England and Wales, which have one of the highest rates in the Western world.[9] All of these countries show a very similar pattern, with divorces in cliff-face ascent after legislative reform then levelling off at far higher rates than before.[10] Marriages are ending earlier the more recently they are contracted, and each age-group divorces faster than the one before. The proportion of marriages dissolving within ten years has increased from 11 per cent for those married in 1971 to 15 per cent for those married in 1981 (one-quarter of those married in 1971 had divorced by 1991).

The proportion of divorces involving children and young people under 18 declined from 78 per cent in 1971 to just under a half in

1996—much the same as in Australia but below the UK level of 55 per cent for under-16s, which has pertained since the mid-1980s.[11] Apart from the big drop in family size, another reason may be that, under current legislation, there is no legal advantage in obtaining a formal dissolution unless one or other of the parties wishes to remarry. Marital property agreements can be sought at any time and decisions over custody, access and maintenance decided irrespective of current marital status or behaviour.[12]

Figure 1:3
Divorce rate per 1,000 married women, New Zealand, 1961 - 2001

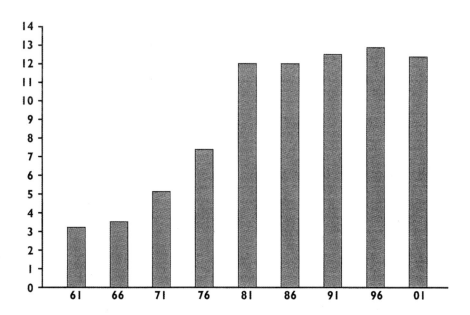

Source: Statistics New Zealand

The rise in sole parents also coincides with the massive rise in the proportion of ex-nuptial births—from eight per cent in 1962 to 44 per cent in 2001 (see Figure 1:4, p. 8). This is higher than England (40 per cent), the USA (33 per cent) and Australia (30 per cent) (see Figure 1:5, p. 9). The result has been that never-married sole parents increased by more than 40 per cent between 1991 and 2001 alone, to become over a third of all sole parents.

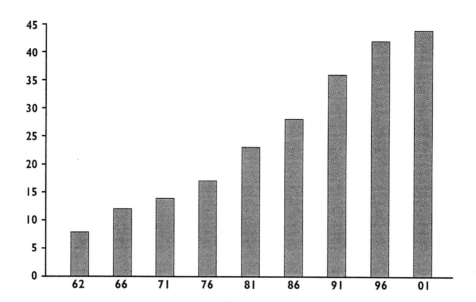

Figure 1:4
Ex-nuptial births as a percentage of all births
New Zealand, 1962 - 2001

Source: Statistics New Zealand

High rates of out-of-wedlock births are accompanied by women's generally low or falling family size, and the total fertility rate has halved since the 1960s (see Table 1:1, p. 10). By the late 1990s, the average number of births per woman, of about 1.9, had fallen below the level required to replace the population, but it has now risen again to something approaching replacement level, partly owing to the higher fertility rates of Maori women. Nevertheless, Maori have experienced one of the most rapid fertility declines of the century.[13]

Figure 1:5
Ex-nuptial births as a percentage of all births, selected countries,
2001 (or latest year available)

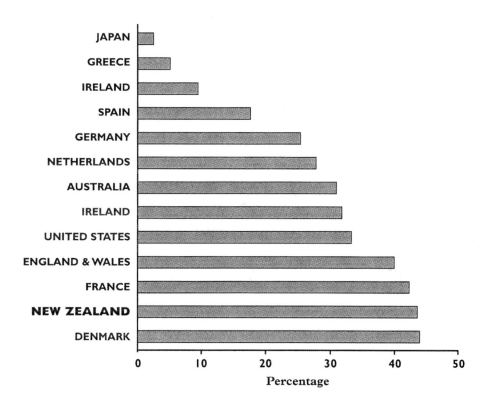

Sources: Eurostat (2002); Australian Bureau of Statistics (2002); Centers for Disease Control and Prevention, US Department of Health & Human Services (2002); Federal Statistical Office, Germany (January 2003); Statistics New Zealand (2002); Office for National Statistics (2002).

Figures for Ireland and the Netherlands are provisional.
Figures for France and Italy are for 2000.
Figures for Greece and Spain are Eurostat estimates for 2000.
Figure for Japan is for 1999.

The decrease in the overall birthrate since the mid-1970s overwhelmingly represents the decline in births to married women.[14] The surge
in the proportion of ex-nuptial births partly represents a big increase
in their actual numbers between 1976 and 2001 from 9,597 to 22,320,
but it also represents a fall in marital births. The marital birthrate in
the 1980s was almost static, then went into sharp decline in the 1990s.
In the year from 1994 to 1995, when there was a slight rise in the
overall birthrate after four years of decline, births to married couples
still fell 2.7 per cent, as those to single mothers rose by 5.9 per cent.[15]
As fewer married women are having second or subsequent children and
more are having no children at all, the rise in sole parents is comple-
mented by increasing numbers of couples without children—now
almost a half of all couples. These are not simply 'empty nesters' whose
children have flown, but represent the increasing postponement and
rejection of parenthood.[16]

Table 1:1
Average number of children born to women in New Zealand,
1962 - 2001

Fertility rate, women 15+

1962	1965	1971	1975	1981	1985	1991	1996	2000	2001
4.19	3.54	3.18	2.37	2.01	1.93	2.1	1.96	2.01	2.01

Fertility rate, Maori women 15+

1962	1965	1971	1975	1981	1985	1990	1996	2000	2001
6.18	5.71	5.05	3.28	2.47	2.2	2.19	2.6	2.53	2.5

Source: *Demographic Trends*, Table 2.8

While the age of married mothers has moved steadily upwards, unwed
child-bearing is mostly and increasingly to young mothers. New
Zealand has the third highest rate of teenage births amongst OECD
countries (behind the US and the UK) and the third highest teenage
abortion rate (after the US and Hungary) (see Figure 1:6, p. 11).[17] The
UNICEF report, from which these figures are taken, draws attention
to the way in which New Zealand's position in the ranking is affected
by the high teenage birth rate among Maori (74 per 1,000 compared
with 30 per 1,000 for non-Maori). Without the Maori component, New
Zealand would fall significantly in the ranking of teenage births.[18]

Figure 1:6
**Births and abortions per 1,000 females aged 15-19,
selected countries, 1996**

Combined number of births and abortions to women
aged below 20 per 1,000 15–19 year olds.

Source: UNICEF, *A League Table of Teenage Births in Rich Nations*, 2001, p. 20.

At the same time, a greater proportion of women of child-bearing age
are single and therefore 'at risk' of having births outside of marriage.
Of women aged 20-24, 60 per cent were married at the 1971 census. By
1981, this was 41 per cent (the 1940s level). By 1986, it had fallen to the
nineteenth century level, of 30 per cent. By 2001, it was 9 per cent.[19]
Age at marriage in New Zealand is higher than at any time since the
1920s.[20] With marriage rates falling (see Figure 1:7), births to single
women, which were rising anyway in absolute numbers, were bound to
represent an increasing proportion of total births. The number of births
to women aged 15-49 who were not legally married increased from
around 37 per 1,000 in the mid-1970s to 47 per 1,000 in 2001. This is
despite the rise in abortions to a record high, of 16,410 in 2001, a 100
per cent increase since 1986. More than a fifth of all pregnancies are
terminated by abortion. Sixty per cent of them are carried out on
unmarried women (nearly 70 per cent of whom are under 25).

Figure 1:7
Marriage rate per 1,000 women aged 16 and over,
New Zealand, 1961 - 2001

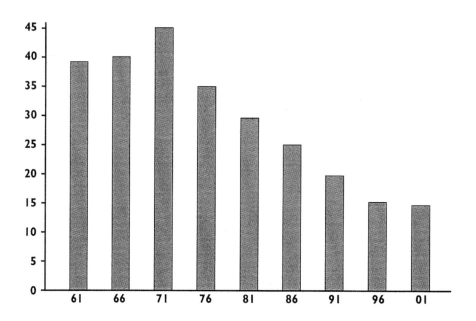

Source: Statistics New Zealand

On census day 1961, half of all men aged 25-34, and two-thirds of those aged 35-44, were married and raising two or more children. Even larger numbers would pass through this phase during their lifetimes. The percentage of males never married in the 20-24 age group increased from 63 to 93.3 per cent between 1961 and 1997: for the 25-29 age group it rose from 29.7 per cent to 66.3, with a similar rise for those aged 30-34 from 16.9 per cent to 37.8 per cent.[21] Remarriages have fallen as well as first marriages, even if these have increased as a proportion of all marriages throughout the 1970s and 1980s. The rising number of sole parents is not the only result of a falling marriage rate: one-*person* households have doubled since the 1970s and became 22.9 per cent of the total in 2001.[22]

Falling marriage rates are not fully accounted for by the rise of cohabitation. Thirty per cent of women aged 15 to 44 years in all 'partnerships' were unmarried in 2001. Divorcees are becoming increasingly likely to cohabit rather than remarry (representing over a quarter of cohabitees), and the relative proportions marrying directly or cohabiting first have been reversed for younger women. However, two-thirds of all women under 30 were unmarried and not cohabiting in 2001, compared with 53 per cent in 1981.[23] The overall Maori cohabitation rate was already relatively high in 1986 at over 11.6 per cent for people aged 15 and over, and had risen to 17.3 per cent in 2001, but this has not made up for the fall in the proportion not living with a spouse.[24]

One reason cohabitation is not replacing marriage is that it tends to be short-lived. This is why there are so few cohabitations in the population at any one time, even if many people embark upon it.[25] In the UK the median duration of a childless cohabitation is 19 months, before it leads to a birth, marriage or terminates.[26] By three years, three-quarters of women have had a birth, got married or dissolved the union. After ten years, only about five per cent are still cohabiting (and 8.7 per cent of those who have their first child in cohabitation). This is similar for America, where about 45 per cent of the cohabitations of those in the National Longitudinal Survey of Youth ended either in marriage or dissolution by the first year, 70 per cent by the second year and 90 per cent by five years.[27] The Australian Family Formation Project also found that around a half of cohabitations end after two years in either dissolution or marriage, and three-quarters by four years.[28] Cohabitations are less likely to lead to marriage than in the past. In contrast, dissolving the union or having a child have become far more common for younger people. Although a greater proportion of US cohabitations end in marriage, similar trends are recorded in that country.[29] The nature and meaning of cohabitation may change over time, so that this may move from being (usually) a prelude, or alternative to marriage, to become a 'live-in' liaison, which younger people are increasingly likely to end by separation.

As such, cohabitation delays—and, it seems, impedes and probably prevents—marriage, in New Zealand as elsewhere. This is because cohabitation has become the dominant mode of first partnership: in 2001 more women under 25 were cohabiting than were married (76 per cent), reversing the position in 1986. But, since cohabitations break up at a higher and faster rate than marriages, this leaves more people 'unpartnered' in the longer term. After a first cohabiting partnership has dissolved, the median duration to the next partnership is five years in the UK, leaving marriage surrounded by longer periods of partnered or unpartnered singlehood over the lifetime. After the first or subsequent 'partnership' breaks down, many people may not try again.

The historical exception to present trends is usually given as the much parodied and 'untypical' 1950s and 1960s, when early and nearly universal marriage became the norm. Present times are then cast as a return to previous patterns. For example, between 1901 and 1911 more than 80 per cent of people aged 20-24 had not married. The 1996 figure may be higher, at around 90 per cent, but claims are that this falls when consideration is taken of cohabitations or *'de factos'* (making nearly 30 per cent 'partnered').[30] However, present *de factos* may have nothing like the survival rate of the later marriages made in the early twentieth century.

Cohabitation is also a speedy route into sole parenthood, since the processes by which families are formed act as important determinants of family survival. By 1996, nearly a third of Maori children with two parents were with unmarried couples compared with 14 per cent in 1981.[31] (The general proportion of children with cohabiting couples rose to 13.5 per cent.)[32] The proportion of ex-nuptial births with paternal information on the registration form increased to over three-quarters by 1996 and the proportion jointly registered at the same address rose to nearly 43 per cent by 1996, suggesting cohabitation.

The use of the term *de facto* and even *'de-facto* marriage' for cohabitation, suggesting that this is marriage, in reality, minus the documents, and that, whether married or not, the participants are all equally 'partners', obscures many important distinctions and understandings that bear upon outcomes. While it may be the official belief that '... many children today are born to and raised by couples who may never marry each other',[33] the 'raised' is often doubtful. Neither the objective evidence on the outcomes of cohabiting unions nor the expectations of those involved indicate that cohabitation is a stable alternative to marriage.[34] Estimates for the UK, where nearly three-fifths of first births outside marriage are born in first cohabitational unions, are that about 40 per cent of these dissolve to produce a never-married lone mother within five years and a half in ten years.[35] While cohabitations with children have a slightly lower dissolution rate than those without children, ultimately more of these dissolve compared with cohabitations of childless women, because children actually reduce the chances of marrying. Thus: 'child-bearing within cohabiting unions does not signal longer-term commitments' even if it does 'signal longer cohabitations'.[36]

Worldwide evidence is that existing cohabitations *with children* tend to break up at four- to five-fold the rate of marriages.[37] In the Christchurch Child Development Study, cohabitation is a foremost risk factor for breakdown of the child's family in its first five years. As many as 43.9 per cent of *de facto* couples separated, compared with 10.9 per cent of married couples.[38] Even teenage mothers who have a child within marriage are more likely to still be with their first 'partner' in their 30s than those who began parenthood as cohabitees: one in two compared with one in three in the UK data. Australian data on parents 18 months after the birth of a child show that 19 per cent of cohabiting couples had already separated, compared with only two per cent of married couples—a difference of nearly ten-fold. Where parents wed after the birth of a child, about 15 per cent of these marriages break up within five years, compared with 38 per cent of the relationships of continuing cohabitees.[39]

When a fertile cohabiting union is converted to marriage, the parents are less likely to split up than if they continued as cohabitees, but the children are still more likely to see their parents eventually separate than those born in marriage, something which applies worldwide.[40] In Britain, 75 per cent of couples who wed after the birth of a child were still together five years after the birth, compared with 92 per cent of the married and 48 per cent of the cohabitees. Less successful cohabitees have more unstable relationships compared with those who enjoy better socio-economic conditions in the British data, just as the less materially successful among the married are particularly vulnerable to divorce. If economic circumstances worsen from one year to the other, both have 50 per cent more chance of breaking up, and conversely, 50 per cent more chance of surviving if conditions improve.[41] However, with economic and other factors like age and duration controlled for, the odds of dissolution are still at least twice as high for cohabiting couples compared with married ones.

The substitution of cohabitation for direct marriage is also implicated in the postponement of—and possible relinquishment of—motherhood, especially given that the fall in the birthrate is accounted for by declining marital births. This might particularly help account for the large fall in fertility for women aged 20-29. While there has been a big increase in children born to the unmarried, and while this may be linked to more widespread cohabitation, cohabiting women have lower fertility than comparable married women. Larger numbers and proportions of non-marital births may reflect increased exposure to risk, which is nonetheless accompanied by a higher rejection of parenthood than within marriage. In New Zealand, 40 per cent of cohabiting couples have children, compared with 57 per cent of married couples. Almost half (46 per cent) have only one child, compared with a third of married couples, who are also more likely to have three or more children. (Married women averaged 2.6 children, and women who cohabit recorded 1.2 in the 1996 census.) This cannot be explained by the younger age profile of cohabiting couples, although this may be an important reason why more are likely to have a child under five than married couples. [42]

Marriage Can Disappear

As fewer adults enter into marriage, more leave it in divorce and separation, and more and more avoid it with single parenthood or cohabitation, marriage can disappear.[43] This has already largely happened amongst American blacks, for whom it ' has become just a temporary stage of life ... preceded by a lengthening period of single-hood and followed by a long period of living without a spouse ... a long stable marriage is the exception, rather than the rule'.[44] In 1940, blacks in the USA in every age group were more likely to marry than whites. In 1960, three-quarters of African American children were born to married couples, and over two-thirds of black children lived in two-parent homes. By the 1990s, most black children (54 per cent) lived with a mother only, another three per cent with a father only and seven per cent with neither parent. Some 58 per cent of black sole-parent mothers have never married. Only about one third of divorced or separated black women remarried within ten years of marriage breakdown, compared with almost three-quarters of non-Hispanic whites. Only 27 per cent of African American children aged 12 to 18 years old lived in their parents' first, intact marriage—something which has occurred within a very short historical time period.[45]

This is 'not a racial anomaly or localised pathology', but something that can happen to other groups, other societies. It will soon be the Maori reality. In 1996, just under 35 per cent of Maori aged 16 and over were married, compared with almost double, or nearly 63 per cent, 20 years before. The proportion who had never married increased from 29.4 per cent to just over 50 per cent.[46] And, if what has happened to the black American family is not much different from what is happening to the American family as a whole, the same applies to the generality of

New Zealand families. Maori are moving into the same position as American blacks and we might expect to find that New Zealand European families will increasingly resemble present-day Maori families.

The Fission in the Nucleus of the Family

The downward trend in fertility has been swifter in New Zealand than elsewhere, given a relatively higher birthrate in the 60s and 70s than in other developed countries. However, the population still grows by 1.1 per cent a year compared with 0.4 per cent for England and Wales, or by 6.6 per cent between 1991 and 1996 (double the previous inter-census period). Net immigration accounted for 39 per cent of this growth, mainly from China, Taiwan, Korea, and Hong Kong as well as from the UK, Japan and India. (In the previous period 1986-91, departures exceeded arrivals.)[47] While migrants initially increase the working-age group, they subsequently swell the numbers in older groups. In turn, their birthrates rapidly fall to the level of the host population. The number of elderly is expected to grow from 12 per cent in 1996 to 17 per cent in 2021, and to 26 per cent by 2051. They will outnumber children two-to-one. Assuming medium levels of fertility, mortality and an annual long-term net migration gain of 5,000, New Zealand can expect its youth population (aged 12-25) to drop from 21 per cent of the total population in 1996 to 18 per cent in 2021 and to 15 per cent in 2051. In 1966, for every 100 working-age persons aged 15-59, there were 21.7 people aged 60 or over. In 1991, this was 25.1; by 2031, this will be 45.5. The number of people in the labour force for every superannuitant will be halved—from 4:1 to 2:1.[48]

It is as trite as it is profound to note that the survival of any society depends upon its ability to reproduce itself physically, socially and culturally, and its fortunes upon the qualities of the next generation:

> [T]he adult heterosexual relationship is inherently, if not inevitably, generative. We must assume that societies which have survived could not have allowed this generative, and regenerative, centre to remain 'unsocialised'—to be without rules, to be disordered and uncertain and to put reproduction at risk. The young must not only be brought into the world, there must be *regular* and predictable arrangements for their care; they must be socially 'placed' or 'legitimated' lest they become unmanageable and dangerous aliens. This cannot be, without great risk, a haphazard and brief process.[49]

Human beings depend upon a lengthy educative process to equip each generation with the skills, knowledge and possessions essential for the survival and success of individuals and society. To this end:

> ... kinship units ... provide continuous, long-term care, individual legal identity, rights and obligations in relation to persons, property rights and claims of

descent and inheritance, which serve ... distant interests of social renewal, continuity and culture.[50]

No society could have survived without making sure its children were raised by parents who took responsibility for them and, until some (abandoned) experiments of the twentieth century, no one thought that any other individuals or institutions could take over this responsibility. By producing, caring for, and educating children, families create and contribute to the good of the wider society. In looking after dependents, the family is also the primary welfare institution, just as it is basic to social order and solidarity.

The fission in the nucleus of the family is of a different and more threatening order than other historical changes that, for example, involved a move away from extended families, or towards small families, or from polygamy to monogamy.

2

Dancing on the Grave of the Family

Summary: The decline of the family has been celebrated, rather than mourned, in some quarters. The traditional family based on marriage is described as oppressive, with 'new family forms' offering the opportunity for free expression. In fact, none of these family forms is new: there have always been broken and incomplete families. What is new is the scale of their occurrence. Critics of the traditional family represent it as a minority household type, but this involves the use of artificially restrictive definitions. There is also a rewriting of history which involves the denial that the family based on monogamous marriage was ever the norm in Western society. This is coupled with unrealistic expectations of what the loss of traditional family ties will mean for people in the future, since extended families depend upon nuclear families. Those hostile to traditional families have used Maori to argue that monogamous marriage was an artificial restriction imposed on people who were living happily in informal unions. In fact this misrepresents the history of Maori. Claims that illegitimacy was of no consequence in Maori culture, and that there were no special ties between parents and their biological children, are simply untrue.

Even more remarkable than the speed and scale of family fragmentation in New Zealand has been the insistence that nothing unusual is happening. Just as the nuclear family based on marriage was idolised in the 1950s, so its disintegration is applauded today. While the same can be said about the reception given to similar developments in the rest of the English speaking world, that in New Zealand has been often little short of euphoric. In 2000 Steve Maharey, the Minister of Social Services and Employment, urged everyone to accept that the days of the European-style family unit were long gone. Over two-thirds of children still lived in one, but it was being replaced by new sole-parent, reconstituted and extended families. These deserved support, he claimed, rather than the old family structure. So long as these were 'able to provide love, discipline and sound nurturing, things are going to be OK'.[1]

19

Support for Marriage Abandoned

Nowhere else has the family been so emphatically rejected, and the 'polymorphous perversity' of the counter-culture so explicitly endorsed, with its demands for 'a practical project for the acceptance of diverse sexualities and for the democratisation of the sexual sphere'.[2] Obligingly, the state will service the 'widest possible range of interests and needs' with 'sexuality being an emblem of the diverse society New Zealanders wish to nurture ...'[3] Nowhere has the programme of leftist feminism been so thoroughly pursued, as a 'task ... to provide both the institutional and ideological support for different family forms, and to eliminate women's economic dependence on men and factors which encourage domestic violence'.[4] It might illustrate how trends arrive late, swiftly, and in exaggerated form, making New Zealand 'prey to capture by imported intellectual viruses that—like so many introduced pests and diseases—take hold with unnatural virulence'.[5]

The twenty-first century has been entered with marriage more or less abandoned as a public institution. Its demotion has been speedy, as is the elevation to equal status of homosexual relationships which were illegal two decades ago.

The Property (Relationships) Amendment Act 2001 now requires anybody breaking up from a live-in relationship to share property on the same basis, whether same or opposite sex, if the relationship is three years old (or, in some circumstances, even if it is not—as when there is a child). De facto or same-sex partners can now claim widow or survivor partner pensions, or maintenance from a previous partner. They can challenge wills, or ask to be provided for in the absence of a will in the same way as spouses.

The only quibbles are over 'remaining elements of marriage unacceptable to cohabitants (essentially state control over the duration and the prohibition of concurrent relationships)', where it might seem 'excessively Euro-centric to insist that for a relationship to be in the nature of marriage it must be monogamous'.[6] Thus, the law is still accused of discriminating against de factos by not removing the one man, one woman qualification for formal marriage, which would make for one seamless system. While the Property (Relationships) Amendment Act 2001 draws upon assumptions that marriage and cohabitation are really indistinguishable, it does not define cohabitation using the definition of a relationship in the nature of marriage (or 'common law' marriage)—which would make marriage a reference point. Instead, there is just a checklist of factors to take into account when deciding whether various live-in situations meet the criteria for property division. This will be a considerable source of contention, since cohabitation is difficult to define, and often a transitory and precarious state. (When people are already married, or have serial cohabitations, it seems that chronology comes into play for settlements. Where a marriage follows a *de facto* relationship, the partner would normally get half the 'relationship' property, which would then be split with the spouse and so on.)[7]

Obviously, law and public policy, which previously supported marriage, must now intervene to prevent or eradicate such 'discrimination'. Marriage is no longer a public good, but just another personal 'lifestyle', about which we must remain neutral in comparison to other 'lifestyles'. Otherwise, there will be 'unfair distinctions'. As marriage is no longer considered vital or central to the family unit, so it is no more consequential than any other relationship: no way of living is more socially relevant than any other, or can be designated as a family compared with any other.[8] Even a non-sexual flatmate-type arrangement fulfils most of the criteria and may be deemed a *de facto* relationship, equal to marriage as a 'lifestyle choice'.

At the same time as marriage has been seriously weakened, the law endorses fragile unions, which represent a poor bargain and threat for women and children. There is little indication that policy makers and commentators have any grasp of what marriage is and of its social functions, not least when it comes to raising children. The Law Commission claimed that 'a general policy of preferring marriage (as distinct from other relationships) ... cannot be a legitimate aim as these are very arbitrary distinctions'.[9] Antipathy to the institutions of civil order, which stand for the unity, continuity and creative wisdom of the community, has now turned into incomprehension. The drive against discrimination on the grounds of marital status and sexual orientation and equal treatment for all 'lifestyles' has trumped considerations of what is best for society. Recognition of unmarried and 'gay' cohabitation or 'gay marriage' as 'equal lifestyle choices' marks the end of concerns for social stability and continuity in favour of individual rights and personal satisfaction. Indeed, the extension of recognition and rights to different types of households and relationships has been done precisely to undermine marriage, and empty it of significance and worth.

Ironically, marital consequences are imposed on people who wish to live in uncommitted relationships, rather than leaving them free to choose with minimal interference. Giving cohabitation the same status as marriage not only debases marriage, but subjects cohabitees to conditions they are trying to avoid. (This is to be distinguished from the right to make 'living together contracts'—in contrast to participating in a legal status—so that property entanglements are avoided when the relationship breaks down.) Cohabitation is expressly chosen because it is unregulated, and promises the individual freedom from the responsibilities and restrictions of marriage. The reasons for living together are

reducible to convenience, whether legal, economic, social, personal, or
sexual. While marriage has been social and recognised by others, a
relationship or cohabitation is private, and often geared to having a
companion and/or resident sex partner, for the time being, not a spouse.
In contrast, marriage implies a legally defined institution, where the
law and not the parties establish the rules of entry and membership.
Like a corporation, or private property, this has to be publicly supported by law and culture in order to exist. It is:

> ... one example of the way in which the institutions of society give us access to
> experiences impossible—even unimaginable—without them. They show us how
> our untutored moral sense and natural impulses may be given shape, direction
> and consummation through associations and traditions that are necessarily
> social and which predate us. ... The instinct to mate may be transformed from
> simple coupling and procreation into the many-sided moral-legal-kinship order
> of marriage and family formation, through the tutelage of social rules and
> ceremony beyond the wit or power of discrete individuals to formulate or
> implement; but which, when we exploit what they offer, can greatly enlarge what
> unaided instinct can accomplish.[10]

Marriage offers an alternative way of life to cohabitation, based on the
expressed intention that the relationship will be permanent. This
provides scaffolding for investment in an enterprise, where personal
objectives are replaced by joint goals. We assume that what:

> ... falls within the compass of the law must also fall within the compass of
> justice; so the laws governing marriage and divorce should pass the test of justice
> and procedural equity [which include] conceptions of right and wrong conduct,
> no less in marriage than in any other sphere of life that engages the attention of
> the law.[11]

However, marriages terminable at will and the removal of fault (or
breach) as a consideration in settlements imply no penalty for misconduct or opportunistic behaviour and no compensation for marriage-
specific investments. Given 'no-fault' and non-consensual or unilateral
divorce, the party seeking to preserve the marriage also lacks power or
any bargaining tool.

Eradicating failure to meet marital obligations deletes the obligations and duties themselves, which are inferred from legal remedies in
divorce.[12] With transgression 'impossible in the eyes of the law, notions
of responsibility are mocked'.[13] There is no duty to refrain from sex with
persons other than the spouse, since adultery is not a consideration in
dissolution proceedings, and neither is cruelty or desertion. A spouse
can leave, live apart for two years, and dissolve the marriage without
the consent of the other partner and be treated the same in regard to
the property, children and maintenance, however they have behaved.
There is no requirement or reference to expectations that the marriage
be lifelong; the length being up to one or both parties to decide.

As law withdraws from enforcing marital stability, marriage is no longer special or especially worthy or worthwhile to support compared with any other association. Indeed, no other contract can be broken so lightly. This destroys the rights of the majority to have meaningful marriage, and reduces the options available in life, where 'the bitter irony is that this loss is portrayed as a liberation'.[14] With the rights of marriage given to those who do not accept the responsibilities, so, stripped of distinction, status and incentives, marriage becomes irrelevant. The 'piece of paper' has become just one way of proving the existence of a 'live-in relationship'.[15]

Stretching the Definition Until It Tears

Accounts of family trends typically insist that 'the family' does not exist, it never did (and, if it did, it was a bad thing), and there has been no real change.[16] The élite repudiation of that ideal of a married couple and their children, caring for each other in their own home, which served as a model for people's actions and aspirations, now frees everyone to substitute their own idiosyncratic and self-constructed meanings for the traditional ones. 'The family ceases to be an objective given and... instead, it becomes a project of individuals, thus always susceptible of redefinition, reconstruction—and obviously, termination. Being part of a family is replaced by participation in a personal lifestyle'[17]—to which instability and unpredictability are intrinsic. Even alternatives to conventional family life are seen as moral equivalents or substitutes, so that lifestyles without the care of children, enjoyed before parenthood for most people, or instead of this for some, become an alternative form of family life. With the definition of family stretched to cover any living situation, and where any transitional state is equally a 'family', there is only movement between ever transmuting 'family forms'. This leaves nothing to decline or dissolve, concern ourselves with or do anything about—except to endorse the judgement of history and facilitate current developments. Thus, officially: the '... factors that determine family composition (marriage, divorce, fertility) have changed' and broken 'the link between marriage and child-bearing and created varied and more complex family forms'. Among such 'varied and complex family forms' are 'couple-only families', and 'same-sex couple families'.[18] Moreover, as well as '[b]lended families' (which include children from previous unions), and homosexual unions, there are apparently entirely new 'culturally non-normative families' involving 'child-free couples, those who are single by choice, and those who "leave" the supposedly normative sequence (e.g. due to marital breakdown)'.[19] There are also 'dual-career households where both adults are in paid employment, and the wife/mother is also responsible for the bulk of the housework and childcare', as well as 'three-generational families, laterally extended families, and non-family households'—a mystery category this, since even single people are now 'new family forms'.[20]

If there are new developments for New Zealand since the 1960s, what might qualify are drastically declining fertility, reducing the reproductive role of the family (see Table 1:1, p. 10), and a marked increase in life expectancy, with the prospect of children being outnumbered by the elderly for the first time in human history. In the 1970s, when some people began scouting around for 'alternatives', they envisaged 'communal living and sexual swinging',[21] to which might be added 'intimate friendships/networks, innovation in marriage and multilateral marriage.' David Swain might well say that 'multilateral, or group, marriage is virtually unknown as an ideal', since no society anywhere has had marriage involving more than one individual of each sex. In fact, none of the alternative families eagerly predicted in the 1960s and 1970s has materialised. Communes turned out to be a short-lived phenomenon, whose internal contradictions made them incapable of functioning as any 'family form'. The organisation is loose, or virtually non-existent, the members are typically young and tend to be supported from outside (for example through the welfare system), and each commune does not last very long.[22]

It is the numbers rather than the structures which have changed in recent times, given that 'even the most superficial knowledge of European social history tells us that all the much proclaimed "new" developments have precedents of one sort or another'. Childless couples, single people living alone or together, marital breakdowns, putative fathers and ex-nuptial births have occurred whatever sort of family is regarded as the norm in a society. We have always had families without children living at home (since children grow up and leave), and families where mother is the breadwinner and father stays at home to look after the children.[23] The only essential difference is that 'disruptive human relationships existent since the beginning of social life, but always discouraged or restrained ... have been elevated to family status by a simple semantic change'.[24] If the commonplace existence of couples without children, single people, occasional homosexual liaisons, the step-parent acquired after widowhood or divorce, can be described in terms of 'totally new structures',[25] or a 'multitude of complex living arrangements' whose 'range is enormous and continually evolving and growing',[26] then someone needs to get out more.

Across Cultures and Within Cultures

Because family systems vary from culture to culture, it is often assumed that such systems can be random within one culture. Moreover, because family systems are cultural constructs, and

therefore artificial, they must be 'unnatural', wrong and to be relinquished. It is claimed that '[e]ven the definition of family is questionable because the nature of the family changes constantly'.[27] Such
notions parallel others from the 1960s, when the socialisation and
education of children were denounced in terms of an abnormal and
repressive process, since this involved the 'imposition' of a culture on
one generation by another. We are meant to be surprised, even shocked,
that while:

> Sexual intercourse, childbirth and breastfeeding, and even the nurture of the
> young, may be 'natural', ... their context, regulation and practice are socially and
> culturally shaped. Indeed, much of our family life has been invented.[28]

So what? Human beings create the conditions for their own existence,
given their unique capacity to make and observe rules. It can be argued
that it was with the transformation of procreation from biological
processes into morally and legally validated institutions of kinship and
marriage that social organisation emerged in our evolutionary history.
Institutionalised fatherhood is purely the creation of society, exemplifying the rule-making and rule-following without which no culture, and
no human association, is possible.[29] This also tells us that, while
kinship practices vary from society to society, the functions they serve
do not.

Within a society there tends to be a single standard guiding mating,
reproduction and child-rearing, elaborately structured by morality, law,
convention and economy, which is not replaceable with 'a pluralistic
conception of domestic lifestyles'.[30] The characteristic of many of the
living arrangements which are now elevated to the status of 'family
forms' is precisely their lack of permanence and structure. Some lack
any capacity for reproduction. No society has been, or could, be
perpetuated by 'single-person households', or 'same-sex couples'—not,
that is, until cloning and other reproductive technologies become widely
available.

Pointing out that families 'made up of two parents ... account for
merely 40 per cent of all household types' (which one would have
thought was quite a lot), a sneering commentator lines up against them
the 24 per cent without children, the 10 per cent of lone parents, the 19
per cent of one-person households and the six per cent of households
with two or more unrelated persons.[31] He has omitted to notice that
people get older, and—unless spouses die together—they are going to
be widowed, and that children grow up and cannot avoid being single
adults while they are unmarried and childless couples before they
procreate, or if they cannot. With smaller families and longer lives, the
period spent as a couple-and-children unit gets shorter. Even if
everybody got married, stayed married and had children, we would still

have many people alive after their children had grown up and left home, many single people yet to marry or never to marry, and many couples existing prior to having children.

Another way in which dominant opinion has been running ahead of the statistics in its eagerness to announce the demise of the family, is by employing ludicrously restricted definitions of a 'nuclear' or 'traditional' family. Thus, to qualify as a nuclear family, there must be:

> ... a male breadwinner, a female caretaker, and (ideally) two children (one of each sex, the boy being firstborn). This kind of family often seems to be regarded as 'normal'. It is not normal—cross-culturally, historically, or even statistically—in our pluralistic society but it suits a variety of political and religious commentators to assume or argue that it is.[32]

Parents with three children, parents with all girls, and parents with an older girl, do not qualify as a nuclear family, and nor does a family with a mother working in the baker's shop from nine to noon. Moreover, anyone who appears to attribute validity to this 'cornflake' model stands accused of condemning other 'family forms'.[33] Thus, the indictment runs, if we have 'a common belief that the nuclear family —a man, woman and their children—is the normal or natural family', then, by implication, we see the 'single-parent/solo family; adoptive family; child-free/childless family; dual-career family; the reconstituted family; homosexual relationships; the lesbian family; the low-income family; the problem family; the Maori family' ... as 'unnatural, abnormal, deviant'.[34]

In preference to the traditional, nuclear family, the empirical fact of different living arrangements is now elevated into a new morality of 'diverse family forms'.[35] The nuclear family unit then becomes 'a middle age myth'[36], even 'a short sighted and simplistic one', deserving the label of 'the idiocy of the normative nuclear family fallacy'.[37] As formal marriages and cohabitations have become officially treated as equivalent arrangements this is described as a 'value judgement which reflected the changing social reality', when it is nearer the truth to say that social reality has been ordered to fit a value judgement.[38] Even if a majority of children still grow up in one,[39] it is continually maintained that only an unrepresentative rump now live in the conjugal, nuclear family. As 'out of mode',[40] this supposedly exists only in the imaginations of those set upon projecting a nostalgic ideal onto the real world. At the same time, the 'gay family' is seen as a popular, spontaneously emergent 'family form', before anybody knew how many, if any, actually existed. But then the aim has been to 'challenge' definitions of family that involve adults of both sexes (or even children).[41] With 'gay families' endowed with such enormous importance, Minister for Social Development, Steve Maharey proudly announces how 'households with two same sex parents had risen from 0.1 to 0.2 per cent between 1981 and 2001.[42]

Projections of current trends not only have the family swept off the map in the near or far future, but even negate its existence in the past: 'the relative security and long term nature of marriage in the 1930s and 1950s may in fact have been an aberration—caused by a transient combination of low mortality, late age at marriage and low divorce rates—rather than a norm'.[43] Apparently:

> ... there is, and has long been, a diversity of household types in Aotearoa/New Zealand, and 'the family' does not exist. Notwithstanding its non-existence, until quite recently, a variety of social policies and services have been designed on the assumption that the nuclear family is the predominant family form. It is not.[44]

Such claims for New Zealand draw upon wider assumptions that the:

> ... West has always been characterised by diversity of family forms, by diversity of family functions and by diversity in attitudes to family relationships not only over time but at any one point in time. There is, except at the most trivial level, no Western family type.[45]

Or if there was, Marxist/feminist dogma dismisses the Western family as a product and prop of capitalism and a comparatively late development. Since something so disgusting can hardly be the 'basic and fundamental social unit', the 'community and neighbourhood' serves as well, not forgetting *hapu* and *iwi*.[46]

However, families are different from 'household types' and communities and neighbourhoods do not produce and rear children. If their own continuity and persistence is dependent upon families, then so are their cohesion and solidarity dependent upon sentiments of responsibility, commitment and belonging that have their origins in family relations. Marriage has always been used to build 'society's infrastructure, its bridges of social connectedness'.[47] In Maori society, inter-group marriages were seen to '... increase group solidarity by re-uniting lines of descent [from a common ancestor]'. Tending to tie communities together '... they are sometimes called *Taura* (ropes), and were condoned or even sponsored. Peace negotiations ... often included marriages between the parties to the truce, in an effort to ensure the permanency ...'[48]

The Persistence of the Independent Conjugal Household in Western Culture

Far from there never having been a Western family type, the monotonously familiar basic unit for the bearing and rearing of children has been the independent conjugal household, where the husband and wife head up a separate residence—from the thirteenth century or before.[49] There has not been a system on the classic Chinese model, where a number of brothers and their wives occupy a compound ruled over by the eldest male. Neither has there been polygamy, where different

wives and children occupy a harem or separate huts in an enclosure,
nor a marriage system where a woman marries several brothers.
Severe economic circumstances, as in the 1930s, are typically associated with delays and declines in marriages and births, or more single
and childless people, while times favourable to family formation, as in
the couple of decades after the Second World War, see rises.

The 1950s and 1960s may have been historically unusual given the
very high and very early rates of marriages and births,[50] but a pattern
of near universal marriage was present in the mid-nineteenth century.
Pioneer women also had very high birth rates, as seen in Australia,
Canada and the United States, as well as New Zealand, having more
babies by the age of 25 than any cohort since, even those of the 1950s
and 1960s. By the end of the nineteenth century, there was some
contraction as the average age at first marriage rose, then began to fall
again in the early 1900s, with a temporary reversal in the 1930s. Early
settlements in New Zealand contained a predominance of men,
although this can be exaggerated since there were 90 women per 100
males by 1896 and women made up about 43 per cent of the population
overall in the latter half of the nineteenth century.[51] Indeed, a particular pioneer form of nuclearity developed, given that the wider kinship
group was frequently missing. Not only did the family have to turn to
itself for assistance and support, but the relatively late arrival of
industrial production put a premium on self-sufficient and cohesive
family life.

In spite of this, there is the continued recycling of notions of a
natural, eternally fixed rate of marital breakdown, which divorce
simply 'brings ... out in the open, shattering the myth of the idealised
family'.[52] We are continually reminded that divorce is merely a legal
event in the process of marital breakdown and that while 'more people
are seeking divorce, this does not necessarily indicate that more
marriages are unstable or that more are breaking down'.[53] We 'forget
that, in the past, marriages were not long-term/permanent arrangements either: the difference was that death rather than divorce was the
major terminator of relationships'.[54] If there is a problem, given that the
'major difference between death and divorce as the terminator of
relationships is that ... the divorced parents are both still living ...', this
can be overcome by envisaging the two-parent family stretching 'from
within one household to across two households'.[55] Unfortunately,
notions that death used to quickly come along and do the job divorce
has to do today are hardly endorsed by the fact that divorce becomes
less likely the longer the marriage lasts, and the fact that there is an
increase from one cohort to the next in the proportion divorced in each
age-group.[56] Half of the marriages dissolved in 1997 lasted less than

12.6 years, while the lowest risk of divorce, at seven per cent, was for marriages which had lasted over 30 years.[57]

A similar assertion is that '[m]arriage has not gone out of fashion, merely been repositioned and taken a different form'.[58] Apparently, it is 'not at all clear that formal marriage was always the norm, at least outside bourgeois and élite groups'. So now, long-term cohabitation has returned to perform 'the same general familial roles of emotional commitment and a base for reproduction as marriage did, at least during the babyboom ...'.[59] However, a minimum of demographic knowledge makes it crystal clear that formal marriage *was* the historical norm, considering that the illegitimacy rate in England and Wales hovered between three and six per cent for centuries until the 1960s.[60] That marriage has ceased to be regarded as central to the family and society in present times, has no bearing on its status as the ideal and the reality in the past.

Now it seems that the presence of exceptions no longer proves, but obviates, the rule. The need for fathers is denied, given that there were widows, forsaken wives 'seeking support from charity', or 'fathers absent overseas in the Second World War'. Such 'anecdotes underline the fact that fathers have not always been central to family processes ... throughout history and across cultures many children have grown up to be well-rounded adults without this influence'.[61] However, anecdotes can always be found that are compatible with any theory. Wars are emergencies, and widows, or deserted wives, have been objects of sympathy and charity, precisely because of the precariousness of young life in the absence of a father's support. Marriage is an age-old and universal framework for the ordering and understanding of family organisation, parental perspectives and behaviour, which creates obligations between the adult parties, their kin, and the couple and their children. For women, biological and social parenthood invariably coincide. For men, there is a gap which is closed by marriage, where the 'necessity of imposing the bond of marriage' is 'practically and theoretically due to the fact that a father has to be made to look after his children'.[62] Therefore: 'In all known human societies, extant or historical, men and women have entered into formal reproductive alliances between individuals of opposite sex. In other words, they have '*married*', where 'couples forge a powerful commonality of interest' analogous to that existing between blood relatives.[63]

Cohabitation not only differs from marriage in terms of relative stability, length, satisfaction, health outcomes, and acceptance of parental responsibility, but present-day cohabitees, especially male cohabitees, have economic, health, social and sexual behaviour patterns that are more like those of single than married people—and often attitudes to match. This makes it more realistic to see *de facto* unions as an alternative to being single, rather than marriage substitutes. Well over 90 per cent of married men and women are monogamous over a five-year span, compared with around 43 per cent of cohabiting men and 60 per cent of cohabiting women in the UK.[64] While there might have been a general increase in children born to the unmarried, and while this may be linked to more widespread cohabitation, cohabiting women everywhere have lower fertility than married women.[65] Since cohabiting men often want the freedom of single men, they may not relish the arrival of children. In Sotirios Sarantakos' Australian study, 38 per cent of cohabitees had children living with them, but only 29 per cent of these were born into their unions: most belonged to previous marriages or relationships. None of those who had children had planned to do so.[66] Similarly, abortions are nearly four times more frequent with pregnancies involving cohabiting rather than married women in the UK. New Zealand has both high abortion and cohabitation rates. Nearly 60 per cent of women who had an abortion in 1997 were 'never married', and over 47 per cent of women who had an abortion had never borne a child.[67]

Myths about Maori

A complement to claims that 'the family' was a 1950s aberration is the insistance that New Zealand's original inhabitants managed to do without marriage, families, and even particular parents, and that the high rates of unwed births, solo parents and *de facto* unions among Maori are a return to traditional practices—which perhaps they have never really relinquished. If the 146 per cent increase in Maori sole parents within 15 years is not being blamed on 'the lack of sex education and knowledge, and access to contraceptives ... because of the legal and social constraints imposed on single females', then the 'ex-nuptial birth classification is based purely on a culturally specific view of marriage. The status of these children in Maori society is different from that of their counterparts in other cultures.'[68] Apparently: '[i]llegitimacy is virtually of no importance, for one is a child of the lineage, not of any particular set of parents. Adoption is widespread and it is an open and public act of generosity in sharing children.'[69] This extends into claims that lone parents generally have exchanged the enclosed, suffocating nuclear family for extended families into which the children are warmly absorbed: whether 'Pakeha, or if she is Maori or a Pacific Islander of whatever age, then she will most commonly be a sole parent who lives not as a total isolate, but in a wider household with other adults, frequently her own parents'.[70] But, among Maori: 'the child has many parenting resources, many more than are implied by the term "extended family", which connotes extension from the nuclear basis of the household to include a few grandparents and the odd aunt and uncle and possibly their offspring'. The 'many, many parents' are 'all persons older than one's own generation', including 'all female relatives of the age of one's biological mother' and ' males on both sides of the lineage, mother's and father's, [who] are functionally equivalent in terminology and parenting role'.[71]

Such assertions have parallels with similar claims in the UK and US, where the high ex-nuptial birthrate of present-day blacks is attributed to the high regard African Caribbeans supposedly have for lone-parent families and consensual unions. They are part of a pattern of 'multiple mothering', or 'shared child-rearing' in extended matrifocal families, and, as such, a sign of strong family life rather than an undesirable modification'.[72] Such statements illustrate how black sole parenting became 'a precious cultural contribution which cemented ... a valuable political alliance with progressive elements in the white population', who conscripted Afro-Caribbeans as their champions, rather than 'just a pragmatic accommodation to a harsh environment'. Indeed:

African Caribbean women who lived as single mothers found themselves increasingly celebrated by white liberals as superwomen, who demonstrated that it was possible to manage without men. Ideas rooting this family form not only in responses to slavery, but also more positively and fundamentally in the heritage of African ancestors, were utilised to construct new theories in which African Caribbean populations became lionised as the nurturers of matriarchal institutions which the post-imperial, libertarian-socialist world order required.[73]

Maori are similar 'exotic models for ... developing sexual radicalism' for New Zealand. As already noted a quarter of a century ago: 'There is a widespread tendency to praise certain meritorious attributes ... in the ancient Maori and to ignore or even deny those attributes which are distasteful and unpleasant to our culture. The effect is to make the Maori more acceptable to our culture than he was in fact.'[74]

The present tendency to fantasise aspects of the Maori past reflects the hippy dream of the counter-culture. Love, otherwise 'locked up in the family', is drizzled over all children, who are the responsibility of the 'community', not the property of the selfish, narrow nuclear family. This is feminist primeval bliss where, before the invention of patriarchy, no man had an interest or investment in any particular child, but nonetheless contributed to a common pot which supplied all children—by whoever sired. In contrast:

... in predominantly Anglo-Saxon countries, such as New Zealand, there is an underlying ethos of individual responsibility such that the man who is supporting his children asks why he should also, through his taxes, support another man's children. It is unlikely that this applied in traditional Maori society where the whanau rather than the father accepted responsibility for its

children. Problems of financial support for Maori sole parents and their children
are more likely to result from the general low income level of Maori or the
breakdown of the whanau system following urbanisation.[75]

Maori certainly applied terms for parents, children and siblings to
many relationships. For example, the term for father was used for
father's brothers and cousins, since kinship terminology was classificatory. The individual accepted as kin anyone who descended from a
common ancestor and, in the parental generation, all males—or
brothers and male cousins of both parents—were 'father' or *mantua* and
all females were 'mother' or *whaea*. However, the 'real' mother or father
was distinguished in practice and linguistically by adding 'other'.
Moreover, the Maori terminology did not identify kin according to
genealogical distance nor distinguish father's kin from mother's, but
grouped them on the basis of sex and generational level and, in the case
of peers, according to seniority of descent.[76]

Marriage was highly valued, because of the economic interdependence and other advantages for the individuals concerned, and because
it produced legitimate heirs to perpetuate and strengthen descent lines
and groups. Pre-marital sex had to be discreetly managed and not
contravene incest regulations and barriers of rank (not easy in small-
scale societies). However, children 'born on the *Takapau whara-nui*, the
wide-wefted sleeping mat of lawful marriage, were clearly distinguished
from those born out of wedlock' and a 'definite stigma did attach to the
illegitimate child, suggesting that pregnancy would determine marriage'.[77] Marriages were usually made by the kin groups on each side,
the 'alliance and exchange' aspect of marriage being as, or more,
important than producing legitimate offspring and enlarging the
kinship group.[78] A man could make a public proposal on the *marae*
(community assembly ground), bringing a wide range of kin into the
discussion, or the couple could deliberately arrange to be discovered
sleeping together. This forced the family that considered itself most
injured (usually the girl's) into forming a *taua muru* (plunder party),
which raided the other group and carried off goods in compensation
(perhaps for the loss of her services as well as the irregularities of the
marriage). This assuaged wounded feelings and, by publicising the
marriage, validated it, since 'the essential elements in the marriage
contract were firstly that ... the whole community should know that the
young couple were setting up in permanent sexual partnership'.[79]
Separation was a matter for the wife and husband's families, not
individuals. If a woman returned to her kin, they would decide who to
give her to next.[80]

This illustrates a basic difference between marriage and cohabitation. Whatever the feelings the couple have for one another, cohabita-

tion is essentially a personal and ultimately provisional agreement between two individuals which does not acknowledge any wider responsibility or long-term commitment.[81]

The nuclear family may not have existed as an independent unit among Maori, but it was a distinct sub-group within the framework of the *whanau*. This common household was an extended one, with an older male, his unmarried children and married sons and their families. The multi-generational aspect is often exaggerated, considering that few people survived beyond 40. But the relationship of husband, wife and children had certain features which were not shared with other members of the *whanau*. Sexual rights were exclusive, and 'after marriage there was no toleration of liaisons, at least as far as women were concerned. This was essential because of the importance of pedigree in the bilateral system of descent which required that parentage be well established.'[82]

For human beings, it has usually been vital to have a complete set of kin relations, or affiliations that span both sexes, and go across and down generations. These ties told you who you were, gave you your place or reference points in the world, and were the basis of your inheritance from it:

> Legitimacy is nothing more nor less than the orderly transfer of social meaning across the generations. Remember that children are the ultimate illegal aliens. They are undocumented immigrants to our world, who must be socialised and invested with identity, a culture and an estate. By conferring legitimacy marriage keeps this process from becoming chaos.[83]

Parents bore responsibility for their children's education and the blame if they turned out badly, even though other kin, especially the grandparents, played a considerable part in the children's upbringing. Ties of affection were expected to be stronger between parents and children than with other members of the household. They occupied a defined part of the sleeping house, or had a separate one of their own. Personal possessions and craft tools, ornaments, hunting gear etc., were made for individuals and their children, not for other members of the extended family. Before a person died, they divided up their land and personal possessions amongst their own children. It was usual for someone standing in the right classificatory position to marry the widowed spouse or adopt the orphan—an important form of social security where able-bodied adults frequently died in war or childbirth. Since 'all members of the village are of one lineage' they were 'in that sense of one family'.[84]

By the 1940s, it was being reported[85] that young Maori ignored the attempts of elders to arrange matches, but lifelong monogamy was the ideal, most married in church and there were no cases of divorce in the community being studied. The usual way of handling marital failure was non-legal separation, followed by the establishment of an informal union. About 30 per cent of households were three-generational and 58 per cent consisted of parents and children only. Like Europeans, people tended to be indifferent to relations more than two generations back or more distant than first or second cousins.

Moving on to a study of a Maori community in the mid-1950s,[86] no people in Kotare were divorced, although 14 per cent of couples recognised as married lived together, because someone was married to another person. While 15 per cent of children lived with someone other than their biological parents, all 'knew' their real parents. Most foster parents were elderly; parents often reclaimed their children, and foster children often suffered from behaviour problems, as they do elsewhere. Of 98 households, only six were three-generational, and housed 12 per cent of the population. A further report in 1958-59,[87] involving a sample of Auckland Maori, included a fifth of households where a person lived alone. Only 14 per cent were part of a three-generational household. However, there were only two divorcees and only eight per cent of couples lived together without marriage.

Such accounts are reminiscent of those from British working-class communities in the first half or more of the twentieth century. People lived in fairly close proximity to kin, but did not wish to live with them unless it was absolutely necessary: 'The Maori people in Rakau did not consider such an arrangement desirable, though of course no one would refuse to offer their parents accommodation should the old people need it.'[88] On marriage, usually following a not unwelcome pregnancy, women expected to manage their own household. The husband spent time away from home working and with his age-mates, while the wife devoted herself to household duties. When, in the early 1960s, married Maori women from the Wellington area[89] were asked where they thought children should live after marriage, 62 answered 'well away from their parents'; 19 'in the same suburb', and 15 'close to parents'. Overall, city Maori stressed the importance of the nuclear family as against links with the wider family, and resolved tensions between the families of origin and procreation in its favour. An overview of studies of Maori families from the 1940 onwards concluded that:

> Everywhere the nuclear family was shown to be the most common type of household, but a significant proportion of households consisted of either a nuclear family with kin boarders or a three-generation family including either the parent(s) of the householder or his wife, or one or more married children with spouse(s) and offspring. Far from being the preferred type as in pre-European times, these extended family households were regarded as temporary arrangements due to economic difficulties. They tended to be short-lived or to change in composition as junior couples achieved a separate house. Because of this and because they were larger than average, a relatively large proportion of the Maori population had lived in such households at some stage in their lives.[90]

By the end of the twentieth century, with Pakeha anti-family activists firmly in the saddle, it was decided that 'an autonomous nuclear household is not the goal of such [Maori] families' and that there was 'no place attempting to impose such a model' on those who ought to be housed 'in communities where extended and multiple families are both important and common ...'[91] Those romanticising extended families tend to forget that the pattern established in Western Europe, where a married couple head up their own independent household, rather than move in with a parent or other kin, has been allied with greater prosperity, individual freedom and higher status for women, compared with oriental and tribal societies. In the latter, arranged and child marriage often applies and young couples (especially the women) lack privacy and domestic latitude and are subject to their elders.

It is not apparent that the modern rise in sole parenthood so prominent amongst Maori means that children are being absorbed into extended families. This is overplayed. In 1996, around one-quarter of Maori children lived in extended households—leaving nearly three-quarters living with simply one or both parents, as were over 80 per cent of all New Zealand children. Of those with two parents, over 16 per cent of Maori children lived in households that *included people other than their parents*, and nearly 40 per cent of children of sole parents.[92] Those living with others *who qualified as 'extended family'*, were respectively nearly 14 and 28 per cent—a decided minority in each case. There is no extended family without the nuclear family. If Maori communities traditionally derived support from a wide network of family members, so now there is 'a comparative lack of support available from partners and grandparents, caused by the relative absence of older Maori and lower than average marriage rates'. This is 'an indication of a community under stress in which relationships have become increasingly informal'.[93]

As already noted, present Maori family developments towards sole parenthood and casualised relationships follow much the same course observed for UK Afro-Caribbeans (and US African Americans).[94] For younger people, the strong trend is towards adults living alone as single men or lone parents, rather than as part of any group (the lone-adult household rate for Afro-Caribbeans born in the UK runs at 56 per cent compared with 22 per cent for those born in the Caribbean, and 25 per cent for white British, despite far more older people in the last two groups). While welcoming some independence, Afro-Caribbean women report being overburdened by multiple demands of work, children and other commitments.

Fantasies about the Future

On a par with progressive fantasies of multi-mothering or shared parenting is the related suggestion that serial family disruption and single parenthood are creating caring, supportive gaggles of people, wider than kin, who will be with us throughout life:

> ... how will the family of the future be characterised? It will typically have a long four-generational stem and an unpredictable accumulation of lifelong friends, in-laws left over from first marriages, new half-kin from remarriages, godparents and godchildren. It will be frequently quarrelsome, and critical, but respectful of each member's independence and united in adversity. Let's take it from folklore and christen it the 'maypole family', long and thin, and with any number of strands winding and unwinding around it. A powerful and supportive structure, it will be, in the vast majority of cases, the first resort in a crisis.[95]

There is no evidence to date to support this sentimental nonsense. Rather than people accumulating lots of extra relatives as sources of support, the extended family is less likely to be able to help, since its numbers are often depleted by lone parenthood, particularly where the natural father never had, or has lost, contact with his children. Without marriage, fewer people are tied in committed and socially sanctioned ways to any obligations of support. Parents who experience marital breakdown are less likely to feel supported by relatives compared with intact families, just as their own obligations to in-laws are substantially weakened after divorce.[96] Children are also more likely to lose touch with grandparents and other relatives after experiencing family transitions, particularly if these are paternal kin.[97] As lone parenthood passes through more than one generation, the result is 'an almost exponential collapse of the number of supporting relatives'.[98] When there is more than one transition, this loss of contact extends to former step-parents, half-brothers and half-sisters.[99]

Marriage breakdown is not necessarily compensated by new relationships. The love of step-parents for their own biological children is often very different from what they feel towards their step-children. The tie is conditional or contingent on the survival of the marriage or relationship with the natural parent and would probably end if this finished. The contribution towards their step-child(ren)'s development often lacks the automatic, imperative quality of support for natural children. The same applies to step-grandparents. While step-parents may be—benignly or otherwise—'non-engaged', the remarriage of either parent is likely to further erode, if not sever, the child's relationship with the original father. In turn, the remaining parent is more likely to be uninterested or take a less active role in parenting than if they were a lone parent or part of the original couple. This tends to persist into adulthood. A custodial father's remarriage is associated with significantly lower relationship quality in adulthood between the child and both the biological mother and the stepmother.[100]

It often sounds as if people's living arrangements which depart from that of the two-parent family are the result of some kind of decision to create a new social order. After all, the common 'explanation' for family changes, is that these are personal lifestyle 'choices'. This may be why government is held to be incapable of influencing developments, since people simply do what they want to do. However, where people end up is not necessarily where they wanted to be. Outcomes may not represent the 'first-best' choice of those involved.

It is often said that '[c]ouples do not divorce just because there is a law that allows them to do so: the motivation precedes the act that legislation makes possible', and that both divorce law reform and the upsurge of divorce afterwards just reflect the way that 'legislative changes were brought in to accommodate an existing need and attitude change'.[101] As such: '... the law is ineffective as an instrument of change in the area of family life ... Just as the law is not effective in initiating changes in traditional values, neither can it prevent marriages from breaking down.'[102] In turn, legislators and policy makers are presented as slavishly obeying the wishes of the population, or being swept along by historical necessity, as when the state is described as being 'forced to modernise its legal code so that it more closely corresponds to reality. Despite its concern with preserving the family, it has no option but to let broken marriages be terminated.'[103]

However, human beings are seldom 'forced' to do anything, and it is irresponsible to speak of 'no option' if a course of action is being pursued with known, or suspected, adverse consequences. Human beings are peculiar creatures who can hardly avoid making choices among the various alternative possibilities of action or inaction which are available. Anyway, it is not evident that policy on the family has been led by popular pressure or 'circumstances and changes in values so that reform merely catches up with established practices and demands'.[104] Furthermore, it is fantastic to claim that these popular 'demands' somehow involved an understanding of 'the interests of the couple, their children and society as a whole'.[105]

Legal and other policy changes are seldom brought about by popular pressure or attitude change, but rather represent élite agendas, or the pet projects of those strategically placed in the political arena to get their way. At most, reformers may hitch their wagons to particular strands in current behaviour or attitudes in preference to others and, in so doing, bring about changes well beyond the aspirations or desires of ordinary people—changes which further alter behaviour, followed by attitudes, as the incentives structure changes. Often, legislation has been proposed by unseen officials, often without public debate, and even in the face of a majority of submissions against it, as in the cases of homosexuality and rights for *de factos*.[106] If, supposedly, the 'growth in unmarried cohabitation and the increasing acceptance of homosexual partnerships are changing the social and legal landscape in New Zealand',[107] such 'acceptance' is from the top down and then acts as justification for further acknowledgement. Even if ordinary people approved greater freedom for individuals to extricate themselves from unwanted marriages, for example, the unintended (from their perspective) impact of divorce law reform has been to undermine the commitment norms that promoted marital co-operation. Necessarily, the 'institution of marriage may become unstable if it is impossible to signal commitment', particularly 'given the failure of the law to deal with fault/breach', making the growth in cohabitation 'nothing more than a rational response to rather messy marital laws'.[108] There is greater support among ordinary people for conventional marriage (or heterosexuality) than is often acknowledged, and policy makers have given disproportionate emphasis to libertarian views.

People are often unaware of the extent to which law affects their lives, not least through the incentives structure it imposes, and the moral assumptions it embodies, imposes and reinforces.[109] Corporate law affects the behaviour of corporate executives. The rules of soccer influence a game of football. The rules of entry into and exit from marriage affect the behaviour of people, as for any institution. The law is not neutral. It does not just reinforce the way a person is going, but endeavours to change behaviour, as law codes have done since time immemorial. The value now ensconced in marriage law is of the radical autonomy of the individual, which precludes the possibility of a fixed, permanent lifelong commitment. As marriage is redefined as 'a time-limited, contingent arrangement rather than a lifelong commitment', revocable at will by either party, this becomes part of the moral economy of people, shaping their attitudes and expectations. Changes in 'the rules for ending marriage inevitably affect the rules for marriage itself and the intentions and expectations of those who enter it'.[110] The incentive to invest resources—both personal and financial—is diminished. Independence is anticipated and, as the cost to one or both parties of pursuing activities inconsistent with the marital agreement is reduced, marriage may be used as a base from which to make forays into pools of alternative partners. The essential element of contract law—that those who break an agreement must compensate for the loss imposed on affected parties—has been abrogated. If conduct has no influence upon the subsequent division of resources, there is no financial constraint on opportunism, or strategic behaviour within the family, no penalty for bad behaviour, and no protection or leverage for the party who keeps their side of the bargain. It is 'no accident that cohabitation emerged as a widespread phenomenon at exactly the same time marriage was being demoted from a permanent commitment, severable only for cause, to a temporary, fully revokable arrangement, terminable at the will of either spouse'.[111] Promises never made seem more worthy than promises broken. Marriage declines further and the law endeavours to address the very conditions it has helped to create.[112]

The notion that marriage break-up is ultimately a beneficial experience has become deeply entrenched.[113] As much as the two-parent family based upon marriage is seen by élite opinion as a ridiculous charade that is on the way out, so its death promises a plethora of opportunities. With the 'monocultural middle-class masculine construction of family life ... disintegrating', these exciting 'changes offer the possibility of a greater variety of family options for everybody, even middle-class Pakeha males'.[114]

The Fantasy of 'Responsible Parenting'

It is increasingly suggested that the demise of marriage can be reconciled with reliable child-rearing through the separation of commitment to a child from commitment between parents. In this way, the 'family can be preserved even if the parents don't choose to live together any longer, unlike New Zealand where the family is virtually automatically broken up'.[115] As unmarried and married fathers and mothers would have the same rights and the same obligations, people would move in and out of sexual relationships, while continuing to 'parent' children in different households. The 'co-parents' can support their children's development while moving on to make a more satisfying life for themselves. This 'family apart' or 'responsible' parenting promises to undermine the very idea of the 'single parent', as well as making marriage and two-parent families irrelevant:[116] 'child-rearing involves two parents, whether or not they live in the same household, and whether or not they are the biological or social parents of other children in their present household or elsewhere ...' The ambitions of the sexual revolution can be met, such as the 'right of all family members to seek economic and emotional independence while avoiding putting restrictions on the aspirations of others'.[117] In contrast, the custody pattern where children live with one parent is blamed for adversarial conflict, resistence to paying child support, domestic violence (attributed to access issues), poorly adjusted children, high costs to taxpayers, and the high unemployment rate of non-custodial parents.

However, the call for 'responsible' or 'shared parenting' is another indication of the way in which male mating patterns are moving in the direction of serial polygamy with women who bear their children or bring other men's children with them into sequential unions. The attempt to redefine fatherhood in ways that make no reference to marriage is another sign of the drift away from child well-being, as influence over men is 'lost in the unregulated market of interpersonal negotiations set up by alternative values'. Women 'cannot readily avoid responsibility for children', but men 'can run away from parenting *unless* there are strong social sanctions preventing this' and they have to make a more explicit public decision to become fully committed.[118]

Good Times Ahead?

When present developments first got underway, the predictions were of improved outcomes: 'young women who bear children out of wedlock are not being stampeded into unwise and premature marriages because of guilt feelings about sexual intercourse, or the probability—or actuality—of pregnancy, and this is a good thing'. The consequences were nothing to worry about, rather the reverse, for, apart from a 'healthier' attitude to sex, it also meant swapping 'unhappy marriages, neglected children, and future psychological and psychiatric problems' for the 'smaller problems of illegitimacy'.[119] Not everyone agreed. As the results started to come in, the Domestic Purposes Benefit Review Committee 1977 felt that it 'should be emphasised' that a number of investigations had already indicated how 'illegitimate children who were neither adopted nor legitimised were more likely than other children to appear before court for misconduct and ... because of parental inadequacy ... illegitimate children who are not adopted or legitimised are vastly over-represented in the population of state wards'.[120]

But such misgivings have been apt to be drowned out by claims that exciting prospects for the grown-ups do not mean any disadvantages for the kids.[121] With a poll showing that 60 per cent of respondents think that children need both parents to grow up happily (down from 69 per cent ten years before), Gabriel Maxwell, senior researcher in the Office of the Commissioner for Children, observed how it partly reflected 'the gradual percolating down of information from research, which shows that children can grow up perfectly unharmed by being in a solo-parent family'.[122] Indeed, the 'new trends bring marital and familial relations a newfound integrity', not least because the notion of an enduring 'marital tie is simply inconsistent with a society which stresses the rights of the individual to seek fulfilment [and] ... dissonant with the views of true sexual equality'. As it is: 'the family is not breaking down, just being measured against new standards'.[123]

3

The Rise and Fall
of Family Policy

Summary: An industrial economy with market wages does not, in itself, take notice of family size, and can impose a stark choice between relative poverty with children or higher material living standards without them. Western nations have therefore traditionally implemented a range of measures to protect the family. New Zealand was no exception when it came to protecting the family's economic security and maintaining some parity in living standards between those with and those without dependent children. However, these measures were replaced with targeted assistance in a most dramatic way. No other country adopted such an extreme agenda as New Zealand. Once near the top, New Zealand sank down to the bottom of the international league, in terms of assistance to couples with children. Parenting outside marriage became the only form of child-rearing that society remains willing to subsidise substantially. The timing and extent of the 'baby boom' of the 1940s, 1950s and 1960s, and the 'baby bust' which followed, must be seen in relation to changing social policy. Falling birth rates, the avoidance and delay of marriage and parenthood, an ageing of the population, are all linked with the fate of the family, the welfare system and conditions in the labour market. There is no morally neutral tax or welfare regime. Each rewards some kinds of behaviour and penalises others, while reflecting certain assumptions and promoting particular values.

Child-rearing makes substantial and simultaneous demands in terms of money and time, reducing earning potential just at the period when expenditure is rising. A family with two young children needs over 50 per cent more income than a childless couple to maintain the same material living standard and about three times more than a bachelor.[1] An income that provides a reasonable standard of living for a single person may maintain a family in little more than penury, although 'many welfare analysts leave this factor entirely out of account in their use of the terms "wealthy" and "high income" in the context of family earnings and taxation'.[2]

41

A deeply ingrained and long-standing assumption has been that people should refrain from having children unless they can care for them properly—or unless the mother is married and the father can support them. It has also meant not embarking on marriage and child-bearing unless a living standard could be preserved something like that enjoyed as an unmarried, childless person, or at least a living standard regarded as acceptable at the time. This is the folk basis for 'responsible parenthood'. If income is insufficient, the general view has been that people should restrict their fertility. Reproduction at the subsistence margin is ill-advised or downright irresponsible. Groups ensure their survival and success by limiting procreation to adults expected to have the best chance of providing for their children, and the Western system developed on the basis of attaining a certain living standard in an independent, conjugal household.

On the face of it, this all seems to impose impossible conditions, considering the costs (including loss of earnings) of having children. Moreover, it has seemingly become increasingly unattainable as the cost of rearing children has risen so drastically. In a farm economy children often make a net contribution to family income from a relatively young age. Shifts from agriculture to urban work mean that families have to purchase housing, food, clothing, and other necessities, and invest in their children for a longer period, which make the cost of supporting each individual child more obvious. Laws restrict child labour and, in mandating education, sharply reduce children's potential economic contribution. Higher educational attainments have become increasingly necessary for occupational success, thus extending the dependency period into adulthood. This development is unique to the twentieth century, where American studies show that for people up to 22, two-thirds of food and clothing costs are accumulated from age 16 upwards.[3] It also has third-party benefits, while making the family bear the costs of the child's upkeep as well as the losses of their potential economic contributions. Higher incomes over time have also increased the opportunity cost of forgoing paid work to care for children.

Expenditure also bunches. Not least, the desirable home that is often viewed as a prerequisite for having children must be acquired at the same time in the child-rearing cycle, so that it competes with parent-hood for resources. Moreover, economic growth increases expected standards of consumption, so that desirable goods and services increase along with the level of expected parental investment.

An industrial economy with market wages does not, *in itself*, take notice of family size, and does not accommodate or recognise familial needs and responsibilities, imposing the stark choice between relative deprivation with children or higher living standards without them.

Everything else being equal, a man with four children and a bachelor will receive the same wage for a day's work, despite the vast difference in their burdens. It is those unencumbered by dependents who are advantaged in the competitive struggle, or best situated to maximise their discretionary time and income. The single person is merely self-maintaining. Lacking the costs of replacing the social infrastructure, those without children can afford better and bigger property. Those without children may be all the better provisioned by putting their money into retirement, not offspring. If they do not, their old age will still be provided for in modern societies from compulsory exactions from other people's children, whom they have not had the expense of rearing.

Horizontal Equity

Historically, various devices have been constructed to shelter the family from full immersion in the industrial economy. A multitude of adjustments in the structure of employment, taxation and services, have been built up and varied over time in developed societies. These endeavoured to ensure that, on the whole, most of those who acted prudently would have resources in terms of time and income to rear a smallish family without privation or undue strain. The principle, based on the understanding that effective income is reduced by multi-dependency, is called *horizontal equity*.

New Zealand was no exception. Probably nowhere else in 'the core of the radical world of welfare capitalism'[4] was family policy so thoroughly, and so generously developed.[5] To describe the forms this took is not necessarily to advocate a return to the tax, welfare or labour market regimes of any past period, but simply to try to understand the extent to which public policy has changed since then.

With increased reliance on income tax, most systems of direct taxation in the world have, or have had, earned-income relief, for the earner, dependent children and for a dependent spouse. The recognition that both low initial earnings and multi-dependency meant reduced ability to pay taxes was seen as fair and progressive. Exempting bands of income from taxation in relation to the numbers it supported helped to prevent tax-induced poverty—where people have to get a welfare supplement to pay a tax bill, because they cannot afford tax and the upkeep of their families at the same time. In New Zealand, exemptions for dependent children and a non-earning spouse were first introduced in 1914 and 1933 respectively. These exemptions would have lowered taxes to five per cent of gross earnings for a young family man of median earnings in the 1940s. New Zealand was the first country to have state-funded family allowances. These were initially introduced in 1926 for low-paid workers for the third child and subsequent

children, in 1941 for all children in the family and, by 1946, all income
limits were abolished as the Family Benefit became universal. A
woman with two children received each week the equivalent of a full
day's pay for a labourer, while one with four children received about
half a labourer's net wages. The family's total entitlement would have
represented 111 per cent of gross median earnings for men under 35
with two children, or a negative tax rate of 11 per cent. Only those in
higher income brackets would have contributed much to income
taxation and, even then, few families with three or more children would
have paid anything in the 30 years after the war.[6] The pattern was
paralleled in Australia. In 1950, a single person at average weekly male
earnings (AWE) paid seven per cent of their gross earnings in income
tax, a one-income, two-child family paid two per cent and a four-child
family nothing. In 1960, a family earner with three children would have
paid no income tax until reaching 120 per cent of average weekly
earnings. With Child Endowment added, only families above 150 per
cent AWE paid any effective tax, and high family earners paid
considerably less tax than earners without dependents on the same
income.[7]

The tax burden started to move upwards in the 1970s. In comparison
with earlier decades, a higher proportion of total tax revenue was
raised through income tax with a commensurate reduction in the
relative importance of taxes on spending and property. The tax burden
shifted onto families, in New Zealand as elsewhere. Allowances were
not uprated and, as wages rose with inflation, so real disposable
incomes were eroded since the tax rates were progressive. By the 1990s,
a young single-income family in the middle of the income range paid
nine times as heavily in 'effective' tax as did an identical family in the
1950s or 1960s.[8] By the 1990s, Australian families had seen a similar
ten-fold tax rise for families, compared with a three-fold increase for
single persons, with the effect of child dependency on family income
being virtually disregarded.[9]

In New Zealand, there are now no income tax exemptions, for self,
spouse or children, making statutory tax rates the same for singles and
couples, married or unmarried, with or without children.[10] As cuts in
higher tax rates have also reduced progressivity in the tax system, this
favours childless high-earners and the parents of older children who are
on high incomes: fathers of young children tend to have low incomes. By
1986, the median earnings for a man aged 25-34 were $18,560. Only
$52 were covered by the 'employment-related expenses' exemption, and
this family was considered 'too affluent' for help from the Guaranteed
Minimum Family Income (for low-income families with at least one
parent working at least 30 hours per week, or 20 hours for a lone

parent). The family, however, qualified for Family Support which abated on joint family income in excess of $14,000 a year at the rate of 18 cents in the dollar.[11] In 1947 the universal Family Benefit was 7.7 per cent of average weekly earnings, in the mid-1970s it was 3.2 per cent, and, in 1991, 1.1 per cent, before it was extinguished. Parents lost more, on average, in terms of disposable household income, at every level, from all social policy changes in the 80s and early 90s, than households without children.[12]

The Royal Commission of 1972 was the 'quintessence of the conventional wisdom of about this time ...' in failing to discuss family income.[13] Elderly people got more political attention, and a generous National Superannuation replaced the Aged Benefit and Universal Superannuation in 1976.[14] The age of eligibility was reduced to 60 and the level of superannuation for a retired couple was increased to 80 per cent of the gross average ordinary wage. As promised in its 1972 election manifesto, the Labour Government undertook a nationwide survey of the financial and material circumstances of people over 65 years of age. However, the vast majority of the poor or hard-pressed were found in families.[15] Around a fifth of families, which would be two-parent families, had incomes insufficient to attain the minimum income level set for pensioners. Overall, the material standard of living of families with children was 13 per cent below the national average on equivalised measures. The childless were 23 per cent above average and the elderly already had incomes above average.

Nowhere else had family policy been so thoroughly and so generously developed as in New Zealand, and nowhere else had it been so drastically swept away. What survived was a reputation as a social laboratory.[16] 'Targeting' was reinforced as the guiding principle in welfare policy or the provision of a 'safety net' for the 'needy', essentially designed to avoid hardship. This has little to do with family policy, although families—in that they have more bodies to support—are likely to make up the bulk of the subjects of relief. Indeed, means testing became something applied primarily to families. The programme of 1990 included proposals to target superannuation on the poor elderly. Since this generated opposition, the newly elected National government settled for an increase in the superannuation surcharge, a three-year freeze on superannuation levels and an acceleration of a timetable for putting the age of eligibility back to 65 years. In 1961, of the 6.4 per cent of GDP directed at young adults by way of cash benefits or through housing schemes, only one-fifth was rationed through tight means testing. By 1986, this was three-quarters of a smaller proportion. Help for families now came largely via the income-related Family Support, payable to beneficiaries and low-income workers. Even this scarcely rose with inflation in the 1980s. In the 1996 tax cuts, Family Support was increased, but still remained below the 1986 real level. Some health subsidies that were previously universal were now restricted to low-income families through the Community Services Card. Student tertiary allowances became targeted on the basis of family income, with students deemed to be dependent on parents up to 25 years of age. An Independent Family Tax Credit, only paid to low-income families in the full-time workforce, was instituted. By the 1990s, expenditure on income-related support for families was a very minor budgetary item, at under one per cent of GDP (not including the Domestic Purposes Benefit).[17] Once near the top, New Zealand sank down to the bottom of the international league, in terms of assistance for children.[18] By the mid-1990s it vied with Spain, Greece, Portugal, and Japan to pay the lowest.

At a half of average earnings, New Zealand became the sixth most generous country out of 18 in terms of the total child support package for a couple with two children aged one and three years at this income level (assuming 100 per cent take-up rate of benefits and using purchasing power parities to compare countries). This diminishes very rapidly as income or family size increases. At one-and-a-half average male earnings, New Zealand, the United States and Spain were the only countries to offer negative assistance to a couple with two young children (since couples with children face additional health and school costs). Parents are left with lower net disposable incomes than childless couples or singles. Only in the USA, Australia and New Zealand are children's healthcare costs targeted on the basis of income, and only in the USA and Japan is there a change in school costs at higher income levels.[19] Many former tertiary students who had student loans and who are parents also pay the tertiary study loan repayment of an additional ten cents in the dollar on the income tax rate in respect of an annual income over $15,964 in 2003/04.

The Mother/Child/State Family

Paradoxically, the demise of family policy makes it pertinent to ask 'what sort of family does the state support?' The reply is that 'parenting outside marriage [became] ... the only form of child raising that society remains willing to subsidise substantially'.[20] The Domestic Purposes Benefit (DPB), effective since 1973, came in with the shift to a targeted approach. Many of the families in greatest need were sole-parent families headed by women. In effect, the state took on the role of male breadwinner. The DPB replaced a group of benefits for unsupported women, including emergency support for unmarried mothers and assistance for deserted wives. These involved discretionary decisions about an applicant's level of need for essentially emergency assistance, which was placing increasing pressure on social security staff. In contrast, the DPB satisfied set criteria and did not require moral judgements. It was precisely to provide an alternative to work for the parent without spousal support for, if 'the husband cannot or will not pay, then social security should come in at an earlier stage'.[21] Women continued to qualify as a 'woman alone' after ceasing to care for children and until the Aged Benefit and/or Universal Superannuation was received. Improvement in the 'adequacy of benefit incomes in the 1970s, aimed at supporting sole parents as full-time caregivers, therefore came at the cost of reduced incentives to maintain attachment to the labour force' and reduced expectations that husbands should support their former spouses and their children.[22] The 1972 Royal Commission on Social Security explained:

> The common pattern of life in our society is that family responsibilities are shared by two parents, with the man being the main breadwinner ... The female sole parent is not only deprived of the help a man might be expected to give in the care of the children, she is deprived (in whole or in part) of his financial contribution and her responsibilities in the home limit her ability to earn an adequate family income.[23]

The DPB soon moved from being an exceptional means to deal with the consequences of the collapse of the family unit as an economic entity, to exemplifying a new and enlightened way to provide for women and children, where they 'are no longer in the position of having to be dependent themselves on other income-generating adults. This is one of the greatest achievements toward equality of the sexes, if not the greatest ... women and their dependent children are no longer at the economic mercy of husbands and fathers ... .'[24]

The other side of the state's willingness to dissolve marriages is this collectivisation of the costs. Prior to the 1970s, the law imposed rights and duties on spouses, which reflected the wider social interest—not only in social stability, cohesion and continuity, but in financial independence from the state. Spouses had rights of divorce against partners who refused to provide or work for the household, and husbands a duty to maintain their wives during the marriage and upon its dissolution.[25] The Matrimonial Property Act 1976, had the effect of securing men's income against claims by ex-wives and, until the Child Support Act, first-marriage children. Property had to be divided equally without reference to future support and irrespective of who would have to house and care for the children, regardless of contributions and the relative loss of future earning ability. (From 2002, the 50-50 asset split can be varied to remedy any perceived economic disparity arising from the relationship.) Since enhanced earning power and future income were not deemed matrimonial property, there was no sharing of the rewards from investment in human capital or return on investment in a husband/wife partnership.

Responses to the 'inequality of equal division' through maintenance awards were rare and spouses have been expected to assume responsibility for their own support within a short time of dissolution. Maintenance was not a right derived from marriage, or a form of compensation for defaulting on the marriage contract, or in lieu of expected returns from the continuing marriage. Based on a 'modern marriage' stereotype, as well as 'no fault' divorce, each spouse was assumed to participate equally in the jobs market, where all women were self-sufficient with a male career structure.[26] Either they had no children, or no difficulty providing both care and an income adequate to pay for housing, their own support, child-raising costs and their own retirement. Estimates from the US are that 'no-fault' divorce settlements reduce maintenance for women and children by about a third compared with situations in which fault is a criterion.[27]

In 1987, legislation eased access to the DPB by dropping the requirement that sole parents identify the other biological parent and allowed men to qualify in their own right. The outcome of Ruka v Department of Social Welfare (CA43/96, October 1996) in the Court of Appeal gave an entitlement to DPB when the mother lived with a man. Financial interdependence now had to be established as a necessary component of a *de facto* relationship in the assessment of claims. This did not exist unless the parties had a personal commitment to financially support each other.

Since the DPB appeared as the logical complement of sexual freedom, the Child Support Act 1991, enforcing the liability of absent fathers, was criticised for reneging on the state's promise to pick up the costs of incidental reproduction. It gave:

> ... little recognition ... to the effects of repartnering and reconstituting families. The thrust of the child support legislation is to give priority to the first family, the one which no longer exists [sic], even if this puts a second family at risk. And yet the consequences, both legally and socially, of relaxed divorce laws, coupled with a growing acceptance of the free entry and exit of *de facto* relationships, is that new families and marriages will be formed. In one breath, the law encourages the formation of new relationships, while in another breath it frowns on them.[28]

Indeed, feminists have not been slow to point out how the provision 'of minimal state assistance in place of the male provider has been inadequate' and to blame the state for 'a growing proportion of our children ... growing up in relative poverty'. It was time for 'the breakdown of the policy assumption of women's financial dependence on men' (as if that had not largely happened already), and for the state to 'rationalise its acceptance of divorce and the increasing diversity of family types as a fact of life and reorganise the way children are provided for financially'. This might be done by paying mothers and children a generous independent income, irrespective of their connection with any particular man, or movement in and out of 'partnerships'. Since moral connotations no longer attached to various patterns of sexual behaviour and their consequences, so the 'reality of the family structure and lifecycle in the later twentieth century western world' must be fully funded and fully integrated into policy making by the recognition of 'non-traditional family types as institutional rather than deviant'.[29] As such, this perspective now receives the backing of men demanding formal recognition of the fact that a man has no paternal responsibility if he did not expressly want a child. Hence: 'before decisions are made about custody, access and financial support from the non-custodial parent, it should be necessary to establish whether there was a parental contract between the biological parents'. If it is established that there was no mutual decision to have and keep a baby, then the father should have no financial or other liability. After all, the 'decision to keep an embryo will be that of the mother alone. With the existence of the "morning after contraceptive" there need be no risk of pregnancy to a woman from a casual sexual union.'[30] Clearly, the 'sexual revolution, feminist proselytising, and the expansion of government entitlements' dovetail nicely with 'the sexual creed of selfish males'.[31]

Spending on sickness, unemployment and lone-parent benefits may be seen as a redirection of former spending on housing and family benefits. At the same time, couples with children have become major net contributors to government finances. For families with a mother under 30 years old, taxes, in 1996, were three-fold the levels of income transfers and eight-fold where the mother was aged 35-39. Retired households and sole parents are net gainers from the welfare state in terms of all transfers (cash benefits, health, educational and other transfers). They represented 32 per cent of households in 1997/8, received 56 per cent of government expenditure, and paid 16.5 per cent of taxes. Couples with children pay more in taxes than they receive from the transfer system, particularly where one partner works more than 30 hours per week. Twenty nine per cent of households are couples with children but they pay 40 per cent of taxes. The biggest contributors to revenue are older couples with children.

Whose Welfare Does a Welfare State Look After?

Family policy measures have come to be regarded as an anomaly, critiqued on grounds of vertical equity objectives, as if egalitarianism had been their primary purpose. It is often suggested that maybe such measures were misplaced, or a muddled, inadequate means to redistribute wealth, leading to both left and right getting lathered up about 'wasted wealth' that was not 'targeted' on the 'poor', or given instead to those who 'did not need it'. Socialists have objected that the welfare state did not redistribute income and wealth as they had hoped, and was little more than a smokescreen to disguise the failings and contradictions of capitalism. They have been joined by conservatives, claiming that the middle classes benefited more than the 'poor', by making more use of education and tax breaks. If the system does not do 'what it is designed to do—make sure only those in need of a benefit receive a benefit', then it must have got waylaid or misappropriated.[32]

A once common understanding of a 'welfare state' was that it assisted people at vulnerable points in their lives to meet the needs of child welfare, age, sickness, widowhood, and unemployment. It had its beginnings at the turn of the twentieth century, and bloomed roughly between 1930 and 1970. A desire for more certainty and security was accentuated by the experience of depression and war. But, as David Thomson explains, Socialist or Christian demands to equalise the life-chances of those who did badly out of the market's allocation, by passing resources from rich to poor, or to impose a sharing or pooling of resources for redistribution, never had much appeal:

> A limited degree of such redistribution might be welcomed, perhaps if it brought some arrogant wealthy people to heel, or removed the ugliest and disruptive effects of poverty. But, for the majority, the Robin Hood approach to sharing income held few promises and many threats if pressed too far. Their hopes for personal betterment would be thwarted if opportunities to get ahead were closed, or if others came to think of them as rich and hence to be penalised.[33]

Instead, the welfare state was more popularly seen in terms of a national insurance system which safeguarded the individual against risks or misfortunes which threatened living standards. As the individual's needs varied enormously over a lifetime, so resources are moved from one phase to another, smoothing out the peaks and troughs. Those who have few resources at any stage in life could be given assistance drawn from the pooled resources of those richer than themselves. For the majority the welfare state would mainly help move resources across time, temporarily rather than permanently, between one age-group and another, as individuals went through life. Horizontal equity measures dovetail with such considerations.

Even so, the impetus for giving parents support, here as elsewhere, often went beyond any income maintenance or insurance principle. Health and education provision involved investments in further generations necessary for the perpetuation of society and the public good, as well as personal well-being. In turn, family allowances were favoured in that they had labour market objectives. They avoided the disincentive effects on the workforce participation of family providers associated with selective poor relief. Given that they also removed pressure on the wage rate by fathers of families, or made possible equal wages without impoverishing the breadwinner's children, they frequently antedated welfare states and were often paid on a firm or industry basis, or by local authorities, as well as trade and professional associations (on an insurance basis), in continental Europe, the USA and Australia (where the earliest payments were made to fathers from a levy in the Commonwealth Public Service in 1920).[34] The way in which Family Benefit was treated separately from other benefits indicates how it was not seen as a major or proper part of the social security structure, in New Zealand, or in the UK.

It is helpful to see family protection measures as something which were incorporated into fiscal and welfare systems, industrial and commercial organisations, professional and private insurance systems and government strategies, in different ways at different times. In the twentieth century, the state came to assume enormous powers to manipulate employment and pay, implement anti-inflation strategies, set interest rates, control foreign exchange and much more. Whether this is practically, or ideologically, seen to be good or bad, is beside the point. What is pertinent here is that all policies shift resources from one group to another, affecting the life-chances of individuals. From the 1930s to 1960s, they worked to assist young adults and their children, in what has been referred to as the 'wage-earners' welfare state'.[35]

The advent of 'targeting' might appear to be a return to a nineteenth-century concept of a more limited role for the state in welfare.[36] But such a judgement—whether made in approval or condemnation—overlooks the way in which considerations of family protection would have been pursued even then. Competition between family members for work, with its downward pull on wage rates, was discouraged by restrictions on child and female labour in the nineteenth century, and gender-based wage differentials. Dealing with the 'problem of wages', the Industrial Conciliation and Arbitration Act 1894 set the concept of a basic minimum wage. Since the:

> ... 'average employee' of the time was male, and since his 'normal needs' included his domestic responsibilities, a 'fair wage' was construed as one wage sufficient to support a wife and two or three children at a reasonable level of comfort.[37]

In the Harvester Judgement of 1907, the Australian Commonwealth Court of Conciliation and Arbitration laid down the guiding principles of the family wage: that organised society owed the family breadwinner a sufficient income to support a decent standard of living for a normal family, a reference point in NZ legislation in 1936.[38] In turn, the:

> ... aversion to heavy tax burdens on average working families, and, hence, strong preference for reliance on progressive income taxes, followed naturally from the

conception that wages from employment were the legally established minimum required for a civilised existence. ... the closely intertwined set of preferences for redistributive instruments on both the expenditure and revenue sides of the tax-transfer system gave the wage earners' welfare state in its heyday a distinctively egalitarian or 'radical' cast.[39]

While male employment and remuneration were foremost economic and social concerns aimed, not least, at ensuring the security of the household, women's pay was a frivolous consideration.

However, what men command on the market affects the value of the woman's homemaking. When he has a higher earning capacity, and the husband gives his time to paid employment, this makes housework 'cheaper' when supplied by the wife. Increases in the husband's earnings raise the value of the wife's time at home. A result is that the number of children is strongly negatively related to the wage-rate of wives, while positively related to the earnings of husbands.

Fiscal Policy and the Family: the Crisis of the Welfare State

In the post-war world, full employment and housing policies were pursued in complement to this guidance of wages, in the interests of family protection. As the 'fulcrum of the welfare state ... the employment of every able-bodied male represented an historic compromise forged in response to the 1920s depression when measured unemployment rose to 12 per cent of the labour force'.[40] The state was assumed to have the means, and the duty, to avert unemployment. From early on, Antipodean states had followed a policy stance of 'domestic defence', involving strong regulative intervention in the economy, but with less direct state ownership of business than in Europe.[41] Immigration controls helped to ensure a tight labour market (a family protection device well known in the pre-industrial world)[42] and, with a regime built upon the preservation of labour scarcity, women exited the jobs market at marriage.[43] From the late 1930s, vigorous import controls were adopted. When economic activity slackened, public money was used in an attempt to create employment, and displaced workers could be helped with retraining and movement to new communities.[44] Aiming to ensure that employment was not controlled from abroad, the Reserve Bank was created in 1933, nationalised, and used to regulate financial relations with the outside world.[45] To describe these measures is not necessarily to endorse them, or prescribe them for other times and places.

Earning an income took precedence over consumption,[46] and earning an income meant providing for families. Certain borrower interests had primacy over those of lenders. Since the 1890s, governments assisted buyers by borrowing and lending at low rates of interest. By the early 1960s, home ownership had become a welfare good to be provided through subsidised or interest-regulated loans. In 1960, three-quarters of young families were eligible for loans to meet 60 per cent of the price of a modest house at a subsidised interest rate of about half the market rate. The most dramatic instance of the equation between home ownership, welfare and family[47] was the way that, from 1958, parents could also 'anticipate' a portion of the family benefits they would receive in the coming years, as a lump sum, so that a further 15 to 20 per cent of the cost of buying a house could be met in this way. As a central element in a family's economic and social security, and in the context of the family wage, home ownership 'attached a "man" firmly to a job, to a piece of land, and to a social group; it established a base for "his" family, and so to a network of neighbourhood institutions, such as church, school, and voluntary society'.[48]

Those who benefited married earlier and in greater numbers than generations before them, and had many more children than their own parents had in the 1920s. No wonder 'New Zealand's "baby boom" was to be more striking and longer lasting than that seen almost anywhere else, for our new welfare state was perhaps the most distinctly youth-oriented of all'.[49] Since the 'economic measure of the Standard Family, a man aged 25-35, his wife and two small children' was 'the unit for which the welfare state was designed', this 'reflects a set of beliefs central to New Zealanders' perception of themselves and their society'. Its situation 'provides one means of testing the achievement of the welfare state in terms of its own ideals'.[50]

Nations doing well in the first half of the twentieth century fell back thereafter. As the oil crises of the 1970s hit industrial countries, so inflation and debt grew and economic growth fell away. In the English-speaking world, the pressures meant a major reappraisal of the role of the state. A central theme was the Keynesian welfare state as a subversive force which undermined the values of individual initiative on which an efficient market system rests, particularly given the loss of export markets. Privatisation was a reaction abroad to statism. In New Zealand the target was the state's regulatory activities, as obstacles to competitive efficiency. From operating one of most closed economies in the non-communist world from the 1930s, New Zealand became 'one of the most open and internationally exposed'. Wholesale corporate restructuring, a glut of labour, and slow adaptation by labour markets 'translated into higher unemployment, less tax revenue, and greater pressure on state resources. The crisis of the welfare state had begun.'[51]

The Family is Abandoned to Its Fate

Reorganisation and sluggish economic performance, with persistently high inflation contributed to a reduction in New Zealand's per capita income relative to that of other developed countries. All sectors of the community were adversely affected. In addition, these economy-wide developments, combined with the elimination of tax-related and other measures of support for families, and a large increase in the level of New Zealand Superannuation weakened the position of families relative to that of the elderly. The wage earners' welfare state ended.

The arbitration system, which once sought to relate wage rates to family responsibilities, (among other factors), had become a mechanism for promoting women's remuneration by the 1970s. Similarly, for Australia, the nexus between the basic wage and the needs of the average family remained until 1967, when it was replaced by a minimum wage determined by individual needs. Equal pay for women followed in 1974. Such radical changes were unaccompanied by any review of support for families, unless the extinction of the 'family wage' for men is seen as met 'by the introduction of state-guaranteed income for divorced and unmarried mothers'.[52]

Deregulation of the financial sector accompanied that of the labour market. As the old consensus governing lending disappeared, with it went the practices and regulations which favoured young borrowers, as inflation was fought by making borrowing expensive. In the last quarter century, the cost of a modest first home, relative to the net incomes of young adults, rose between four and six times.[53] In 1961, a majority of two-child families would have qualified for Family Benefit Capitalisation grants equalling about 20 per cent of the price of a modest house. By 1985 it was seven per cent for a poor minority and in 1986 the scheme ended. In the 1960s, all families would have been eligible for a first mortgage from the government; by the 1980s this applied only to the poorer half. If a family were not disqualified by income, it would have paid around two-thirds of the open-market interest rate and then the full rate as the scheme dissolved. As rentals for state houses were raised to 'market rates', housing reforms in 1993 brought about a rationalisation of all former assistance into an income- and assets-tested Accommodation Supplement.

The demise of family policy brought the level of parental expenditure involved in the production of children into direct conflict with the penalties which make child-rearing economically foolish. Not only the timing and extent of the 'baby boom' of the 1940s, 1950s and 1960s, but the 'baby bust' which followed, are hard to explain without reference to economic upheavals and changing social policy. Falling birth rates, the avoidance and delay of marriage and parenthood, an aging of the population, are all 'linked with the fate of the Standard Family and the welfare state which once served its interests', and are correctly seen as '"logical" adaptations to the underlying shifts in economic fortunes.'[54]

Parents and Poverty

With family size at the lowest level ever recorded, families with children are the lowest income group, measured by average, after-tax income, and single people and couples without children the highest. About 26 per cent of children were in households that were in the lowest income quintile (bottom 20 per cent) of the population in 1996, with 23 per cent in the next-to-bottom quintile, and only 11 per cent in the top quintile. Nearly 50 per cent of people below 15 years of age are in households in the bottom third of the income distribution, while less than 15 per cent are in the top third. Couples without children (not counting those over 65) account for around a third of all households in the top household income quintile.

The growth in the number of sole parents has clearly altered the structure of poverty over time: accounting for 19.4 per cent of New Zealand poor in 1998 compared with 10.2 per cent in 1984 (on the 50 per cent of median, equivalised household income, before housing costs). Not least, an increasing disparity in overall income between sole-parent and two-parent families betokens greater reliance on benefit income for lone parents (and on double incomes for two-parent families), with falling relative incomes for those on benefits.[55] In 1996, only 22.3 per cent of sole parents had income from sources such as wages, salary and interest and had not received income support, compared with 66.4 per cent of two-parent families, only four per cent of whom relied entirely on income support.[56]

Being young, having children in the household, having fewer workers, less income and less education, are important in making people vulnerable to poverty, and sole parents have more than their share of these characteristics.[57] They lack the support of another parent and women with children to care for often do not have the leeway to earn at a reasonable and consistent level. Employment doubles the income of UK lone parents, but it is still only about two-thirds that of one-earner couples.[58] Unwed mothers will go on to perpetuate their poverty, because parenthood, particularly early in life, damages career growth and economic security. Young UK mothers (before age 23) are particularly likely to be receiving means-tested benefits over ten years later, to be in social housing, to have no qualifications and poor mental or physical health.[59]

Unemployment, reliance on state benefits and disability are also common characteristics of divorced populations, not least because many men do not have the resources to support sets of children from serial marriages.[60] Data on cohorts of US women divorcing from the late 1960s through to the late 1980s show overall declines in household income of around 35 per cent on separation and declines in per capita income of at least 20 per cent (and up to 35 per cent for black women in the 1980s).[61] Families had, on average, low incomes before disruption and even lower ones afterwards. Children whose fathers left home were nearly twice as likely to end up below the poverty line compared with children who stayed in stable two-parent families (21 per cent versus 12 per cent). Federal statistics for the late-1980s indicate that the percentage of children coming from disrupted families whose mothers claimed public assistance increased from five per cent just before separation to nearly 20 per cent over two years afterwards, and food stamp receipt increased from 9.4 to over 24 per cent.[62] Similarly in New Zealand, 'Half a house and no income do not pay the bills'[63] and, unsurprisingly, one study of 500 family court clients found that over a half went on the Domestic Purposes Benefit following marital breakdown.[64] Confirming the Scottish, US and Australian experience that mothers are seriously disadvantaged by 'clean-break' settlements,[65] the average incomes of non-custodial males increased by 41 per cent after separation (from a baseline of half the household income before separation), and that of custodial females decreased by five per cent. Six months later, nearly 60 per cent of men had an income over $30,000, but three-quarters of women had less (while, on average, the households of these women contained two children), and 86 per cent of custodial parents had moved at least once. However, the favourable position of the ex-husband may not persist even if he does not acquire a second family. Worsening health, loss of social status and work often follow on marriage breakdown.

Work-Rich and Work-Poor Households

Certainly, non-work is likely to mean low income and/or welfare dependency, and the 'workless household' factor is strongly implicated in the risk of child poverty. As elsewhere, New Zealand sole parents have increasingly contributed to the growth in workless households. But couples with children have also seen a significant increase in worklessness. When men move out of work, women tend to move out with them, or are already not working. Thirty years ago, 92 per cent of British children lived with two parents of whom at least one worked. By 1995/96 the proportion outside such families had risen from eight to 29 per cent, faster than the official unemployment rate and the highest in the European Union, not least with the growth of lone-parent households.[66] Two out of three working-age households with persistently low incomes, and six out of ten children with persistently low incomes, had no parent in employment.[67] One in five Australian children were also in workless households.

The underlying trend is for workless households to increase even during periods of job growth, with a substantial and growing proportion of long-term non-employed.[68] Workless households increased over two-

and-a-half-fold in New Zealand between 1986 and 1996,[69] so that 20,652 children under five years with no parent in the paid workforce became 53,547. Overall, nearly a quarter of all children, or 23.4 per cent, lived in a household that had no one in paid work in 1996. For Maori children, the figure was 41.2 per cent.[70] Of the 27 per cent of all families with a child under five with no one in paid work, 72 per cent were sole-parent and 28 per cent two-parent. Only about 25 per cent of European and 18 per cent of Maori sole parents were in paid work of any kind. In contrast, about one in three of mothers in two-parent families were employed full-time, and over 80 per cent of fathers, 86.5 per cent of whom were either in work or seeking it—although this figure had been over 95 per cent in 1986.[71]

Two-Parent Families are Poor Too

However, while there are many social security beneficiaries among the poor, there are also a large number of households with children which are primarily dependent upon market incomes.[72] In turn, while a large proportion of lone parents may be poor or on low incomes, they *do not constitute the majority of poor or low-income families*—even if child poverty is often seen as not only intrinsic to, but exclusive to, lone parenthood. Of course, growing up with a sole parent clearly makes a difference to a child's chances of being brought up in poverty, compared with a child in a two-parent family. It is approximately four times greater in Australia, five or six times greater in Canada and eight times greater in Germany.[73] But while in 1998 sole parents made up 17.7 per cent of New Zealand's total poor population on the 60-per-cent measure, and 19.4 per cent at the 50-per-cent measure (before housing cost adjustment), couples with children made up respectively 21.1 and 27.2 per cent.[74] Given that this most 'functional' family type has suffered significant income declines, these cannot simply be attributed to a movement towards sole parenthood.[75]

Moreover, poorer two-parent households often break up and become poor sole-parent households.[76] Men with higher incomes can more easily afford to be married, and better-off families are more likely to stay together. This makes family structure a consequence as well as a cause of poverty. Contrary to the feminist thesis that the 'notion of a male breadwinner supporting a dependent wife and children has disadvan-taged women in most ways',[77] *male earning power is tied to a lower likelihood of family poverty*, even if the labour supply and income of other household members is important to transitions in and out of poverty.[78] Children in mother-only families will have substantially less income available from their fathers than children living with both parents, for whom male earning power will also be linked to living standards. Over the 1980s in the US, it is calculated that about one-third of the increase in child poverty was attributable to the rise in mother-only families. The other two-thirds is accounted for by declining income, and historical analysis strongly suggests that employment insecurity and low earnings, not least for fathers, are prime determinants of the levels and the trends in childhood poverty.[79] Childhood poverty rates and trends have been affected directly by an increasing proportion of children living with jobless or low-income fathers, and indirectly by the effect of male joblessness and low income on fostering the rise of mother-only families through divorce and out-of-wedlock child-bearing.

Is the Family Self-destructing?

The dominant or preferred explanation for the dramatic changes in family trends has no time for any relationship to changing family fortunes. Instead, the story is that social policy has simply followed, or even failed to catch up with, a popular retreat from family life. Women and children have been put 'at the risk of poverty', because 'higher divorce rates, lower fertility rates, the prevalence of single-parent families, greater female participation in the work place and a larger proportion of elderly persons, have moved society away from the single breadwinner in a nuclear family that the welfare state was designed around'.[80] This is back to front. Far from these trends making a 'welfare state' geared to 'the single breadwinner in a nuclear family' moribund, it is more likely that the collapse of family policy amid the economic dislocation of recent decades precipitated or, at least, facilitated such demographic developments.

Changes in family structure reflect marriage and children postponed or forgone. A major reason for the growing *proportion* of out-of-wedlock births is, after all, because there are fewer marriages and fewer babies are being born to married women. Between 1971 and 1981, the proportions of married women who had been married at least three years before having a child rose from 16 to 40 per cent. The proportions delaying having children for five or more years rose three-fold. Woman born in the mid-1950s had 1.7 births by 30, or 40 per cent less than women born in the 1930s who had, on average, 2.7 children.

Establishing a career, buying a house, marrying, having a child, become widely spaced activities for prudent individuals. Arguably, student loans will impose more constraints on having children. Moreover, to the list of desirable goods with which children compete has come the expensive 'must have' of the big retirement. A pension may no longer be seen as a stipend for the declining years when work is obviated by the incapacities of age, but a sizeable fortune for the 'decades of golden leisure' while one is still fit. Women who have children may decide to take up or stay in employment in the middle years to help pay for their children's tertiary education. Saving for their own retirement does not have priority.[81] Yet, those who spend effort and personal income in raising and educating children have no better claim to their future production than the neighbour who made no such investment. As adults with just one child or none at all are so favoured during working life and in old age: 'given the ethos of modernity, *parents behave highly rationally by not producing more children than they believe they can afford or find time to raise.* Any other behaviour would jeopardise the welfare of the family and the well-being of the children.'[82]

The Feminisation of Employment

As well as cutting down on the numbers of children, parents also try to maintain or raise living standards by pushing more labour onto the market. Fathers may work longer hours (with 46 per cent of full-timers working 50 or more hours a week in 1996).[83] Women's increasing opportunities have promoted the growth in married mothers' labour market participation.[84] For example, in the USA only 10 per cent of children lived with a mother in the labour force in 1940. By 1990, it was nearly 60 per cent. For up to 25 per cent of children in two-parent families with working mothers, these mothers were working out of necessity (and 40 per cent on the relative poverty measure of half average income).[85] Despite general unemployment and declining rates of employment for sole parents and single women, employment rates for New Zealand mothers in two-parent families where the youngest child was aged under one year increased from one in eight to one in four between 1976 and 1986, and then to around a third by 1996. From being below the OECD average in 1960, female labour-force participation was above this by 1990. For children aged one to four, a half of their mothers were in full- or part-time work by 1996.

Many of the jobs created in the 1990s went to secondary earners. Between 1986 and 1996 there was an overall decline in people employed 30 hours or more a week of two per cent, while those employed part-time increased by 71 per cent, and over two-thirds were female. However, a trend towards full-time work is more established for New Zealand mothers than for those in the UK.[86] The separate taxation of married people, combined with a progressive tax scale, encourages families to raise disposable income through the workforce participation of both spouses, in contrast to nations where joint taxation lowers the benefit derivable from mothers earning additional income outside the home.[87]

Employment, as well as poverty, has become 'feminised'. The economic restructuring and downturn of the 1980s did not impact negatively on women's employment as in the case of men. The total number of people employed full-time dropped by nearly 100,000 between 1986 and 1991, but the drop for women was almost a third of that for men—at 4.5 compared with 12.7 per cent.[88] As economic conditions improved in the early 1990s, the percentage growth in women employed full-time was nearly twice the increase (or 22.4 per cent between 1991 and 1996) experienced by men. This was due, not least, to men's concentration in manufacturing and extractive industries that were especially hit by restructuring and recession, compared with service sector work, which was comparatively insulated.[89] Similarly, the advance in women's market incomes, absolutely and relative to men's, reflects a fall for men as well as an increase for women.[90]

A Triumph for Women?

Tribulations of the male provider, together with growing equality in the workplace, ought to have produced greater protection for women and made it more possible for them to provide for themselves and their children—according to feminists, anyway. This has not happened. Wide-scale female employment, with equal wages and opportunities, has helped undercut the ability of one earner to maintain a household, sole- or two-parent at the living standard now expected. While the limitations of the one-adult unit make it less likely to be in a position to supply one fully-employed person, couples are able to supply two earners as living standards gravitate towards a two-income norm. In a sample of 3,000 British families with net income below 140 per cent of the ordinary rate of public assistance, 35 per cent of two-parent families rose above this poverty line a year later, compared with 11 per cent of lone mothers. It was overwhelmingly those two-parent families with two earners who did so.[91]

There has been the fallacious notion that, with equal pay and opportunities, women would somehow bring in a 'family wage'—an impossibility, since this depended on labour market restrictions that privileged men's jobs. While economic opportunities for married women might have been gradually increasing after World War Two (not least because the supply of single women fell because of earlier and more universal marriage), men's wages and employment opportunities were increasing as well. In the 1982-1996 period, wages adjusted to equality through lower, unisex rates in which men largely sustained the falls.

Double Income: No Kids

With the growth of female employment, children have come to impose a great and historically unprecedented cost in terms of lost parental income, at the same time as both their direct costs and competing

attractions have grown.[92] Initially, the postponement of children after
marriage, with the woman making profitable use of her marketable
skills before withdrawing from work, seemed to promise couples the
chance of starting a family off on a higher living standard than they
might have had on the basis of the man's wages alone. As equal pay and
the elimination of gender differentiation further increased women's
labour force participation, by pushing up their earnings as men's fell,
a dedicated two-income strategy became increasingly necessary to
maintain living standards. This is probably the most effective contraceptive ever devised. Child-rearing became a most expensive use of the
mother's time in terms of the returns forgone from virtually any paid
occupation. Recent work on first-time mothers in the UK reveals how
more than one in three delayed children because they were afraid that
they could not cope financially; another quarter feared for the job
impact, and nearly a half delayed telling their employers because they
feared how it would be received.[93] A third felt pressurised to work
harder during pregnancy than ever before, and much the same
proportion believed that they would now be passed over for promotion
and pay increases.

As decisions to have children are negatively correlated with the
wage-rate of wives, while being positively correlated with the earnings
of husbands, so the rise in women's net earnings in relation to men's
has probably made a major contribution to the way in which births
have fallen below population replacement levels in many countries.[94]
With higher women's wages, the incentive for wives to work outweighs
the disincentive for them not to, even when their husbands may be as
highly paid—although the decline in home production will offset some
of the gains in income. Many men have found it possible to make good
some of the loss with extra effort, reflected in the discrepancy between
the earnings of married men and those of single men and women,
although this is interpreted as women being 'denied' equal wages.
Nevertheless, the higher a woman's earnings, the older she is at the
time of her first birth and the smaller her family.

There is no morally neutral tax or welfare regime. Each rewards
some kinds of behaviour and penalises others, while promoting certain
assumptions and values. In the past, compensatory measures not only
reduced the standard of living penalty and the opportunity costs of
child-rearing but upheld its esteem. When families have lower living
standards or are more impoverished compared with those without
dependents, both may come to believe that there is little or no value
placed on raising children. Childless couples and singles can have
financial stability, a comfortable home, and early retirement as the
expression of material attainment, while parenthood is identified with

disruption, change and deprivation. Parents 'do without', or 'give up' their social lives, jobs and spending on themselves, and 'never stop being responsible'. Childlessness represents 'freedom to be independent adults who pursued their own interests' for those who have 'weighed up the responsibilities of money and commitment and sacrifice and counted themselves out'.[95] In sum: children are more trouble and expense than they are worth.

Economic uncertainty is only part of a wider climate of apprehension about family life. Not only do parents identify 'a lack of money as a key impact of having children',[96] but non-parents put stability of a couple's relationship along with economic considerations near the top of the factors that influence child-bearing.[97] Increases in divorce rates lower marital fertility.[98] As the advent of no-fault divorce makes the marriage contract unenforceable, the prospect is not only fewer marriages, but fewer children, more investment in individual careers, as well as more opportunistic behaviour in marriage leading to more divorces.[99] As marriage becomes illusory, it is risky to bring children into this relationship, both because divorce is difficult for them and because children will reduce women's earning potential.

4

War Is Declared on the Family

Summary: Claims that we can no longer 'afford' to support the family are unconvincing. Whatever the size of the pot, the way in which resources are allocated shows a society's scale of priorities. When war was declared on the Standard Family in the 1970s it was conducted by an unholy alliance of left and right, sexual liberators and feminists, who believed that the overthrow of the institutions of family and marriage would bring emancipation and self-fulfilment. Those hostile to the idea of supporting the family often speak as if family trends occur irrespective of public policy or economic changes. However, they are no more beyond human influence than other social or physical phenomena, and no less likely to reflect the influence of a changing public policy environment.

When the old family-benefiting measures were eradicated, no new ones took their place. With the passing of old corporate society, nothing 'protected the standard of living of children when the conflict over resources intensified. It could easily have been done, but it has not been done.'[1] There were no compensatory measures to safeguard the family economy with the advent of the equal wage and equal opportunity labour market. When the economy was being restructured, dealing with the issues without a family policy meant that the losers from economic rationalisation were bound to be families and children. In 1991, the Change Team on Targeting Social Assistance saw little amiss whereby '82 per cent of two-parent families with pre-school children will be worse off ... compared with 100 per cent of families with tertiary students and 89 per cent of other two-parent families with children' as a result of its proposals.[2]

But were family-benefiting measures affordable? After all, the nations which had been comparatively rich for at least half a century then experienced slow growth and sank down the league table of affluent nations. 'Now it could seem that such public generosity was no longer economically practicable, or even that past generosity was amongst the causes of present discontents.'[3]

63

However, often family-protective and -benefiting measures were historically operated in far more straightened circumstances, this makes it difficult to argue that they are a luxury which only rich societies, with ample surpluses, can afford.[4] While it may be true that countries with higher GDP per capita tend to have higher levels of child support, New Zealand became an international outlier and now has considerably lower support for children than countries with similar GDP. In turn, there is little relationship between all social expenditure as a proportion of GDP and the level of child support packages.[5]

The Triumph of Age over Youth

Big pot or little pot—what it is spent on is a matter of choice. This is not to deny that there has been real fiscal constraint. To a greater or lesser degree, there always is. But judgements about what is or is not politically acceptable or sustainable are also statements about the priority given to the objects of expenditure.[6] New money was found to expand the benefits of the elderly, while governments were able to eliminate or charge for things used mainly or exclusively by younger people. By the early 1990s, the elderly absorbed 10-11 per cent of GDP, two-and-a-half times the level in the 1960s, while they increased as a proportion of the population from 12 to 15 per cent.[7] At the same time as family benefits waned, the old acquired a generous superannuation scheme, with a reduced entitlement age, irrespective of future fiscal difficulties—although the realisation that this was an extravagance too far led, in 1979, to benefits linked to the net of tax average, instead of gross, wage and, in 1989, to the lesser of wages or prices.

Such political ageing is evident in many modern states. Given rising numbers of elderly people in relation to declining numbers of young, this might suggest that the pressure on resources would make their situation unfavourable, since their cost to the state is so much greater. However, public decisions are influenced by the power of interest groups, and power is partly a function of size. Moreover, the larger the role of transfers going to growing groups and the bigger the role of government in delivering these, so, paradoxically, the more advantageous it is to be in an expanding dependency group.[8] Everyone in their forties and above, or half the electorate, has a clear personal interest in enhancing provisions for the aged, since they will shortly benefit. We all have to grow old, while childhood is behind us, and anyway, nobody 'has' to have children. There are increasingly well organised and successful elderly lobbies, while a greater proportion of the population is becoming single or childless, so the concerns and issues of parents fail to carry the weight they once did.

If the Domestic Purposes Benefit is the only provision which is remotely analogous to the old 'family wage', this is closely allied with the rise of the sole parent it supports, and their disproportionate dependence upon an expanding means-tested and selective benefits system. Given the 'rapidly vanishing social stigma attaching to both ex-nuptial births and marriage breakdowns', the 1977 Review Committee on the Domestic Purposes Benefit observed: 'the solo mother in particular is now even acquiring a certain status which in time could place our traditional two-parent basic family unit in jeopardy'.[9] It was those not in the labour force who had increases in real incomes in the 1980s. Across the decade, families with a parent in full-time employment experienced the largest percentage declines in equivalent income, whether one- or two-parent.[10] Accompanying this has been the trend for the proportion of families with a parent in full-time employment to decrease while the proportion of families with no parent in work increases. Similarly, for Australia over the 1980s and early 1990s, single people and sole parents received increasingly favourable treatment by the state, as did elderly people, with their share of taxation falling in relation to their share of the population, and their benefits increasing. In turn, 'the proportion of households that are single persons and sole parents increased rapidly over the period that the proportion of families with dependent children decreased. It is hard to believe that changes to the taxation and social security arrangements are not part of the explanation.'[11]

It might be maintained that those in family-building age groups, or the married, are 'richer' in modern times and therefore do not 'need' help. In the 1940s, families were 'richer' than in the nineteenth century, but they still had considerable assistance channelled their way. However, for many young adults in the 1970s and 1980s, the decline in real purchasing power was probably as great or greater than that suffered during the Great Depression, just as present fertility levels are well below the minimums of the 1920s and 1930s. The shifts in favour of the elderly have been so great as to more than counter-balance their earlier withdrawal from the workforce, while households with children receiving little in the way of government transfers are the most affected by adverse market conditions.[12]

History suggests that channelling resources to one group or another is a self-reinforcing process, in which more goes to those already doing comparatively well. Between 1936 and 1945 the real purchasing power of the Standard Family doubled, and a widening array of public services meant that its 'true' income increased even further. The period ended with 'both governing and opposition parties determined to raise the incomes of young adults, furnish them with expanded free public services, promise much improved job security through working life'. But, 'fifty years on, two decades of declining youthful fortunes end with both government and opposition parties deliberately promising less in future'.[13] Older people must not have disappointed expectations, but 'their successors ... can save harder, work longer, avoid having children—or simply learn to live with less'.[14] Affluence seemingly dictates that more should be available in old age as this has become a time for greater consumption and leisure.

Accounting for the way in which Australia, New Zealand and the UK as 'social policy innovators on a major scale' became united by the common 'status' of 'welfare state laggards',[15] David Thomson attributes the termination of family policy to processes inherent in modern welfare states. The economic woes of the 1970s and after were a catalyst. Initially, welfare provisions purported to treat all people equally during their earlier lives, upon the trust that one generation would cede its place to a second, and so on, if the exchange was not to break down. When the welfare generation was young, priorities were such that older people paid most taxes, received little in housing assistance and were forced to lend at fixed low interest rates.[16] But the rules were rewritten: those 'born in the 1920s and 1930s were the major beneficiaries in the 1940s, 1950s and 1960s, and they are now once again the winners'. As a large cohort of children born after the 1940s was about to enter adulthood, the first generation refused to relinquish its place and obligations were swept aside.

However, family- or 'youth-' benefiting measures are older and wider than any idea of a 'welfare state' and, anyway, the change in the proportion of older people in the population by the 1970s was not so large as to account for such a swing against the young. In the 1930s when electorates were already ageing, the government reduced pensions, as well as reducing mortgages and interest payments owed by younger to older people, since the earnings of young people fell. The prime concern was 'to manage the labour market, or a collective undertaking to create jobs for adult men and to protect their wages, which supported dependent women and children'.[17]

If governments used to be generally more mindful of 'family impact' considerations, then family-benefiting measures were, in large part, a recognition of the long-term social benefits from investments in a further generation. This applied to free, secular and compulsory education in 1877; secondary schools in 1902; together with the Plunket Society for infant care (1907); a school medical service in 1919; and the continued development of child medical care in the Health Act 1920. The Arbitration Court, which set the minimum 'family wage', was perceived to be both 'an instrument for raising the downtrodden and for improving the stamina and character of the coming generation'.[18]

Creating the social infrastructure of a future society is a key to understanding family policy in the past and its absence today. At the very least, a successful society produced enough children to sustain itself. Maternal and child welfare and health services outside the poor law, and school-based medical and nutritional provisions for children, were introduced in the UK, together with revamped child tax allowances, in the aftermath of reports on the condition of youth, just as the establishment of the Royal Commission on the Birth Rate in Australia in 1903 led to the introduction of the Commonwealth Maternity Allowance in 1912.[19] Ensuring that children could make a positive contribution was particularly vital when it came to rebuilding nations in the aftermath of war (and for securing the co-operation, if not rewarding that section of the population shouldering the war effort). If anything was worth perpetuating, and if family life was personally desirable and socially essential, then there was no question of whether or not this was affordable—it had to be. By putting money into education, early health and housing programmes, and child endowment, society 'made vital statements about its values and priorities'.[20] Children are necessary for the works of any and every lifetime to survive. Without inheritors, experience, wisdom and knowledge are void. It was for the same reasons that marriage was encouraged for the social good and defended against both individual and state demands. The parliamentary speech of the minister introducing the Joint Family Homes Act 1950, (exempting married couples from gift duties, stamp duties and death duties in relation to such homes and providing some protection against claims by creditors or an assignee in bankruptcy), emphasised: 'that it is true to say that family life is the basis of our civilisation, at any rate so far as the western nations are concerned, and the object of this bill is to help in promoting and maintaining the happiness of married life.'[21]

The desirability of family-oriented policies after the First World War was underscored by falling fertility and the trailing off of immigration, a 'barometer of the health and attractiveness of the country'. The average New Zealand marriage in 1860 had produced eight births; in the 1920s and 1930s this was 2.5. Many people were not marrying at all, and one in five marriages was childless, provoking 'widespread fears of lasting and irreparable damage to the nation, perhaps of its slide into oblivion'. But rather than celebrating 'new family forms', or mocking the married two-parent family on its way to oblivion, the matter in hand was how to encourage families of two, three or four children. The minority status of that section of the population engaged in child-rearing was traditionally an argument for protection. Shrinkage of this group called for support, not denigration. No doubt these 'anxieties may now seem quaint, and the nakedly racist language deeply offensive, but the worries were intense and widely felt in a nation which had created for itself an image of youthful vigour as an attractive alternative to a tired, aged Europe'.[22]

An Unholy Alliance of Feminism, Marxism and Sexual Liberation

By the 1970s, war had been declared on the family. The Standard Family became an object of derision and hate: enemy number one in the counter-cultural struggle against social order and revolt against the legacy of Western civilisation. Maoists, feminists, Neo-Malthusians, sexual liberators, devotees of street 'hobo' culture, new hippies and old Bohemians 'all found a common enemy in the ... family'.[23] Marriage was declared sexually restrictive, and the primary focus of female oppression, as the Marxist preoccupation with the working class was transferred to blacks, women, and homosexuals. Mutual obligation seemed the antithesis of freedom, and the family the chief instrument of a pernicious process of conditioning, which enslaved individuals to do the system's bidding. The overthrow of the institutions of family and marriage would usher in self-fulfilment, self-actualisation and true liberation.

There are foundation myths. One tale, repeated *ad nauseum,* is that women are engaged in useless, unrecognised and unrewarded toil for others' benefit. In past and rosier times: 'our ancestors were not in such a bind, as their agricultural work was considered productive and essential'. Then, out of the blue, 'a division of labour was created and with it the creation of new jobs for men. With this came the emergence of private property, power, the patriarchal family and the subsequent decrease in the importance of women's work'. This was the 'great historical defeat of the feminine sex. Women soon became the private property of their husbands which eventually led to both social and economic dependence'. Thrown in for good measure: 'Capitalism is another reason why women end up in the domestic realm doing all the childcare and the domestic work.'[24] Not only are the differences between men and women deemed cultural ones, 'constructed out of social and power relations', but 'sexual identities, sexual desires, and sexual practices have less to do with hormones and biological drives and rather more to do with historical and cultural factors. Procreative hetero-sex is no more "natural" than homosexual acts or bisexuality. Heterosexuality simply has the weight of ideological and material privilege behind it.'[25] Moreover, 'it should be noted that the interest and involvement in sex by children is socially constructed and has varied historically and in different cultures,' there being 'no empirical or anthropological evidence to support this theory [that children are uninterested in sex]'.[26]

If what was considered normal in other times and places 'now seem[s] quaint', if not abhorrent and 'nakedly racist', it has even been questioned whether it should be considered normal to have children.[27] It follows that what must be engineered is a transition to the 'no-child "family"'.[28] According to Jan Cameron, further reductions in fertility have to be brought about 'by increased rates of childlessness', which might be a 'difficult reproductive strategy to adopt in a society which [already] has low fertility preferences'. The question is 'how existing prejudices might be overcome', since people still persist in having and wanting children,[29] and '... to understand why people have children and to work out what the social conditions might be that are necessary for any increase in voluntary childlessness as a new mode of family type' [*sic*]. To expose and explode 'the values intrinsic to the construction of parenthood' involves redefining 'categories of culture', like parent, and showing how these are 'voluntaristic constructions, rather than something intrinsic to the human social condition'.[30]

Needless to say, the demise or removal of anything that allowed a repugnant institution such as the family to thrive has not been unwelcome. If 'the sexist assumptions of the wage-earners' welfare state have been subject to a slow process of dissolution over the past two decades [then this] is a gain not a loss for social development in Australia and New Zealand',[31] is the gleeful verdict. The left lauds the post-war state as a 'progressive force' for protecting 'unions, workers, the sick and the aged', and subsidising the 'national wage bill, by paying for the health, education and retirement costs of workers'. Virtually 'every sector benefited ...: cheap loans for farmers, import controls and high tariffs for manufacturers, cheap timber for pulp and paper companies, and cheap power for industry in general'. But, in protecting families, the state was 'traditional, conservative, and even reactionary'. What else might be expected when 'National ... depended on farming and small businesses for much of its mass base. These tended to be family-based enterprises that fostered patriarchal, authoritarian and commercial attitudes'.[32] Moreover, the state's real role in the 'social democratic consensus 1935-66' was 'to further both capitalist accumulation and sustain the legitimacy of the state's own power by maintaining public order, in part through the patriarchal family'.

In this discourse of paranoia, public order is described as being 'particularly problematic when trying to deal with the increasing financial and social burden of the "victims of social disruption"', particularly 'the elderly, the destitute and the deserted' (even if, by all appearances, the post-war decades seem extraordinarily unproblematic). However, the powers that ruled you and fooled you decided that by 'fostering a greater and more rigidly defined domestic role for women, the state could impose domestic order on men and children'. (The implication being that disorder is good for men, children and presumably, women as well.) Supposedly, the Cult of Domesticity 'reasserted the obligations of individuals to care for kin and reinforced the nuclear family'. Women would not otherwise have cared for their children unless forced by 'the economic and ideological factors which define this work as largely the responsibility of women'.[33] In turn, 'the appropriated labour of women as carers for the young, the old, ill or differently abled [sic] ... perpetuates the marginalisation of women from the paid workforce and their confinement to unpaid domestic labour'.[34]

As family provisions were tools of environmental degradation (in supporting children) and patriarchal oppression (in enabling mothers to stay home), if these are withdrawn, women would be forced into the workforce for their own good and children would not be born, so saving the planet.

Repudiating interdependence, feminists turned questions of family policy away from help for families, to one of the rights of mothers to an income that made them independent of men. The functions of child-rearing lost recognition when performed in the context of the conjugal family, as this came under concerted attack. If the provider role was dismissed and denigrated as a drag anchor keeping women subservient, unable to compete and out of employment, then the maternal role oppressed women by keeping them dependent on men. Allowances for the caring parent, like the dependent spouse rebate in Australia or the married couple's allowance in the UK, have been especially singled out for attack for providing 'wealthy' men with 'free' housekeeping. 'What it meant for women themselves, or for children, was apparently of no moment. ... [and] far from being free, a mother at home costs the family the value of her potential earnings as well as her living costs.'[35]

Instead, child-rearing has meant childcare, since this 'involves a shift of emphasis from a focus on the child to that of women'. Childcare 'challenges the existent values that mothers should care for their children ... challenges the economic structure by enabling more women to be part of the workforce ... challenges the power relationship within the home, the community and the state by providing an alternative means of child-rearing that society finds threatening'.[36]

Above all, the cry to 'recognise the diversity of family types, including those formed outside of formal marriage'[37] and repudiate any policy acknowledging two parents or male providers, has meant basing policy on the independent sole mother. But, even here, the Domestic Purposes Benefit can be cast as part of the plot to force women to 'engage in full-time child-rearing and domestic responsibilities'. (Apparently, 'the Government recognised that unless it provided for lone mothers, this group would be forced to "compete" with men on the labour market and "neglect" their children'.)[38]

Feminism has not only applied the language of Marxism to relationships between the sexes. A reassertion of old socialist concern for the 'poor' and appeals to fiscal justice condemned family support as handouts for the 'wealthy' (unless these made it easier for mothers to work).

On the assumption that the welfare state was just about vertical redistribution: 'Middle class capture became a convenient yet unsubstantiated "explanation" for the failure of the welfare state to achieve equity and justice for all ... .'[39] Yet, the demise of family policy and the advent of 'targeting' or vertical equity as 'social justice ... meant egalitarian poverty for the family, and spiralling wealth for those without dependents'.[40]

Values influence welfare and tax policies, as well as flow from them. Both the refusal to assist married families and the unprecedented growth of a welfare system for sole parenthood are related to upheavals in values at élite level. These have affected popular morality, not least through behavioural changes attendant upon the changing incentives structure. Francis Fukuyama believes that culture changes too slowly to explain the Great Disruption in Western nations,[41] but it can change very rapidly at the instigation of social élites who are easily drawn to new ideas. The 1988 Royal Commission on Social Policy was a missed opportunity to examine family policy at a crucial juncture. While claiming that '[u]rgent attention needs to be given to policy formulations, co-ordination and implementation' since '[f]amily is too important to be left to chance and mismanagement', the author of the submission on family indulged in a chaotic reverie trying to 'grasp what it [family] means in New Zealand in the late 1980s':

> Family is a complex process. Family is beyond words—wordless. It exists as hugs, sighs, touches. It means sharing bad patches, a joke, laughter, celebration; juggling time and energy. It means staying home when you want to go out; listening and not hearing; looking, and not-seeing. It means exploding with love, pride, pleasure—and feeling bitter, angry left-out, misunderstood—all at the same time.[42]

In a long march through the institutions, the radical philosophies of the 1960s have become established wisdom. Anti-family activists got themselves and others of like mind into the bureaucracy and onto commissions where they could determine what is politically acceptable. The withdrawal of normative affirmation from the conjugal family not only facilitated the abolition of recognition for dependents in the tax and benefit systems, in favour of relief for the 'needy' and the 'casualties'. The absence of over-arching values, or basic guiding convictions about the worth of family life, also encouraged the occupation of the field by sectional interests, as lobby groups came to have a disproportionate influence on government. With no counter-weight to self-interest, and as the resources available for redistribution shrank, the vacuum left by family policy became an arena where interests met, struggled and divided the spoils. Without anything worthwhile to preserve or perpetuate, children cease to be a social investment and become a drain on the public purse, to which seniority, if nothing else, has a privileged claim. As a long-term perspective evaporated with the dissolution of any vision of a future, what need or purpose is there for children?

However, even with anti-family engineers instrumental in sweeping away family protection measures, and effectively abolishing marriage, reflexive oppositionalism still dictates that the state be portrayed as 'playing a major part in reinforcing families and maintaining inequality within them'.[43] The enemy is still with us, in the form of a terrible right-wing challenge to progressiveness where 'moral authoritarianism', or the 'moral right' is stopping women having abortions and children having sex, with a 'very restrictive view of the appropriate outlet for sexual desire', that is inhibiting the free flowing 'exploration of sexual practices, identities, desires and relationships'.[44] By supposedly upholding the family against a tide of popular rejection, policy makers are 'doing their society a disservice'.[45] They must instead emulate 'other societies and periods in history where there have been moves to promote social change and more fully utilise women's labour in the paid workforce. For example the Bolsheviks in the USSR after 1917, who made 'divorce easy to obtain, abolished maintenance payments, provided state childcare and legalised abortion'.[46]

The Dust of Atoms

The attack on the family was followed by the anti-statist challenge in the English-speaking world. If nothing else, market individualism seemed to offer a neutral refuge from such a contentious and painful subject, and it might even save money. Those with no particular axe to grind against the family, and even fond allies, could justify abandoning it to its fate. Family policy, whatever form this took historically, could be construed as collectivist meddling. The notion of children as simply a private choice and not a concern of social policy could even signify recognition of the autonomy and integrity of the family, which might give it strength in a world of interfering social engineers anxious to subvert or pre-empt parental functions. Families might be all the better off if whatever had sustained then through time was taken away. At the very least, this could do no harm since the family had the capacity to endure and survive anything that history might throw at it.

While the family once received protection from the full impact of market imperatives and radical individualism, now it was translated into their terms. The flattening of the tax structure, irrespective of dependents, demonstrated how raising children was just another act of consumption, no different from keeping a dog, running a car or acquiring a video:

Perhaps the most important reason parents have children is that children function ... as a consumer durable. Like a refrigerator, children last and deliver consumption benefits over a considerable time span. There are also pleasures in playing with them, watching them learn and grow, and loving them and having them love you. There is also the pleasure in generational continuity—the idea that we live on through others with whom we are both socially and biologically related—and seeing the pleasure they give their grandparents and other relatives.[47]

By the same token, the childless derive benefit from children only if they are fond of them, like seeing horses in the field or ducks on the pond. Otherwise, children lack utility for anyone other than their parents, or have none that would justify any financial exemption or allowance for dependents. This would amount to an unwarranted 'subsidy' from those who have chosen to go without this particular acquisition. Not least, this all suggests a static, as much as an a-social perspective, where people stay the same age all life long, and are entirely self-sufficient and independent of other human beings, in their own self-created, self-contained and self-serving worlds. However, sooner or later, people need help and it has to come from other people.

Such views about children as optional and alien, complement the abandonment of civic institutions like marriage, with all the social consequences, in return for individual rights to equally valid 'lifestyles'. In turn, the notion of the child as a mere commodity, without any communal basis or worth, is companion to the belief that freedom lies in the sheer fact of choice, not upon the choices and objectives made or acquired in terms of important aims and values. There is no belonging to some continuing, and pre-existing, social order, which is important in what we are, and what we do. Instead, notions of choice and commodities are being applied to anything in which human beings have their being, antecedents and posterity, and without which there would be no choices to make or commodities made.[48] That 'society' does not exist in the collectivist sense of an entity separate from the social existence of human beings has been read to mean that people inhabit a world of autonomous and self-regarding individuals, or live in a solipsistic vacuum—which by definition is mono-generational—with random living arrangements and sensory experiences disconnected from each other, the future and the past. Parenting, then becomes that 'expensive hobby' or 'irrational desire', or a meaningless activity or eccentricity and, as such, a distraction and drain upon the maximisation of the discretionary time and resources which enable us to live for ourselves alone. It is also part of the way in which family life is publicly relegated to a matter of taste or inclination in a world of competing sexualities. In the world where 'everybody has their own definition of family', which can always be redefined, reconstructed and discarded, there are none to protect.

Where children are regarded as consumer goods for their owners' enjoyment, and parents make no contribution to society, it seems to follow that a 'good case can be made that those who do not have children are fiscally exploited', when we '[c]onsider the vast amounts spent by the state on child health, education, housing, and income support—a transfer from the childless to those with children'.[49] However, parents as well as the childless pay taxes and charges, and often pay more than they receive in 'child subsidy'. In turn, much of the 'child subsidy' that is so often cited relates to services like education and health care that convention, morality and law insist that children receive. Economically, children might be more accurately seen in terms of capital, than consumer, goods (which might infer that parents should have sole ownership of the proceeds of their investment). So far as I am able to tell, there have been no proposals or plans to charge the 'child-free' for the use of other people's children to keep their world going—which would amount to an enormous bill (consider national defence).[50] There is much here to consider and little sign that it has been given much thought.

The Family Floating Free

Family trends as the sum of personal decisions have long-term consequences for everyone. However, just as the notion of family decline is steeped in controversy and is still not intellectually respectable,[51] so neither is the idea that family trends are sensitive to economic and social conditions. (This is curious considering the prevalence of beliefs that 'cash out' family behaviour in economic terms, as when children become consumer options.) This shades into the notion that these are beyond understanding and certainly beyond human influence. This makes government helpless in the face of exogenous developments and that, even if family measures were affordable, which they are not, they would not work. At this point, accusations about wanting to return to the 1950s are usually thrown in for good measure.

The orthodoxy that the family somehow floats outside of social and economic factors, immune to their influence, certainly draws upon a legacy of popular psychology, where social behaviour is but a shadow play of internal, emotional dynamics. In turn, the founding fathers of twentieth century sociology, like Tallcott Parsons, downplayed the economic and social functions of the family along with the influence of the social and economic conditions on family building.[52] Yet, as David Fergusson observes, while most 'popular lay accounts of family breakdown emphasise the importance, for example, of psychological attributes (and particularly "communication") in sustaining marriages', it is 'difficult to reconcile these claims with the findings which suggest that family survival is strongly influenced by sociological factors'. The reality may be 'that interpersonal skills and other attributes may only contribute to successful marriages if the prerequisite social and structural conditions exist for these skills to be applied fruitfully'.[53] Private lives are never separable from the surrounding social and economic environment, and it is these, as much as the internal emotional dynamics of relationships, that may influence the formation and dissolution of families.

To emphasise the economic factors which influence people's decisions about marriage and child-bearing is not to say that money is the only consideration, and that various causes, whether economic or otherwise, are mutually exclusive. Indeed, one cause may enhance the effect of another, as we see with the interaction between the structure of welfare benefits and changing male marriageability, or long-term welfare dependency and the development of an intergenerational culture of poverty.[54] It is also not to say that family life and the values located in this primary moral domain are reducible in economic terms. Marital outcomes, for example, may be seen as the result of the respective attractions to be found in and outside a relationship and the barriers to their realisation, economic and otherwise.[55] The considerations of men and women are strongly affected by the relative gains each would experience by moving from single to couple status, just as the degree of dependence of each party on the relationship depends on the relative costs that each would experience should it end. Income and ownership, family status, similarity, attachment, affection, companionship and sexual enjoyment, compete with the attractions of independence, other partners and alternative sources of economic support. The barriers and alternatives which significantly affect the probability of instability being translated into separation relate to financial expenses, legal and religious constraints, obligations to the marital bond, the pressures from kin, community or other primary groups and the ties and responsibilities towards dependent children. Relative attractions are clearly crucial and, we have to ask why people do not form or stay in families, just as much as why women become sole parents. When people argue about the effects of benefits on divorce, remarriage or out-of-wedlock births, they often assume that the gains from marriage are static. This is unlikely to be the situation in the real world, where prospects are constantly changing.

Thus, I turn first to considerations of what prospective and actual husbands have to offer, as the incomes of men, before and after taxation, will play a role in the attractiveness of marriage compared with going solo with or without children. Factors like the ease or difficulty of finding a spouse with stable employment, or rising or falling levels of male earnings, might have substantial effects on marriage and birth patterns, even in the absence of public assistance for unsupported mothers. We must not neglect what is going on with men as the missing husbands and fathers, anymore than we should let a preoccupation with the predicament of sole parents lead us away from how families generally are faring.

Section B

Marriage and Money:
the Consequences of Family Breakdown
for Personal Wealth and the Economy

5

When Men Don't Bring Home
the Bacon

Summary: Worldwide evidence indicates that men and women have a preference for the husband as the main wage-earner, even if wives work. Research consistently links male employment to family formation and marital stability. Men who can't support a family are unlikely to get married. If they do marry, and their earnings are insufficient, they are more likely to get divorced. Changes in the labour market have shrunk the pool of marriageable men, thus encouraging cohabitation. Maori men have been especially disadvantaged. Until 1987 they were more likely to be working than non-Maori, but then their unemployment rates began to rise, especially for young men, of whom 40 per cent were unemployed by 1991. At a time when the labour force requires higher levels of skills, over 60 per cent of Maori and Pacific people have problems with literacy. Young Maori men have death rates which are three time higher than those for Maori women, with car accidents and suicides accounting for two-thirds of deaths. Maori represented 18 per cent of the prison population in 1950, but nearly half by 1989. There is a two-way process. Without marriage, men work less. The male drop-out from the labour market is now widespread throughout the English speaking world, and runs parallel with the rising numbers of welfare-dependent sole parents. Large percentages of single and divorced men are unemployed and the employment gap by marital status is increasing. Just as families without men need far more help than those with men, so men without families are far more likely to need assistance themselves. Marital status is not only a proxy for a man's attachment to the labour market, but also for greater willingness to invest in human capital. Cohabiting men do not exhibit the same labour-market behaviour as married men. Marriage provides a focus for striving. Feminists have welcomed the 'release' of men from the 'treadmill' of the labour market, on the grounds that they will have more time to be caring husbands and fathers, but the opposite is more likely to be the case: work is pivotal to the male role, and out-of-work men are less likely to be involved with their children—if they are there at all.

Social convention has long demanded a reasonable economic standard of living as a prerequisite for marriage, and a man's earnings are still often regarded as a family's primary support. The idea that men must be the economic mainstays of families survives, alongside the insistence that women have access to equal opportunities and wages, and despite the removal of the mechanisms which once were intended to ensure that the labour market delivered a 'family wage' to male workers. Worldwide evidence indicates that men and women have a preference for the husband as the main wage-earner, even if wives work. Men provide and women contribute; fathers fit family commitments around their work, while mothers fit work around their family commitments.[1] Even where politically correct researchers assiduously avoided the tabooed term in a study of fathers' roles, '"provider" ... was used no less than 135 times in the sample of 140 interviews. "Breadwinner" was also common, cropping up 40 times ...'.[2]

When it comes to women, there is considerable ambivalence concerning the appropriateness of both partners contributing to household income, and even less consensus on women's primary interest or priority, especially in non-European Anglo-Saxon countries (US, Canada, Australia and New Zealand).[3] A substantial minority of women prefer segregated family roles, where married women have a primary responsibility and commitment to home and family. Another minority would choose to be earners throughout their lives and compete in the labour market on the same basis as men. Many more 'enter the workforce as secondary earners: they expect (or hope) to be supported by a husband for most of their adult life, so that they only supplement his earnings rather than being a co-equal earner'.[4] These women make up the largest group in any country and may reach 80 per cent of all adult females.

If the responsibility of being the main wage-earner is a man's responsibility, then employment decisions tend to be framed with reference to the way in which the labour market and the tax and benefit systems shape and constrain efforts to fulfil this role. A 'good' job is still often inseparable from one which will go much of the way to support a family adequately. There must be some ability to predict the future in terms of employment and earnings, otherwise it becomes difficult to make the kind of long-term plans involved in family building, and enduring relationships with women will be avoided.

Working Men More Likely to Become Husbands

A long line of demographic and ethnographic research consistently and directly links male employment to family formation and marital stability. The more encouraging the economic conditions, the earlier and more commonly will people marry, with a pool of securely employed males usually a necessary condition for a viable marriage market.[5] Historically, marriage rates like birth rates have always declined in times of economic hardship, as during the Great Depression. Men's marital fortunes are tied up with a whole range of political, economic and social factors, including government expenditure on higher education, the nature of labour markets and military obligations, as these affect their perceptions of the viability, costs and benefits of marriage.

Without a 'decent' job, men are undesirable spouses. A report on attitudes of women with ex-nuptial births noted how they 'wanted a man who would be a responsible breadwinner and father but their current boyfriends did not live up to this ideal and most of these women preferred to have their baby on their own rather than compromise their standards'.[6] Nearly 80 per cent of US women in the 1990s thought that a well-paying job was an essential qualification for being a husband.[7] Few girls imagine a future where they are the sole or main provider for a dependent family:

Wendy: Any particular quality that you'd be looking for ... [in a man]?
Rachel: He'd have to be good-looking and he'd have to be kind and he'd have to have a good job. That's it really.
Wendy: Which would be the most important out of these?
Rachel: A good job.[8]

Women are particularly likely to consider marriage when a prospective husband earns more than some minimum threshold. This seems relatively resistant to change in the face of fluctuating opportunities. The overall fall in wages of black American men after the 1960s did not lead women to scale down their expectations. The smaller numbers of men marrying in the 1980s were those who had been fortunate enough still to have incomes close to the level of the 1960s.[9] Analysis of US census data between 1940 and 1980, as well as population surveys for 1985-7, showed how, for example, a $100 increase in weekly earnings raised the odds of marriage for young men by about 30 per cent (or 20 per cent for those aged 30-39).[10] As men's earnings fell by 20 per cent between 1972 and 1989, with less educated young men, black or white, most affected, marriage rates followed a roughly parallel course,[11] with the employment and earnings effects remarkably similar in every age group.[12] Similarly, the ongoing 21 cities survey shows how economic conditions are foremost when it comes to family formation. Afro-American women hold particularly traditional expectations of male roles and, when men do not work, women do not marry.[13] Women's economic independence, in itself, may delay, but not diminish women's desire for marriage.[14] Moreover, women do not want a mate with lower economic prospects than their own.

Labour Market Upheavals Undermine Men and Marriage

Where a smaller percentage of men hold jobs, their earnings are lowered, or their future prospects become unpredictable and precarious, these developments reduce the economic gains from marriage as they undermine men as providers.[15] Each US economic downturn after 1970 led to intensified growth in mother-only families, suggesting that recessions may account for about 30 per cent of their overall increase between 1968 and 1988, and about 50 per cent of the increase involving divorced or separated mothers.[16] The decreasing ability of men to make sufficient and stable provision for families has likely had a pivotal role in generating high rates of non-marriage, family breakdown and a rising proportion of children without fathers on both sides of the Atlantic, and in the Pacific.

In 1986, over 90 per cent of men aged 25-29 in New Zealand were participating in the labour force, and nearly 93 per cent of men aged 30-34. By 1996, the figures were respectively nearly 79 and nearly 81 per cent, and the big decline of men in couples occurred in the younger age groups. Despite growth in the economy until 1996, there was no overall growth in the labour force participation rates of men.[17] Those aged 15 to 24 comprised 14.5 per cent of the New Zealand population in 1996, yet they made up 40 per cent of people unemployed and actively seeking work. This pattern, established by the mid-1970s, reversed that of the 1920s and 1930s when the young figured lightly among the unemployed. (In 1936, 14 per cent of males unemployed were aged under 25, while more than 50 per cent were over 50.)[18]

The groups with lower qualifications had the lowest employment rates between 1986 and 1991, with the 'no qualifications' group experiencing a further drop in employment to 1996, while those with highest qualifications had rising employment. The workforce participation rate for men aged 25-54 years with no formal qualifications declined four-fold the decline for those with post-school qualifications.[19]

The relatively well-paid, full-time jobs for semi-skilled or unskilled male workers lost between 1970 and 1990 were a major entry point into the world of work for youngsters without the skills or paper qualifications for white-collar work.

Not long ago, a man consolidated his position and rose up the hierarchy with incremental increases in earnings as he gained experience. This often coincided with the growth in family expenses. The new de-regularised labour market is one where long-term security of tenure has often given way to short-term and 're-negotiable' agreements at all levels, in public services, banking and finance, as much as in industry, with no automatic progress up a salary scale with age.

Where young men grow up without expectation of the kind of stable employment 'around which traditional models of working-class masculinity were organised' there are particular obstacles to couple and family formation at the bottom of the socio-economic ladder,[20] with men neither in paid work nor in couples. The disparity in marriage rates between employed and jobless men has probably grown over time. US work suggests that men with stable work are now twice as likely to marry as those without. In 'earlier years, the social stigma of illegitimacy counter-balanced economic considerations in the decision to marry. [Then] ... marriage rates dropped precipitously among chronically jobless men as couples no longer felt obliged to legitimate the birth of a child for social reasons'.[21] Women's growing ability to control their own fertility, and the emphasis on their exclusive rights to decide if, and when, they have children, have weakened men's sense that they are morally obliged to marry their pregnant girlfriend. The fact that what used to be regarded as the prerogatives of the married state, like sexual companionship, are now routinely available to unmarried people reduces the opportunity costs of remaining unmarried or of not searching for a spouse until a career has stabilised or job been secured—if ever. More people will settle for the next best thing or least worst option, even if only a small minority would have actively pursued it. Women who would otherwise have been likely to remain childless spinsters, if potential husbands were scarce, now smoothly move from *can*, to *may*, to *will* have a baby alone—with the state providing a basic income. From several directions, the beliefs that marriage, children and families are inextricably linked, and tied to the adult work role,[22] were undercut within a short space of time; and young men lost the 'taken-for-granted project for life of responsibility for their own wife and children. Their expectations had ceased to be automatically geared to unavoidable parenthood.'[23]

Sustained economic recoveries may eventually have some positive impact on the low-skilled unemployed, as in the US in the 1990s, but the economic decline of low-skilled workers seems unlikely to reverse itself, as 'demand ... has plummeted to the lowest depths in human history'.[24] The rise of the working mother, anxious to keep her employment to a minimum necessary to meet basic commitments, may have helped companies to 're-structure' with contingent workers and '... many have designed new jobs with the new women's labour force in mind. The new labour force of mothers has proved an attractive, reliable, workforce to many service industry employers compared with unqualified young male school-leavers and at the same, or sometimes lower, cost.'[25] Over the 1980s and 1990s, there was virtually no growth in 'elementary occupations' for prime-age men, compared with that for women.[26]

The pool of marriageable men, and therefore couple formation, not only decreases when male unemployment increases and male earnings decline. Couple formation also declines when women become more educated and qualified. Increased female workforce participation combines with increasing male non-participation to accentuate the decline in marriage rates.[27] At the bottom of the income ladder, welfare income subsidises the marital search process for lone mothers, just as unemployment payments enable the unemployed to search longer for a better job. Further up, women's education and earnings reduce the economic need to marry early and allows them to take longer finding a suitable spouse. But as women still seek to 'marry up', this also means that the pool of marriageable men with the same or better professional status is severely reduced.[28] The marriage squeeze on men, which started when a large cohort entered collapsing labour markets, may be followed by a marriage squeeze on women. This is driven by higher female education and increased labour-force participation, as well as higher divorce rates and less incentives for men to marry, given their access to uncommitted sex and convenient live-in arrangements, encouraged by female competition for eligible men.[29] Where there is a relative oversupply of women, men will also be less inclined to marry. When they do, they will be less committed to existing marital relationships. Women will be more likely to pursue career goals which decrease further their chances of marrying men with comparable socio-economic characteristics. Among black Americans, not only is the marriage pool for black females severely restricted, but divorce is high, black females have high educational and occupational status compared with black men, and very low rates of marital births.[30] (In the UK, black men's hourly pay is well below that of black women, and their unemployment rate is double that of whites of the same age.)[31]

Out of Work, Out of Wedlock

While income makes marriages, its loss breaks marriages. At any point in a marriage, joblessness substantially raises the chance of divorce. Labour market changes may aggravate financial hardship by adding to marital instability. The husband's unemployment was associated with a 70 per cent increase in the risk of marital breakdown the next year for British cities in the 1980s.[32] In a recent study of the growth of lone parenthood, couples were three times more likely to separate if the man was unemployed,[33] and twice as likely in the six years of the British Household Panel Study (1991-97),[34] with the husband's economic status topping the list of factors associated with separation in the Economic and Social Research Council's programmes.[35] The higher the husband's earnings, the less likely are couples to part.[36] In Australian samples, young men in the lowest income group are nearly one-and-a-half times more likely to be divorced than those in the highest income group.[37] While falling marriage rates are a major factor in the failure of young men to form couples, for older men (over 34), marital break-up accounts for more than half of the overall growth in male isolation from couples in New Zealand over the decade from 1986-1996. Moreover, the growth of marital instability during this time is largely accounted for by couples where the man has no post-school, or only trade, qualifications. As with the link between marriage and education, the association between low divorce-proneness and high husband-education tends to disappear once income level is considered, as do occupational differences. Even research on the survival rates of marriages after application for divorce has shown an inverse relationship between the fate of the application and the husband's income.[38] Moreover, while men in high status groups have a below-average propensity to be divorced, they also have an above-average likelihood of re-marriage if they do divorce.

The weak economic position of the young father provides a strong link between pre-marital pregnancy and the breakdown rates of subsequent marriages.[39] While pre-school children generally tend to deter divorce, in lower-income families the presence of a young child and all the additional economic demands is correlated with break-up.[40] Young fathers who are able to improve their economic position have noticeably higher marital stability, while downward mobility in the husband's occupation after marriage increases the chances of divorce, even in earlier New Zealand data.[41] Later in the life-cycle, an important reason (explaining half the association) why older people and those in longer marriages are less apt to divorce, is 'material interest'. As married couples accumulate assets, the barriers to divorce mount.[42]

An increase in men in the family-building stage with insufficient resources to support a family above poverty level, if at all, means that wives have to bring in income. Factors which frustrate or reduce specialisation at home also reduce the gains from co-operation. Even as there has been a rapid increase in dual-earner families, marriages where the husband is the main provider are still less likely to break up compared with those where both partners are unemployed, employed full-time or there is role reversal.[43]

Not only the erosion of the significance attached to marriage, but the declining influence of religious, moral and legal obstacles, including stigma, to marital dissolution and illegitimacy, has left individuals freer to respond in the face of the apparent advantages and disadvantages of various options. At the bottom of the class ladder, the likelihood of divorce or separation may be higher than the chances of re-marriage.[44] As sole mothers remain single longer than formerly, women with reliable benefit income, over which they have full control, and a public tenancy, may have few economic incentives to find a live-in or 'official' partner. Retaining autonomy and having a boyfriend is preferable to relying on a low wage-earner or claimant.

Cohabitation Takes Over from Marriage

Those vulnerable to the vicissitudes of the economy are also more likely to avoid marriage in favour of casual and conditional relationships, precisely because these enable people to keep their options open. A man in a poor economic situation is more likely to cohabit, and couples are less likely to commit themselves in the face of uncertain prospects, or when the economic gains from marriage are low or negative. Prudence has dictated that a couple should wait until they are financially secure enough to 'afford' marriage, without which children should not be produced. In the past, this meant attenuated courtships. Now they can move in together and even produce children while the nuptials are put off or abrogated in the absence of the financial security felt necessary for marriage. Cohabiting couples with children are generally more likely to be of low socio-economic status compared with childless cohabitees and married couples with children. Unemployment of fathers, worklessness among couples and receipt of unemployment benefit and income-related family support have run at roughly double the rate for cohabiting, compared with married, couples. Over a third of cohabitees fall into the lowest income quintile, almost twice as many as the proportion for married parents, and the proportion of cohabitees among couples declines progressively up the income scale.[45] (Lone parents coming out of cohabitation have a greater chance of receiving means-tested benefits, compared with those coming out of marriages.[46])

The picture is similar in other English-speaking countries.[47] In the US, the 1996 poverty rate for children living in married-couple households was six per cent, but 31 per cent for children living in cohabiting households, much closer to the rate of 45 per cent for children living with lone mothers.[48] Around a quarter of children in cohabiting families, like 30 per cent of those with single mothers, had mothers who received public assistance. On average, cohabiting couples with children have only about two-thirds of the income of married couples with children, mainly due to the fact that the average income of male cohabiting partners is only about half that of married men.[49] Economic differences persist even when factors like parental education, race, parental age and age of children are considered. Not only is a selection effect present, but when men marry, especially when they have children, they tend to become more productive; working and earning more than their unmarried counterparts. In turn, the private transfer of wealth, particularly from family members is considerably lower for cohabiting, compared with married, couples.[50] There is clearly less willingness to transfer wealth to 'boyfriends' than to 'in-laws'.

High-status and high-resource parents, concerned perhaps at the possible loss or 'leakage' of wealth, may discourage children from cohabiting and pressurise cohabiting offspring either to marry or break up.[51]

For many cohabiting parents the passage into marriage is often associated with financial resources or labour market advantage, and as people acquire assets which they can bequeath, or something to transact, such as houses, savings and pensions.[52] The higher the man's earnings, the more the chances are of the union being converted to marriage and the less the risk of dissolution. Along similar lines, Australian research shows how employment reduces the chance of first cohabitation for women, while increasing the chances of marriage.[53] Means-tested benefits may discourage marriage, and encourage more low-income people to operate as two singles, one with children.[54] As cohabiting parents tend to have a less successful socio-economic profile than married parents, this contributes to their overall higher breakdown rates.[55] However, the greater propensity of married parents to stay together is not just 'a function of their relatively more successful circumstances',[56] since cohabiting parents break up at much *higher rates* at similar income levels.

The worst economic profiles are found amongst men who have neither married nor cohabited more than sporadically with the mothers of their children.[57] Such men are seen as more or less useless and superfluous. At a group discussion for single mothers:

> ... a young woman who had recently discovered she was pregnant entered the room in tears, explaining that her boyfriend had just ended the relationship. One of the mothers offered the following advice: 'Nay pet, shut your crying. If you're having a bairn the last thing you need is a bloke hanging around ... you'll be right.' The conversation which followed confirmed the opinions of most of the women that the men in their worlds were of little help in terms of parenting, and less in terms of financial support. Noticeably, only one of the 40 women interviewed ... had continued any degree of relationship, albeit platonic, with the father of her child. This was the only one of the fathers to be in stable employment.[58]

Minority Men Especially Disadvantaged

Family behaviour may provide a barometer of economic dislocations. In 1965 Daniel Patrick Moynihan first drew attention to a rise in family breakdown and illegitimacy among American blacks which augured badly for their advancement.[59] These communities were being drastically affected by changes in agriculture, industry and migration. As black urbanisation overtook that of whites by 1950, this made blacks extra vulnerable to the impending post-industrial changes that were to transform the opportunity structures of cities. The joblessness of black men was almost indistinguishable from that of white men in 1955.

Between 1975 and 1989 there was a 15-25 percentage point difference, suggesting that the increasing racial gap in joblessness was a major cause of the increasing racial gap in the proportion of all children living with sole mothers.[60] The increase in sole parenthood was tied to the falling fortunes of two-parent families, where the stresses on one encouraged the formation of the other, making the rates of female-headed families in American cities inversely related to the income of intact families, so that one rose as the other fell.[61]

In the post-war period, the manufacturing bases in New Zealand cities created a need for labour, resulting in rapid internal migration of Maori from rural areas or small towns and, in the 1970s, a wave of migration from the Pacific Islands.[62] Up until 1987, Maori were more likely than non-Maori to be in the labour force. Maori participation rates then began to fall below those of non-Maori, with unemployment reaching a high of 27.3 in 1992.[63] In December 2002, the Maori unemployment rate was still 11.4 per cent, three times the non-Maori rate of 3.6 per cent.[64] With young men worst affected, the unemployment rate of Maori men aged 15-24 years approached 40 per cent in 1991 (the rate for non-Maori was nearly 20 per cent).

With major employment areas such as manufacturing and forestry in decline, experience and skills were not transferable to the jobs created in the expanding service sector. (Even in 1996, the proportion of Maori employed as plant and machine operators and assemblers was twice that of non-Maori, and accounted for nearly a quarter of employed men.) While the estimation is that 20 per cent of the adult population have very poor literacy skills, over 60 per cent of Maori and Pacific peoples are functioning below the level of literacy required to effectively meet the demands of everyday life. Gender disparity in the qualifications of the employed and unemployed is greater for Maori than non-Maori, and a larger proportion of unemployed Maori men (59 per cent), and employed Maori men (41.6 per cent) hold no qualifications compared with their female peers (51.4 per cent and 34.8 per cent).[65]

For those in employment, average earnings for Europeans are significantly higher, largely reflecting the difference in education levels, and they are more likely to be in two-income couples (as a cause and effect of marriage). Relative to Europeans, Maori earnings and incomes have declined since the early 1980s,[66] and Maori men are over-represented in the lowest 25 per cent of men's income distribution.[67]

While employment, earnings and income changes have particularly depleted the supply of marriageable Maori men, disparities in male and female death rates for the age group 15-24 are also particularly marked, being nearly three times higher for males than their female counterparts. Motor accidents and suicides account for over two-thirds of deaths.[68] Even when adjusted for population changes, the rates of imprisonment have more than doubled since 1950. In 1950, Maori were only 18 per cent of prison inmates but, by 1989, nearly a half of all prisoners were Maori. Migration weakened the *whanau, hapu* and *iwi* support networks basic to social control, further to be undermined by disintegration at the family nucleus.[69] Idleness and inactivity are not the way to develop the skills and aptitudes necessary for self-support and success, but are rather associated with drug and alcohol abuse and crime, with younger men both perpetrators and victims:[70] 'locked into a vicious circle from which it is difficult for individuals to extricate themselves'.[71] A 'behavioural resistance to work builds over the life course as welfare dependence becomes a way of life: the length of any job becomes ever shorter and the likelihood of finding such men in work at all declines'.[72]

Do Non-Working Men make More Caring Fathers?

A man's position in the family is strongly related to his external position: fathers 'earn their place' in the family by providing.[73] Men themselves often do not see how they can be good fathers without being good economic providers. Other involvement is additional, not a substitute. However, it has increasingly been suggested that providing is somehow antithetical to any 'commitment to involved fathering'.[74] Researchers comment on the way in which the inability of unemployed or low-paid men to 'show their love through material provision signified loss of self-respect and indeed a threat to identity. Such men did not take the opportunity to assume a more active and involved style of fathering.'[75] However:

> ... the male breadwinning role has been regarded by most members of the social research community as a reactionary phenomenon which no right-thinking person would *want* to analyse sensitively and constructively. Many research projects explicitly treat women's economic independence as a self-evident, uncontested public good, in terms of which the persistence of male attachment to economic providing sticks out as a problem and an embarrassing obstacle to social progress.[76]

Feminists are now joined by 'new men' who complain that the traditional father was trapped, and excluded from doing the caring by having to earn. Therefore, men who have lost their jobs and 'continue to cling to traditional notions of gender' should 'positively adapt to their new situation' like the men 'wanting to change' into male mums.[77] Therefore, the eradication of the breadwinner will bring a change in 'fatherhood from income generating to loving and responsible'.[78] Men themselves are seen as desperate to be homemakers or child-carers. Not only is the rejection of marriage attributed to 'women escaping the hold of patriarchy. It is also men who have woken up to the trap of marriage that kept them on the breadwinner treadmill and separated from home life.'[79]

In contrast to the view that earning somehow prevents men nurturing their children (as well as being oppressive), breadwinning is basic to involvement with children and domestic participation, and thus pivotal to the paternal role. Men who are not family providers are far less likely to be making any other contribution. Men freed from work are liberated from family life. Men—particularly lower-class men—are more likely to make a positive contribution to the development of their children, as well as their support, when they are employed. Fathers in low-income, black US families who are satisfied with parenting, employed and contributing financially, have young children with better cognitive and language competence, and fewer behavioural problems. 'Employment and financial contributions serve as markers of a father's commitment and support': men with 'economic resources are more likely to be involved with their children and to be accepted by the mother and her family'.[80] In contrast, the National Longitudinal Survey of Youth showed how father-care was detrimental, particularly to the development of young boys in low-income families. Many of these fathers were unemployed—often with their own emotional problems.[81] As observed of young, single, and largely unemployed non-resident fathers in Tyne and Wear, England, it 'was difficult to determine to what degree "being there" involved moral and emotional support or physical availability'.[82] In 'the absence of the more traditionally defined role of provider', the men projected future scenarios 'when they would be needed', which seemed to centre on fantasies of drinking partners, or teaching a boy *how to look out for his self not get shoved around*.[83]

Irrespective of parents' actual involvement in paid work, few people (including most women) want role reversal. Mothers everywhere take care of young children. Changes in the labour market may cause changes in family work patterns, but not in assumptions. Few men and women see equality in terms of an absolutely equal division of the same tasks, but rather as mutual respect, commitment and reciprocity over time. Moreover, if one wage is not sufficient to support a family, it is not going to stretch further if the man rather than the woman stays home.

In Geoff Dench's multicultural work on fathers' roles, men with traditional values (understanding 'family' as a network of interpersonal rights and obligations, whose members have responsibilities to provide reciprocal supports for each other), were far more likely to be the main or sole providers than those holding alternative values (to whom divisions of domestic labour are sources of inequality and injustice and personal choice and autonomy are basic to a fair society). Only 40 per cent of 'alternative-values' men were in work of any kind, compared with 68 per cent of 'traditional' men. Forty per cent of 'alternative-values' men lived alone; few were ever married or had children and, if they did, they were far more likely to be absent fathers.[84] Among Afro-Caribbeans this was accompanied by the most far-reaching adoption of alternative lifestyles in terms of the lowest marriage, highest unwed birth and lone parenthood rates. Also present were the highest rates of sexual conflict and sexual polarisation, as well as marginalisation of men, who were highly likely to be unproductive (47 per cent were unemployed), apathetic and generally peripheral to household and community affairs.[85]

Married Men Work Harder

Changes in employment affect family patterns, but changes in family patterns influence employment and earnings—of men as well as women. Male marriageability depends on employment and income. But marriage itself promotes male labour-market involvement and success, while non-marriage means downward mobility. The support a man can offer a family depends upon a number of factors, over which he may have little control, but economic responsibilities for family members provide an impetus to work. While the feminist view is that men 'use' their families for personal gain, husbands tend to see work as the means to improve the conditions of family life, or securing a standard of domestic living rather than occupational progress *per se*. Recent research in the UK confirmed the obvious:

> Jo: How important is work to you?
> Roger Green: My work? It isn't. The only reason I've ever worked is to get money to er provide—that's all. No—work's been a bind. (Father of three, service engineer).[86]

In the Maori community at Rakau, described in the 1950s:

> ... the wage workers of the community do not feel motivated to work by either economic or social insecurity. Security is not valued consciously because it has become an accepted part of the background of work. Family needs and the means of acquiring property are the chief incentives to work.[87]

Traditionally, in working-class communities, marriage carried with it the right to be treated as adult and independent, and to be seen as socially adequate. Young husbands 'felt they were now no longer simply youths out for a good time, but mature and responsible citizens'.[88] Marriage was:

> ... inextricably linked with responsibility; indeed, marriage confers autonomy on the individual *because* it also confers responsibility. The act of getting married is, therefore, both liberating and restrictive. A job is no longer merely an activity which provides an income; it has become the means of sustaining a household and of carrying out those responsibilities which define adulthood.[89]

Juxtaposed with this, is a long-standing undercurrent of male protest at marriage as financially burdensome, restrictive and sexually repressive. This antedates modern feminism, although it's manifestation in the 'hobo' street culture provided inspiration and content for the nihilistic counter-culture of the 1960s. Here, the bread-winning role is an onerous, emasculating burden and the 'good provider' the dupe and drudge of women and children. The struggle between 'respectable' and 'rough' working class was played out in 1950s Rakau where:

> Young men who have no family responsibilities compete with one another in buying fine clothes, guitars, motor bicycles, or other goods. Their affluence is soundly criticised by the older people who think their money could be put to better use. There is not much surplus money once they marry and have a family. Some young men try to maintain their bachelor spending habits after they marry, but most settle into a responsible pattern of purchasing the goods their families need.[90]

Labour market detachment amongst men is now widespread throughout the English-speaking world. Showing a steady upward trend compared with the cyclical movement of unemployment, this shadows the rising numbers of welfare-dependent sole parents. The duration of time men spend out of the labour market is becoming longer as the rate of non-participation among prime-age males (aged 25-55) increases. There was a slight increase between 1961 and 1986 and then a sharp rise as, by 1998, nearly nine per cent of prime-age males were non-participants, well above the five to six per cent who were unemployed.[91] About a third not participating in the labour market are non-European. The Maori position parallels that of black men in the UK, where there is a tight link between men's job and marriage prospects. Afro-Caribbean men's high unemployment rate and low pay may be owed, not only to poor educational qualifications and a lack of work experience, but to few family commitments.[92] If black men have qualifications, are attached and do not live in a run-down area, then their prospects are the same as a similar white person's.[93] For both, a young man living on his own is about twice as likely to be unemployed as one who lives with a 'partner'.[94]

Marital status is a significant predictor of joblessness and of the length of time men spend without a job. An employer dismissing workers may favour the retention of men with families over single men.[95] However, results from a large US sample of young white men aged between 16 and 31 show that married men were between 58 per cent and nearly 94 per cent more likely to leave joblessness at each point in time than single men. (This compares with being from 12 per cent to 14 per cent more likely to find a job for each additional year of schooling.)[96]

For New Zealand, as elsewhere, the employment gap by marital status has increased over recent times.[97] According to the 1991 census, only around 40 per cent of male non-participants aged 25-54 were living with a spouse or 'partner', while around ten per cent were with parents, and another nine per cent were living as sole parents. A low level of formal education increases the likelihood that they will be isolated from both family and work.[98] In 1996, 90 per cent of prime-age men who were living alone and had a degree or higher qualifications were in paid work, compared with only 66 per cent without formal qualifications.[99] The only counter-movement to the increasing alignment of male employment and marriage involves a distinction between young men in couples, with and without children. Observed elsewhere, this may be owed to the disincentive effect of means-tested benefits for low skilled and low paid people with children.[100]

The position is almost identical to that in the US[101] and the UK, where it is increasingly apparent that large percentages of single and divorced men are unemployed or otherwise economically 'inactive'—an aspect of the way that, by the mid-1990s, over 40 per cent of single adult households had no earnings, up from 24 per cent two decades before.[102] Men at 33 years old were six times more likely to be 'economically inactive' and over twice as likely to be unemployed if they were separated, divorced or widowed compared with the married. Never-married men were three times more likely to be unemployed or economically inactive and to derive all their income from state benefits.[103] Similarly, the Family Resources Survey shows an astonishing 42 per cent of single men aged 40-59 not working, as well as 47 per cent of divorced men, compared with 13 per cent of married men with children. There was a four- to five-fold difference in the proportions of single and divorced, compared with married, men, receiving income support. Non-resident fathers are far more likely than fathers in general to be unemployed, poor and dependent on means-tested or health related benefits.[104]

Average increases in the per capita income recorded for separating or divorcing men, compared with women, should not distract from the trailing off of male earnings and employment. The protective solidarity given by the ties and responsibilities of marriage and parenthood is less available to or accessible by people who live in isolating circumstances. Men 'living by themselves may find it difficult to lift themselves out of unemployment, and quickly degenerate into inadequates and misfits'.[105] If families without men need far more help and transfers than those with men, so men without families are far more likely to need assistance themselves. The fragility or absence of family responsibilities easily promotes a 'child-like dependence in the family setting, or as welfare-supported loners', becoming a burden to 'families, the community and society generally'.[106] Young men who have never worked, and adults out of work for longer than two years, have low prospects of ever leaving income support.[107]

Marriage and Human Capital Accumulation

Marital status is not only a proxy for a man's attachment to the labour market, but also for greater willingness to invest in human capital, as studies continue to document the greater growth in earnings for men after marriage than before.[108] Single men earn much the same as single women, sometimes not so much, but married men earn more than single men, single women and married women.[109] Not only were nearly 87 per cent of New Zealand fathers in two-parent families in the labour force in 1996, nearly 95 per cent were working more than 30 hours a week and nearly a half of full-time workers put in 50 hours or more.[110]

The greater economic productivity of married men is not simply explainable by the way that men in more precarious economic positions are less likely to marry. When US researchers tried to discover why married men earn more per hour than single men (the 'marriage premium'),[111] and experienced faster wage growth for the first ten to 20 years of marriage, or why marriage increased by 50 per cent the probability that recent hires would receive top performance ratings, this was not attributable to factors like union membership, experience, occupation or education.[112] Simply: marriage provides a focus for striving. Since a man now has something to work for, he must keep going, do well at the job, and grasp opportunities for advancement.[113] As married men increase their objective human capital endowments more rapidly than single men, the returns are used to support the marriage.[114]

Over time, the marriage premium may have fallen.[115] There are indications that younger fathers are more likely to work longer hours to raise family earnings.[116] Women have reduced incentives to invest in their spouse's earning power where the male/female wage gap is narrowing, where high divorce rates reduce the pay-off from investing in marriage, or where they have a wage advantage—as with American and British blacks.[117] In turn, while married women may work more outside the home as an insurance against marital breakdown, the marriage premium for husbands is reduced the more hours a wife works, and declines as divorce approaches.[118]

Cohabitation Differs from Marriage

The tendency for married men to earn more than single men by being more productive and successful at work is missing or far lower for cohabiting men.[119] Men in more precarious economic positions are less likely to marry, and cohabiting men with children also tend to be less well qualified and educated. However, male cohabitees have rates of economic inactivity that resemble single and divorced men. A third aged between 25 and 39 were unemployed or out of the labour market in the British Household Panel Study, compared with 14 per cent of married men with children.[120] Since cohabitation is more provisional and unstable than marriage, specialisation in tasks and responsibilities is less rational. The initial advantages of well educated people are likely to be reinforced by the greater likelihood of better educated people to be in couples, and to be legally married. However, marriage also 'involves a commitment. That commitment is perhaps an epiphany upon saying the words "I do", perhaps a gradual change in experience leading to a penumbra of changes that ultimately result in the formation of human capital'.[121]

By closing the gap between natural and social parenthood, marriage has traditionally tied a man's position in the wider society to the proper performance of family duties. Within marriage wives are likely to offer help, advice and pressure to do well—not least because higher husband-income increases their own options. Marriage will also increase productivity by significantly reducing negative health behaviours, like drinking and substance abuse.[122] In contrast, cohabitation represents freedom from the constraints and demands of marriage, particularly where there is an inability or unwillingness to take on the responsibilities, and potential liabilities, involved with commitment.[123] In turn this generates the expectation that 'family-like' relationships are temporary, and so unworthy of the investment of time and energy, which the parties are less likely to give or require.[124] The uncertainty makes investment much riskier even than in contemporary marriage.[125]

No Need for the Unmarried to be Seedless or Celibate

Historically, the pattern has been childlessness in marriage and celibacy outside on the part of the long-term poor or hard pressed.[126] Sudden upward surges in bastardy are associated with economic downturns in earlier periods, but these have been passing blips, owed to the disruption of marital plans, rather than sustained movements.[127] In pre-industrial times, a not insubstantial proportion of the population never married, being often servants in other people's houses or casual and mobile labourers. The population was more than adequately replaced, as those who married, even when late, had lots of children. Now, those who marry increasingly have few or no children, given the dependence on double incomes, and those who do not marry, do not have to be seedless any more than celibate. The state will fund their reproduction, albeit at a relatively low standard of living.

6

Targeting the Needy— and Creating More of Them

Summary: While it has become difficult for men to support families, so the welfare system has made it easier for women to have children without having a husband. The rising level of benefits for sole parents has accompanied an increase in the number of them, wherever this has occurred. As rising levels of welfare expenditure have caused concern, the answer has been seen in terms of 'targeting' the really 'needy'. Unfortunately, the more tightly that social assistance is targeted, the more swiftly it must be withdrawn. This lowers the incentive to take a job. At the same time, for those in work there is a disincentive to increase earnings because income-related benefits will be abated, and because the benefits system takes into account different household sizes, when the tax system does not. The combined effect of the 'employment trap' and the 'poverty trap' is to lock people into a perpetual low-income zone. Meanwhile, there is no recognition of the 'self-reliant family' since a man who does the best he can for his children receives no external affirmation or encouragement. Yet, he saves the state the cost of providing for his children, while helping to provide for other men's—carrying, unaided and unrecognised, the cost of a new generation, while funding the retired. One of the consequences of a 'pathological' approach to the family—targeting all assistance on those with problems—is that it assumes other families do not have problems. By depriving them of assistance such a system can actually cause more family fragmentation. When governments 'target the needy' the iron law of welfare is activated. An income-related benefit creates incentives for individuals to change their behaviour to continue qualifying, and for those on the margin to make themselves eligible, so that the system creates more dependency than it resolves. As economic circumstances have made it difficult for married couples to support children, while making it easier for poorer single women to do so, the result is that a big fall in marital fertility is allied with an increased propensity of single women to have babies.

When the destabilisation of male earnings is accompanied by prog-rammes supporting broken families, parenting outside marriage becomes a viable option and there is likely to be a shift from one welfare system to another. The development of a system of public assistance and extra benefits for UK lone mothers in the late 1970s coincided with a considerable rise in welfare dependency. Australia saw an enormous upsurge in the dependent numbers and a subsequent rapid rate of increase, after the six-months qualifying period was removed in 1980. (The numbers rose five-fold in ten years.)[1] By 1991/92 the federal government was providing about ten times as much support to children of separated parents as to children in intact families.[2] In America, the level of Aid to Families with Dependent Children (AFDC) and welfare participation rose together. Originally AFDC was designed for widows, but changes in the qualifying rules meant that all a mother had to do to be eligible for assistance was not work and not marry an employed man. Between 1963 and 1972 the average real benefit (for a family of four) increased by 35 per cent, with Medicaid, housing, school meals, food stamps and other benefits adding to the welfare package. The percentage of sole mothers going on the AFDC programme increased from 29 per cent to 63 per cent. There was also a 50 per cent rise in the number of female-headed families.

The Attractions of Targeting

After New Zealand had developed an elaborate system of selective and means-tested relief for the needy, debate on the causes and conse-quences of poverty was soon overtaken by concern at the rising numbers drawing income-related benefits, the increased duration of benefit receipt, and possible inter-generational cycles of dependency. Approximately 20 per cent of working-age adults were dependent on social security benefits as their primary source of income by the end of the twentieth century, compared with two to three per cent 30 years before.[3]

'Targeting' is popular with people of all political perspectives. The immediate attraction is, as always, 'the need to ensure the maximum welfare gain at the least fiscal/economic cost' as advised in both the 1984 and 1987 Treasury briefing papers.[4] Where 'promoting equity' means restricting help to those in 'real need', or the 'genuinely needy', the idea is that eliminating payments, exemptions or services for the better-off ensures that redistribution to the poor can become more generous and effective. This is justified because of the 'costs on the economy of paying large sums of money to those not in great need. There is also an equity issue. It seems unfair for the taxpayer to support the rich while at the same time paying the poor less than could otherwise be afforded'.[5] (The suggestion is that the 'taxpayer' is a being apart from the 'rich' and the 'poor'.) Offering a seemingly cost-effective way of alleviating poverty, targeting promises to reduce total expendi-ture, while greater benefits flow to low- or no-income people. In contrast, universal systems appear 'deeply regressive when the economy demands cuts in the bad times, because the sacrifices hit both rich and poor equally'.[6] (However, expecting the 'rich'—i.e. those not under the benefit line—to carry all their costs without recognition, while funding the 'poor', may provoke resentment at free-loaders as much as sympathy for the unfortunate.) The process impacts disproportionately on middle-income groups with children, rather than the 'rich', so that:

> ... concentrating welfare on those below the poverty line, while affording no tax relief to family earners, ... means [that] a large bracket of family incomes is levelled to a single minimum family income. This represents the perfect realisation of welfare's social justice principle that no family should receive tax or other recompense of the extra costs of family members, if its net income would thereby rise above the current level of welfare benefits for a family of its size and composition. The fact that taxation reduces the *majority* of families to ... welfare levels of income, while it leaves all earners without dependents *well above* the single welfare income, is apparently of no moment for social justice.[7]

From centre left, selective benefits are often construed as a form of income redistribution—the true goal of a welfare state. By definition, a share-out is easily affordable. Holding governments responsible for the living standards of their people, the poverty lobby's 'solution is to devise ... transfer policies which ensure comfortable real incomes for all, irrespective of their employment or family status'.[8] These are owed as of right and involve no reciprocity, where 'the capable, responsible and powerful state should serve programs to incapable, irresponsible and powerless people on the ground'.[9] It might look like 'a completely artificial means of living', a 'gammon economy', that requires no 'work, initiative, struggle, enterprise, contribution, effort', but those who receive are always seen as deserving, and the system that gives is always seen to be denying.[10] In the nihilistic perspective of the counter-cultural feminist, all obligations or concerns of one person for another are abhorrent anyway. If women and children are supported by the father, not only are they seen to be 'controlled by the main earner', but 'their dependency also has the effect of controlling the person who is obliged to provide'.[11]

Unfortunately, the more tightly that social assistance is targeted, the more swiftly it must be abated. Similarly, a government that wants to increase benefit amounts without helping more people than before, has no choice but to increase the rate of withdrawal. This lowers the incentives to take a job, by reducing the rationality of work and respect for the law—hence, the 'employment trap'. Providing someone with an income-substitute for employment is, by definition, a discouragement to work—and it will be greater the larger the benefit in relation to possible wages.[12] It is hardly surprising that there is a positive relationship between the overall real wage rate and male labour force participation, and negative relationships between the level of government transfer payments, or total income from non-wage sources, and male labour-force participation.[13] At a time of declining real living standards or falling earnings, the overlap of benefits with wages, especially for those with children, is likely to be particularly acute.

In turn, it may become counter-productive to increase earnings (especially if taxes are imposed at the same time) as income-related, in-work benefits are abated—thus the 'poverty trap'. The benefits system takes into account different household sizes, when the tax system does not.

The pious belief may be that those 'less well-off than they used to be ... may decide to work longer hours to restore their previous standard of living'.[14] Some do. But Treasury economists have not been blind to 'a general rule, [that] the more people facing higher effective marginal tax rates over longer ranges of potential income, the greater the costs to society and the greater the probable loss of output'. Indeed: 'An indication of the effect of such scales is the fact that very few people are in jobs with an income at the level when the maximum rate of benefit abatement applies ...'.[15] As 'the combined effect of taxation and abatement of in-work benefits as ... earnings rise ... [leads to] a barrier both to increase work hours and to efforts to advance in the labour market, this may have the effect of trapping workers in a perpetual low-income zone'.[16]

The tendency is to dismiss this as a smaller price than the 'opposite problem posed by the high cost of universal schemes', where the 'tax burden must be greater' and the disincentive of high tax rates generally 'needs to be contrasted with the specific disincentives of high effective marginal tax rates on recipients'.[17] But does one bear comparison with the other? Or is a tax rate approaching 100 per cent at low earnings different from, for example, 40 or 50 per cent in the top income decile? Anyway, tax concessions can represent revenues foregone rather than spent by the state. Children's costs are relatively constant, regardless of family income. Children in high-income families take up proportionately less of income than in poorer families, but then tax allowances are also less significant at higher levels. It is not so much whether universal programmes, like education and health, benefit the 'rich', but whether the 'rich' are net beneficiaries or net contributors.[18] The available evidence suggests that they are net contributors.[19]

The more provisions that become means-tested, the more people face a range of measures, with differing entitlements depending on family type, age, assets and income. Very high withdrawal rates can result, sometimes over long income ranges. Even at the point of abatement, there are more losses to face, like the Community Services Card which disappears with the end of eligibility for Family Support. To cope with this, there arose a vision of a seamless, global system of abatement of all social assistance and services. Recognising that targeting of income support, housing assistance, education and health, would lead to 'cumulative effective marginal tax rates ... possibly well over 100 per cent', or more money lost than received with each extra dollar earned, it was imagined that the 'solution to this problem is to carefully integrate the scales of assistance and abatement of assistance for the various areas'.[20] So, through the development of 'family accounts', one form of assistance would phase out after the previous assistance had been fully phased out, in order of benefits first, then Family Support, then health assistance, followed by any other service where help might become means-tested (like education), and, finally, the (tertiary) student allowance.[21] While support would be reduced as family income rose, it was imagined that the system could be designed in such a way that people would always be better off earning additional income and moving smoothly from dependence to independence. As those who do not 'need' assistance begin to meet the costs of 'their own demands ... at the same time, [they] contribute to the costs of those services for the less fortunate'.[22] The family account proposal was not implemented, not least because it was unrealisable.

No Recognition for the Self-Reliant Family

The opposite side of the coin to the 'needy' recipient is the completely self-reliant, 'responsible' or 'self-sufficient' family, meeting all its 'care, control and support responsibilities',[23] well beyond childhood. The income necessary to stay above the poverty line obviously varies according to the number of people who depend upon that income. It is much easier for a single person to be self-sufficient than a family which, even when it has a higher income, may be providing for four or more times as many people, and considering that the arrival of a child pre-determines other choices in the following decades. If those with dependents must compete against unencumbered individuals, while making the same contributions to the revenue (and perhaps meeting the involuntary costs of services like health and education which it is ordained that children receive), then the way to meet all responsibilities, and the route to virtue, is simple—do not have children.

The nature of the 1991 proposals to make the 'core family' responsible for its members bears no relationship to the reality of the family in the market economy. As one commentator puts it: 'One of the consequences of the pathological approach to families is that it assumes that all other families are unproblematic ... the bigger issue of the adequacy of the incomes of all families with dependents could be ignored.'[24] The result is that what has no existence in one context becomes a reality only where the costs of child-rearing thrust people below a certain threshold—and the state is obliged to help. It is rare for a modern waged economy to deny recognition of family or reproductive costs, (unless these plunge parents under the poverty threshold). These costs are normally accommodated or mitigated in the labour market, housing market, the tax or welfare system, goods or services. To espouse a goal of 'self-reliance', which would throw off any such 'burden of welfare' is a dramatic social experiment, or an adventurous and highly ambitious policy to embark upon. The result may not be 'self-reliant' families, but fewer families, with the consequence that the individual faces a solitary life without supports. More people may live alone, putting redistribution within households in decline, with the effect that more people actually rely on government as the principal source of income and services.

The contradiction at the heart of the system is that, while it has the 'self-reliant' family as its goal, it ranks people's care and support of children or each other as no more meritorious or worthwhile than breeding poodles; no more deserving of recognition than collecting stamps. Once the good father was defined both popularly and politically in terms of the good provider for his wife and children, and incentives and sanctions were so arranged that he received public approval and recognition. Now, the state 'assumes that the demand for parental togetherness is "price inelastic"'. With financial well-being decreased by marriage, this is transformed from an institution designed to protect children into one which particularly penalises lower-income parents whose children would benefit from it most. A man may try to do the best he can for his children without complaint—an activity which receives no external affirmation or encouragement and is deemed as worthwhile, or worthless, as boating. Yet, he saves the state the cost of providing for his own children, while helping to provide for other men's—carrying the cost of a new generation, while funding the retired.[25]

If mutual support is a private choice, this might at least indicate that a couple should be treated as two self-sufficient individuals. But it is assumed that a non-employed married woman is supported by sharing in the employed spouse's income—while the government refuses to treat marriage as a partnership by splitting and taxing the main income in equal shares. Denying that marriage is a business partnership for taxation purposes, a judge for the Taxation Review Authority declared that what the husband 'subsequently chooses to do with that income is entirely his own affair, but the tax on that income is paid at the point and at the time of derivation'. The unemployment benefit is also calculated on joint income, so if one partner earns extra income the total couple-rate is reduced by the relevant amount and the remainder divided between the two. Each must then sustain themselves separately on less than they would receive if they were actual singles, even if the man treats his share as personal spending money, while the woman meets collective expenditure as her responsibility. However, the DPB is nearly as much as the unemployment benefit for both parents together (or only $30 less), making the total amount of benefits payable to a four-person family significantly higher if the parents separate. Where a couple can present themselves as a lone parent, plus a single person, they will do far better.[26]

Almost by definition, targeted welfare programmes will channel support to families that deviate from the norm.[27] While other targeted assistance is for poorer families, whatever their composition, the DPB specifically supports sole parents as essentially the only recognised family type. The state accepts the responsibility to provide a basic living when one parent goes solo without resources, or contributes towards someone to look after the children while she earns. If families separate, or fathers do not support children, aid is provided from taxes largely levied upon intact families. The system can be indicted as 'unfair to self-supporting families in that it violates the common taxation principle that an income should be taxed in proportion to the number of individuals dependent upon that income'.[28] If 'the family is to be efficient in what it does, it needs a solid basis of organisation, resources and commitment, as do all organisations for efficiency'.[29] The responsibilities of men who stay with families would be acknowledged, rather than discounted or penalised, and a 'universal allowance for dependent children in the tax system ... would ensure for all children an equal, minimum level of net "income", *irrespective of the incomes of their parents*'.[30]

More Welfare, More Lone Parents

As the sole-parent population has expanded,[31] so the non-beneficiary sole-parent population has declined.[32] As one in four families became a sole-parent family, so one in every five families became a sole parent supported by an income-tested benefit. Numbers on the DPB rose sharply, from just over 17,000 in 1975 to over 37,000 in 1980 to nearly 95,000 in 1990,[33] and to over 110,000 in 2000. By 1976, 60 per cent of sole parents were collecting DPB or widow's benefits, in 1986 three-quarters were, and, by 1991, this had peaked at 89 per cent.[34] By 1996, 86 per cent of non-widowed sole parents received DPB.[35] The parents of over 19 per cent of all children received the DPB in the year to March 1996 (and 36.7 of Maori children), compared with 17.4 per cent in 1991. Around a third of those receiving DPB were Maori in the 1990s, compared with 12 per cent of Maori women aged 20-49 in the population. Some 80 per cent of sole parents also receive the housing subsidy, or the Accommodation Supplement, along with 60 per cent of the unemployed (but few low-income workers). Indeed, if the number of sole parents receiving domestic purposes, widows, unemployment, sickness, invalids, or emergency benefits are combined, they accounted for 85 per cent of the sole-parent population counted in 2001.

The larger numbers forming the lone-parent population in the 1980s and 1990s were more likely to claim benefit compared with their 1970s counterparts, and the increase in lone parents accounts for the great majority of the increase in DPB numbers. By the end of the century, nearly three-quarters of sole-parent DPB recipients had been on this for more than a year, and nearly a quarter for over five years, with a creeping increase in duration over time.[36] Between 1981 and 1991 the number of male DPB recipients rose by nearly 500 per cent (and from 4.2 to 9.7 per cent of recipients). Around a half of sole fathers might be beneficiaries in 1991, compared with only one in six as late as 1981.[37] The proportion who were Maori rose to 42 per cent. (After the cutting of DPB levels in 1991, the male proportion of all recipients fell back to just under nine per cent, and was back to over ten per cent by 2000.)

Demonstrating one of the biggest international differences between the employment of sole parents and parents in couple-families, 84.3 per cent of New Zealand two-parent families had fathers in the paid workforce, and 58 per cent had mothers in the workforce in 1991, when unemployment peaked. However, 73 per cent of female sole-parents were not working (87 per cent where the youngest child was under five), and a further 11 per cent worked part-time. Three-quarters of children in sole-parent families were without a resident parent in any paid work, compared with over one-quarter of all children. In 1976, 25 per cent of sole mothers were in full-time work.[38] Moreover, while 44 per cent of sole fathers were working full-time in 1991, compared with only 17 per cent of sole mothers, their rate had also fallen substantially, from 81 per cent in 1976 (and to only 25 per cent for sole Maori fathers in 1991). The proportion of sole fathers who were not employed at all increased from 17 per cent in 1976 to 52 per cent in 1991 and had fallen little by 1996.[39] Even non-Maori sole fathers had a probability of being out of the labour force which was more than double the rate for single men, already markedly higher than for married men.[40] About 70 per cent of workless sole fathers became long-term non-participants (over a year or more out of the labour market).

As in the US and UK, separated/divorced sole parents have the highest employment rate.[41] While never-married sole parents are particularly likely to have a child under five and to be young them-selves (more than half of all children living with never-married fathers have fathers under 30) they are still more likely to be out of work irrespective of these factors.[42] The unmarried sole parent is, of course, the fastest growing 'family form', with those not in the labour force also tending to have a higher average number of children. Moreover, as the workforce participation rates of married and/or cohabiting women, as well as previously married women, have grown, those of never-married women (not just mothers) have fallen, except in the over-45 age-group.[43]

This has been part of the way that numbers receiving basic welfare benefits nearly trebled over little more than a decade (and not counting those drawing supplements for the working poor). Overall beneficiary levels were very low until the introduction of DPB in 1973. In 1996, 400,000 working-age people were state-dependent, or 18 per cent of the working-age population, compared with five per cent in 1975,[44] and nearly a half had been on public assistance for over one year. Twenty-eight per cent of all children aged 0-15 years and 14 per cent of young people aged 16-17 years were children of welfare beneficiaries. In the mid-1980s this had been 12 per cent of children. Those on sickness, invalids and DPB continued to grow even when those getting unemployment benefit fell back in the mid-1990s. Expenditure on the DPB overtook that on unemployment benefit by the mid-1990s, both in total and per benefit recipient. (However, the numbers receiving a disability allowance rose three-fold simply between 1990 and 1996, when benefits granted rose four-fold. Where there are a range of means-tested and selective benefits, benefit cuts and benefit scares lead to benefit reshuffling.[45])

In parallel, around seven out of ten UK lone parents came to obtain all or much of their income from public assistance (or income support) by 1989. Over a half of all social security spending on families in 1998 went to lone parents, more than one-and-a-half times the unemployment budget, and more than the total costs of the higher education system.[46] Over half of the income of lone parents is from social security benefits, compared with only eight per cent for two-parent families.[47] Increasing numbers of working-age people came to claim long-term sickness and incapacity benefits, with a five-fold rise between 1972 and 1994.[48] In Australia, the benefit take up among sole parents rose from 57 per cent in 1974 to a peak of 84 per cent in 1986, then declined in 1990, as labour-force participation increased, but leaving nearly three-quarters of sole parents claiming the parenting pension for low-income families.[49]

Overall, the percentage of final income which New Zealand households earn from market income has declined,[50] and the proportion that is saved has fallen, at the same time as the gap between tax paid and benefits received has narrowed (although the tax system relies less on direct personal taxation, after the introduction of the goods and services tax in 1986). Benefit income increased from 1982 to 1996 as a proportion of gross income (particularly for those with no formal qualifications) from six to 15 per cent. Those in the lowest 40 per cent of market income received over three-quarters of benefit income, as they doubled their proportion of government transfers in the late 1980s.[51]

The Iron Law of Welfare

Unfortunately, when governments 'target the needy' the iron law of welfare is activated. A dollar of income-related benefit does not simply add a dollar to a needy person's income, but creates incentives for individuals to change their behaviour to continue qualifying, and for those on the margin to make themselves eligible. The size of the target increases, since a 'social transfer increases the net value of being in the condition that prompted the transfer.'[52] This necessarily weakens any constraints on getting into any particular condition and any incentives to escape it, so that the system creates more dependency than it resolves. The 'needy' are not a finite group, neatly separated off from the majority of 'well-off' or 'rich' people.[53] There are always 'others on the other side of the cut experiencing similar pressures'.[54] Familiarity and example mean that there is a strong association between having a welfare-dependent birth, for example, and the receipt of public assistance by sisters, mothers and other members of the family, as people learn to regard the state as the place of first resort when in need.[55]

Parallel to the way in which 'confiscatory taxation' diminishes incentives to greater effort,[56] welfare encourages people to be deceitful as well as inactive and to keep work and relationships 'off the books'. From the 1991 census, 68 per cent of lone parents were on the DPB, but the figure was 88 per cent if Department of Social Welfare records were used.[57] The welfare package includes not only the level of cash benefits, but factors like the ease of getting it and its long-term reliability compared with uncertain market income, as well as supplementary or associated entitlements.[58] Dependability of benefit income is very important to people's decisions about whether or not to work (and, by implication, whether to marry).[59] Even if financially advantageous, insecure work may be unattractive compared with a benefit that is difficult to reinstate.[60]

In turn, while some children escape the welfare dependency of their parent(s), many more than in the general population are also captured by it.[61] Young people whose parents are dependent on income support payments, for any time, are more likely to leave school early, be out of work and be receiving income support themselves—something particularly affecting indigenous people.[62] In the UK, among couple-households with an adult child in 1991, the child was in employment in 69 per cent of dual-earner households, but was employed in only four per cent of no-earner households.[63]

Non-work Passed Down Through the Generations

Work is not just a matter of availability, but of the kind of information, association and commitment promoted by parents' present and past employment. With a sole parent (or couple) on public assistance, the children grow up in an environment where no-one is working, and they are mainly or wholly dependent upon outside sources of support. While such children are familiar with the welfare system as the provider of first resort, there is no working role model which provides attachment to work and acquaintance with working behaviour. Everywhere there is a significant relationship, between both aspirations and 'right' attitudes, and whether other family members are on public assistance or unemployed.[64] In the UK, where the female head is unemployed, children were three times more likely to become unemployed adults than those in couple-households—with no declines in their rate of joblessness over time. This is paralleled by the Utrecht Study of Adolescent Development[65] where Dutch youngsters from sole-parent families are far more likely to be unemployed or otherwise out of the workforce than those from other types of family. Poor children learn early not to work: 40 per cent of UK children in two-parent and earning households have a part-time job, a third in income support families and a quarter in lone-parent households.[66] This bodes ill for minority employment patterns given that, in 1996, 30.4 per cent of Maori children lived in a sole-parent family where the parent was not employed compared with 10.8 per cent of non-Maori children. Indeed, 17 per cent of Maori children living with two parents had no parent in employment, compared with 7.8 per cent of non-Maori children.[67]

At first glance, means-tested and selective benefits are eminently appealing—not least because 'cost saving' translates as immediate savings to welfare budgets. Little attention is paid to the dynamic consequences, or to the behavioural change which makes the historical record so appalling. If the Department of Social Welfare laments that the 'continued existence of high levels of dependency may result in the development of an "underclass", and generate social friction, stigmatisation, and loss of public confidence in the welfare system',[68] it is re-learning the lessons of the means test in history. More recently, Charles Murray linked the upsurge in drop-out from the labour force, welfare dependency, family dissolution and illegitimacy—that 'demographic wonder, without precedent in the American experience'[69]—and the way in which the numbers of the US poor stopped shrinking in the early 1970s and began to grow. Benefits for lone mothers discouraged providers from remaining as the family support, and their availability militated against the formation of the family in the first place. The result is a circular process: men do not strive to be good providers and women do not expect it or put pressure on men to behave responsibly. A licence to earn while on welfare is not just an incentive to work. It provides 'a much stronger incentive for women who were not on welfare to get on it and then become trapped in it'. The net effect is to raise the value of being eligible for welfare and thereby, 'via a classic market response, increase the supply of eligible women'.[70]

After the declaration of the 'War on Poverty' in 1964, the following decade saw a growth in public assistance in the US far exceeding the real increase in household income. It converted the low-income working husband into a financial handicap.[71] As the family was eligible for an expanded package of help as a result of the father's actual or staged desertion, this could mean an immediate increase in economic well-being. Yet people in female-headed families were a growing proportion of the non-aged poor, constituting over a third by 1980. They were also more likely to be persistently poor, and the children were more likely to become welfare dependent themselves.[72] Short-term gain is long-term loss. What may have seemed a tempting option at the time precludes any advance, and 'any teenager who has children and must rely on public assistance to support them has struck a Faustian bargain with the system that neatly ensures that she will live in poverty the rest of her days'.[73]

Making Even More Poor People

It is questionable whether so much dependency reduces poverty, despite claims that targeting the 'needy' and the 'casualties' makes for a direct hit on poverty, as well as being a cost-cutting exercise. Benefits just 'for the poor', result in more 'poor' people, just as benefits restricted to the unemployed or sole parents result in more unemployed and unmarried parents, accelerating the division into two-income and no-income households.[74] While cash transfers may be '"better targeted" ... [this] clearly failed to stem the rising tide of overall inequality ...'.[75] Sole-parent households were among the major gainers from redistribution. Between 1981 and 1990, sole-parent households showed income rises compared with two-parent families, and increased their benefit support by an average of 31 per cent—but still remained among the lowest average disposable incomes of all household types. Despite benefit cuts, sole-parent households even gained from income transfers (in terms of the proportion of income received in benefit) in the early 1990s. Yet, by real average household, equivalised disposable income, sole parents were worse off in 1991-1996 than before (as were young couples with children).

Maintaining incentives and relieving poverty may be incompatible objectives. To reduce the number of claimants and make substantial savings, 'assistance has to be [low and] phased out at a fairly low level of income'.[76] In a classic move to decrease the pattern of 'permanent dependency on the state', the levels of sickness, DPB and unemployment benefit were cut by between five per cent and 27 per cent from April 1991,[77] age-limits imposed and eligibility rules tightened. Unfortunately, reductions affect the poorest people, while work incentives remain so low that they discourage those on welfare from work and, at the same time, alienate those who work for little wages. Anyway, benefit cuts have the lowest impact on least skilled, least educated and long-term beneficiaries, who have the worst labour market prospects.[78] This also prompts a search for absolute measures of poverty.[79] However, all 'needs' are flexible and culturally relative, and one society's or age's poverty is another's superfluity. Poverty is difficult to define without reference to social perceptions about what constitutes a basic or even 'adequate' level of living.

Noting that the reforms of 1991 fell hardest on low-income households, while tax cuts benefited higher-income households, those preoccupied with equality, asked: 'if exactly the same amount of money spent in the tax cuts had been distributed primarily to the lower and middle-income groups, rather than the top 40 per cent, would this not have better met the OECD policy management goal of equity and efficiency?'[80] The answer is no, as the recipients would have been better off than those above them. The analysis was faulty, since when 'it calculated the cost of increasing incomes of the poor, it failed to consider the implications of the proposed change for those above the poverty line'.[81] Those affected would have no incentive to earn, and every incentive to reduce their efforts, since any reduction in market income would be offset by an increase in supplementing benefits. This exposes the way that: 'Ultimately, the welfare lifestyle is based on a pretence: that persons of working age deserve a guaranteed minimum income not far short of average earnings, which has been earned not through their efforts but by those of others.'[82]

What is so easily ignored is that people do not just get into poverty, but also manage to climb out. Had 'the mother and father remained together, poverty begun before the household composition changed might not have continued, and poverty begun after the change might have been avoided'.[83] Couples make income gains over time, and are clearly more successful in improving their circumstances than sole parents.[84] Low-income mothers who divorce are more likely to have stagnant incomes over the following years, compared with those who stay married, and divorced or never-married fathers are more likely to continue with low or no earnings compared with men living with wives and children.

While couples with children numerically make up more of the hard pressed than sole parents in the low-income statistics at any one time, there is movement outwards, while sole parents accumulate and make up a greater proportion of the long-term poor. Couples exit from welfare dependency at roughly double the rate of lone parents. In the UK, after five years, around two-thirds of workless couples with children have at least one adult in work, but only one-third of lone parents will be working.[85] The proportion of couples with children who were in the bottom three income deciles in 1991 was 29 per cent, while the proportion for singles with children was 64 per cent. The proportion of couples with children in the bottom three deciles six years on was eight per cent, for lone parents it was 29 per cent. Research on the patterns of income and expenditure of beneficiaries and other low-income groups in New Zealand show that the group with the largest rise in income over time is couples with children. (The lowest was single adults living alone.[86]) Similarly, the US longitudinal data from the Panel Study of Income Dynamics[87] shows how the educational level of the household head and whether the household is headed by a single female have large effects on exit and re-entry rates to poverty, and whether poverty is a transitory or a permanent state. Rates of marriage appeared to be the single most important influence on poverty status in the long run. If black women had the marriage pattern of white women, their far higher poverty rate would be almost halved.[88]

Marriage can supply two earners, or a second earner who can enter the labour market or increase their labour supply when income is insufficient.[89] Financially, as in other ways, marriage is a risk-reducing institution, or system of co-insurance, where spouses share their economic and social resources and act as a small insurance pool in the face of the uncertainties of life. In the UK longitudinal study of lone parents over the 1990s, those who prospered in new relationships had acquired working partners and were themselves in paid jobs.[90] However, individual earnings have a small long-term effect on prosperity compared with marriage. This expands the repertoire of economic possibilities, including access to another income stream, while family disruption diminishes access to income and property. Australian research found that economic recovery for divorced women was attributable to re-entry into the full-time workforce and, even more, to re-partnering.[91] What will not bring prosperity are subsidies for childcare or the rent.

All the evidence supports Charles Murray's 'set of modest requirements' for avoiding poverty: 'get married and stay married', as well as 'get a job—even if initially low paid—and stay in it' and, 'whatever else ... a poor woman ... ought not to have a baby out of wedlock'.[92]

If poverty is to be relieved and incentives maintained at the same time, this has often been better achieved through allowances for dependents that are not withdrawn as work is entered or income rises, so that the floor of wages is always above the ceiling of relief. Such assistance is not at risk if individuals take casual or temporary jobs, or foregoing the certainty of a guaranteed income stream. The experience of history is that general recognition for the costs of dependents removes far more people from poverty than do means-tested transfers.[93]

There has been little apparent awareness of the implications of policies which increase the levels of need that they are meant to meet—or none beyond the reiteration of how costs will be reduced by reviewing benefit levels, tightening eligibility and 'enhancing targeting of social assistance to those most in need',[94] or to that elusive category of the 'truly poor'—the victims[95] that incentives cannot touch.

As policy has ossified, the dream of making all provisions for child-rearing 'needs-based' has collapsed. Despite the optimistic notion that assistance could be discretely phased out service by service, techno-cratic ways of preventing the cumulative impact of overlaps in income tests for different provisions became self-defeating. With the system becoming so complex as to be unintelligible, the comprehensive 'family accounts' project was abandoned in 1993 with the realisation that global abatement was impossible. Attempts to target services such as health and education floundered.

Indeed, making parents pay directly for health and education, as the two remaining services still generally provided for children, would be particularly problematic given that the 'general climate of poor incentives in New Zealand is, perhaps, an indication that the limits of redistribution are being reached', or that 'the limits of targeting have been reached'.[96] James Cox suggests that if these are phased in then it might require compensatory help in the 'form of tax credits that are available to all families'. Should these be a step too far, we might depend on 'income growth and general tax reductions'.[97] However, this does not take into account the way that much of the general sum of tax reductions would go to those not only on higher incomes but without dependents. Leaving parents to pay for (compulsory?) health and education would further widen the living standards gap between those with and without children and would adversely affect older people in poor health. Australia, on the other hand, began to move away from targeting for families in the late 1990s. This reflected a more positive stance by government towards marriage and child-rearing, with expressed concern over the extent of family breakdown and its consequences.[98]

Good Prospects for Girls?

With good economic prospects, teenage girls have something to lose by having a baby, and are motivated to defer having children, in the same way that the pursuit of living standards has acted, for centuries, as the great family planner of the Western world.[99] But this is not the case for those whose earning capacity is low and who may not be able to better themselves much, if at all, through employment. The Domestic Purposes Benefit Review Committee found in 1977 that 'in many instances ... the amount of money that can be received from the benefit is higher than what a girl herself could earn in normal employment'.[100]

Lower-class women have often started child-bearing early in life anyway, with motherhood traditionally providing an identity and positive role. A woman might not now be able to achieve this at all if she waits for marriage. Ex-nuptial births are overwhelmingly concentrated among the least educated women, or those least likely to be able to support themselves and their babies.[101] Over 46 per cent of children from sole-parent households in New Zealand in 1996 had parents with no qualifications—much the same as in the UK.[102] Nearly a third had only a school qualification.[103]

If women can marry the state, men may feel that they are free from an obligation to stay with their wives, or have no cause to assume parental responsibility to engage in sexual relations. While poorly qualified women are more likely to have traditional notions of marriage as an exchange of services in return for resources, the DPB encourages both parents to see themselves as independent of each other.[104] After all, provision for sole parents came in as part of the freeing-up of sexuality from consequences and social controls. This is allied to the ways in which ex-nuptial births and casual relationships rise in tandem with the ease of preventing and terminating pregnancy. Modern birth control emancipates men from norms requiring them to look after a woman who becomes pregnant. If she does not get rid of a pregnancy when she has the chance, then reproduction is a woman's choice, a woman's right and a woman's problem. As this also makes informal partnering, or live-in sexual companionship, routinely available, so it enables men to 'escape from responsibilities by leaving relationships or re-negotiating them when children are born'.[105] The emphasis on personal choice and the optional nature of family roles further argues against the 'acceptance of the traditional convention that men should support families', particularly given the rhetoric about women's independence. The 'altruistic reasons ... (not to mention welfare back-ups)' are 'for standing aside to let women do things for themselves'.[106] Being an unwed mother living on a state-guaranteed income may seem more desirable than being a single woman without children or a mother living with an undesirable man.[107] Women may have:

> ... very little money but they did not generally feel particularly worse off ... Moreover, some women found themselves able to work and support their families, particularly if they had help from their relatives (in the form of

childcare) and help from the state (in the form of family credit). These women felt little need to find a male partner/breadwinner. Other lone parents, who were reliant on income support, would have liked to find a male breadwinner but few seemed to be around. Generally, the lone parents interviewed felt they no longer needed a man to support them.[108]

Dual Fertility Markets

Non-marital fertility, like marital disruption, is often not the 'first-best' choice of the people involved, but the 'least-worst option'. The dissolution of such measures as supported the family up to the 1970s means that those who obey the traditional behavioural norms about family building may not only be far less likely to have out-of-wedlock births or become dependent on public assistance, but also to have fewer children or *none at all*. Where economic imperatives have made it difficult for married couples to support children, while making it easier for poorer single women to do so, the result is dual fertility markets.[109] The choice for some people is not simply between an acceptable living standard without children or relative poverty with them, but also marriage without children or lone parenthood with them. In essence: '... policies were put into place which ensure that families will be dysfunctional in one way or the other'. If 'the family is intact and capable of supporting itself, we withdraw all monetary recognition of the fact that its income must support several persons' needs' and 'so force it into unnecessary financial stress and into recuperative efforts (e.g. children in childcare while both parents work) which pick at its foundations and *raison d'être*'. Otherwise 'we give welfare payments that indict families as not economically self-sustaining, and that persuade family members to see themselves as dependent, or potentially dependent, on the state.'[110] The Change Team on Targeting Social Assistance accepted as much, but concluded that those who were unhappy about either this, or the disincentives to working and earning, were simply enemies of targeting:

> Someone who believes ... that, to encourage families to stay together, two-parent families should receive the same assistance as one-parent families, would not support targeting. Nor would someone who thought that, to encourage work effort, employed families should receive the same assistance as unemployed families. Nor would someone who thinks it is unfair that employed adults in middle-income families should face an EMTR that is higher than the top income tax rate.[111]

Suitable Work for Mothers?

The assumption has grown that the public interest in reducing the cost of dependency and women's independence can be equated if sole parents get jobs to enable them to work their way off benefits. There are grand claims that women's increased participation in the paid workforce would not only result 'in better use of their skills and experience' but:

increase production and consumption, reduce the disparities for low-income earners, and so benefit women, households, businesses and the economy. Resulting reductions in the number of women on state benefits would reduce the cost of income support. This is to the benefit of all New Zealanders.[112]

For a long time there had been few expectations of beneficiaries beyond requiring them to demonstrate eligibility. The work test was first applied in 1997, when those with children over 14 were required to seek part-time work or undertake part-time training or education.[113] As extended in 1999, sole parents with children over 14 were required to seek full-time work, and part-time work if their youngest child was aged between six and 13. The work test was, however, withdrawn by the Labour-led government in March 2003.[114] Unlike the US, where a major factor in joblessness is assumed to be the lack of motivation to find or take work, the belief in New Zealand, like the UK, is that joblessness results from external barriers. Under one model, people do not work because they have decided against it. Under the other, they are excluded. Unsurprisingly, mandatory programmes outperform voluntary ones because they make more recipients go to work.[115] Work incentives, or training for better jobs, government jobs, childcare, or letting beneficiaries keep benefits when earning 'do not cause large numbers to rush forward and work who were not working before. That is why most experts have abandoned such proposals in America, even on the left.'[116]

For their part, women want either a part-time job that does not affect their benefit or a well-paying full-time job that, among other things, more than pays for the costs of childcare.[117] Women prefer not to work when children are small, and then to work part-time with children at school.[118] Mothers may be less sensitive than men to incentives, since work competes with the attraction of being with their children, whose care they may not trust to a third party. If lone parents have withdrawn from the workforce, as the numbers of employed married mothers has grown, there may be a greater correspondence between preference and practice in their case.[119] Welfare recipients may not be particularly motivated to solve childcare problems. The difficulties are illustrated by the Compass project. Piloted from March 1994 to March 1995, 1,122 people participated, but only 14 per cent of participants were no longer receiving a benefit and for only eight per cent was this due to being employed.[120] Those citing the availability of child care as an obstacle to work are a minority of workless sole parents: around 15 per cent of women not seeking work in 1994/5 could not find suitable childcare.[121] In 1987, a Transition to Work Allowance encouraged long-term beneficiaries to move into employment by ensuring that, at least for the first three months, they would be $20 per week better off working than on benefit.[122] It failed—uptake in 1992 was 43—and was abolished in 1996.

Allowing recipients to earn on the side (a 'disregard'), or have benefit withdrawn at a gentler rate as earnings increase, is another classic move to circumvent the problems of targeting. It is politically more acceptable than slashing entitlements—particularly as there is always pressure to let more people into the target zone. Instead, we get 'broadening target populations', where political expediency adds a new layer to the eligible population.[123] Programmes are less selective, more expensive and far more are caught in complex abatements, and will take longer to earn their way out of entitlement. This hardly fulfils the objective of making as many as possible 'independent' of the state.'[124]

The process has a remorseless inevitability about it. In the UK, as general support for children in the tax and benefit system fell in the early 1970s, it became pointless for many low-paid providers to work. This 'unemployment trap' was met with Family Income Supplement for the working poor. To make it lone-parent friendly, it was paid for part-time work of a minimum of 16 hours. Clients then stuck at the high rate paid for minimal earnings, and, like income support for the unoccupied, it increasingly became a benefit for sole parents. So an extra supplement was paid for working over 20 hours. As so much was withdrawn, and taxes imposed as earning rose, it was still pointless to raise income (especially as benefits were also available for housing costs and local taxes). To reduce withdrawal from over 70 per cent (or 90 per cent if other reliefs were added) to something closer to 50 per cent, a Working Families Tax Credit was introduced. This extends further up the earnings scale. The extra people who have been brought within scope of the benefit will take longer to earn their way out. It is estimated that nearly a half of all families receiving the US equivalent, the Earned Income Tax Credit, would be better-off without the subsidy because they have less income in total as a result of working less hours. Subsidies for part-time work that encourage people to get a job in the first place may discourage recipients from improving their skills or seeking promotion, and so increasing their long-term earnings capacity.[125] They also discourage family formation, since subsidy levels are the same for one- and two-parent families.[126]

In New Zealand, as elsewhere, extending benefits up the earnings scale to cut the income loss from their withdrawal further down, pushes high EMTRs (effective marginal tax rates) further up the income range.[127] It still reduces work incentives because of high levels of abatement, and has higher administrative costs,[128] so that 'the changes have not entirely succeeded in overcoming the problems they were aimed at addressing'.[129] Moreover, in providing incentives for sole parents to earn, the dual abatement regime increased incentives for sole parenthood. For sole parent beneficiaries, earnings between $80 and $180 per week became subject to a 30 per cent rate of loss, instead of 70 per cent where gross income exceeds $80 a week for couples.[130]

Making sole parents 'self-sufficient' usually involves shifting them from one set of benefits to another:

> ... instead of reducing the fiscal cost of income support by the full amount of benefit that is no longer being paid, part of the cost will simply be shifted from income support programmes to the tax credit programmes. Many beneficiaries who move into employment as a result of welfare-to-work programmes will be equipped only to carry out low-skilled work, which means both that they will command low wages and that their prospects of income growth are low. Taken together these facts mean there is likely to be a significant demand for in-work benefits from former beneficiaries and that many will need this additional assistance for long periods. [131]

Instead of being housewife and full-time mother in relation to the subsidising state, a mother becomes a secondary or supplementary earner to this primary provider. Either way, the state has come to provide role substitution and endeavours to make up economically for the lack of a second parent. The low ability of many welfare mothers does not bode well for educational qualifications, or raising wages. In general, the effectiveness of training or work experience for dependent groups is low,[132] particularly given its expense and the problem of matching with projected job requirements.[133] It is said that lack of 'high quality, low-cost childcare' is another 'of the more significant barriers to self-reliance for sole parents',[134] but then 'high quality, low-cost childcare' is a contradiction in terms. Its expense (even if the personnel could be found to provide it) would out-run the worth of the mothers' labour elsewhere.[135] The women put into the workforce will likely move from 'home-production' to doing similar work for the government or service industries, or staffing the administrations that manage it. This may add little to the sum total of output properly measured. All would have existed before, as one woman fries burgers, while another minds the baby of a woman working in the public sector to care for the parents of other women who are looking after other people's children. Between 1991 and 1996 alone, the number employed in the early childhood sector doubled from 9,000 to 18,000, overwhelmingly women. This was over four per cent of total jobs created in the economy and, in absolute terms, was far higher than the growth in manufacturing employment, a traditionally male domain.[136]

Whatever the numbers of mothers who turn up for jobs, this will not improve the prospects for future family formation. For some, the answer is bigger benefits, as well as improved labour market opportunities, with maybe a universal basic income. Objections that 'if financial support for sole-parent families is too good it will encourage divorce and sole-parent families' are dismissed for inferring that 'sole-parent families are not as good as two-parent families'.[137] But US evidence suggests that whereas income from work appears to improve children's outcomes somewhat, welfare income reduces their chances of graduating from high school, years of education, sons' work and earnings and young children's test scores. Other work shows that child support improves children's educational attainment more than income from welfare or mothers' work.[138] Best of all for the child is an earning father living at home.

Sole parents may not be very successful at improving their circumstances whether their poverty is carried from a poor two-parent family into a poor one-parent family, or results directly from family break-up. Early, unwed child-bearing has more far-reaching consequences in terms of adverse outcomes for the lives of mothers than does their experience of childhood poverty.[139] It has been self-evident through the ages that a mother on her own is not self-supporting, which is why raising children has devolved on groups, with the progenitors committed through marriage.

The Awkward Question

Is it possible to deplore the spiral of welfare dependency, while at the same time treating family structures as optional? People have much to lose in the long term when economically efficient behaviour is deterred or discouraged by immediate or short-term costs. Economic dislocations pose threats to family stability, when this is people's best protection, and the state's biggest bargain, in constrained circumstances. This makes it a short-sighted policy to withdraw support from productive family behaviour in favour of the subsidisation of disintegration, which facilitates a mass movement from a relatively cheap and efficient form of living and child-rearing to a comparatively expensive and inefficient one. Family developments are not just 'choices' affecting the individuals involved, but have knock-on effects on the larger and future society—not least, through the effects on future generations.

Section C

**Coping with the Fall-Out:
The Consequences of Family Breakdown
for Children, Adults and Communities**

7

The Consequences for Children

Summary: There are many adverse consequences for children resulting from the lack of involvement of the two biological parents. Mortality and morbidity rates are higher, and such children are more likely to have serious accidents. The risk of child abuse is higher for children in non-traditional households, with the presence of a step-parent being the strongest risk indicator. Children from broken homes perform less well at school. They are more likely to experience problems of mental health, poverty and relationship breakdown as adults. It is sometimes claimed that differences in outcomes for children in traditional and non-traditional families can be accounted for by the poverty of single-parent households, but studies which control for income find that this cannot explain the wide differences.

If the nuclear family is as oppressive and unhealthy as the triumphant anti-family movement maintains, then its decline ought to be beneficial for everyone. Not least, children ought to be doing much better in all the 'new family forms'. Arguing, in 1994, that 'it is not only "problem families" that are a cause for concern', but how '"normal" families ... are also a site of serious structural social problems', one commentator called for ways to reduce the abuses and inequalities of the 'heterosexual nuclear family', and argued that it was 'important that both diverse family forms and alternatives to family life be encouraged and explored'. Indeed, she claimed that 'evidence shows that it is possible to rear physically and mentally healthy people outside families as we know them'.[1] As there are fewer heterosexual nuclear families around, and more 'diverse ... alternatives', then outcomes should be getting better, and problems diminishing.

Unfortunately, problems associated with changes in family structure are now such that even official sources describe them as threatening to 'become entrenched and endemic without action to support families and improve their functioning'.[2] When the Education and Social Science Committee reported on children at-risk in education through truancy and behavioural problems, it drew attention to an increase in dysfunc-

119

tional, at-risk families, which produce at-risk children, unable to benefit from schooling, and thus a widening 'cycle of disadvantage'.[3] Similarly, the Department of Child, Youth and Family Services (CYFS) refers to as 'many as 95,000 children and young persons' living in families characterised by 'factors such as low health status, psychiatric disorders, severe marital stress and conflict, no attention to pre-school education and a strong likelihood of family violence'. The service was 'struggling with increasing numbers of highly disturbed children and young persons and, not infrequently, with disturbed parents'.[4] Their children are 'those whose problem behaviours dominate and preoccupy the attentions of schools, welfare agencies and the police, and who in later life will develop serious anti-social behaviours and associated difficulties'. It is suggested that five per cent of families in New Zealand are in a 'cycle of disadvantage', and a further 45 per cent of families 'may be at risk of becoming severely disadvantaged given a combination of adverse events and reduced capability'.[5]

It is claimed that while:

> ... ineffective parenting can be found in all family structures, and in all ranges of socioeconomic and ethnic groups ... adolescents in families experiencing parental separation or divorce, economic loss, maternal employment, parental remarriage, a move to a new area and a new school, may be most at risk for exhibiting maladaptive coping behaviours.[6]

If these factors have increased, then a connection seems obvious.

Studies controlling for a host of other variables cannot make the effects of family structure disappear, or make the results go in the opposite direction.[7] A large number have accumulated based on large, nationally representative surveys, with longitudinal designs which follow children from different backgrounds into adulthood, using standardised measures and increasingly sophisticated statistical techniques. As Sara McLanahan and Gary Sandefur put it:

> ... we reject the claim that children raised by only one parent do just as well as children raised by both parents. We have been studying this question for ten years and in our opinion the evidence is quite clear.[8]

All research indicates:

> ... that children who grow up in mother-only families are disadvantaged not only during childhood or immediately after their parents' marital disruption, but during adolescence and young adulthood as well. Moreover, the negative consequences associated with family structure extend across a wide range of socio-economic outcomes.[9]

The extent to which parental separation puts children at a disadvantage appears remarkably consistent across different locations and over time, with many adverse outcomes having roughly double the prevalence among children from disrupted families compared with intact families.[10] Typically, in the Western Australian Child Health Survey of 2,737 children, the proportion with low academic competence was 30 per cent for sole-parent families and 17 per cent for couple-families.[11] The recent survey into the mental health of children and adolescents in Great Britain found that, whereas ten per cent of all children aged 5-15 years had a mental disorder, the rates were running at double (16 per cent compared with eight per cent) among children in lone-parent as compared with couple-families, and at 15 per cent for those with a step-family.[12] Children living with cohabiting couples were more likely to have a mental health problem, as distinct from those of married couples (or 11.2 per cent to 7.3 per cent). Nearly one in five boys of lone parents had a mental health problem, with most having a conduct disorder. (For girls, it was one in eight, equally distributed between conduct and emotional problems.) Fifty per cent of children with a mental disorder had at one time seen the separation of their parents, compared with 29 per cent with no disorder. In turn, 37 per cent of those with a mental health problem, compared with 21 per cent of those without, lived with a lone parent.

Matters of Life and Death

The disadvantages for children not brought up by their two original parents begin at birth and are reflected in the infant mortality rate.[13] It appears to be a world-wide phenomenon, repeated from Jamaica[14] to Finland.[15] Children are also likely to die at a higher rate—something associated with father absence in the historical record, even in circumstances where resource levels were maintained.[16]

Health effects, including significant increases in injury rates, and higher rates of hospitalisation for children whose parents separate or never marry compared with those remaining in an intact family, are also recorded worldwide and occur independently of social background and income.[17] For the US, children living with a lone adult report a higher prevalence of limited activity and higher rates of disability, more hospitalisation and poorer health.[18] New Zealand does not seem to be an exception. In the Christchurch study the trends were most evident from a five-year longitudinal follow-up study of hospital admissions as a result of accidents or infections.[19]

Family Breakdown and Child Abuse

New Zealand is in the top six industrialised nations in terms of deaths from child abuse and neglect of children under one year of age.[20] In the year 1999-2000 some 26,000 young people under 18 years were referred to the Children and Young Persons Service for Care and Protection. In the previous year, 1998/9, there were 10,800 substantiated cases of abuse, neglect and problem behaviour notifications.

Children from backgrounds of family disruption comprise a majority of the victims of all major forms of active child abuse, physical, emotional and sexual.[21] Neglect of children is twice as high for separated and divorced parents, compared with the continually married.[22] In particular: 'The presence of a step-parent is the best epidemiological predictor of child abuse risk yet discovered'. This runs the gamut from sexual molestation to fatal batterings, and is statistically independent of poverty, maternal age and family size.[23] Out of 52,000 child abuse cases reviewed for the US, 72 per cent involved children in a household without one or both biological parents, even though these households comprised roughly a third of all households with children.[24] In the early 1970s, when family fluidity was far less advanced than today, nearly 20 per cent of a group of 255 New Zealand children with non-accidental injuries lived with a step-parent in contrast to 9.3 per cent of a comparison group of 108 children with accidental injuries.[25] Similarly, the Australian Institute of Health and Welfare[26] reported in 1994/5 on 30,615 substantiated cases of child abuse and neglect. Step-children were involved in 21 per cent of cases, although less than 4 per cent of children lived in step-families. While 81 per cent of children lived with biological parents, they accounted for only 30 per cent of cases. A child living with a mother in a *de facto* relationship with a man other than the child's father, or with a husband who was not the child's father, was at least five times more likely to be abused than one who lived with both married parents. The rate of sexual abuse of children in *de facto*-couple families is more than three times the rate in natural or adoptive families. A high proportion of child killers in Australia are either step-fathers or the mothers' boyfriends, and represent a disproportionate risk for children, particularly in the early stages of a relationship.[27]

This is not simply a phenomenon of developed societies. Among foraging South American tribes, 43 per cent of children raised by a mother and step-father die before their fifteenth birthday, compared with 19 per cent of those raised by two genetic parents. Historical demographic analysis shows similar results in European peasant societies of the past, where child mortality rose after a widowed parent remarried. Poverty is more strongly associated with neglect but cannot account for the high risks of abuse in step-parent families.[28]

A step-father with no blood ties to the children is not only more likely to kill or ill-treat them than the biological father, but the risk from a man without either a blood or legal tie to the children in the household appears greatest of all.[29] To an extent, marriage increases commitment to the father role in men who are not the biological fathers of the children in the household, and it brings into play the incest taboo. Leslie Mangolin's work for the University of Iowa into reported cases of non-parental child abuse found a half of the total inflicted by boyfriends, although they provided only two per cent of all non-parental childcare. Among cases of non-parental child abuse in lone-parent homes, 64 per cent of the perpetrators were mothers' boyfriends, from whom the risk of sexual abuse was particularly high.[30]

Fragmented families also afford poorer protection from opportunistic males in the area, so that 84 per cent of all cases of non-parental child abuse occurs to children from sole-parent homes. The enhanced risk of abuse outside the home parallels the higher accident rates of sole-parent children. This may be a factor in the earlier sexual activity and pregnancy rates of girls of sole mothers, since many young teens report being coerced by older boys.[31] Unfortunately, the recent report on child abuse and neglect produced jointly by Child, Youth and Family Services (CYFS) and the Ministry of Social Policy was dismissive of the 'large body of evidence' suggesting 'that the incidence of reported child maltreatment is over-represented among single-parent families and blended families'. Instead the reported abuse and neglect are accounted for by the 'higher levels of surveillance' from neighbours and welfare agencies that sole parents supposedly experience. The 'causes' are drained away into a 'complex interplay between different factors that may act at the level of the individual, the family, the community, and the cultural system.[32]

School Performance

International surveys of educational performance show how the underachievement of boys, particularly in relation to reading, is a problem for the UK and New Zealand. In 1998, roughly a third of school leavers had less than year 12 qualifications. Children from separated homes perform less well in school-based skills than those from intact homes, and problems often persist into adulthood, as seen in studies from the UK, the US, New Zealand and Australia.[33] American data from the National Health Interview Survey on Child Health in 1988 showed how—even after adjustment for other economic, social and demographic variables—family structure was related to academic performance. Children from disrupted marriages were more than twice as likely as those living with both biological parents to have been expelled or suspended, while those with a never-married mother were more than three times as likely to have had this experience.[34] Those from two-parent families are generally least likely to truant or be disruptive at school.[35] Recent work on six rounds of the International Social Science Surveys/Australia showed how children whose parents divorce get, on average, about seven-tenths of a year less education than children from intact families. This is a statistically large difference, similar to ones from US data, and the loss is for children who are otherwise comparable, economically and otherwise.[36] The loss is not ameliorated by remarriage. The results are consistent with the argument that the loss of parental encouragement, support and control has a detrimental effect on educational success. While family structure tends to be more related to the attainment of formal qualifications and school behaviour than actual intellectual differences, some evidence links father absence with lower cognitive test scores for young children. By age 13, there is an average difference of half a year in reading abilities between children of divorced parents and those who have intact families.[37] In some samples of young adults, divorce is connected with low educational attainment as much or more for women as men.[38]

Greater acceptance of divorce, unwed births and sole parenthood, and the reduction of the stigma as more children experience divorce or live with one parent, might be predicted to ameliorate any adverse effects. However, even those anxious to put the most optimistic construction on the evidence, concede that '... the lessons from the United States ... are not encouraging. Their experience of a higher divorce rate over a longer period of time has not resulted in improving outcomes for children.'[39] A combined analysis from the three UK national cohort studies—the National Survey of Health and Development, the National Child Development Study and the Education Study, shows that the disadvantage in educational qualifications has remained constant for children born from 1946 through to 1970.[40] Although the prevalence of having no qualifications and of having fewer than five O-levels has decreased with each birth cohort, the relative risk of a poor educational outcome associated with parental separation has risen slightly.[41] The Australian data also suggests that the educational differences due to divorce have increased over time.[42]

The Same Patterns on Both Sides of the World

Both the New Zealand Christchurch Health and Development Study and the UK National Child Development Study provide for large-scale and detailed study of the impact of different environments on children of similar parents, by following and comparing adopted and non-adopted children born to single mothers.[43] Generally favourable conditions prevailed in the New Zealand adoptive and biological two-parent families, compared with those of non-adopted children born out of wedlock, who had lower levels of childhood activities and pre-school education, poorer healthcare, greater residential change, more parental separations and more unresponsive, punitive mothers. The single mothers had low levels of education and qualifications, more difficulties with child-rearing, and greater numbers of stressful or negative life events.[44] Similarly, in the UK, adopted children had the most advantaged mix of family and social circumstances and children of single mothers the least. Only one per cent of the adoptive mothers showed 'little or no interest' in their children's education in non-manual homes, compared with four per cent of the mothers of children born in wedlock and 21 per cent of those of out-of-wedlock children.

At 11 years of age,[45] one in three of the UK's out-of-wedlock children were living with a lone parent or in 'other situations': one in six had been in care and one in three families was receiving public assistance. One in ten of the born-in-wedlock children were no longer living with both natural parents. Very few adopted children had experienced a family break, only four per cent of families received public assistance, and both middle- and working-class adoptive families usually maintained or improved their circumstances over time. The out-of-wedlock children again showed the poorest social adjustment, and the difference with those born in wedlock was only slightly reduced when allowance was made for environmental factors.

While the three groups in the Christchurch study at 14-16 years[46] did not differ significantly for mood disorders, anxiety, or suicidal behaviour, oppositional and defiant behaviour was marked in 36.7 per cent of adolescents of single mothers, 21.9 per cent of those from adoptive families and 14.2 per cent of those born into two-parent families. Self-reported offending rates were respectively 42.6 per cent, 28.1 per cent and 20.3 per cent. The rates of difficult behaviours in adoptees were higher than expected given the generally advantaged characteristics of their adoptive families, but lower than expected given the characteristics of their biological parents, with the same pattern for achievement and ability.

For the parallel British National Child Development Study, at 16 the out-of-wedlock adolescents still had the highest rates of difficulty overall, even after allowances were made for material and social factors. The difficulties of the adopted group were less marked than earlier on; the deterioration in their adjustment between seven and 11 did not continue into adolescence. The out-of-wedlock children were by far the most likely to have completely separated from their homes and to have spent time in care where, 'for many ... the picture is one of continuing material disadvantage and an increased likelihood of family instability'.[47]

A similar picture is reflected in US data from the 1988 National Survey of Child Health[48]. Biological children in intact families repeated grades less often than any other group, saw mental health professionals less and had fewer behaviour problems than all other groups. This group was followed by those adopted in infancy, who did better than those adopted later, or born outside marriage and raised by a single mother. Adopted children generally did better in educational attainment than single-parent and grandparent-raised children, and enjoyed health similar to that of those from intact families.

Delinquency and Family Disruption

Serious violent offending has increased more rapidly than other types of crime in New Zealand. Rape and sexual violation offences rose 10,936 per cent between 1948 and 1995, and robbery by 6,848 per cent, as the population grew by 115 per cent. Between 1981 and 1991, the number of robberies and serious assaults trebled, sexual attacks doubled and homicides increased by 70 per cent, with a dramatic upturn in 1992-93. While there might be some problems with the data, the amount of crime committed by the age group 10-16 seems to have risen considerably in the 1990s. The number of 14- to 16-year-olds apprehended for violent offences was reasonably static between 1987 and 1992, then almost doubled in the four years from 1992 to 1996 (1,813 to 3,195). The proportion of youth (10-16) apprehended in relation to total reported crime stayed constant at around 22 per cent over the 1990s, while the proportion of children and young people in the population declined. A study of a cohort of New Zealand males aged 10 to 24 found that around 25 per cent appeared in the adult or youth court on one occasion and that over a half of these re-offended on at least one other occasion.[49] Of those offenders whose first offence is between the ages of 17 and 19 years, 75 per cent are reconvicted within five years.

It has long been known that severely disturbed or delinquent youngsters usually have very adverse backgrounds, with chronic levels of family disruption. Although children in divorced and step-families show a broad range of social, emotional, academic and behavioural problems compared with those from intact, original families, the most marked and consistent problems are those relating to oppositional and anti-social behaviour.[50] On a standard checklist, about a quarter of US adolescents in divorced and step-families were above the cut-off point for behaviour problems, in contrast to the ten per cent in intact families.[51]

Estimating that about three per cent of New Zealand school pupils exhibit severe behavioural difficulties, David Fergusson's 20-year Christchurch Health and Development Study, using a cohort of 1,265 children born in 1977, illustrates how these are related to a complex of adverse factors centring on the family. Those 15-year-olds whose problematic behaviour includes early sexual activity, conduct disorder, police contact, and substance abuse,[52] tend to come from generally disadvantaged backgrounds with low parental education, parental criminality, young parents, low socio-economic status and particularly high rates of family instability, ex-nuptial births and single parenthood.

They entered a lone-parent family at birth in 40.7 per cent of cases, compared with 5.8 for other teenagers, and 55.6 per cent were the result of an ex-nuptial birth, compared with 14.3 per cent generally. A quarter of those in this most disadvantaged part of the sample developed early onset multiple problem behaviours and 87 per cent had at least one behavioural or mental health problem by 15. Only 13 per cent were problem-free teenagers, compared with 80 per cent in the most advantaged 50 per cent of the sample.

In parallel, the Cambridge Study of Delinquent Development, the main British study of criminal career development, tracked the development of anti-social behaviour for inner-city males, mostly born in 1953. Delinquents tended to have convicted parents and siblings (less than five per cent of the sample families accounted for half of all the convictions). Up to the tenth birthday, they were more likely to be hyperactive, impulsive, unpopular, to have broken homes, harsh parents who were uninterested in education, low intelligence and poor attainment. The best independent predictors of convictions up to age 32, after anti-social child behaviour was excluded, were a convicted parent, daring, large family size, separation from a parent, and low junior school attainment. The background to an anti-social personality itself lay in earlier anti-social personality and separation from a parent, low intelligence and attainment, plus convicted, unemployed, uneducated fathers who were uninvolved with sons.[53]

The other New Zealand longitudinal study from Dunedin shows that children exposed to family changes, single parenting and discord are more likely to become anti-social and delinquent.[54] Research completed in 1995 analysed the case histories of 109 recidivists (a half had committed at least six offences in one year), aged between ten and 13 years (29 per cent were European, 58 per cent Maori and ten per cent Pacific Island).[55] In 38 per cent of cases, crime was intergenerational. In 34 per cent, the family was involved in drugs and alcohol abuse and, in 76 per cent of cases, the parents had difficulty coping. While 60 per cent of these youngsters had suffered neglect, physical or sexual abuse, and 80 per cent had schooling problems, only 17 per cent of the children came from stable backgrounds, and 65 per cent had experienced at least one change in caregiver or family constellation. In Australia, 62 per cent of recidivist car thieves, average age 16 years, had dead or separated parents; 50 per cent lived with relatives or in care; 57 per cent were lacking parent or adult support; and 76 per cent were neither employed nor at school.[56] Exploration of the degree and varieties of parental deprivation (defined as the loss or absence of one or both parents for at least a year before age 15) amongst 'abnormal' (and usually institutionalised) adult populations, compared with samples drawn from 'normal' Australian populations, revealed that the worst

affected group of disturbed prisoners often had experienced the virtual
if not total collapse of their family structure after the loss of the father
or both parents.[57] Their families were belaboured by strife, with
institutional care prominent and recurring. A similar story is told for
persistent young offenders in the UK, where 15 of the 74 successfully
interviewed were living with neither parent, five with their fathers
only, 32 with their mothers only and 22 living with what are described
as two parents, but including step-parents, mother's boyfriends and
grandparents. The degree of family disruption is under-represented,
since young offenders with the most disordered lives are difficult to
trace.[58]

While there may be young people with as chaotic backgrounds who
do not get into trouble, this does not alter the fact that such disrupted
backgrounds are far more common among the seriously delinquent than
the law-abiding. In turn, while possible congenital characteristics
shared by the child and the parents may lie behind the problems of
both, and while inappropriate socialisation practices may be both a
cause and effect of the child's maladaptive behaviour, environmental
adversity has an additive and not just an interactive effect. Connections
exist generally between disrupted family background and lesser
degrees of criminality or socially problematic behaviour. A sample of
500 files within the Christchurch Police Zone, detailing offences for
1999 committed by children and young people, showed that 65 per cent
were committed by youngsters from homes without the birth father.[59]
Such associations between broken homes and delinquency have been
demonstrated consistently over a century. However measured or
recorded, higher rates of aggressive behaviour, criminal offences,
behaviour referrals, behaviour problems at home or in school are seen
from early childhood to early adulthood. The associations are particularly strong for boys.[60]

The Cambridge Study of Delinquent Development showed that
delinquents were not only more likely to be born out of wedlock, but
there was an overall doubling of the risk of delinquency where homes
were broken by divorce.[61] There were particularly high rates of parental
separation among the 50 men who had been convicted as juveniles and
adults.[62] In the longitudinal Oregon Youth Study boys who had been
through divorce by the age of ten were more likely to be anti-social. This
was especially marked where they had step-fathers, with their chances
of arrest double those living with both biological parents.[63]

Elsewhere, children with step-fathers were more likely to demonstrate the most disruptive behaviour, and those living in intact married
families the least.[64] At the 16-year-old follow up of the National Child
Development Study, the main longitudinal study of child development
in Britain, eight per cent of boys with both natural parents had been to

court at some time, but 16 per cent of those with lone mothers and 19 per cent of boys with step-fathers. Those who had dealings with police or probation officers were respectively nine per cent, 17 per cent and 20 per cent,[65] and similarly for the 1946 birth cohort.[66] The US National Longitudinal Survey of Youth, where boys who were between 14 and 22 in 1979 have been followed through to their thirties, also shows how those raised outside of an intact marriage are, on average, more than twice as likely as other boys to go to jail. This is after controlling for many background variables like mothers' education, family income, number of siblings, intelligence and neighbourhood factors, such as the proportion of mother-only families, unemployment rates and so forth. The study covers one of the first youth cohorts to have experienced high levels of father-absence during childhood and high rates of youth violence, with rising prison populations during adolescence and early adulthood. Boys raised by unwed mothers were about two-and-a-half times more likely to be imprisoned. They spend more time without a father compared with those whose parents divorced in their teens, who were about one-and-a-half times more likely to be imprisoned.[67]

Similar results are found for hard-to-manage pre-schoolers.[68] Altogether, 27 per cent of youngsters with problem behaviours which persist until age nine, 21 per cent of improved youngsters and only four per cent of controls were living in lone-parent or step-families. Moreover, early family change and disruption predict age-nine attention deficit disorder. Again, the results are similar to those from the Dunedin study, where children whose behaviour problems remained stable from ages five to seven lived in more discordant families, characterised by higher rates of marital separation and lone parenting, poorer family relationships, and more maternal symptoms of physical and psychological distress, compared with children who had improved or who were never identified as having problems.[69]

Unfortunately, the groups with the highest rates of family fragmentation and disruption, who already have the highest participation rates for criminality, are expanding groups which will progressively become a higher proportion of the population. In the 1990s, the rates of offender-apprehension for violent offences for those under 30 were almost as high, and in some age bands higher, for Maori youth as for European, although Maori represented less than one in four of the younger New Zealand population. Maori rates of juvenile offending are over five times those for non-Maori.[70]

From Disadvantaged Children to Disadvantaged Adults

The effects of divorce and sole parenthood continue to be evident in adulthood, with poorer psychological adjustment, lower socio-economic attainment and greater marital failure than adults reared in an intact family. A longitudinal, national sample of US children born between 1965 and 1970, whose parents separated or divorced before 16 years of age, and for whom there is data from all three waves of the nationwide study,[71] showed that, even after controlling for variations in parental education, race, and other child and family factors, 18-22-year-olds from disrupted families were twice as likely to have poor relationships with their mother (30 per cent compared with 16 per cent), or father (two-thirds compared with 29 per cent), to show high levels of emotional distress or problem behaviours, to have received psychological help, and to have dropped out of high school at some point (at double the rate or those from non-disrupted backgrounds). School-based problems had more to do with emotional and behaviour problems than learning difficulties. Girls were at increased risk of early sexuality, teenage pregnancy and non-nuptial births and of themselves divorcing. The effects are stronger for those whose families were disrupted before five years old.

Adult children of divorced parents have significantly more mental health problems than do adult children of intact families,[72] something seen in the strong link between parental divorce during the middle and late childhood years (ages seven to 16) and adult mental health status in the British National Child Development Study, with a substantial 39 per cent increase in the risk of clinically significant psychological problems. Maladjustment also rose when there was family 'restructuring' and, even more, when time was spent in public care.[73] It is particularly in early adulthood that the risk to women's mental health becomes evident.[74] Among subjects born in 1946 from the UK's National Survey of Health and Development, and last interviewed in 1989-1990 at 43,[75] there was still a doubling of the proportion with high depression scores among women who had undergone earlier parental divorce and a strong link between coming from a divorced family and being divorced oneself. The plight of offspring faced with the financial consequences of their own divorce may provoke or exacerbate mental health problems, since divorced parents provide less in the way of economic support to adult children than do intact families. However, neither the extent nor magnitude of the effects of financial hardship are anywhere near sufficient to explain the extremely high level of symptoms. If very high rates of depression found for women who have undergone both parental and adult divorce 'truly reflects causal influences' then the 'upward trend in divorce rates seen in many developed countries would be doubly implicated as a factor serving to increase rates of depression, particularly in women.'[76]

Not just women, but men are also more likely to have long-term problems. Men from divorced families in the British 1946 cohort were proportionally more likely to be out of work by their mid-30s, both as a matter of choice and as a result of mental and physical disability (having a three- to five-fold incidence of mental illness compared with those from intact families).[77] Twice the expected proportion were in the lowest income bracket after controls for class of origin and early abilities. A middle-class child was half as likely to go to university and the same applied to a working-class child's likelihood of passing examinations. As poorer prospects made men insecure workers at the lower end of the job market, this sabotaged their chances of both acquiring or retaining mates. Being far more likely to be single also increased their chance of being unemployed, and of dropping out of the workforce entirely.[78] In the 1958 UK cohort, men who experienced divorce as children were also twice as likely to be unemployed at age 33 (14 per cent to seven per cent), and to have experienced multiple spells of unemployment, with the differences coming mainly from those whose parents divorced before they were seven. After educational test scores in childhood, the most powerful predictor of adult outcomes was family type, followed by father's interest in schooling, contact with the police by age 16, and experience of childhood poverty.[79] The deficit in qualifications for men from divorced families was somewhat reduced by considerations of financial circumstances in childhood as well as early intelligence and behaviour, but this did not apply to the relative lack of higher qualifications. In parallel for the US, the recent Occupational Changes in a Generation Survey showed that a non-intact family background increased the odds of sons ending up in the lowest socio-economic stratum at their first occupational destination by over 50 per cent, and over 30 per cent for their current position.[80]

How Much Does Money Count?

It is very commonly argued that family structure *per se* has no negative consequences for children, and that adverse outcomes are entirely due to low income. In turn, the unspoken if not explicit assumption is that the low income, and hence the adverse consequences, may be laid at the door of the state's failure to provide for sole parents. Whilst not denying that many sole-parent households are poor, many studies have shown little or no relationship between economic circumstances and outcomes. In Sanford M. Dornbusch and colleagues' work on the control of adolescents, measures of social class or parental income and education did not affect the consistent relationship between mother-only households and higher rates of deviance.[81] In the National Longitudinal Survey of Labor Market Experience, the longer the time spent with a lone parent, the greater the reduction in educational attainment. Controlling for income did not noticeably reduce its significantly adverse effect on men—only women. And, while living with a lone parent had the greatest negative impact in the pre-school years, income had no effect on this timing.[82]

In the Western Australian Child Health Survey,[83] a child with a mental health problem was present in 23.1 per cent of couple-families compared with 39.2 per cent of lone-parent families. There was a struggle to provide necessities in respectively 2.8, 5.0, and 15.3 per cent of original couple, step-families and sole-parent families and an unsafe neighbourhood was experienced by 4.0, 4.8 and 9.2 per cent. However, family income was not significant in predicting child mental health status, while marked family discord, family type and parents' disciplinary style all were: 83 per cent of children with mental health problems could be classified correctly on the basis of significant family discord, family type and parents' disciplinary style. When children from families in the National Study of Child Development (UK 1958 cohort) who experienced a fall in status after separation were contrasted with those from families that did not, equal rates of delinquency and psychosomatic or emotional problems were found in both groups.[84] There are also disadvantages in educational attainment between children of divorce and those who remain with both original parents in the UK, irrespective of social class at birth, or socio-economic status before separation.[85]

In Sweden, children of sole parents are not poor and so suffer no disadvantages compared with children from intact families, or so we are told. However, according to the Swedish Commission on Educational Inequality, which studied 120,000 students between 1988 and 1992, children who had been through family dissolution showed lower educational attainment at 16 than children in stable two-parent families. Children of lone parents did better than did children living with two unmarried adults, and children of widow(er)s better than children of divorced parents.[86]

Parental remarriage, often associated with a very marked improvement in economic circumstances, is not associated with any consistent improvement in children's behaviour or performance.[87] If the educational attainment, or the behaviour, of the children of lone parents is only affected by their income, then we must expect that outcomes should be the same for children of two parents in the same economic position. This tends not to be the case. The 1988 National Health Interview Survey on Child Health, involving 17,110 US children aged 17 or under, found that anti-social behaviour, anxiety and depression, headstrong behaviour, hyperactivity, dependency, peer conflict or social withdrawal were higher at lower income levels, and then tended to diminish up the income scale for children in all circumstances. However, within income bands, from the lowest to the highest, the differences between children of one- and two-parent families persisted.[88]

Distinctions by family type obtain amongst the poor as anywhere else. Analysis of a sample of 300 nationwide care and protection notifications to the New Zealand Children and Young Persons Service, and a further 300 youth justice notifications for 1995, revealed that 59 per cent of the former and 51 per cent of the latter were the children of income-tested beneficiaries, compared with expected population percentages of 27 and 19.[89] However, most of these notifications were not simply from poor or low socio-economic backgrounds, since 42 per cent of those who were the subject of care and protection notifications and 35 per cent of the youth justice notifications were also the children of Domestic Purposes Beneficiaries (compared with the expected population percentages of 19 and 12) and lived with sole caregivers. A higher than average proportion of Maori were in both populations of beneficiaries and those coming to the attention of the CYFS, (with Maori women about three times more likely than non-Maori women of parenting age to receive DPB).

Sara McLanahan and Gary Sandefur consider that 'it would be inappropriate to compare children with similar income levels' if 'we want to measure the *total* effect of family disruption on children'. They see 'low income as partly the *result*, as well as partly the cause, of family disruption', thus to compare children with similar income levels would 'lead us to underestimate the consequences of single parenthood'.[90] Only after estimating the total effect do they then explore how much of the effect of family disruption is due to loss of income, for whatever reason. They calculate, for example, that income accounts for between 40 and 50 per cent of the overall difference in high school drop-out rates between children from mother-only and two-parent families in one prominent American sample.[91] Analysis of three other longitudinal US surveys showed how family income accounted for between 13 per cent and 50 per cent of the relationships between growing up with a lone mother and becoming a single parent in adulthood, depending on which sample was used, and whether one looked at blacks, whites or Hispanics.[92] Between 50 per cent and 87 per cent of the difference is unexplained by economic factors. McLanahan's own analysis of the data from the Panel Study of Income Dynamics showed how differences in income accounted for up to 25 per cent of the intergenerational cycle of lone parenthood (and so not for 75 per cent).[93]

The higher the ratio of children to adults, the more attenuated parental attention is likely to be, and this probably accounts for the frequent finding that children from large families at all levels do not do so well educationally compared with those from smaller families. Parental investment in children is affected by parental ability to combine resources of time and money to produce achievement, and this will depend upon parental skills, education and intelligence. In the survey of 13,135 British five-year-olds for the Child Health and Education Study it was found that children of lone parents and those from families with five or more children had poorer linguistic ability, compared with those from two-parent and smaller families. Children with the lowest scores lived with grandparents and in foster homes and were likely to have come from disrupted backgrounds.[94]

The role of income in accounting for outcomes at all has been questioned. Income may be a proxy for other variables. Once children's basic material needs are met, characteristics of the parents become more important to how they turn out than anything additional money can buy.[95] An attempt to unpack the effects of parental socio-economic status on educational outcomes for boys of divorced mothers found that achievement was affected by parental occupation and parental education, as mediated by home environments that encouraged skill building. The income aspect of SES had no influence.[96]

8

Why Children Don't Do So Well in 'Alternative Family Structures'

Summary: Some people argue that, in analysing the problems experienced by parents and their children, we should concentrate on 'processes' not 'structure'. In other words, the family type (lone-parent, step-parent etc) is not important—only the quality of the parenting that takes place. In fact, it is not possible to turn structure and process into rival concepts claiming our allegiance: they go together. The problems of 'process' result from one of 'structure'—one parent, usually the father, is absent. Two-parent families act as a group: one parent monitors and supports the other. The negative outcomes experienced by children of divorced parents cannot be wholly attributed to conditions which existed prior to the divorce, like arguments. Except in cases of high conflict, children can cope with parental arguments better than they cope with divorce. When sole parents re-partner, forming step-families, it might be thought that problems would be reduced, as the child acquires two adult carers instead of one. In fact, step-families have problems of their own, resulting from internal rivalries and an unwillingness of step-parents to 'invest' in bringing up other people's children. Because social science deals in probabilities, and cannot predict with certainty the outcome of a particular case, the risks of family breakdown are dismissed.

The evidence that children do not, on average, fare so well in arrangements other than the traditional, two-parent family is now overwhelming. We still need to ask why this should be so. Is there something about 'alternative family structures' that leads to poorer parenting?

Trying to Separate Process from Structure

The most long-standing and well worked reason for rejecting the roles of family composition and transitions in outcomes is economic, and relates to poverty and lower social class. As research has begun to show that this is not the case, it has been concluded that the real subject of enquiry should not be family transitions or structure at all. Instead: 'children's well being is more a functioning of parenting and relationship processes within the family than it is a function of household

135

composition or demographic factors'. Sexual orientation has recently been added to 'family structure' so that, while it 'might be argued that certain kinds of family interactions, processes, and relationships are beneficial for children's development, ... parents need not be heterosexual to provide them. In other words, variables related to family processes (e.g., qualities of relationships) may be more important predictors of child adjustment than are variables related to family structure (e.g., sexual orientation, number of parents in the home)'. Since 'sensitive parenting in creating secure attachment ... does not stipulate the necessity of any particular family constellation or structure',[1] it follows that parenting of a sufficient quantity and quality can be provided equally well from different relationships, different addresses.

Thus, it is possible to re-cast many of the associations or 'statistical connections [between solo parenting or family disruption and more adverse outcomes] as ... the result of indirect influences over the way that children are socialised'.[2] For example: 'hostile coercive parent-child relationships, inept parental discipline and supervision, and parental yielding to child coercion (negative reinforcement) are associated with aggression and externalising behaviours in adolescents'. This 'interacts with non-compliance in children to produce escalating cycles of coercive exchanges between parents and children that lead to child aggression and anti-social behaviour'. The outcome is that children 'exhibit unregulated aggressive behaviours and a dearth of social and academic skills that often lead to association with anti-social peers and greater risks for the development of more serious externalising behaviours in adolescence'.[3] Thus, once the quality of relationships with parents and their willingness to supervise their children are taken into account, the influence of family structures disappears.

> The majority of well-designed studies ... find that family structure—the number of parents in the home or the fact of divorce—is not *in itself* the critical factor in children's well-being. In both intact and other families, what children need most is a warm, concerned relationship with at least one parent ...[4]

However, process and structure are so closely interrelated as to be virtually inseparable. Consider the role of fathers.

Highly Involved Men and Dad Deficits

Father involvement in older children's lives, especially boys, has repeatedly been found to foster positive development in terms of educational achievement, career plans, and the prevention of lawlessness.[5] Even such small matters as willingness to go with the mother and discuss the child with teachers have large measurable results on achievement.[6] The Tomorrow's Men Project[7] found that can-do boys—with a positive attitude to life, combining confidence, optimism and self-motivation—are more likely to live with dad, compared with low can-do boys. A can-do attitude amongst boys is linked to school ethos, a positive parenting style (which is empathic and supportive), high family togetherness and highly involved fathering (in the sense of spending time with a son, talking about worries and showing interest in schoolwork). Can-do boys commonly report highly involved men (HIM) in their lives (91 per cent with HIM are can-do boys). But 72 per cent of those with dad deficit (DD) are low can-do boys. Compared with boys with DD, those with high level fathering are more likely to care about social and community issues, to have strong ideas of right and wrong, and to consider or imagine themselves as a father one day. Only a quarter of those boys with HIM have one or more problems (depression, being in trouble with the police and being anti-school), compared with two-thirds of those with a DD, where more than one in ten have all three.

Similar associations between positive paternal engagement and outcomes in children aged 5-18 in two-parent families emerged from the US National Survey of Families and Households.[8] For both boys and girls, it meant lower levels of personal and social problems and better sociability. In boys, it also predicted better school behaviour. All results were irrespective of positive mothering, race and socio-economic variables. Among boys and girls who claimed a bad relationship with their fathers, twice as many had ever offended compared with young people who claimed to have had a good relationship. In a long-term follow-up of black US teenage mothers and their children, father presence had large effects on adjustment in adolescence.[9]

The effects of early father involvement are evident in adulthood: children of affectionate fathers are more likely to be happily married in their 40s, to report good relationships with friends, and be mentally healthy.[10] At the same time, adults who had a father present in the early and adolescent years are more companionable and responsible.[11] Obviously intact marriages strongly affect the probability, even the possibility, that a child will have a good relationship with a father. The continuance, let alone quality, of the child's relationships with his or her natural parents is affected by whether they are divorced or whether the child knew each parent from the beginning. Fathers who live in separate households often have a low level of involvement with their children, become less altruistic towards, or less closely identified with them over time, less aware of their needs, and less willing to share their income with them. The younger the children at the time of divorce, the more likely the father is to drift away from regular contact.[12] By adulthood, the relationship quality with divorced, non custodial fathers and that of children who have never lived with their father, is much the same.[13] Some fathers develop new emotional attachments which supersede previous commitments. Only a third had frequent, regular contact in the Tripp and Cockett study.[14] Typically, as in the US National Survey of Children, nearly one half had not seen their non-custodial fathers in the past year, as 'marital disruption effectively destroys the ongoing relationship between the children and their biological parents living outside the home in a majority of families'.[15] Even where there is contact with a non-resident father, it is arguable whether or not it makes any difference to the child.[16]

While we know that family structure on its own is not a predictor of child development, it is a proxy for those factors that directly affect children's well-being. Economic status or poverty are also structural, but their effects usually depend upon intervening variables. These might be the characteristics of the relations that accompany marital dissolution or intermittent cohabitation (for example, decreased attention, affection and communication), as well as the task overload of single parents.[17] Income, neighbourhoods, resources, educational level, supervision, attachment, and so forth, supply reasons why some children do not do so well as they might in other circumstances, but these factors are, in turn, affected by the presence or absence of a parent. It is not so much that family processes make family structure irrelevant, as that 'the differences in family processes associated with parental divorce and remarriage are critical for the child's social and emotional development'.[18] All in all: 'it borders on educational malpractice to tell students that process matters, but structure does not, as if these concepts were somehow competitors for our ideological allegiance, rather than descriptions of two closely interrelated aspects of family life'.[19]

Where one parent is absent from home, he is not only less likely to be spending time with the children, but this may also reduce the availability of the mother because she has to do many tasks performed by fathers in two-parent homes. The remaining parent may spend less time on primary childcare activities, with comparatively less affection, supervision, and attention and a comparative lack of household order, activities and predictable regimes. Lower levels of parental involvement and supervision, which are found more frequently in mother-only homes, affect everything from help with homework to the monitoring of adolescents' social activities.[20] Social and economic investment in the children may fall, not just because there is less income, but also because the mother may be more likely to centre her life elsewhere. Her own social and sex life, courtship and boyfriends may compete for attention with the children, and her reference points are more likely to shift away from the home.

As paternal absenteeism generally lowers levels of contact between adults and children, so family life becomes more sparse and perfunctory. While nothing is more strongly correlated with delinquency than the number of delinquent friends an adolescent has, time spent with a family is capable of reducing and even eliminating peer influence.[21] The motivation toward delinquency generated by one social environment (peer culture) is neutralised or counteracted by another (the family) by inhibiting the initial formation of delinquent friendships. Family time has a significant effect on all self-reported delinquency, particularly weekend family time. Parent-child attachment may indirectly affect delinquency, because it inhibits the development of delinquent friendships by either reducing opportunities to associate with deviant peers, or influencing the kind of friends adolescents have. (It does little to reduce delinquency among those who already have delinquent friends.) The immediate pressure of peers on adolescents is so great that peer-induced pressures to violate the law can only be overcome by avoiding the company of delinquent peers altogether.[22]

If any factor is primary in the genesis of anti-social behaviour in all forms, it is encompassed under the heading of discipline, or rather the lack of it.[23] Parental control may be weaker in a one-parent family, simply because monitoring or supervision is more difficult for one person. Moreover, divorced mothers may make fewer demands of children, and use less effective disciplinary strategies than married mothers.[24] In the Western Australian Child Health Survey,[25] parents of almost 20 per cent of children in sole-parent families expressed the need for outside help in disciplining their children in comparison with seven per cent in couple-families. A sole parent may be less capable of providing supervision, and *if* poor supervision is linked to delinquency, then there is an unavoidable link between disrupted families and criminality.[26] Given that sole mothers have less input into their children's decisions than married parents, adolescents may consequently be more susceptible to peer pressure, and thus more likely to engage in anti-social behaviour, be non-compliant, and lack social skills.[27] As the child ages, parents and teachers may abandon any attempts to set and enforce limits in order to avoid confrontation. This is all likely to be magnified where the child has a behaviour disorder. David R. Offord's study of all juveniles placed on probation by the juvenile court of Ottawa-Carlton in the mid-1970s found that intact families had a significantly better chance of keeping anti-social behaviour under control than lone parents if there were no other parental disabilities like mental illness, criminality and welfare history.[28] Elsewhere, men who had come from unbroken homes with serious conflict (often with alcoholic or criminal fathers) were more criminal than those from either unbroken or broken homes with affectionate mothers.[29] But, 'supervision, a form of control more likely to occur when a child was raised by two parents, accounted for a reliable proportion of the variation in crime'. Loving mothers were more likely to supervise, but then so were two parents and, 'comparisons indicate that boys were more likely to be supervised if they had intact homes and were less likely to be criminal if supervised. The data could be interpreted as suggesting an indirect criminogenic effect from paternal absence'.[30] Unaffectionate broken homes provide very low levels of supervision. In one study of families in high-risk inner-city neighbourhoods, only six per cent of children from stable (no broken marriage) and safe (supervised) homes became delinquent, compared with 18 per cent from homes which were either unstable (broken marriage) or unsafe (lack of supervision). There was a 90 per cent rate from homes rated as both unstable and unsafe.[31] As Dornbusch and colleagues report, while it is true that the presence of other adults, like grandparents, brings household control levels closer to those of the two-parent family so, by the same token, 'the raising of adolescents is not a task that can easily be borne by the mother alone'.[32]

The absence of monitoring by parents and 'over-investment' in peer relationships that accompanies the withdrawal of adolescent children in divorced mother- and step-families from home relationships, may also lead to poorer competence and education compared with those whose parents are in stable marriages.[33]

Being a Group

In two-parent families, each parent can help to make up for the deficiencies of the other. Being a group involves a qualitative, as well as a quantitative, difference. It is an aspect of the way in which the family acts as a social unit. Observing how, in the research, the frequency of visitation by non-custodial fathers is unrelated to child adjustment, Paul Amato[34] suggests that paternal commitment and the 'paternal effect' may be heavily dependent upon marital commitment, since:

> For many men ... marriage and parenthood are a package deal. Their ties to their children, and their feelings of responsibility for their children, depend on their ties to their wives. It is as though men only know how to be fathers indirectly, through the actions of their wives.[35]

It may not make sense to ask whether mothers or fathers have a greater influence on children's development. Instead, it may be more meaningful to think about the mother/father/child triad. Not only may fathers play their most important role in children's lives as a member of the marital partnership, but as the supportive behaviour of fathers improves the quality of their wives' parenting skills, a 'similar observation can be made of mothers. They play key roles in their children's lives through their relations with their husbands.'[36] Certainly, 'without the marriage structure, men often seem unable to maintain their perspective as fathers or to hold in view the needs of their children'.[37] Like other institutions, marriage brings order to people's lives and provides reference points outside of individual consciousness which shape attitudes and give coherence and direction to behaviour—making it significant in its own right.

If lone mothers themselves are more likely to abuse or neglect children compared with married women then, as with any enterprise, standards are maintained, performance improved and excesses checked through the expectations and responses of other people. Not only can two biological parents sharing the same household monitor the children and maintain parental control, but:

> ... just as important, the parents can also monitor one another and make sure the other parent is behaving in appropriate ways ... Having another parent around who cares about the child increases the likelihood that each parent will 'do the right thing' even when otherwise inclined. In short, the two-parent family creates a system of checks and balances that both promotes parental responsibility and protects the child from parental neglect and, sometimes, abuse. This is an important function of social capital within the family.[38]

Social isolation and a lack of support systems have been noted as reasons for child abuse and neglect becoming a problem of increasing magnitude as tribal peoples adapt to more private, Western modes of living. When reference is made to the movement of Polynesians from a profile of low to high child abuse, this is accounted for by the way that, traditionally: 'Potential abusers cannot get away with it ... elders intervene directly to require that parents impose punishment or exercise proper control, when needed, and step in when parental conduct gets out of hand.'[39] Thus '... nothing is more likely to disturb and disrupt the Polynesian child-rearing system than nucleated suburban living'. The child who does not have a network of 'individuals beyond the biological parents who are concerned about his or her welfare is at increased jeopardy. Child-rearing as a group concern: 'both ensures general standards of childcare and prevents idiosyncratic departure from those standards'.[40]

However, having concerned kin within range is not the same as child-rearing being a 'group concern'. The hypothesised picture of traditional child-rearing as one where 'many people actively participate and assist in child-rearing' is often little more than a hippy dream projected onto tribal society. As child-rearing is described as moving indoors, and coinciding with the way in which one person has to be 'all things at all time to all their children', that one person increasingly does it alone, without the presence of anyone, indoors or out, to offer support or restraint.[41] The shrinkage of the circle of others is nowhere better illustrated than by marital disruption.[42] Those on their own do not receive the feedback which encourages and tells them that their efforts are right and worthwhile, and neither are they policed and corrected by another concerned parent.

Parents who have themselves been abused or spent part of their childhood in care are far less likely to repeat a pattern of parental inadequacy if they have a supportive spouse from a 'normal' background. When they parent alone, this corrective mechanism is absent and the likelihood is that problems are added to, rather than withdrawn from, the cycle of disadvantage.[43]

Already There?

It is widely believed that:

> ... many of the so-called effects of divorce are actually conditions that existed prior to divorce ... inter-parental conflict, lack of parenting such as emotional support and practical help and guidance—perhaps due to the parents own post-divorce adjustment process.[44]

In the British National Child Development Study, it has been possible to trace the effects of parental divorce on mental health from age seven, through ages 11, 16, 23 and 33.[45] Early on, it was suggested that much of the apparent effect of a parental divorce on children's emotional problems between seven and 11 and in later life could be attributed to characteristics of the child and family prior to divorce, or before age seven.[46] Later, as the divorce and non-divorce groups aged, their differences widened. At 33:

> Many of the relationships of family type during childhood to the adult outcomes remain virtually untouched by the addition of the controls ... extra-marital births, multiple partnerships, and homelessness for both sexes, malaise and unemployment for the men, and lack of qualifications and low income for the women, change very little and are often large.[47]

Parental divorce might set in motion a train of circumstances that affects individuals' lives even after they have left home, married, and entered the labour force, or trigger events such as early child-bearing or curtailed education which, in turn, affect adult outcomes. US data from over 81,000 people in 37 studies, comparing over-18s from divorced or separated families and those whose biological parents had been continuously married,[48] suggests that parental separation has broad negative consequences for quality of life in adulthood. The outcomes primarily affected psychological well-being (depression, low life-satisfaction), family well-being (low marital quality, divorce) and socio-economic well-being (low attainment, income and occupational level), leading to '... a pessimistic conclusion: the argument that parental divorce presents few problems for children's long-term development is simply inconsistent with the literature on this topic'. The effects are weakened by controls for pre-divorce factors, but the 'fact that any effect is observed, given the length of time involved, is noteworthy'.[49]

It's the Fighting

A familiar way to discount the bearing of family composition and transitions on outcomes is to claim that: 'child behaviour problems associated with parental divorce are best understood as the result of inter-parental conflict rather than changes in household composition or structure as such'.[50] This seems to preclude effects due to the breaking of attachments or departure of one parent and, indeed, it has been widely promoted and become accepted wisdom that it is better to separate than to inflict a conflictual relationship on children.

Inter-parental conflict is hardly beneficial to children's development. It is estimated that between 25 and 70 per cent of those exposed to physical conflict between parents manifest clinically significant behaviour problems.[51] However, children go through considerable distress when their families break up, so that the effects of conflict vie with those of separation.[52] Separation, or the threat of separation, keeps pushing through as a detrimental factor in the lives of children involved in marital disruption. The younger the child at break-up, the poorer the outcomes.[53] John Tripp and Monica Cockett found that it is family reorganisation, particularly involving the father's departure, which is the main adverse factor in the lives of children involved in marital break-up. This, not financial hardship or marital conflict, led to poor health, educational and social effects, and the more transitions children experienced, the poorer the outcomes.[54] In the Netherlands, the well-being of adolescents from stable and conflicted intact families has been compared with that of those in a one-parent family or step-family after divorce. The best results for physical and psychological health, 'relational well-being', and employment situation, were for young people from stable intact families. Those in one-parent families fared worst and those from conflicted families fell in-between.[55]

Ronald Simons' data from families in the Iowa Youth and Families Project and the Iowa Single Parent Project seems to bear out the analysis of Cockett and Tripp.[56] Parental divorce increased boys' aggression and delinquency because it reduced the father's involvement and increased the mother's depression, which disrupted her parenting. Boys' depression was related to mothers' depression, pre-divorce conflict and quality of mothers' parenting. Divorced, non-residential fathers were less likely to help their children solve problems, to discuss standards of conduct, or to enforce discipline, compared with fathers in married families. However, parental divorce was inherently distressing and depressing for boys, regardless of the quality of parenting or level of parental conflict. Interestingly, there was no association between conflict in continuing married families and children's emotional or behaviour problems. It has been suggested that either marital conflict is unlikely to be as severe as pre- and post-divorce conflict, or that conflict has little impact on children unless it is perceived as threatening the parents' marriage and is a precursor to divorce. Again, the threat of parental loss, rather than parental conflict, is disturbing to a child.

The Western Australian study seems to underline these findings. Children whose parents had a poor relationship with each other were better off on average than children living in lone-parent or reconstituted families where there were good adult relationships.[57] Judith Wallerstein and Julia Lewis, in their study of the long-term consequences of divorce, found that the nature and level of conflict in marriages were similar in families that divorced and in a comparison group of intact families from the same neighbourhood. Failure in their own relationships was lower for those whose parents stayed together and it is speculated that, despite serious marital problems, the children had a better sense of how to behave in marriage, or how to co-operate and solve problems, even when this meant not being 'like my parents'.[58] It has been demonstrated elsewhere that marital conflict which does not concern children or is resolved constructively and non-aggressively, even if frequent, does not adversely affect them.[59] Children who involve themselves in their parents' conflict, or take on responsibility, have higher levels of depression, anxiety, hostility, and lower self-esteem than do children who do not. Children who use coping strategies that distance and distract them from their parents' conflict, or accept that it is none of their business, fare better than those who perhaps make unsuccessful attempts to end conflict.[60]

It is often axiomatically assumed that divorce finishes conflict, when this may initiate conflict where it did not exist before, raise the level or sustain it at high levels. Moreover, why assume that conflict is only found in two-parent families, and not in lone-parent homes—whether it is continuing conflict with the ex-spouse or partner, with new 'partners' or other third parties, or between parent and children? Simons and colleagues emphasise how children from divorced families have more problems, not least because their parents are less likely to engage in competent parenting and more likely to be in conflict than those who stay married.[61]

The Christchurch longitudinal study recorded the number of occasions for which the child's parent figures had separated for a period of three months or longer between nought and ten years, the number of parental reconciliations (following separation) and changes of parents that the child had experienced during the period, whether as a result of family breakdown or death, or remarriage or reconciliation.[62] Also recorded was whether the parents had engaged in prolonged arguments during the previous year, and whether the child's mother had reported being assaulted. Exposure to parental discord was associated with higher risks of offending, particularly where combined with early conduct problems. Family change in the absence of discord did not lead to increased risk of self-reported offending between 11-13 years. If this seems to underwrite the view that, where there is discord, it may be in the child's best interest for the parents to separate, there are important qualifications. The life history of children following parental separation showed that within five years nearly three-quarters had experienced parental reconciliation or parental remarriage, and over 50 per cent of these 'second passage' families broke down.[63] While separation 'may lead to the short-term removal of the child from a discordant situation, it may also have the secondary effect of placing the child at risk of exposure to further family discord'.[64]

Beliefs that divorce is more a remedy, than the cause, of adverse outcomes (which owe themselves to conflict in marriage), take it for granted that divorce only ends conflicted marriages. But as divorce becomes increasingly acceptable and commonplace, it removes a growing number of children from two-parent homes that still provide many benefits. Children are likely to be exposed to many stresses, such as moving homes, changing schools, conflicts over post-divorce arrangements, and declining household income. Divorces in the past (when marital dissolution was uncommon and occurred only under the most troubling circumstances) may have freed children from home environments that were especially aversive. In contrast, many divorces today (when marital dissolution is common) subject children to stressful experiences with few compensating advantages. A 15-year study by Paul Amato and Alan Booth[65] found that less than a third of divorces involved high-conflict marriages. It was after divorce from low-conflict marriages that children were particularly likely to become adults with increased psychological distress, reduced happiness, fewer ties with kin and friends, and reduced marital quality.

> If divorce were limited to high-conflict marriages, it might be in children's best interests. But with marital dissolution becoming increasingly acceptable, people are leaving marriages at lower thresholds of unhappiness now than in the past. These are the divorces that are most likely to be stressful for children. ... Consequently, we conclude that the rise in marital disruption, although beneficial to some children, has, on balance, been detrimental to children. Furthermore, if the threshold of marital unhappiness required to trigger a divorce continues to decline, then outcomes for children of divorced parents may be more problematic in the future.[66]

While 'conflicted' families are invariably seen as two-parent families (who ought to split up), ongoing conflict is highest in lone-parent and step-parent families. In the Western Australian Child Health Survey,[67] nearly 18 per cent of original families were involved in serious arguments, compared with 28 of step-families and nearly 30 per cent of one-parent families. Those involved in drugs/legal strife were respectively 4.3, 10.7 and 14.8 per cent, and for a child reported to be frightened by someone's behaviour, it was respectively 3.5, 7.8 and 11.5 per cent. Families with high levels of discord were twice as likely to have a caregiver with a history of mental health problems (23 per cent to 12 per cent). But sole parents were more likely to have been treated for a mental health problem, at 27 per cent, compared with a parent in 12 per cent of two-parent families. Children in sole-parent and step/ blended families had their higher risk of mental health problems further increased compared with children in original families marked by discord or problematic disciplinary style.

Child-rearing often deteriorates under the stress of divorce.[68] Negativity between mothers and children is certainly highest in lone-parent households, and child behaviour problems are associated with maternal negativity.[69] Unsurprisingly, the quality of the relationships that divorced fathers have with sons, often troubled during divorce, worsens significantly afterwards.[70] When conflicted parent/child relations are added to poor supervision or monitoring of children, this increases the probability of involvement with delinquent peers. The emotionally distancing effect that divorce has on relationships with both parents is stronger than for conflict and unhappiness in intact marriages.[71]

As lone women with pre-school children appeared to have multiple stressors with which to cope, the high levels of strain led to counter-productive control attempts, and the children's subsequent non-compliance.[72] Moreover, in sole-parent families there may be less clear boundaries between the parental and child sub-systems (where children understand that they are not responsible for and need not involve themselves in their parents' strife or problems).[73]

This should suggest that, even where there is a reduction in conflict with marital dissolution, there may not be a reduction in disorder. If family change leads to involvement in a delinquent peer group, through lowered monitoring and supervision, then less discord may not help at all—leading to the production and prolongation of behaviour problems in middle childhood and adolescence.[74]

Can Step-Parents Improve the Situation?

Today's sole-parent families are often tomorrow's 'reconstituted' families. As a family moves from having one parent to having two, it might be expected that step-families would solve or reduce many of the problems associated with solo parenting, not only by increasing income, but also by reducing task overload, and increasing supervision of children.

A close supportive relationship with a step-father is certainly associated with fewer behaviour problems, greater social responsibility and higher achievement in boys, especially pre-adolescent boys. But this may be difficult to attain,[75] given breakdown rates.[76] As already noted: children who experience several changes of family structure have particularly adverse outcomes.[77] The Christchurch study, like others, demonstrates that those who encounter multiple family situations are at greater risk of developing more anti-social and aggressive behaviour.[78]

As it is, there is an overall 'absence of a remarriage benefit for children in step-family households'.[79] In the prominent three-wave US study,[80] adolescent children in divorced lone-mother families and step-families formed through remarriage consistently did less well for behaviour, competence and education than comparable children in stable marriages. Over a two-year study period positive relationships between adolescents and step-fathers declined, with increased withdrawal and anti-social behaviour towards mothers. All major longitudinal studies in the UK and US not only suggest that children with step-parents have high distress levels at 16,[81] but also that they are as or more likely to be involved with crime compared with those with lone parents.[82] For example, the 1987-88 National Survey of Families[83] showed how children living in step-father households are over twice as likely to have behaviour problems at school as children with biological mothers and fathers (26 per cent *vs* 11 per cent). After controlling for economic factors, children in step-father households score significantly worse than those in lone-mother households in areas of sociability, school performance and behaviour problems, something noted elsewhere for teen births.[84] These differences remain after adjusting for differences in family conflict. In the US National Longitudinal Survey of Youth, boys raised outside of an intact marriage are, on average, more than twice as likely as other boys to go to jail. But the rate rises three-fold for boys with step-parents—the same level as those with no parents and from far more difficult circumstances.[85]

At the very least, the well-being of step-children tends to lie closer to that of youngsters with lone parents than to those with two original parents. In a major Dutch study of the life-course of 2,500 youngsters aged 15 to 24, those from stable two-parent families had the best results for physical and psychological health, relationships with others and employment, and those with one parent the worst. The children in step-families were closer to the one-parent children for psychological problems, and closer to the two-parent children in physical, relational and employment matters.[86]

Weaker Ties in Step-Families

The formation of a step-family tends to stress all family relationships, whether between parent and step-parent, step-parent and step-child, and between step-siblings.[87] Such tensions and difficulties may lie behind the fact that, as in the Christchurch sample, over a half of 'second-passage' two-parent families break down within five years.[88] Accounts abound of relatively loveless, unsatisfying and ambivalent step-relationships; lacking in warmth and support compared with biological relationships[89] and becoming more, not less, negative over time. Observers find step-families less cohesive than intact families, with relationships less positive,[90] and children from both lone or step-parent families seeming to be more involved with delinquent peers and susceptible to anti-social peer pressure. In the first wave of the Non-shared Environment in Adolescent Development Project,[91] step-fathers' hostile behaviours were not only more important predictors of deviancy than those of biological fathers, or of mothers or siblings, but association with delinquent peers was greatest among boys in step-families, whose homes were marked by more conflicted, negative relations, and less monitoring and control.[92] This all replicates findings from D.J. West's and D.P. Farrington's longitudinal study of London youths.[93]

Indeed: '[m]ore pervasive than reports of conflict ... are reports of disengagement. Nearly every observer describes step-parents' [typical] parenting style as disengaged.' In turn '... perhaps one-fourth to one-third of adolescent step-children disengage themselves emotionally and physically from their step-family'.[94] In the UK National Child Development Study, almost twice as many step-fathers as natural fathers (33 per cent to 18 per cent) showed little or no interest in children's school progress. Only 24 per cent, compared to 45 per cent of natural fathers, were very interested, whatever their social class. Step-father families were also most likely to want the children to leave school at the earliest possible opportunity, and had the lowest aspirations for employment.

Moreover, just as single or divorced mothers were comparatively uninterested in their children, the same was true for remarried mothers, especially where they had sons. (Only 24 per cent were very interested, compared with 43 per cent of mothers in unbroken families.)[95] In the US National Survey of Families and Households, remarried and cohabiting mothers are the least involved with their children. They share fewer meals, read to their children less often, are more lenient and supervise less, and participate in fewer activities.[96] Much the same came out of the first wave of the Non-shared Environment in Adolescent Development Project, where mothers in step-families also show significantly higher rates of negativity than those in other family types.[97] Moreover, mothers who live with a 'partner' are more lax and less involved with their children than mothers who remarry, just as married step-fathers are also more likely to assume parental responsibilities than 'partners'.[98] The Children in Families Study reported significantly less support for children or teenagers in Australian step-families, with reading ability, self-esteem and self-control below those of children in other homes.[99] This difference in investment probably explains the way that offspring of mothers who remarried had lower educational achievement (by over one year) than those whose mothers did not remarry in the Study of Marital Instability Over the Life Course.[100]

As step-parents and boyfriends help to push their partners' children towards premature independence, there is an early termination of parental responsibilities—found despite all controls for economic circumstances.[101] By the mid-1990s, a half of Scottish young people under 19 with a step-parent had left home, compared with a third of those who lived with their birth parents.[102] All sources in the English-speaking world record a major change in the circumstances in which young homeless people leave home. Submissions to the Australian Burdekin report on homeless youngsters from numerous refuges and surveys in different states showed how these came overwhelmingly from step-families or lone-parent households.[103] By the 1990s, a majority of single homeless in the UK were young people aged 25 or under.[104] Most 'leave their parental home because of household conflict and only a small minority of young people choose to leave'. Even in the early 1980s, the main reason young homeless people had left their 'last settled base' was to find work.

When Joan Smith and her colleagues reported on their in-depth study of homeless people aged 16 to 25 in 1998,[105] they found that two-thirds had experienced family breakdown, often combined with the arrival of a step-parent or mother's boyfriend(s), and a quarter had spent time in care. In such households: 'the obligation to support may simply not be there, whatever the combined earnings of the couple ... One of the major causes of youth homelessness is [now] the ... re-marriage or re-partnering of their own parents.'[106] More than half reported physical abuse from step-fathers—whether long-standing systematic abuse, growing violence or major confrontations where the young person was seriously assaulted. Young women also reported sexual abuse, as well as abandonment or physical abuse from a birth-parent in reconstituted households, or neglect from lone mothers with a series of boyfriends. A half also experienced mental health problems —depression, self-harm and suicide attempts and the associated factors were much the same as those which had driven them away from home: 'abuse—sexual, physical, verbal—or neglect/rejection by the mother or failure by her to protect them from abuse'.[107] Of course, 'there were some caring parents in the disrupted households' just as 'there were a few abusive parents among non-disrupted households ... but they walked a fine line between their loyalty to their children and to their new partner'.[108] The same pattern has been found for under-16s, who were three times more likely to run away from step-families, and twice as likely to run away from a lone parent, than were children living with both birth-parents.[109]

The effects of having a step-parent persist well into adulthood, not least because going back to the parent's home is not an option for those who find themselves with housing problems. When young people from intact households leave home, even as a consequence of their own bad behaviour, this is often not the end of family support.[110]

How Much Effort Will Step-Parents 'Invest' in Bringing Up Other People's Children?

Attempts to explain why children in step-father families do worse than children with their original two parents, and often no better than children in lone-mother households, cannot account for the differences simply in terms of conflict.[111] Even when children in the least conflicted step-father households (about 25 per cent of all children in this type of home) are compared with children in their original two-parent households or with sole mothers with average levels of conflict, the former still do worse on many important indicators of well-being.

In general, loss of a parent through widowhood, rather than divorce, separation, or unwed motherhood, is not associated with the same adverse outcomes, or not to anything like the same degree. Those who are most disadvantaged by parental death are those whose surviving parent remarries. It is most obvious in the lack of educational qualifica-tions and early transitions to adulthood, with early employment, home leaving and early parenthood.[112]

All societies are pessimistic about child-rearing by non-relatives. Adoption is the only exception where the object is to provide the couple with a child and the child with parents. For the step-father, the object is the mother, not the child. There are likely to be many households which benefit from having a step-parent's 'help to re-construct a more solid family life than existed beforehand',[113] and many treat their step-children well, accepting their share of upbringing costs. But, this does not amount to having the same love and commitment as genetic parents, and being prepared to invest the same costly personal resources. Step-children may have negative utility, since offspring from a previous union militate against the mother having more children by subsequent consorts. Less committed to the child's welfare than biological fathers, step-fathers are less likely to serve as a check on the mother's behaviour. Rather than assisting with the responsibilities of parenting, a step-father may compete with the child for the mother's time and attention, or his efforts may be rejected or undermined by the mother because she does not trust his judgement. Children may resent sharing their mother, or maintain loyalty towards their father. In cohabiting unions, issues of authority and trust are even more problematic. Thus: 'From the child's perspective, the arrival of a boyfriend or step-father does not represent a "second chance" as much as it represents a foreclosure of the first and only chance.'[114] Discriminating in favour of one's own young is a human characteristic. Parental love is an onerous commitment and it cannot be fully activated by pairing up with someone who already has dependent children. Enormous differentials in violence are the most dramatic consequence of this difference in feelings.

The idea that step-children are not loved equally with genetic children is likely to be regarded as distasteful; for example: '[t]here is something about the association between step-parenthood and child maltreatment that appears to be uniquely unpalatable, and we have witnessed some curious attempts to make it vanish'.[115] It has been put down to poverty, stereotyping, to children having to 'make the transition from a long-term stable situation with one parent into a two-parent household',[116] to the step-parent role being 'incompletely institutionalised' (so that people do not know what they are supposed to do) or to society not accepting the equal validity of all 'family forms'—where failure to develop the norms that would enable step-family relationships to function successfully is blamed on the endorsement of the biological nuclear family.[117] However, there is a lot more to social action than role-playing or having the right script. Step-parents 'do not find their roles less satisfying and more conflicted than natural parents because they don't *know* what they are supposed to do. Their problem is that they don't *want* to do what they feel obliged to do ...'[118]

Why Does it Affect Some but Not Others?

The consequences of family dissolution and fragmentation are obviously not uniform for all children, in that adverse effects are not inevitable or present in all cases, or necessarily along all different dimensions of well-being. It is difficult to see how this could be otherwise, since so many variables are involved, and people are not genetically identical. While living with just one parent (or step-parent, or in a cohabitation) increases the risk of many negative outcomes, it is not the only cause of any of them.

However, findings that children growing up with lone parents may do less well than those with married couples are apt to be simultaneously condemned for dooming, or sentencing, all children in one category to do badly *and*, at the same time, for being misleading. Because the adverse effect is not present in 100 per cent of cases, suggestions are that there is nothing whatsoever to worry about, and that 'parents (and professionals) should be aware of the successful adjustment made by the majority of children who experience parental separation'.[119] However, in the social and behavioural sciences, or medical epidemiology, researchers are not looking for strict, exceptionless laws, as in physics, but probabilities. This means something which occurs at a significantly higher rate in one group compared with another, and whose distribution is not due to accident or chance. It is not a sign of failure that we do not know who precisely is going to be adversely affected, although further comparative investigations could narrow this down. We know that 100 per cent of smokers are not going to get lung cancer, but this does not make smoking any less a significant risk factor in populations. To dismiss findings because there are exceptions is to demand impossible standards that would abolish social and medical investigation altogether. Findings are group averages. Measures of the frequency of any characteristic in different groups greatly overlap and there is no problem showing good results at the best end of the worst distribution, and bad results at the worst end of the best distribution. It is easy to make the contrast between children who grow up in a loving one-parent family and children who grow up in two-parent families and are neglected or abused, but it does not invalidate evidence that both situations may not produce the same proportions of good and bad effects.

In David Fergusson's 20-year Christchurch Health and Development Study,[120] only a quarter of the children in the most disadvantaged five per cent of the sample developed early-onset multiple problem behaviours. Less than seven per cent of children of beneficiaries in one year are the subject of Child, Youth and Family Services (CYFS) notifications for care and protection or offending, even if more than a half of actual notifications are for the children of income-tested beneficiaries, mainly lone mothers, or nearly three-fold their representation in the general child population.[121] Genetic endowment may play some part in increasing susceptibility and predisposing young people to multiple problem behaviours, but a disorganised, disrupted family environment also clearly has a significant role to play.

Research findings as to whether or not there are differences are essentially distinct from the evaluations of whether any discovered or discoverable outcomes are socially and morally desirable or not. However, people do not usually accept that delinquency, or educational failure, or a heightened rate of mental instability, or downward social mobility, are desirable. Often, adverse findings tend to be minimised, unlike those which, for example, deal with pollutants, diet or disease. However, as we have seen, the risk of negative outcomes for the children of divorce and single parenthood is double or more, and: 'In epidemiological terms, the doubling of a hazard is a substantial increase, greater than that associated with many well-known medical risk factors. The increase in risk that dietary cholesterol poses for cardiovascular disease ... is far less than double, yet millions ... have altered their diets because of the perceived hazard.'[122]

Premature Celebration of 'Alternative Family Structures'

Commenting on the 'enthusiastic' nature of much of the scientific, professional and popular literature 'about emerging alternative family structures', D.M. Fergusson adds that:

> ... the dismal statistics emerging from this longitudinal study tend to suggest that this enthusiasm may have been premature or misplaced ... While the traditional nuclear family may have limitations as a child-rearing institution, it is open to very serious debate as to whether the alternative of short-term family structures which involve successive transitions between single-parent and two-parent families will prove to be as effective as a child-rearing institution. Certainly our results suggest the need for family policy makers to be cautious about accepting enthusiastic claims about the desirability of alternative family structures until the viability or otherwise of these structures has been assessed on the basis of carefully collected empirical evidence.[123]

Understandably: 'persons who positively evaluate recent trends in family structure tend to be reluctant to admit that those trends may have negatively affected the well-being and socialisation of children and adolescents'.[124]

In turn, it is often considered unnecessary to offer any reason for rejecting evidence, apart from sneering dismissals which cast aspersions on the motivations of those who believe that such facts deserve consideration. A neo-Marxist orientation persists from the radicalism of the 1960s among social affairs intellectuals and commentators; or a relativism where there is no right or wrong either factually or ethically, but only ideological orientations that serve the (malign) powers that be. The problems that evidence may help explain or elucidate are often themselves seen as unworthy of attention in the first place. Not least their reality is rejected. Concern over youth crime is dismissed in that 'offending has existed for a long time. It is not a recent phenomenon.' If anyone notices, then what we really 'witness [is] the construction of a moral panic'.[125] Anybody who may not be quite blasé over family and social trends is *ipso facto*, it appears, in a blundering state of terror—there being 'moral panics' breaking out everywhere, not to mention the 'moral panics of yesteryear'.[126] So how big does a problem have to become before it is proper or appropriate to notice? Not only robberies, burglaries and murders, but also plagues, Jew-baiting, massacres, wars, and mining accidents have also existed for a long time. Does this make them unworthy of attention, and is such attention 'moral panic'? The balance of discussion deserves to shift from ideology to research-based information, so that policies affecting families are informed by the facts.

Family conditions affect adults as well as children, and their role goes largely unacknowledged even when it comes to top-priority concerns like domestic violence.

9

Problems for Adults

Summary: New Zealand has an unusually high rate of domestic violence. While feminists have criticised marriage as patriarchal and a threat to women, domestic violence is far more common amongst single women and women in cohabiting relationships. One reason is alcohol abuse, to which unmarried people are more prone. New Zealand also has a high male suicide rate, particularly amongst young men. Suicide rates of both adults and children are correlated with divorce rates, with never-married people having three to four times the suicide rate of the married.

Domestic Violence and the Decline of Marriage

New Zealand is the only country to have a national family violence prevention agency which co-ordinates education and sanctions. It seems that around 80 per cent of violence is family violence,[1] and that this accounts for nearly a half of homicides. The cost of domestic violence in 1994 was estimated at $1.2bn a year[2] in terms of the services used, on the assumption that one in seven families is affected. The Women's Safety Survey 1996[3] suggests that two per cent of women with current partners and 22 per cent of women with recent partners (within the last two years) had experienced ten or more acts of abuse, and ten per cent of women with current partners and two fifths with recent partners reported four or more acts. Within the previous year more than a quarter of Maori women and a tenth of non-Maori women with current partners reported at least one act. A half of the women who had experienced violence by their current partners and more than three-quarters who had experienced violence from recent partners rated it as 'very serious' or 'quite serious'.[4] A survey of 2,000 men reported similar figures for violence against female partners.[5] This all indicates much higher levels of violence against women than in other English-speaking societies.[6]

Concern about family violence has waxed and waned historically.[7] A reason for the concerted action programme may be that the problem is easy to 'conceptualise as one which largely affects women and which is clearly the result of male behaviour'.[8] However, as the issue re-entered the policy arena with the modern feminist movement, domestic violence became a crime typifying marriage (and requiring its eradication), rather than just a deviation from the norm that might be corrected legally. According to feminist analysis, wife-beating is a reflection of patriarchal norms, where the family is 'the site of a good deal of domestic and sexual violence ... this violence is a result of the very structure of the family and its relationship to other institutions in society'.[9] Thus it is maintained that violence against women is not only socially approved, but mandated or embedded in legal, medical, occupational and educational institutions. Accordingly, 'the marriage license is a hitting license',[10] whereby '... men who assault their wives are actually living up to cultural prescriptions that are cherished in Western society'.[11] The 'increasing number of women and children seeking shelter in refuges from male domestic violence lends support to the radical feminist perspective of the nuclear family as the source of oppression for women rather than the ideal unit of social organisation'.[12] Apparently '[a]busive relationships, are ... only the most extreme manifestation of the problems of inequality within the family'[13] which start with the housework, advance through unequal pay, and end in murder. There are complaints that the dangers of the family based on marriage are not sufficiently appreciated, nor is its abolition advanced enough for safety's sake.[14] Therefore, with less marriage and more informal unions, there should be less wife-beating and child abuse.[15]

However, 'within the field of violence against women a simplistic feminist analysis has meant a failure to address certain issues'.[16] There is neglect of violence within lesbian relationships (due to their idealisation), even though lesbian batterers 'display a terrifying ingenuity in their selection of abusive tactics, frequently tailoring the abuse to the specific vulnerabilities of their partners'.[17] There is neglect of women's violence towards men and boys. In addition, there is the refusal to acknowledge that marriage may be more protective than abusive.

Throughout the English-speaking world, single women are more at risk of violence than 'partnered' women, and women in casual or informal relationships are more at risk than married women. In the Western Australian Child Health Survey,[18] 1.8 per cent of principal caregivers in couple families mentioned violence in the home, but 8.2 per cent of lone parents. The level of parent/youth conflict doubled for lone parents, and quadrupled for child abuse; doubled for alcohol abuse and tripled for drug abuse. US cohabitees experience more disagreement than their married counterparts and they also report more fights or violence.[19] The US crime victimisation rate for two decades up to 1992 showed how violent crime affecting females aged 12 or older was 43 per 1,000 females for unmarried women, 45 for divorced and separated women and 11 for married women.[20] Only 29 per cent of the violent crime towards women committed by intimates involved a current spouse, while 42 per cent involved boyfriends or 'partners' and another 12 per cent an ex-spouse.[21] Marital status as a predictor of abuse was ahead of race, age, education or housing conditions in data examined by an agency of the US Department of Health and Human Services. Unmarried women were three to four times more likely to be physically abused by their boyfriends while pregnant than married women by their husbands.[22] Confirming its earlier findings, the US National Family Violence Resurvey showed that almost 35 out of every 100 cohabiting couples experienced a physical assault during the previous year, compared with 15 per 100 married couples and 20 per 100 dating couples. Cohabiting couples had the highest rates for violence towards women, towards men and involving both partners. For 18 out of every 100 cohabiting couples, both were violent, double the rate for dating and married couples. For minor violence committed by both partners, cohabiting couples had roughly double the rate of other groups, and six times the rate for severe violence. Even after controlling for education and occupation, the marital status difference in assault rates remained, for male and female violence and for minor and severe violence. A similar picture is presented by US men charged with domestic violence. The most frequently cited relationship was cohabitation (48 per cent), the second was divorce or separation (27 per cent). Few violent men were married.[23]

Across the Atlantic, the British Crime Survey of England and Wales for 1997[24] shows that while the average chance of experiencing violence in the year was 4.7 per cent, young men aged 16 to 24 were most at risk, at 20.9 per cent, followed by lone parents, at 11.9 per cent. The proportion of adults who were victims of violence in their living arrangements came to 2.7 per cent of the married, compared with 6.4 per cent of cohabitees and 11.9 per cent of lone parents. The 'high overall risk of violence among lone parents' is 'solely because they are far more likely to be victims of domestic violence ...', when over half of assaults were 'in-house', and another third involved acquaintances. Moreover, 42 per cent of these single-parent households reported being victimised more than once in a year, which is higher than rates for low income, social renters, private renters, or people living in areas of high physical disorder (33.5 per cent). It bears out figures for the London study of maternal depression,[25] where solo mothers experienced more than three times more domestic violence than married mothers (45 per cent *vs* 13 per cent).

Unfortunately, New Zealand data, like that from the Women's Safety Survey 1996, does not distinguish violence in cohabiting and married 'partnerships'.[26] Family violence is given a crucial role in the 'perpetuation of the cycles of crime and violence' and adverse ' behavioural, developmental and social effects on children'[27] in a Strategy Paper on Crime Prevention, and there is mention that 'a considerable amount of research has been accumulated on the circumstances in which it takes place ...', but there is silence on its relationship to family structure.[28] However, the Hamilton Abuse Intervention Pilot Project (HAIPP) recorded the relationship between victim and assailant in cases where the child(ren) of either had been present during an assault. Only in 27 per cent of cases were they married, and in a further four per cent of cases, previously married, compared with 36 per cent in current 'partnerships' and 13 per cent in previous 'partnerships.'[29] Moreover in the case of protection and non-molestation orders under the Domestic Violence Act 1992, only 35 per cent of the 96 per cent of the orders granted against men have involved husbands, compared with 50 per cent relating to *de facto* partners. Even given that the *de facto* partner figure includes men in same-sex or other 'close relationships', and even allowing for hypothetical differences in action women may take against cohabitees, but not husbands, the ratio between the two is considerable in relation to their proportion in the population.[30] The high prevalence of domestic violence in 'recent' rather than current partnerships in New Zealand may underscore the results of a small-scale UK study of cohabitation breakdown.[31] While the women spoke of violence as a major reason for giving up on the relationship (as did recently part-nered women in the New Zealand Women's Safety Survey 1996) the men identified criminal behaviour, taking or dealing in illegal drugs and drinking problems.[32]

If young women, those lower down the socio-economic scale, and beneficiaries (like low-income solo mothers) are far more likely to report abuse, so are Maori women,[33] with the same ethnic difference present for severity of abuse.[34] Moreover, the reported incidence of abuse of Maori and other Polynesian children is far higher than that of Euro-pean children.[35] At least 30 per cent of care and protection notifications relate to Maori children and young persons,[36] who are only 12 per cent of those under 16 years of age. Referrals for elder abuse studied between 1996 and 1999 also show how Maori made up a significantly high proportion.[37]

A parallel might be drawn for the US. While it is arguable, in the face of ambiguous results, whether child abuse is higher among American blacks than among whites, the rates of black spousal violence are higher than for other ethnic minorities and whites (twice as high in the first instance, and four times in the second).[38] Race differences could be due to income and employment status, as well as differences in cultural expectations and values surrounding violence, although there are no simple reasons why domestic violence is common among some peoples, and not others. Rates are found to be five times higher among US families below the poverty level than among families in higher income brackets, with severe violence against spouses twice as likely from unemployed men as from those working full-time.[39] (In the Hamilton study, fewer than half the assailants were in employment.) However, as black American men are still more likely to hit women and engage in severe violence against them, so they are more approving of hitting women.[40]

Domestic violence is prevalent in the South Pacific. In some cultures, as in Papua New Guinea, it is assumed that all men beat their wives.[41] Violent homes tend to make violent adults, and these help to create a society in which people use violence as a means of problem-solving, expression and gratification. Societies in which warfare, feuding and conflict have been prevalent also tend to have high levels of domestic violence—in contrast to those where conciliation and self-control are valued. Traditionally, violent confrontations were common in Maori society.[42]

People violent in one context are likely to be violent in another. Men engaged in domestic violence are significantly more likely to be violent toward non-family members and significantly more likely to have arrest records for criminal offences generally. With continuity between childhood aggression and adult violence, the best early predictors of later spouse assault in the study of criminal careers are having a convicted parent, unpopularity, daring, separation from a parent and low intelligence.[43] Indeed, US work illustrates how men in families in which children and women are assaulted are five times more likely to have also assaulted and injured someone outside the family, and to have an arrest rate 3.6 times higher than their less violent counter-parts.[44] In the Hamilton Abuse Intervention Project,[45] where Maori were about five times more likely to be involved in domestic violence as assailants and three to four times more likely as victims compared with their proportion in the locality, over half the assailants (53 per cent) had a criminal record for a violent offence.

Cohabitation and Domestic Violence

However, family structure varies by ethnicity, as well as being related to domestic violence. Since 'investigations [have] revealed that ... physical assaults may be more common and more severe among cohabiting couples [and given] ... that cohabitation as an alternative living arrangement has steadily increased since 1970, more individuals may be at risk not only of minor violence, but severe violence'.[46] Couples with multiple cohabitational experience seem to be particularly prone to

report violence.[47] Cohabitees tend to be younger, less likely to have ties
to groups and organisations, less bound to their relationships, more
likely to be depressed and to have alcohol problems.[48] They may guard
against participating in organisations as much as being tied to
partners, since these involve being subject to others' expectations and
possible restrictions, which are threatening to the freedoms they enjoy.
In Australia, Sarantakos found that not only were there more cases of
violence, and protracted violence, among cohabiting couples and those
with pre-marital cohabital experience (compared with married couples
without cohabital experience), but more tolerated and justified violence:
'cohabitees, especially women, seem to tolerate in their partner types
of behaviour which marriers consider unacceptable. Drugs, drinking,
social deviance and sexual freedom are often accepted more in a
cohabitation environment than in a marriage ...'[49] Significantly, the
most common cited trigger for violence mentioned (by a third of women)
in the Women's Safety Survey 1996[50] was their 'partner's drinking'.
Vindicating the image of the 'drunken bum' as the prototypical 'wife
beater', a combination of low occupational status, drinking and
approval of hitting women is associated with a very high likelihood of
abuse (or a rate 7.8 times greater than rates for white collar men who
drink little and do not approve of hitting women). Heavy drinking, like
dominating women and physical force, may be a means of asserting
power and control in a relationship, or demonstrating masculinity. The
indictment of male alcohol consumption as a prime cause of cruelty
towards women and children has long historical antecedents. Modernisation is associated with rising alcohol consumption—a leading reason
given for the increase in domestic violence throughout the Pacific.[51]
Unfortunately: 'cohabiting relationships are associated with lifestyles
that include problem drinking and ... a commitment to conventionality
is made only after marriage. Likewise, the role of spouses in exerting
social control over behaviour arises only after marriage, not during
cohabitation'. Even after controlling for prior levels of problems and
unconventionality, as well as many other factors, cohabitation is
strongly associated with alcohol abuse.[52]

Cohabitees are more apt to report that ending their relationship
would have more positive and fewer negative consequences than do
those who marry directly or cohabit and then marry.[53] The married
have greater material, social and psychological investment in the
relationship, and more to lose.

There may be more conflict and violence in cohabitations because
some cohabit rather than marry to keep their independence, only to find
that there are frequent arguments over rights, duties, and obligations.
Fathers may insist that they behave like single men without responsibilities, while women speak of fathers as refusing to take their

responsibilities seriously and settling down.[54] Since, across societies, marriage is the 'single most reliable, and relied upon prescription for socialising males', and bringing order and meaning to men's lives, the breeding grounds for male violence 'are casual sex, family fragmentation, and non-marital child-bearing, as marriage is deinstitutionalised'.[55]

There is a relationship between network embeddedness (years in the neighbourhood, organisational membership, number of adults in the home, the number of relatives living near, and so forth) and family violence. In New Zealand, the contrast is made with traditional Polynesian settings, where there is mutual surveillance and checks on behaviour.[56] But kin and friends may put fewer constraints on how cohabitees act. Instead of encouraging them to fulfil certain expectations, they leave them freer to lead their own lives.[57] They may also distance themselves from relationships which cannot be placed in the network of kin ties. Such reactions are consistent with the cohabiting lifestyle, which implies that the individuals somehow set or make up their own standards, rather than being guided by the rules of society. The description of 'multi-problem' families in the Strategy Paper on Crime Prevention might as well be one of cohabitation, where 'families tend to be isolated from society. They have problems parenting ... alcohol abuse is common, as is domestic violence.'[58] If networks are more operative for some groups compared with others in providing support and controls,[59] these are going to suffer all the more from the casualisation and fragmentation of relationships. Moreover, the connection between violence and *anomie* may be strengthened where cultural norms are tolerant or permissive of violence and people consider this an appropriate response to stress, anger, grievance or frustration.

Rising rates of *de facto* pairings may be one reason why 'it seems that little headway is being made in achieving the goal of stopping family violence; on the contrary, it appears to be reaching epidemic proportions'.[60] No-fault divorce and no fault 'equal shares' asset division made the marriage contract unenforceable and 'illusory'. This would predict fewer marriages, fewer children in marriage and more opportunistic behaviour in marriage, not least in the form of spousal abuse. Figures from the US suggest that the abolition of fault led to a significant increase in domestic violence.[61] With easy access to divorce without accountability for conduct, perpetrators are less constrained. The continued dissolution of marriage, in law as in reality, then encourages more uncommitted unions.

The same trends affect the control of domestic violence as much as its perpetuation. Since calling the police and arrest 'remain rare strategies of last resort', it is easy to believe that this is 'part of the reason why wife-beating persists ... Until the probability of arrest increases, assailants will continue to receive a *de facto* message that they can assault their wives with impunity.'[62] While 'arrest works best' policies arise out of frustration and demands to 'do something',[63] they also draw upon an experiment in 1980-83 in Minneapolis, the first controlled, randomised test for the use of arrest for any offence. This found that arrest and a night in jail for suspects cut in half the risk of repeat violence against the same victim over a six-month period, compared with other responses.[64] On the strength of these results, police were allowed to make warrantless arrests in misdemeanour domestic violence cases.[65] Replications of the experiment elsewhere found that 'arrest backfired' or increased violence.[66] Arrests had the greatest criminogenic effect among suspects who were both unemployed and unmarried—a consistent finding, which has not been contradicted to date. Among ever-married suspects (including those separated or divorced), full arrest reduced the annual frequency or prevalence of repeat violence, but then only 30 per cent of cases in Milwaukee, for example, involved couples who had ever been married. Among the unmarried, arrest increased repeat violence.

A woman with a marriage licence may have a firm basis for seeking the arrest of an abusive spouse. A woman without one may find arrest causing more violence against her or other women, or at very least not deterring the suspect's future violence. Moreover, unlike formal marriage, the length of cohabitation has no effect on the efficacy of arrest. Thus, the price of a '... modest deterrent effect for the "staked" is a certain and substantial violence-escalating effect for the "stakeless": the unemployed, unmarried, high-school dropouts and black suspects, with each characteristic taken separately'. The pioneering mandatory arrest *and prosecution* policy in Duluth, Minnesota was accompanied by comprehensive court-ordered counselling,[67] which provided the model for the Hamilton violence intervention programme. One five-year follow-up of batterers going through the programme shows that 40 per cent are suspects in a repeat domestic violence incident, either with the same or a new victim—comparable to the recidivism rates in the arrest-only experiments.

Marriage is Good for Women

Despite the strident claims made for the benefits of family decline and fragmentation, there are no recorded advantages. It has, for example, become part of feminist folklore that marriage makes women sick as much as servile and that exposure to the traditional family structure and its 'stereotypical roles' may be personally harmful. 'The high prevalence of psychological stress in women, as demonstrated in many epidemiological studies, ... [is] evidence for women's unhappiness in a sexist society. Mental health statistics ... form part of a standard catalogue of the wrongs of women.' Women's lowered health status is categorically attributed to being out of the workforce caring for children 'and anybody else who seems to need it'. With no doubt, the villain is: 'firstly, the patriarchal nuclear family'.[68]

We would expect legislation to reduce gender discrimination, more working mothers, and rising lone parenthood to have enhanced the well-being of women. The consistent, striking trend across all developed countries in the last few decades is that death rates for all age groups of unmarried (that is single, divorced and widowed) men are approximately double those of married men. However, for unmarried women, death rates are also approximately 50 per cent greater than for the married. Unmarried people in their 20s to 40s experience the highest mortality risks; sometimes ten times higher than those for married people of the same age.[69] Married people not only live longer, and get sick less; but if they get sick, they get better more quickly.

Evidence worldwide suggests that single women and solo mothers have more morbidity—physical and mental. Of all social variables relating to psychiatric disorders in the population, none is more crucial or persistent than marital status, where people living with a spouse are always under-represented in psychopathology.[70] The position of the sexes is reversed in the National Survey of Psychiatric Morbidity, conducted in the UK in 1995, for cohabiting women anyway, who have a much worse neurotic profile than cohabiting men, as well as single or married women (who do best). Women may be unhappy about sexual relationships that lack permanence, where they may have to face the consequences of pregnancy with a man who has made no commitment.[71] In turn, lone parents in the Western Australian Child Health Survey[72] had more than double the mental health problems of parents in couple families. Consistent with findings from previous national surveys, a US study involving 6,573 respondents from the National Survey of Families and Households, with controls for variables like the number of children, income, education etc.,[73] found that married people reported greater happiness and less depression than cohabitees, who reported greater well-being than those who lived without another adult. Those with no divorce reported less depression and greater happiness than those with a history of any divorce, and those with one divorce reported less depression than those with two or more divorces, although women report more depression than men anyway. This all needs to be related to the way that, in the last couple of decades, both sexes in New Zealand have shown increasing rates of psychiatric admission, particularly for drug and alcohol dependence. The increase is greater for women.[74]

This poorer mental health of solo mothers, where acknowledged, is likely to be put at the door of poverty or money problems. A detailed study of the relationship between marital status, poverty and depression among London inner-city single and married (or cohabiting) mothers, over a two-year period, suggests otherwise. While it was weighted in favour of lone parents, their risk of depression was double that of women in couples (16.0 per 100 women years versus 7.9).[75] For mothers as a whole, the risk of depression was almost double among those living in 'moderate' or 'marked' financial hardship. This seems to be almost entirely accounted for by couple-women because, just for the lone mothers, the risk was higher among those not in financial hardship.

Falling marriage and rising divorce rates have made women neither happier nor healthier. Data from America and Britain from the early 1970s to the late 1990s shows that, if anything, the well-being of women has fallen.[76] In turn, investigations show, if anything, that women report greater happiness and life satisfaction than men, particularly when they are married.[77] However, fewer people married may be a major reason why reported happiness in the US has generally declined over time, and satisfaction has been flat in Britain.[78] The greatest depressant of happiness is being separated, closely followed by being widowed. A person whose parents are divorced (by the time the respondent is 16) has a lower level of well-being in adulthood. Women living *de facto* are happier than those who are single, but markedly less than those who are legally married. The amount of happiness bought by extra income is not very big, although it accounts for upward movement over time. To 'compensate' for a major life event such as being separated or widowed, it would be necessary to provide someone with approximately US $100,000 per annum. (To compensate men for unemployment would take US $30,000.)

Suicide and Family Disruption

Suicide has occupied a similar position in the hierarchy of problems for men as domestic violence has for women. New Zealand has a high male suicide rate, which rose from 12.5 per 100,000 for the male population in 1974 to 23.6 by 1993-98 (see Figure 9:1, p. 166). Female suicide rates are also high compared with other countries, but relatively more stable over time, and falling in proportion to male suicides, from a rate of two male for every female to four to one.[79] Male youth (15-24) suicide deaths have also increased disproportionately compared with increases in other age groups, nearly doubling from the mid-1980s.[80] Suicides comprised nearly 40 per cent of male youth injury deaths and over a quarter of female youth injury deaths, where one in 20 incidents of deliberate self-harm result in death for women, but one in four for men. By 1996, the age group 15-24 accounted for 26.6 per cent of suicide deaths and only 15.6 per cent of the New Zealand population.[81] The highest suicide mortality was for males aged 20-24 at 49.7 deaths per 100,000 (for females it was 12.4), while for males aged 15 to 19 it was 29.2 per 100,000 (while for females it was 16.2).[82] The overall Maori youth suicide rate was 59.6 per 100,000, compared with 35 for non-Maori young males.[83] Deaths by suicide and self-inflicted injury per 100,000 males aged 15-24 are higher than Finland (33.0), Latvia (35.0), and Slovenia (37.0), being overtaken only by the Russian Federation (41.7) and Lithuania (44.9).[84]

The risk factors behind serious suicide attempts by youngsters are reminiscent of those for young recidivists, and relate to the extent of an individual's exposure to adverse childhood experiences, limited life opportunities, the extent of psychiatric morbidity, depression, substance abuse and antisocial disorders.[85] Completed suicide in adolescents is the termination of long-term difficulties and dysfunction. Unemployment is not associated with risk when poor educational qualifications, low income, and residential change are taken into account.

The suicide rates of both adults and children are highly correlated with divorce rates. Worldwide, the divorced have a three- to four-fold higher risk of suicide compared with the married. The never-married rates are almost three times the rate of the married.[86] This relationship holds even for the advanced Scandinavian welfare states, indicating that public services may be able to make little impression on the rise in suicides if family structure becomes increasingly unstable at the same time.[87] Marriage has a particularly dramatic effect on the suicide rates for men, where the differential in mortality rates by marital status is huge.[88] Similarly, there is a strong relationship between the suicides of young men and the out-of-wedlock birth rate and the number of persons living alone.[89] Marriage and parenting, with the relationships, responsibilities and obligations these entail, afford a social regulation and social integration that is less available to people living in more isolated conditions.[90] UK figures suggest that over two-thirds of the increase in suicide rates for young men since 1982 can be related to the smaller proportions who are married.[91] Both the rising adolescent and young-adult US suicide trends in the post-war period are related to family trends, such as the annual rate of children involved in divorce and the percentage of female-headed families.[92] There are no direct unemployment effects. The large size of post-war cohorts affects their income levels through labour market competition. This, in turn, affects family indices such as marriage rates, divorce and lone parenting which, in turn, affect mortality.

Figure 9:1
Male suicides per 100,000 male population, selected countries, 1993-98

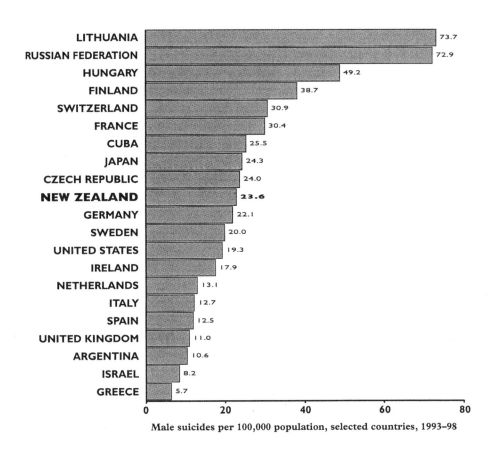

Male suicides per 100,000 population, selected countries, 1993–98

Source: United Nations Development Programme, *Human Development Report 2000*, pp. 251-52.

Exploration of the high suicide risk of the unmarried has suggested that isolation and alcohol abuse are much involved, with increased alcoholism itself related to social isolation.[93] As it is, figures from the US suggest that adults who are separated and divorced are four-and-a-half times more likely, and the never-married twice as likely, to become alcohol dependent than comparable married persons.[94]

10

There Goes the Neighbourhood

Summary: The cohesiveness of local communities declines when marital and family disruption dilute social bonds and reduce the linkages in the network of social control. Marriage gets men off the street and out of the pubs. Single men are troublesome, and difficult for the community to control. Without marriage, society is deprived of the most successful corrective institution ever devised, as so many investigations of criminal recidivism will testify. When men abandon responsibility for their children, many are effectively abdicating from any responsibility in the community. Instead of neighbourhood standards being enforced by fathers, low marriage rates mean a decline of the responsible male and an increasing likelihood that men are going to be net contributors to the community's problems. People do not learn and uphold social rules from outside social relations and responsibilities, but by being in the midst of these and maintaining them because they are their own.

The weakening of informal 'social controls and social bonds lie at the heart of any explanation of crime at the individual level and of crime trends at the aggregate level'. Their decline must explain 'why crime, most of it committed by young people, has increased so much in most developed countries in the postwar period'.[1] With changes in family structure go declines in the cohesiveness of local communities, as marital and family disruption dilute social bonds and reduce the linkages in the network of social control. This control is dependent upon more than the individual child's family. Areas of high family disintegration are places of turbulence affecting all children in the area. Youths may be more likely to know people in trouble with the law and welfare mothers than they are to know professionals, or people demonstrating how success follows from work. The number of unattached people in the community is predictive of crime levels, and US studies show how the percentages of sole-parent households are significantly associated with rates of burglary and violent crime in urban centres.[2] Population density, mobility and the number of adolescents matter as well. What, by itself, does *not* seem to matter is the number of low-income families in a neighbourhood.[3] US liberals like William Julius Wilson[4] have

167

drawn attention to the relations between family fragmentation and crime, violence and civil disorder, and their implications for policing and penal policy, centring on the axiom that, if men fail to marry, they do not settle down. As such, unemployment and poverty are associated with high levels of criminality and violence when mediated by family disruption. For the US, the association between homicide and unemployment is negligible: divorce is the most powerful predictor of homicide rates.[5] In turn, a city's divorce rate is a better predictor of the robbery rate than measures of arrest and sentencing, and regardless of economic and racial composition.[6]

If the neighbours of sole parents are more likely to be victimised than the neighbours of two-parent households, then, in turn, sole-parent households are more likely to be targets for crime.[7] It became clear in the Western Australian Child Health Survey[8] that not only was there more intra-family violence and conflict in sole-parent homes, and more drug and alcohol abuse, but a third of lone parents reported being a victim of theft, assault, malicious damage or some other crime in the last three years, compared with 20 per cent of couples. Only two per cent of caregivers in original families had been arrested or charged with an offence other than a minor traffic violation, compared with ten per cent of lone parents and nine per cent in step-families. While young American black men with sole parents are twice as likely to engage in criminal activities compared with those raised by two parents, growing up in a neighbourhood with high rates of family fragmentation triples the possibility.[9]

Where Crime Becomes 'Normal'

A most intriguing aspect of crime is its astoundingly high variance across time and space.[10] Neighbourhoods put youths into close proximity to others, whose behaviour will influence them directly. The delinquency of temporary law breakers is dominated by group solidarity more than individual motivation to offend.[11] Peer contacts operate to recruit young criminals and create information flows about criminal techniques and the returns to crime. Peer groups help create high crime levels by stigmatising law-abiding behaviour.[12] Crime, like unwed births, is initially stigmatising, but as the number of criminals rises, the average criminal becomes a 'normal' member of society.[13] Weak social bonds lead to criminality, which creates environments that cause a further weakening of social bonds.[14] A study of criminal behaviour in the US across cities and precincts in New York found that crimes committed by younger criminals involve more social interactions, and less individual design. These higher levels of social interaction (for serious, as well as petty crimes and auto theft), rose with the percentage of female-headed households, suggesting that they relied 'on family instability, not unemployment or schooling or low arrest rates'. If 'the average social interactions among criminals are higher when there are not intact family units', so the 'presence of strong families interferes with the transmission of criminal choices across individuals'.[15] General youth neighbourhood surveillance, intervention in disturbances and control of peer group activities—that often become the overture for more serious crime and gang delinquency—is easier for two-parent families.

Juvenile peer groups are criminogenic in urban societies and their malign effect is accentuated by family disintegration. They militate against the lengthy educational process needed to function and succeed in a complex society. It has been pointed out that Polynesian child-rearing can push independence as a cultural value earlier and earlier. Independence is both a training practice and a Polynesian child-training goal, now almost as lionised by white liberals as the Maori matrifocal extended family. But to lighten their own responsibilities, parents may force autonomy on children to a degree that leaves their dependency needs unmet. Moreover, acting independently may lead children into conflict with neighbours, the school, and the law, and girls into pregnancy. 'Children may be abused for the very acceptance of the independence that their parents seem to have forced upon them. Motorcycle gangs, school drop-outs who seem to form groups that sometimes resemble truancy clubs, runaways from home who squat in deserted houses, monocultural playground gangs often forming a hostile presence within the school environment—all these are negative exemplification of the peer socialisation phenomenon.' It is not just Eurocentric bias which dictates that learning must 'take place at home or at school, ... [so that] when it occurs elsewhere, as in gangs or through the media, it is suspect'. Success anywhere means moving away from peer socialisation, not reinforcing it. It is misplaced to sentimentalise and idealise peer-centred child-rearing, and blame urban 'European social structure and lifestyle' for being 'poorly adapted to accommodate the degree of independence which Polynesians customarily grant to their children'.[16]

Not only delinquency, but also other social problems, like truancy and teenage pregnancy, are clearly contagious and spread through the peer influence to which the children of sole parents are very susceptible.[17] Neighbourhood effects operating through peer influences are important for social and economic outcomes, even when all the youths are living in high-poverty neighbourhoods.[18] Moreover, individuals are also more likely to have a particular behaviour when the proportion of the local population engaging in this reaches a certain threshold or critical mass. This is not just a case of adult role models and sources of social control (or their absence) or the part played (or not) by institutions such as schools, businesses, political organisations, social service agencies, and the police in the community. As neighbourhood quality decreases, 'epidemic' interactions generate a whole much greater than the sum of their parts.[19] There are precipitous increases in social problems at approximately the same point in the distribution.[20] Moreover, one problem has implications for others, so that local violence, for example, reduces educational attainment.[21] In one US investigation, an eight percentage points increase in the proportion of female-headed families in an area decreased educational attainment by about one-fourth of a year, and a ten percentage points increase in welfare receipt reduced schooling by about half-a-year.[22]

In this way, the loss of traditional patterns of work, family and neighbourhood fuels the breakdown of social infrastructure. Educational performance falls and crime rises, while truancy, disorder and youth disaffection undermine efforts to improve schools and communities.

Marriage Gets Men off the Streets

While the effect of family disruption on crime is strongest for juveniles, family fragmentation is related to adult criminality as well, indicative as it is of much instability, disorientation and conflict in relationships. The impact of sole parenthood on the absent men is of immense and fundamental significance for public order as well as economic productivity. The family-man role provides men with incentives for orderly and patient participation in the community just as it is a source of discipline for children. When men abandon responsibility for their children 'many are effectively abdicating from any responsibility in the community. A man who does not recognise claims of dependents on him loses those external demands on himself which could raise him above his own immediate or short-term desires'.[23] Instead of neighbourhood standards being enforced by fathers, low marriage rates mean a decline of the responsible male and an increasing likelihood that men are going to be net contributors to the community's problems. American single men are almost six times as likely to be imprisoned as married men, and the multiple for the divorced is almost as large.[24] They also have a four- to five-fold greater likelihood of being victims of crime. Compared with marriage, work itself probably provides a comparable focus for social integration for only a minority of men. Marriage gets men off the street and out of the pubs:

> Single men are troublesome, and difficult for the community to control. Marriage is an extremely valuable instrument for tying them down and channelling their energies into socially useful ends ... to achieve this end, conventions about

husbanding and fathering typically exaggerate the real importance of the contributions which men make to family life, so that men are flattered into feeling that they are really needed.[25]

Without marriage, society is deprived of the most successful corrective institution ever devised, as so many investigations of criminal recidivism will testify. This traditionally provided much of the explanation of why so many delinquents, even in the roughest areas, 'grew out' of misbehaving or 'drifted out of delinquency'. Boys were 'less driven to prove manhood unconventionally through ... misdeeds when, with the passing of time, they may effortlessly exhibit the conventional signposts of manhood—physical appearance, the completion of school, job, marriage, and perhaps even children'.[26]

Most delinquent groups are unstable, and an important reason for membership turnover has been the shift to more conventional career affiliations that provide the potential for social control.[27] Typically, around a half of a criminal sample dropped out of the criminogenic group in one investigation because they married, went into the services, joined a job-training programme, or worked regularly.[28] Comparing 'retired' criminals with those who were still 'active', a prominent UK study found that 86 per cent of the reformed criminals, compared with only 11 per cent of those still active, had formed conventional bonds with a woman, a job or education. As males aged, the 'two factors of settling down with [unconvicted] female partners and in stable jobs seemed most plausible in explaining the decrease in offending'.[29] When 'males in their twenties [were asked] why they had stopped offending, they often mentioned marriage and the influence of women as well as the fact that they did not hang around so much with delinquent friends'.[30] The influence on offending of a strong marital bond is large and the preventative effect increases over time—as illustrated by an analysis of the criminal histories of 500 US delinquent boys who were followed to age 32.[31] In the first period after marriage, persons who entered into a good marriage had an offending rate 19 per cent less than a person who was one period into a 'not-so-good' marriage. By the second period after marriage, the difference grew to 58 per cent, and by the third period, the difference was 68 per cent.

The disappearance of the custom of early, more or less obligatory, and frequently shotgun, marriage, has changed the life-course of young men. Not long ago, perhaps 'unwillingly and also perhaps unhappily, the young man would ... take on his new responsibilities of fatherhood and marriage ... his friends would be doing the same'.[32] The 'peer groups to which he belonged would break up, as marriage is complementary with time spent in the home and a substitute for time oriented outside the home. Insofar as they continued to meet, it would be in part to reminisce about their lives of a very different past'. A man may now cohabit, but assumes less of the responsibility of fatherhood and marriage 'as indicated especially by the increases in the fraction of men who either have not had children and therefore incurred no responsibility or who have abandoned the children they have fathered ...' The absence of family responsibilities may translate into longer and more intensive education. For others it means a lengthier evolution of peer group activities, where: 'the indiscretions, and worse, of the past will become the forerunners of greater misdeeds in their twenties. With delays in marriage this evolution has a lower hazard of interruption. The peer groups that used to be transformed into groups of old friends meeting but not hanging out together, now linger on ...'[33] Aiming to provide an estimate of the extent, frequency and nature of self-reported offending among young people in England and Wales, the Home Office also attempted to establish not only why some start to offend, but what influences those who stop and sustain a non-criminal lifestyle. It reaffirmed that the variable most likely to have an effect was marriage, which increased the odds of desisting three-fold. However, few males were now married by 25. Young males were decreasingly likely to acquire the means for making a successful transition to adulthood: to 'form new families and eventually become economically independent, socially responsible and self-reliant individuals'. Instead, young men '[a]re at risk of drifting into a kind of perpetual adolescence'.[34] Unfortunately, behaviour due to changes in the marriage age and marriage rate has a multiplier effect, as the behaviour of young men in their twenties influences boys in their teens, providing them with role models that are engaged in escalating violence.[35]

The effects of criminal sanctions depend upon the suspects' 'stake in conformity', or how much they have to lose from the social consequences of arrest, conviction and sentence. Marriage is one such stake, where those who are married are not only less likely to offend, but the ones most deterred by arrest, in part because they have invested more in a relationship they do not want to lose. As we saw with domestic violence, so with all criminal behaviour:

> ... the effectiveness of the criminal sanction may depend upon the strength of the social fabric in which it is used. The weaker that fabric becomes, the stronger the argument to use criminal sanctions in its place: if the family cannot control the problem, let police and prisons do it. But the weaker the social fabric becomes ..., the more danger there may be that criminal sanctions will fail or backfire by provoking anger rather than reintegration.[36]

People often behave differently when they know that their actions will affect the standing in the community of those to whom they are formally connected: 'they have a "project" and are surrounded by palpable reminders of their immediate personal importance and social responsibility ...' Otherwise:

> Men not involved in shielding and supporting find other ways to prove their existence: 'I hurt, therefore I am', is one twisted alternative. The graffiti boy's

proof is, 'I deface therefore I am'. The gangbanger reasons, 'I kill, therefore I am'. The street libertine says, 'I impregnate, therefore I am'. At the other end of the economic spectrum ... are the rows of rich hedonists who can only babble, 'I feel pleasure, therefore I am'. And contrary to feminist claims, these are all expressions of a *stunted*—not an exaggerated—masculinity.[37]

A New Warrior Class?

In communities where sole parenthood starts to become a norm, the state supports the mother/child unit, and a significant group of less skilled prime-age men are isolated from both work and family life as a source of social loyalties and integration. Thus, some people have argued, we have reproduced the historic conditions for a warrior class. There is separation of economic activity from family maintenance; children reared apart from fathers; wealth subject to predation; and male status determined by combat and sexual conquest.[38] Without family bonds, there is no motive for the regulation and control of aggression and self-seeking. The less men are involved with nurturing the next generation, the more violent a culture tends to be.

Feminists are apt to insist that men should not need families or employment prospects to behave themselves. Anyway, why should a woman want anything to do with men as destructive and futureless as so many are? But, if this strategy deprives the child of close contact with half the human race, it also excludes a half of the human race from the means to transcend immediate self-interest. People do not learn and uphold social rules from outside social relations and responsibilities, but by being in the midst of these and maintaining them because they are their own. People have to live and teach the lesson, if they are to know and abide by it. However, the neo-Marxist feminism so prevalent in New Zealand endorses the nihilistic prospect of a society (*sic*) without rules or norms or values or institutions. In this perspective, all constraints, conventions, sanctions, obligations and expectations are perceived as abusive and the manifestations of alien malevolent powers. This includes people's care for each other and their children. To 'critique' something is to explain it in terms of the imposition and machinations of evil and controlling forces, like capitalism or patriarchy. Thus, families are: 'the instruments through which the state could impose domestic order on men and women and, at the same time, relieve itself of the fiscal burden' of 'welfare and social reproduction'.[39]

Since the family role provides men with incentives for orderly and patient participation in the community, the impact of its absence is of large and fundamental significance for positive contributions, as much as public order, economic productivity, and male welfare itself. This may weaken general processes of care and education in society, where one generation exerts itself on behalf of another. When men abandon responsibility for their children, 'many are effectively abdicating from any responsibility in the community', formal or informal, that involves the guidance and welfare of younger people.[40] Communities with pronounced family disruption may experience a weakening of formal and voluntary organisations, many of which play crucial roles in fostering desired principles and values,[41] as well as the dissolution of the affiliative and integrative patterns created by marriage and kinship networks.[42]

The Spread of Concentrated Poverty

The growth and nature of modern disadvantage demonstrates how the 'chief problem for today's seriously poor is no longer social injustice but the disorders of private life'.[43] The population in US metropolitan neighbourhoods, with at least 40 per cent of the residents in poverty, grew by 92 per cent (mainly in central cities and inner-ring suburbs) between 1970 and 1990. The increase was strongly related to the geographical spread of high-poverty neighbourhoods.[44] In the UK, poorer neighbourhoods have also tended to become more run down, more prone to crime and cut off from the labour market.[45] It is estimated that 40 per cent of crime occurs in just ten per cent of areas.[46]

Such processes have a bearing on an observed trend for poorer people in New Zealand to move to rural areas, with cheaper housing. The prospects for employment and economic advancement are lower and they are 'education poor'. In 1996, 14 per cent of geographic areas had 30 per cent or more of men aged 25-59 not in paid work and, in six per cent of area units, 40 per cent or more not in paid work.[47] Analysis of movement to the Wairarapa region showed a jump in the numbers of people on benefits of nearly 100 per cent for the period 1991/1994 compared with the period 1988-1990, as poorer households made up a greater proportion of the migrant population.[48] This is not accounted for by retirement. Many households which are not beneficiaries in their last urban area become benefit recipients in the rural towns, as all beneficiary categories increase, whether sickness, invalids, unemployment and, especially, DPB. Income transfers feed into a cumulative process of disintegration. A similar phenomenon has been described for Australia.

An accelerating disintegrative process, in which lone parenthood feeds into a host of other social problems, combines with the situation of two-parent families for whom there is little affirmation from the wider world. In one telling account from the UK, one-third of an estate's young people were living in households without both birth-parents, while their parents had virtually all lived with both parents. Despite a high proportion of estate parents having no qualifications when they left school, almost all went into permanent employment or apprenticeships at 16 and could contribute to the household, or, if they left, could afford a bedsitter. Young people now went to a youth training scheme, college, or into a succession of low-paid jobs. In the past, young women left home for marriage and motherhood (most had their first child by 22), or employment with accommodation. Now, in a hostile environment, parents in non-disrupted households were 'struggling to control their older children in the context of a social milieu which was totally transformed from when they were young'.[49] They tended to be supportive and aspiring for their children, but coping against external circumstances which led to a greater likelihood of conflict between young people and their parents over drugs, crime and early sexual relationships, in a social and economic climate 'where early and lifelong marriage is rare'. The 'world had changed around them ... They were parenting more than they had been parented themselves, but felt they were able to do less for their children because their children's chances were less than theirs had been.' Young people were no longer 'introduced to a world of work through a mentoring system of older men', who would, in turn, reinforce the values and norms of parents and a wider community. Women from non-disrupted households 'found that sexual relationships did not result in permanent domestic partnerships, instead, they were more likely to settle down as lone mothers'.[50] This is unlikely to help them, their children, the disassociated men or their communities. Endorsing and furthering these developments does a service to no-one.

11

Feedback Loops and the Spiral of Decline

Summary: Family fragmentation has effects which are transmitted from one generation to the next. The children of divorced parents are less likely to marry and more likely to divorce, less likely to have children, and more likely to have them out of wedlock. Teenage daughters of sole parents are more likely to be sexually active and thus become sole parents themselves. Downward social mobility and life on welfare are more likely for both sexes.

Family behaviour is inter-generational. The children of divorce or single motherhood are proportionally far more likely to repeat cycles of divorce and non-marriage than those born to married couples who stay in intact families—seen even in an early study of divorce-proneness in New Zealand.[1] These effects mean that it is not only the parents' receipt of public assistance which is a significant determining factor for whether the daughters become welfare mothers, but the family structure itself. All in all, non-marital fertility and family disruption mean downward mobility over generations and increasing dependence upon public institutions.[2] Poverty and disruption compound each other, so that while low income in childhood increases the likelihood of low income in adulthood, divorce amplifies this and other problems.[3] Families under financial strain not only have a greater chance of fragmenting, but their children have a greater chance of having unwed births (if a woman), or going to prison (if a man), as well as economic failure[4]—with third generational 'spillover' now being observed.[5] But having a sole mother increases the likelihood of girls becoming welfare-dependent mothers, irrespective of parental income.[6]

Prone to Divorce

The consequences for future family formation are the strongest, most indisputable, and perhaps the most important outcomes when it comes to the effect of family structure on behaviour. As exemplified by the Boston Youth Study, the best predictor of whether a youth produces a child out of wedlock are whether his or her parents were married. Also important was having a teenage mother or being on welfare, and all are strongly related to idleness (not being at work, at school or training). It parallels the way that youths with family members in jail when they were being raised are more than twice as likely (25 to 12 per cent) to admit to being involved in criminal activity: those with family members with drug problems are more likely to use drugs and those with more educated parents get more schooling.[7]

Judith Wallerstein carried out one of the earliest studies of the impact of divorce and has followed her sample for 25 years, finding that adult children of divorced parents were less likely to marry and more likely to divorce.[8] They are less likely to have children and, when they do, to have them out of wedlock. Her study has been criticised for not using a random sample. However, the results have since been repeatedly replicated. In the Christchurch Child Development Study, parents reared in a stable two-parent family to the age of 16 were almost half as likely to separate as those who had experienced parental separation before 16 (12.2 per cent to 20 per cent).[9] Similarly, almost double the number of young men in the British Child Development Study who experienced parental divorce saw their own marriage dissolve by their early 30s, compared with 18 per cent whose parents had stayed together (for women, it was over 50 per cent more likely).[10] Multiple cohabitations were over three times as frequent and children born out of wedlock were twice as likely to have extra-marital births themselves.[11] Background conditions, such as behaviour and ability measured at seven years and financial circumstances at seven and sixteen years, reduced the impact on divorce only by a third for men—from 91 per cent more to 63 per cent more.[12] The earlier National Survey of Health and Development, which addressed the same questions with a cohort born in 1946, also found that only two factors were directly and independently related to the probability of marriage breakdown in adulthood. These were parental divorce during childhood and psychological well-being assessed at age 15—confirmed by the later Economic and Social Research Council's (ESRC) research.[13]

Similar findings are reported from the US longitudinal data of the National Survey of Families and Households, where parental divorce increased the odds of disruption for women within the first five years of marriage by 70 per cent.[14] In the Study of Marital Instability over the Life Course, the percentage of marriages breaking down between 1980 and 1992 was 11 per cent in the first marriage where neither spouse's parents had divorced.[15] When wives had experienced parental divorce, the odds of divorce increased by more than half and, when both spouses had experienced parental divorce, the odds nearly tripled. The transmission of divorce across generations is explained by the earlier age of partnership, the greater extent of premarital cohabitation, socio-economic attainment and pro-divorce attitudes and interpersonal problems (related to anger, jealousy, infidelity, and so forth), which interfere with the maintenance of relationships. Cohabitation is linked to subsequent divorce because this is itself selective of the divorce-prone, or unstable people, and those less committed to marriage and favourable to divorce. It also increases susceptibility to divorce, through its effects on attitudes and values about relationships.[16]

Prone to Become a Teenage Mother

The National Survey of Sexual Attitudes and Lifestyles showed that, in the UK, as everywhere else, young women are more likely to become teenage mothers if they have lived with only one parent as a child.[17] Any experience of family disruption for women is associated with early parenthood.[18] Teenage parenthood is associated with larger than average family size, growing up with one parent, being born out of wedlock and having parents who were separated, divorced or widowed. The largest association is with growing up without parents (e.g in fostering, or children's homes). A half of UK teenage mothers also reported that their own mother had had her first child in her teens and a quarter had a sibling who was a teenage parent.[19] They were also more likely to have experienced childhood poverty, have a mother or father who was uninterested in schooling, have been in contact with the police, and have been aggressive as a child. American evidence shows a doubling or more for the likelihood of unwed and/or teenage births or subsequent divorce for daughters reared with lone parents. Economics played little part in the outcomes.[20]

Everywhere, adolescent daughters of sole parents are more likely to be sexually active.[21] Borne out by English research into the lifestyles, mores and attitudes of 13- to 15-year-old school children, those who were sexually active were twice as likely to live with one parent compared with those from intact families. Those willing to cohabit are four times as likely to be sexually active as those unwilling, and a greater proportion of young people whose parents have divorced would consider cohabiting compared with those from intact families.[22] Not living with both parents when 14 years old was associated with multiple recent partners among single white women in the US.[23] Everywhere, family disruption increases the likelihood that children will enter informal relationships.[24] In Britain, young women whose parents' marriages broke down by the time they were 16 years of age are more likely to cohabit in their teens, as well as almost twice as likely to have a child by age 20, and to give birth whilst single or cohabiting.[25] These findings are similar to those for Australia[26] and are altered little, if at all, by the introduction of background controls for childhood hardship, social class and earlier behaviour. All of this is virtually identical to the findings of the Utrecht Study of Adolescent Development,[27] in which children of divorced or single parents more often gave birth earlier and outside marriage, got married or cohabited earlier, had more conflict with partners, and got divorced more often.

Early sexual activity, early marriage or cohabitation are often a refuge from an unhappy or uncaring home environment.[28] Unhappy young Australian men and women, who did not feel acceptable to parents and felt a high level of tension in the home, were far more likely to leave home early and cohabit than those reporting a happy family upbringing.[29] This may be why girls from step-families are even more likely to drop out of school, to leave home early and become teen parents, than those with sole parents.[30] Cohabitation is companionship, a sex life and independence from parents, without the commitment of marriage which suggests intrusion into personal autonomy. In these and other ways, early sexual activity will also be associated with marital breakdown.[31]

Sole parents have more difficulty supervising and maintaining authority and control over adolescents, which leads to high-risk mate selection as well as early pregnancy.[32] Moreover, divorced and single mothers may have less restrictive attitudes towards sexual behaviour than women in intact marriages and be more permissive concerning their children's conduct. Adolescents in sole-mother households are often more aware of parental sexuality than those in intact two-parent households. Adult courtship may overlap with the initial dating and sexual experimentation of their adolescent children, and at a particularly salient time for shaping behaviour, when youngsters are making decisions about their own values and intimate relationships.[33] When recently divorced mothers are dating it affects both their daughters' attitudes and behaviour, and the sexual behaviour of sons, all in the permissive direction.[34]

Not least, daughters who live with sole parents may be more prone to becoming sole parents themselves simply because familiarity makes this seem viable and acceptable, just as divorced and remarried people are more favourable towards separation and divorce, and single mothers more approving of rearing children without fathers.[35] Since changes in attitude often follow rather than precede changes in behaviour, they may best be treated as dependent variables, rather than explanatory factors.[36] It is normal to expect people to become more positive towards a situation after they have experienced it. Parents who divorce or who never marry may also set an example about the desirability or necessity for marriage, so that it becomes downgraded or marginalised for the children.[37] Daughters of US mothers who would be bothered if they did not marry, and think that married people are happier, cohabit at significantly lower rates than daughters of mothers who would not be bothered if they did not marry, and a lesser effect is also observed for sons of mothers who believe married people are happier.[38] The same pattern is found in Australia.[39]

With a series of feedback loops folding into a spiral of decline, a climate of expectations is created in which family trends appear to develop a momentum of their own. Both divorces and unwed births are self-sustaining because they produce an increasing toleration of divorce and unwed births and so a declining commitment to marriage—and thus more divorce and unwed births. As part of the larger process, cohabitation is an important engine behind the decline in marriage as a lasting union, and the primary institution for child-bearing and parenthood.[40] Rampant divorce seems to emphasise the importance of trial runs for marriage in order to avoid disruption, or of holding out for the ideal match to come along, or of avoiding commitment until one is really sure. Informal relationships are encouraged as people try to avoid the stresses and financial losses divorce portends in terms of assets and, for men, maintenance or child support. But cohabitation, or exposure to cohabiting partners, changes people's attitudes towards marriage and increases acceptance of divorce—and thereby increases the likelihood of divorce should marriage occur.[41] The continuing high divorce rate prompts more frequent and early cohabitation, and thus an even higher rate of relationship turnover.[42]

These unintended consequences of what are often attempts to circumvent the hazards of family breakdown have more to do with the actual decline in marriage than any fanciful ideological rejection on the part of the public at large and the invention of new 'family forms'. The increasing trend towards 'consensual partnering' is sometimes interpreted as evidence of emancipation from oppressive institutions, but it can equally indicate 'declining commitment ... of men and women to each other and to their relationship as an enduring unit, in exchange for more freedom, primarily for men'.[43] This collapse of marriage not only means declining investment in children. Serial partnerships actually tend towards 'more separate lives for men and women', showing up not only in lone parenthood, but also in the rapid growth in the numbers of men living alone.[44]

12

Conclusion

Summary: The family is the necessary engine to stimulate human capital in the next generation. In the absence of any policy to prevent the decline of the family, the only acceptable response has been to treat the symptoms—no matter how ineffective these treatments may prove to be. What is needed is a policy of support for intact families, and recognition of the responsibilities of all parents, not just those who are in difficulties. Public policy should signal that family stability is important for children and for society as a whole. Changes to family law and other public policies are necessary to help strengthen the institution of the family based on marriage.

Family Breakdown is a Public Policy Issue

The accumulating evidence about the costs of family fragmentation suggests that we are not dealing with the emergence of alternative 'family forms', but with breakdown and decline of the institution of the family based on marriage. The evidence suggests that the plight of the family owes much to policy-induced changes in incentives. Facilitating 'joint investments' or reinvigorating marriage stands a better chance of reversing deterioration in child well-being, adult relationships and social cohesion than endorsing transient associations, or trying to enforce parental care in the absence of supporting institutions. Not least, this requires a move away from 'no-fault', non-consensual or unilateral divorce. Reform should put some power back into the hands of a spouse who maintains a marriage, in order to underwrite trust and commitment. In such ways we signal that family stability is important for children and for society as a whole; that both parents matter; and that the way in which they meet the child-rearing tasks and their obligations to each other deserve recognition and respect.

The failure to protect families in the face of economic pressures over the last few decades, and the propensity to accentuate the situation over time by allowing their overall tax burden to increase has contributed to the unprecedented weakening of the family as an institution. The change from family policy to targeted or selective welfare has incentivised casual relationships and sole motherhood. This has coincided with the way in which the law has become virulently hostile

181

towards marriage, even though two people of the opposite sex committed to each other provide the optimal environment for rearing children. It is true anywhere that:

> The human capital of a nation is a primary determinant of its strength. A productive and educated workforce is a necessity for long-term economic growth. Worker productivity depends on the effective use and development of the human capital of all its citizens, which means that schools, families, and neighbourhoods must function effectively.[1]

The notion of a randomised collection of individuals who neither have nor aspire to any continuity or allegiance delineates a polity from hell. The family is the primary moral domain, or Emile Durkheim's 'key link in the social chain of being', which mediates between the individual and other institutions. Marriage does not just build society's bridges of social connectedness, it is the crucible of the moral sentiments and values we all rely on: loyalty, commitment, service, promise-keeping and formal responsibility. Filial obligation generalises and operates in ways which support political and legal institutions, providing the 'cornerstone of the social attitudes ... described by solidarity', which underpin mutual trust, social control and cohesion in all societies, to curb the aggressive, destructive and self-centred propensities that militate against their existence.[2] If institutions, particularly the family, in which virtue is developed and nurtured, are not preserved and supported, then this not only puts at risk the welfare of many people, particularly the young, but weakens the foundations of democratic civil society itself.

The lack of family stability has dynamic consequences, causing problems at school, on the streets, in the labour market, and for welfare services. If the 'family becomes less efficient, we become more dependent on other arrangements and institutions for what families cannot manage: more dependent upon the money economy for consumption, more dependent on schools and pre-schooling for identity, values and the training of citizenship, more dependent on government for care and services'.[3] The four aspects officially admitted in New Zealand to be 'particularly worrying' are the 'entrenched nature of families in a cycle of disadvantage, the prevalence of risk factors, the disproportionate number of Maori and Pacific Island families in the risk category, and the failure of several years of economic growth to impact on the numbers of at-risk families'.[4]

Families, and how they function, are one of the main determinants of the development of children's physical, emotional, intellectual and social capacities and the foremost environment for the growth of human competence. However, the first response to increasingly evident problems in these areas is to deny that there is any connection with family fragmentation. Another is to blame everything on the way that policy is supposedly focused on 'the breakdown and attempted restoration of old family structures, rather than supporting the new forms', where we must 'accept that the world has changed and provide for the diversity of families'.[5]

As already observed, this is manifest nonsense. No attempt has been made to restore 'old family structures' if by that is meant the married two-parent family. Instead, just about everything has been done to ensure its demise. In 1996, a rare and startling admission was made in a Post-Election Briefing Paper from the Department of Social Welfare about the need to:

> ... address one of the most difficult social policy issues in contemporary New Zealand: the continued growth in the number of sole-parent families and the appropriate response to the growth. Sole parenthood is associated with negative outcomes for children, in particular when linked with benefit dependence and a pattern of changing family structures. The Strengthening Families project will consider the factors driving this growth, current policy responses, and other initiatives which might be taken.[6]

So far, the only permissible response has been to treat the symptoms, with, for instance, '[p]arenting and home building programmes which support the development of strong families ... [supposedly] raise capable and self-reliant young people, and ... reduce long-term and inter-generational welfare dependence and family dysfunction'.[7] Yet, at precisely the same time, there comes the admission that 'evidence [is] that neither universal and/or standardised services, nor current more intensive social services, are having a significant impact on changing the dynamics of families in a cycle of disadvantage'.[8] Insofar as offending can be prevented, conclusions are that 'short-term attempts at behavioural intervention when they [children] reach adolescence are of limited success', and 'there are barriers to the extent to which the State can intrude in parenting although the State can assume the parenting role where natural parenting is grossly deficient'. In turn, home-school liaison is 'probably too late to impact positively upon the antecedents of problem behaviour' and while external 'controls may inhibit anti-social behaviour ... [they] are unlikely to address the root causes of that behaviour'.[9]

Where, anyway, are all the personnel, or the parent substitutes to come from? For the schooling system itself to address the needs of children at risk, the report of parliament's Education and Science Committee advocated that teachers should be fully trained to recognise such children; support should be provided in the classroom for teachers to deal with at-risk children; and that in- and off-school site intervention programmes should be implemented to modify behaviour. As it was suggested that five to seven per cent of the child and adolescent population have serious mental disorders requiring specialist assessment and treatment, then, given the more conservative figure, specialist services are needed for 40,000 young New Zealanders. However, there has been a persistent short-fall in services for children and young people, due not least to shortages of mental health professionals.[10]

Even if the risk-enhancing effects of some conditions could be counteracted by social services supplied by public bodies, this is a far more expensive and cumbersome way to do what families may provide as a matter of course. Even in the very early years: 'functioning parents ... [are] worth 25 HeadStart programs'.[11] Moreover, even if ameliorative measures were to work brilliantly, problems are being created faster than any 'treatment' could possibly mop them up.[12] The state is being asked to substitute itself as the provider of the missing parent's functions, and make good the loss of social capital for the children. It must also endeavour to provide for the family's role in nurturing those personal values and skills which enable communities to function.

An 'ambulance at the bottom of the cliff' policy is fundamentally inadequate because it does not contain the realistic possibility of halting or reversing the personal and social problems that stem from family disintegration. Of course, we might intervene earlier, with a 'positive approach to protecting children from the negative effects of family dissolution' which provides 'counselling to enable the parents to adjust to their new circumstances'.[13] But, however big the army of counsellors guiding people through their 'family changes', breakups and 'repartnerings', there is no evidence that they will be able to counteract the adverse effects on the children exposed to family 'transitions'.

Unusually, the report of the Education and Science Committee acknowledged that '[i]f solutions exist [to youth crime] they probably lie in the macrosociological changes and processes of social reconstruction which aim to limit the number of seriously dysfunctional and disorganised families in society'.[14]

But again, the taboo on investigating and acting upon the family aspect of social problems closed over this suggestion. The 'adverse social outcomes that involuntarily deprive people of an ability to participate and belong to society', or socially exclude people, are variously listed as child neglect and abuse; educational failure and illiteracy; poverty; unemployment; marginal and insecure employment; sickness and injury; criminal victimisation; social isolation; alienation from political participation and discrimination.[15] We go round in circles. These outcomes and causes relate, in no small degree, to family behaviour, as do the '"resilience" factors that protect against social exclusion'.[16] However, the answer is to tackle 'social exclusion' by 'building capacity, creating opportunities, and tackling existing areas of social exclusion, with measures to reduce child poverty, increase literacy, early childhood education, primary health care, economic development, active employment policy, and improving work incentives ...' Just to deal with child abuse and neglect 'requires not merely treatment and prevention services with individuals and families, but also a range of community programmes directed at strengthening individual and family integration into communities as well as strengthening local communities' capacity to address their economic and social viability and cohesion'.[17] This is beyond the ability and resources of the most ambitious, wealthy and overbearing state to achieve, even if it had a portion of the knowledge and control which might enable it to try.

What, anyway, is a socially *included* individual, who 'participates and belongs to society'? The answer seems to be that, properly serviced, and along with the others in a social and moral vacuum, he or she is free to 'make informed choices and live the type of life that they choose [*sic*]'.[18] Autonomy, satisfaction and self-fulfilment come before the very social bonds that foster personal security, well-being and responsibility. Not only the dubious nature and tremendous cost of the means, but the end desired would seem to be questionable—even if attainable—and feed into the cycle of decline. The undue promotion of an ethic of personal choice tends to 'presage a political economy in which citizens' demands get out of balance with the resources available to institutions of state and public welfare, and, in the end, undermine them'.[19]

The Cultural and Sexual Revolution

The effects of the cultural and sexual revolution of the 1960s are well established in New Zealand and are commonly expressed in attitudes and policy proposals that are hostile and damaging to the survival of marriage and the family, and to the wider welfare of society. This raises the question of whether it is realistic to think that a reversal of policy and attitudes affecting marriage and the family might be achieved. As a large part of this book has been devoted to analysing the depth and scope of the cultural and sexual revolution that has undermined the family, it might be concluded that such an enterprise is doomed to fail.

This pessimistic view is supported by the rapidity with which the government has accorded informal heterosexual and homosexual relationships a legal status that is similar to marriage. The Property (Relations) Amendment Act 2001 renamed and amended the Matrimonial Property Act 1976, which previously applied to spouses on the dissolution of marriage, and extended it to *de facto* couples and same sex couples. The Human Rights Amendment Act 2001 amended a number of acts so that *de facto* and same-sex couples are covered by laws that previously applied to married couples alone.[20] Moreover, claims that statutes and regulations unjustifiably discriminate on the grounds of marital status, gender and sexual orientation may be heard by the Human Rights Review Tribunal, which may make a declaration that a particular act or regulation is inconsistent with the Human Rights Act 1993. In that case, the responsible minister must bring the declaration to the attention of parliament, together with a report advising how the government is to respond to the declaration.[21]

Given current family trends, it is predicted that, by 2010, more than one-half of all European children and three-quarters of Maori children aged under one year will live apart from their fathers. Casual sexual relationships free of commitments are now pretty much routine for many young people. They are depicted in films, on television and in magazines that provide little space for a way of life that places marriage and children at the centre.[22]

The growing realisation of the detrimental effects on children, adults and society of the cultural and sexual revolution, however, provides ground for optimism. The government may be pressed to take action as those effects become better understood. The planned establishment of the Families Commission in July 2004, which was promised as part of the confidence and supply agreement between the Labour-led government and United Future New Zealand, reflects growing disquiet about the state of the family among at least a section of the electorate.[23] Young adults who were affected by marriage breakdown during their childhood and seek a better environment for their children are also a source of optimism.

The cultural and sexual revolution rests on a mistaken view about what individualism and individual freedom truly mean. This error needs to be exposed. The revolution is 'mistaken in equating freedom with release from any and all restrictions and in finding, in every assertion of authority and behind every traditional norm, nothing more than the mailed fist of bourgeois power'.[24]

Freedom to enter into relationships and to exit from them may be seen as a fundamental freedom. Freedom to engage in social relations, exchanges of goods and services, and voluntary co-operation are the basis of a liberal social order. It implies regularity and predictability which cannot be established or sustained in the absence of customs, conventions and rules that inspire confidence and trust in the behaviour of other people. This requires the state to maintain law and order, enforce contracts and establish the right to due process. Unconstrained individualism, exempt from formal and informal enforcement of rules, is a threat to the freedom of others and to a viable social order without which other freedoms—to exchange with confidence, associate with others safely and co-operate with protection against opportunistic behaviour—cannot be enjoyed. 'Human associations must therefore have the means to protect the integrity of the various transactions which are their *raison d'etre*, in the interests of individualism understood as opportunities for personal fulfilment.'[25]

The above approach can be illustrated by reference to cohabitation and marriage. Both rely on voluntary acceptance by the parties of the nature and terms of the relationship. They differ in the kinds of fulfilment they offer and in the constraints, or absence of constraints, appropriate for achieving the promised fulfilments. They also differ in the duties entailed. Cohabitation is expressly chosen because it frees the individual from the responsibilities and restrictions of marriage. The reasons for living together are reducible to convenience, whether legal, economic, social, personal or sexual. Cohabitation is a private arrangement between the parties. If the terms of a cohabiting relationship suit the couple, it is consistent with freedom-under-the law unless a breach of criminal or civil law arises and provided children are not involved. Marriage, on the other hand, implies a legally defined institution where the law and not the parties establishes the rules of entry and membership. Cohabitation and marriage are different forms of association that have arisen to serve different interests, and the rules of each should reflect those differences.[26] The failure of the law to distinguish between them is itself a threat to freedom.

The nature of the relationship between parents is of vital interest to the child. The presence of a dependent child changes the relationship between his or her parents from one comprising two adults who are capable of acting in their interests to one that also involves a third party that is unable to act in his or her interest. A child needs to be protected because of his or her immaturity and vulnerability. If parents fail their child, the government is ultimately the only authority that can act on the child's behalf. It seeks to uphold the interests of the child and to protect society from the consequences that flow from children who are neglected.

Research now shows conclusively that, on average and over time, the traditional family, comprising a married couple of the opposite gender, provides the best environment within which to raise children. This does not mean that sole parents or a couple of the same gender necessarily do a poor job of rearing children—some may do an excellent job. Similarly, it does not mean that the continuation of a marriage is always in the best interests of affected children—this is not the case, for instance, where one spouse, the children, or both, are at risk of harm from a violent spouse. Furthermore, sole parenthood is unavoidable in some cases, such as in the event of the death of a parent. But the clear finding from the literature means that the traditional family should be encouraged so that children are given the best possible opportunity to develop into self-supporting adults who contribute as fully as possible to society.

A first step is to begin to restore the status and dignity of marriage as the key institution for raising children. As Maley insists, for marriage to play 'its part in promoting the well-being of adults and children, the cultural indifference will need to be reversed, the costs of children appropriately acknowledged, and policy neutrality established as between the preferences of husbands and wives for either customary or non-customary domestic roles'.[27]

The Fragile Contract

The institution of marriage cannot be sustained unless it confers privileges and imposes obligations on those who choose to marry that are different from those imposed on people who elect to cohabit or associate in some other way. The failure to honour the solemn promises that a man and a woman make to each other and to the community cannot be ignored, as is the case under no-fault divorce provisions, without rendering such promises meaningless. The most influential result of no-fault divorce law has been to eliminate legal support for norms of lifelong obligation and commitment and for the expectation that individuals will be rewarded for fulfilling normative roles.[28] Restrictions on divorce under traditional law 'strengthened the social norms that encourage co-operative behaviour in marriage by reinforcing the informal enforcement mechanism with legal compulsion'. Hence:

> ... the fact that divorce law created a substantial barrier to exit underscored for each spouse that marriage was a life-long commitment and reinforced the norm of marital loyalty. In general, the legal and normative regulation of marriage under traditional family law formed a coherent and mutually reinforcing system that functioned to enforce obligations and to promote cooperation in marriage.[29]

No-fault provisions made the marriage contract inherently precarious, or redefined marriage as a contingent, provisional arrangement. Marriages are conducted 'in the shadow of divorce', just as all business is conducted under the 'shadow of the law'. Now, marriages begin in the worst possible way. There is no assurance that investments in a costly and uncertain venture will not be lost as a spouse defects. Abusive behaviour is not taken into account in the divorce settlement, so that a dependent may be loath to take action to protect themselves for fear of loss. New Zealand has had very high levels of domestic violence and, until recently, rigidly enforced 'equal division' rules. In this way, divorce failed in its most proclaimed objective—to rid the world of bad marriages. The expectation that when marriage problems occur, divorce is the acceptable way out, is the concomitant of the legislators' belief that behaviour is a symptom, not a cause, of breakdown.

As a recipe for failure, 'no-fault' legislation means earlier and more divorces than there would have been otherwise, since the state's role has moved from protecting marriage to facilitating divorce. Divorce rates rose everywhere as the law changed, irrespective of when it changed. It necessarily shifted underlying assumptions about the nature of the marital relationship, the distinction was blurred between marriage and other forms of cohabitation, and children placed outside the partnership agreement. Marriage was not simply reduced from a status to a short-run contract under no-fault divorce. It is hardly even a contract. In no other area could a contract be broken without any consequential blame attaching to any party, and with no resort to law to apportion responsibility. The essential element of contract law—that those who break an agreement must compensate for disappointed expectations—is abrogated. Making marriage less binding than a job contract, no-fault and unilateral divorce is likely to encourage opportunism, lower the costs to departing spouses and remove protection or leverage from spouses who do not want their marriages to dissolve. Not only need the instigators of divorce incur little or no loss, they may benefit. Altruistic, family-first, co-operative and sharing behaviour is penalised. Individualistic, selfish, personal aggrandisement is rewarded. Should conflict arise, the one who has guarded his or her private interests best will come out on top, so that norms of co-operation, loyalty and sharing have been weakened by the individualistic bias that underlies the law.

The freedom of perpetual choice means that the person must continually expend time and energy to re-evaluate the wisdom of the previous choice, by constantly monitoring satisfaction with the relationship, the quality of the possible alternatives, and the degree of their investment. When people continually compare their marriage with possible alternatives, it will sometimes compare unfavourably and engender discontent. As people are not aware of needs that are being well served, but only of those that are not being satisfied, the grass often looks greener in the next field. Traditionally, the law also had a role in protecting people from themselves, or from their own rash and self-harming actions.

First marriages began to plummet at the same time as the rise in divorce took off. The trends are mirror images of each other. The climb in children born outside of marriage also starts at the same time. This is related to the rise in cohabitation, which itself emerged as a widespread phenomenon at exactly the same time that marriage was being demoted 'from a permanent commitment, severable only for cause, to a temporary, fully revokable arrangement, terminable at will of either spouse'.[30]

The prevalence of divorce may have been partly responsible for the decline in marital fertility, as a lack of confidence in the durability of a marriage would discourage a woman from having children. The woman's contribution to the marriage of rearing children occurs early. She makes 'sunk investment in the marriage and places herself in considerable jeopardy ... typical male incomes increase throughout the working life. Middle-aged husbands, then, can realistically expect a new spouse after divorce, whereas the same is not true for middle-aged wives. Under these conditions it is easy to see why the inability to enter a binding contract is detrimental to the wife.'[31] Women might only enter marriage later in life, after they have acquired property and established themselves in employment, in order to protect themselves in the event of marital failure. As the costs are raised of getting and remaining married, women may work longer hours, and choose careers that may better support them if they are divorced.[32]

Divorce law may affect not only the divorce rate itself, but the gains to marriage. Entering marriage with the assumption that it may only last a short time means that people may not be inclined to fully commit or make the kinds of investments that would be lost should the marriage end. People who feel secure that their marriage will last are freer to specialise and invest in different skills and areas of life in ways that leave both of them better off. A permissive divorce ethic substitutes uncertainty for a sense of secure identity and belonging.

Since the benefits to society of long-term stable marriage are huge, including better health, education, housing, old-age care, crime reduction and wealth accumulation, it is something in which it should invest. In turn, as so much is saved by marriage, society is entitled to tell people that if they are not prepared to make the commitment, then they should not expect the benefits.

The conditions under which marriages may be dissolved, or divorce permitted, are an important issue for the future of the family. The present law recognises irreconcilable breakdown of the marriage as the only grounds for divorce. This ground is established if, and only if, the court is satisfied that the spouses have lived apart for the two years immediately preceding the filing of an application. It enables one spouse to walk away from the marriage and therefore bring it to an end. We need to remove the unilateral aspect and give recognition to the possibility of misconduct in marriage which is presently ignored.

No-fault divorce might be preserved where there is agreement by both spouses that their marriage is finished and where they have agreed on the terms of their settlement and the arrangements for their children.[33] Unlike unilateral divorce, such consensual divorce will enable each spouse to bargain from a position of equality. Otherwise, if consensus is missing, then there could be divorce where serious misconduct during the marriage is something to be taken into account in deciding the terms of the divorce settlement. The first duty of the law is to uphold individual rights, to deter transgressors and to hold perpetrators responsible, as far as possible, for compensating their victims. Thus a wronged spouse should be able to claim compensation by way of a differential property settlement or maintenance. Similarly, equal sharing of assets should not apply where the performance of marital duties, like housekeeping and child care, have prejudiced the future earning potential of a spouse. In the absence of misconduct, settlements should compensate for disadvantage, as is only fair. In turn, as the first responsibility for children rests with the parents, the distribution of assets and maintenance should attempt to ensure that, as far as possible, the children and the custodial parent enjoy at least an adequate standard of living.

Non-custodial parents might be expected to pay higher levels of maintenance than they are required to pay under the present Child Support scheme. This applies whether we are dealing with ex-spouses or ex-cohabitees. This approach would diminish the financial scope for divorced, separated or formerly cohabiting parents to form new families and have more children without providing adequately for those that already exist.

While the law should enforce the obligations incurred through producing children in uncommitted relationships, it has no place in relationships that people make between themselves, whether they be companions, sex partners, cohabiters, or room-mates. When people freely chose to enter a legally defined institution: 'those engaged in it know what ... to expect of one another and what kinds of actions are permissible. There is a common basis for determining mutual expectations.'[34] Among the 'mutual expectations' that have defined the contract and the institution, and which impose limitations on conduct, is the presumption by the parties, and their mutually declared intention, that the relationship will be exclusive and permanent. This crucially distinguishes marriage from cohabitation, which avoids the public promise of permanent bonding that is characteristic of marriage. At the very least, if the rights of marriage are given to those who do not accept the responsibilities and '... cohabitation gets the same material benefits as marriage, marriage becomes stripped of all incentives ...'[35] The recognition and support of unmarried cohabitation, like 'gay marriage', as equal 'lifestyle choices', destroys the rights of the majority of the population to have meaningful marriage. The prime motivation behind the campaign for partnership rights has been the desire to destroy marriage.

Since cohabitation affects the married and the institution of marriage, its recognition needs to be questioned. Increasing cohabitation among parents means that the overall proportion of children affected by the parting of their parents will increase. Instead, it might need to be discouraged in ways that minimise its damage to marriage. It is possible to use judicial concepts in order to accommodate difficult cases without disturbing the fundamentals of family law. Some problems are not specific to cohabitants, be they homosexual or heterosexual. Moreover, cohabitants are, for example, presently as free as anyone else to make wills and bequests and can jointly own or rent their home.

Economic and Social Environment

The family was particularly strong and popular in the decade or two immediately after World War II. A higher proportion of the adult population than ever before was married and the proportion of Maori adults who married was consistently higher than that of non-Maori. The rise in fertility was sharper in New Zealand than anywhere else, and it lasted much longer. The economic and social environment that was so supportive of marriage and the family around that period was vastly different from that of today.

Better economic and social performance has a role to play when it comes to rejuvenating the institution of marriage and the family in New Zealand. Policy changes are required in many areas. The government has adopted the laudable goal of restoring New Zealand's *per capita* income to the top half of the OECD. If this objective were to be achieved within ten years, New Zealand's real GDP *per capita* would need to grow by between 4.6 per cent and 7.4 per cent a year depending on the measure of GDP used.[36]

Sustained unemployment of the breadwinner is a tragedy for a family, especially one with dependent children. A reduction in unemployment, especially among the young, is required to enhance families' financial security and to improve the attractiveness of young people as potential marriage partners. A reduction in unemployment to not more than two-three per cent of the labour force should be achievable with appropriate labour, education and welfare policies.

While improvements in the home environment, particularly by encouraging two-parent families, would be a large help, the performance of schools must also be improved. This requires a revamp of curricula, the adoption of more effective teaching methods, most notably in relation to literacy skills and mathematics, and steps to identify and address promptly poorly performing schools.

The corrosive effects on families and society of the welfare system must be addressed. Although designed with the best of intentions, the welfare system has, over time, helped to undermine the family, the work ethic and social cohesiveness. Furthermore, the cost of welfare imposes a heavy burden on families and other taxpayers. This does not imply any rejection of the need for a safety net for people who would otherwise face hardship, including those who will in any event require assistance (for example, those born with serious physical and intellectual disabilities).

The DPB and Child Support arrangements unduly encourage the break-up of families, lone parenthood, ex-nuptial births, the shedding of responsibility for financial and other support for children by non-custodial parents, and welfare dependency. The proposals outlined on family law would place prime responsibility for the provision of material and other support of children on their parents whether they are married or not and whether they stayed together or split up. Maintenance should be paid direct to the custodial parent and enforced through the courts, making it less attractive from a financial perspective to end a marriage or father a child out of wedlock. These are very different from the arrangements which generally assume a fifty-fifty allocation of marital property without the costs of caring for children and where the state provides the DPB for the sole parent who cares for a child under 18 years of age.

The first priority should be to ensure that non-custodial parents meet the cost of raising their children.[37] Inland Revenue administers the Child Support scheme.[38] A non-custodial or paying parent is assessed annually for Child Support based upon his or her liable earnings. They comprise the parent's taxable income (up to a maximum of $90,823 in 2003/04) less a living allowance which is related to benefit levels. The level of the living allowance reflects whether the paying parent is single or married (including a *de facto* couple) and the number of dependent children living with the paying parent. The rates of payment are 18 per cent of liable earnings for one dependent child, rising to 30 percent for four or more children. A lower rate applies in almost all cases where the care of the child is shared between the parents. The minimum rate of Child Support is $677 a year.[39] The average rate assessed in 2001/02 was less than $1,400.[40]

In some cases the amount that the non-custodial parent can pay may allow the custodial parent to decline paid work altogether and in more cases it may enable the custodial parent to be self-supporting with the addition of income from part-time work and without resort to benefits. Recipients of the DPB were generally required to work on a part-time basis after their youngest dependent child reached six years of age and to undertake full-time work when the child reached 14 years of age. These requirements were repealed in March 2003. Instead, such beneficiaries are required to develop a Personal Development and Employment (PDE) plan. A PDE 'will contain a client's training and employment goals and action points needed to achieve the goals.' It 'will take a broad approach taking account of parenting and family needs as well as training and employment goals.[41]

The new arrangements are loose and discretionary, and mandatory work requirements need to be reconsidered. In Wisconsin lone parents are required to work when their youngest child is aged 12 weeks. The view is taken that a married woman who took time off work to have a baby would be expected to return to work after 12 weeks and lone mothers should be treated in the same way. In France the limit is three years; in Germany part-time work is required when the youngest child reaches school age and full-time work when that child is aged 14 years; in the United Kingdom there is no work requirement until the youngest child is aged 16 years. However, to impose a work obligation on lone parents raises the problem of childcare costs, which could be as high or higher than non-work benefits. Childcare costs are much reduced, of course, when it is mothers of school age and older children who are in the workforce.

New Zealand Superannuation is New Zealand's largest welfare programme. It provides a relatively generous level of support on a universal basis for people aged 65 years and over. As a consequence, higher taxes than would otherwise be the case are imposed on people of working age including families. This problem will be accentuated if the ratio of retirees to those in employment rises as projected. To rebalance the extent to which policy has moved against young families with children in favour of older people, the age of eligibility for New Zealand Superannuation might be gradually increased and the level of superannuation indexed by the CPI. Alternative ways may need to be found to finance non-labour income in old age, or ways other than that of using the current family building generation, with all its costs, to largely fund their elders declining years.

Families that stay together, and those outside as well as inside the means-tested system, deserve support and recognition of their extra responsibilities. Married people are taxed as if they had the discretionary income of childless singles, and are lent upon to generate resources for all other needs. A fair tax system would recognise the costs of dependents, through a system of allowances, rebates or income splitting, so that revenue contributions were related to personal liabilities. This would enhance family security and reduce welfare dependency. If 'the family is to be efficient in what it does, it needs a solid basis of organisation, resources and commitment, as do all organisations for efficiency'.[42] The responsibilities of men who stay with families should be acknowledged, rather than discounted or penalised.

The proposals outlined above indicate the general direction in which policy should move. They are not aimed at achieving ideal outcomes or returning to the environment that prevailed around World War II. Further work is required to develop specific policies. Policy proposals should be fully debated and a period of notice should be given before any changes are introduced, as they affect the long-term commitments that people have made.

No society can survive without making sure that children are raised by parents who take responsibility for them. By producing, caring for and educating children, families create and contribute to the good of the wider society. In looking after dependents, the family is also the primary welfare institution, just as it is basic to social order and solidarity. The effective functioning of families is far too important to society to allow policies that threaten the very survival of marriage and the family to continue.

Notes

Foreword

1   Green, D.G., *From Welfare State to Civil Society: Towards Welfare that Works in New Zealand,* Wellington: New Zealand Business Roundtable, 1996.

2   Green, *From Welfare State to Civil Society,* p. 30.

3   *New Zealand Herald,* 20 November 2003.

4   Stigler, G.J., *The Citizen and the State: Essays on Regulation,* Chicago: University of Chicago Press, 1975, p. 185.

5   *New York Times,* 26 December 1992.

6   Popenoe, D., 'Married to the Idea: But Not Each Other', *American Outlook Magazine,* summer 2002, www.americanoutlook.org.

1: The Fission in the Nucleus of the Family

1   Houston, S., 'The New Zealand Family: Its Antecedents and Origins', in Houston, S., *Marriage and the Family in New Zealand,* Wellington: Sweet & Maxwell NZ Ltd, 1970, pp. 37-38.

2   *Families and Households,* Statistics New Zealand, 1998.

3   Metze, J., 'The Maori Family', in Houston, *Marriage and the Family in New Zealand,* 1970, p. 121.

4   Ministry of Social Development, *Agenda for Children: Appendix 5,* http://www.msd.govt.nz
      Original source Statistics New Zealand, unpublished census data.

5   Statistics New Zealand, unpublished data, quoted in Social Environment Scan, Information and Analysis Group, Department of Social Welfare, June 1999.

6   Fergusson, D., 'Family Formation, Dissolution and Reformation', in *Proceedings of the SSRFC Symposium: New Zealand Families in the Eighties and Nineties,* Canterbury University, No. 20, November 1987, pp. 15-30.

7   Fergusson, 'Family Formation, Dissolution and Reformation', 1987, pp. 15-30.

8   Fergusson, 'Family Formation, Dissolution and Reformation', 1987, p. 29.

9   Haskey, J., 'The Proportion of Married Couples Who Divorce: Past Patterns and Current Prospects', *Population Trends* 83, 1996, pp. 25-36; Haskey, J., 'Children Who Experience Divorce in Their Family', *Population Trends,* 87, 1997, pp. 5-10; Haskey, J., 'Families: Their Historical Context, and Recent Trends in the Factors Influencing Their Formation and Dissolution', in David, M.E. (ed.), *et al.,* *The Fragmenting Family: Does It Matter?,* IEA Health and Welfare Unit, 1998.

10   In England and Wales, the rates peaked with the implementation in 1971 of the Divorce Reform Act 1969 and in 1985 with the Matrimonial and Family Proceedings Act 1984, and in Australia in 1976 with the no-fault Family Law Act. *Marriages and Divorces Australia 1996*, Cat. No. 3310.0. Australian Bureau of Statistics Canberra, ABS.

11   In the UK, the proportion of children affected by divorce continues to rise (to 28 per cent based on 1994-5 data compared with Australia's 18 per cent), even if the average number of children per divorcing couple has fallen slightly, reflecting the fall in family size. Given present rates, two in five marriages will end in divorce and more than one in four children will see their parents part before reaching age 16.

12   Maxwell, G.M., 'Marriage and Divorce; Trends in NZ Compared with Australia and the USA', *The Family Law Bulletin*, June 1989, pp. 7-11.

13   *Maori*, Wellington: Statistics New Zealand, 1998.

14   A way to look at these movements is to calculate the number of children a woman is likely to have over her lifetime while she is single by asking what would have happened if the birth rate for that year had applied throughout the woman's lifetime. In the US in 1960, a typical white woman could expect to have 0.08 unwed births over her lifetime and, by 1987, to have 0.29. This is not a large absolute, but a big percentage, increase. For black women the increase was from 1.05 to 1.43, a large absolute increase but a smaller percentage increase. By themselves, these figures do not suggest a massive rise in unwed births. However, in 1960 both black and white married women could expect to have 3.5 children. By 1987, a white married woman could expect only 1.81 and a black married woman 0.81.

15   As the general downturn continued in 1996, nuptial births fell 2.1 per cent as ex-nuptial births increased 1.7 per cent. *Demographic Trends 96*, Wellington: Statistics New Zealand. With the slight rallying in 1997, the increase among unwed women was over three-fold that of married women. Statistics New Zealand, 1998 personal communication.

16   *New Zealand Now: Families and Households*, Wellington: Statistics New Zealand, 1998 edn.

17   UNICEF: 'A League Table of Teenage Births in Rich Nations', *Innocenti Report Card*, No. 3, Florence: UNICEF Innocenti Research Centre, July 2001, p. 4.

18   UNICEF: 'A League Table of Teenage Births in Rich Nations', *Innocenti Report Card*, No. 3, July 2001, p. 4.

19   Only one in 33 marriages involved teenage women, while in 1971 this was one in three. In 1991, 78 per cent of women aged 20-24 and 39.2 per cent of women aged 25-29 were still single, compared with only 36 per cent and 12.5 per cent in 1961. For those aged 30-34, it was 19.6 compared with 8.1. Similarly, for Australia, a third of women had married by the time they turned 20 in 1972, and 83 per cent by 25, but by 1991 this had dropped to five and 47 per cent, below the figures of 14 and 48 per cent for 1934.

20   In 1997, average age of first time grooms was 28.3 years and for brides
     was 26.5 years, while it had been 23 and 20.8 years in 1971. *Demographic
     Trends 1998*, Wellington: Statistics New Zealand, 1999.

21   Figures are similar in the UK. In 1960, for every thousand men over 16,
     77 got married for the first time (and 82 women). In 1970 it was 86. In
     1992 it was 37 (and 47 women.) This is not accounted for by the rise in
     cohabitation. In 1979, 23 per cent of women were neither married nor
     cohabiting but, by 1993, the proportion was 32 per cent. One in 10 men
     aged 25 to 44 was living alone in 1994, three times the proportion of 1973.

22   From 104.943 in 1971 to 235.986 in 1991.

23   In Australia, 27 per cent of women aged 25-29 years, had never married
     in 1986, but 45 per cent in 1996. The fall in marriage rates has not been
     compensated for by increases in cohabitations. Seventy per cent of women
     aged 30-34 were in couple relationships in 1996, compared with 77 per
     cent in 1986. The share of men aged 30-34 who were 'partnered' in 1996
     was 62 per cent, compared with 71 per cent in 1986.

24   The proportion of women either in a marriage or cohabitation fell from 59
     to 55 per cent in the decade to 1996. Those under 30 living with a spouse
     was down from 39.2 per cent in 1986 to 31.8 per cent by 1996. *New
     Zealand Now: Women*, Wellington: Statistics New Zealand, 1999.

25   Willis, R.J. and Michael, R.T., 'Innovation in Family Formation: Evidence
     on Cohabitation in the United States', in Ermisch, J. and Ogawa, N. (eds),
     The Family, the Market, and the State in Ageing Societies, Oxford
     University Press, 1994, p. 24.

26   Ermisch, J., 'Pre-marital Cohabitation, Childbearing and the Creation of
     One Parent Families', in Jonung, C. and Persson, I. (eds), *Economics of
     the Family*, Routledge, 1997. Also Ermisch, J. and Francesconi, M.,
     Cohabitation in Great Britain: Not for Long, but Here to Stay, Institute for
     Social and Economic Research, University of Essex, 1998.

27   Bumpass, L.L. and Sweet, J.A., 'National Estimates of Cohabitation',
     Demography, Vol. 26, 1989, pp. 615-25; and Willis and Michael,
     'Innovation in Family Formation: Evidence on Cohabitation in the United
     States', 1994.

28   *Australian Family Formation Study*, Melbourne: Australian Institute of
     Family Studies, 1991.

29   Bumpass and Sweet, 'National Estimates of Cohabitation', 1989; and
     Willis and Michael, 'Innovation in Family Formation: Evidence on
     Cohabitation in the United States', 1994.

30   Wertheimer, A. and McRae, S., *Family and Household Change in Britain:
     A Summary of Findings from Projects in the ESRC Population and
     Household Change Programme*, Centre for Family and Household
     Research, Oxford Brookes University, 1999.

31   *New Zealand Now: Children*, Wellington: Statistics New Zealand, 1998.

32 Although the growth itself has been largest for European children (increasing from 6.7 to 9.9 per cent of all children between 1991 and 1996), *New Zealand Now: Children* Statistics New Zealand, 1998.

33 *New Zealand Now: Families and Households,* 1998, p. 21.

34 Ermisch, J.F., *Personal Relationships and Marriage Expectations,* Institute for Social and Economic Research, University of Essex, 2000, p. 20.

35 Ermisch, 'Pre-marital Cohabitation, Childbearing and the Creation of One Parent Families', in *Economics of the Family,* 1997. Lone motherhood via cohabitation more than doubled for women reaching their 16th birthday after 1979. Buck, N. and Ermisch, J., 'Cohabitation in Britain', *Changing Britain,* Issue 3, ESRC, October 1995; McKay, S., 'New Data on Life Events: the Family and Working Lives Survey', *Changing Britain,* Issue 7, ESRC, October 1997.

36 Ermisch and Francesconi, *Cohabitation in Great Britain: Not for Long, but Here to Stay,* 1998, p. 18. The odds of marriage (relative to not marrying) for women who had their youngest child within cohabitation are 67 per cent lower than for childless women in the British Household Panel Study. Marriage rates for cohabiting couples have also been falling in the US, where the proportion of cohabiting mothers who eventually marry the child's father declined from 57 per cent to 44 per cent over the decade from 1987 to 1997.

37 Or at 4.8 times in the British Household Panel Study. Buck, N. and Ermisch, J., 'Cohabitation in Britain', *Changing Britain,* Issue 3, ESRC, October 1995; McKay, 'New Data on Life Events: the Family and Working Lives Survey',1997; Fergusson, 'Family Formation, Dissolution and Reformation', November 1987, pp. 15-30; and Boheim, R. and Ermisch, J., 'Breaking up—Financial Surprises and Partnership Dissolution', Paper presented at the Royal Economic Society Conference 1999, Nottingham.

38 Rates of relationship breakdown were also higher amongst parents who had only been married a short time (risks of breakdown decrease with length of marriage), families in which a birth was unplanned, young parents, parents lacking formal educational qualifications, Polynesian parents (11.7 per cent for whites, to 22.7 for non-whites) and those of semi or unskilled economic status (5.8 per cent for professional and managerial to 23.9 for semi-and unskilled). Fergusson, D., 'Family Formation, Dissolution and Reformation',1987.

39 Quoted in *To Have and To Hold: A Report of the Inquiry into Aspects of Family Services,* 1998.

40 Kiernan, K., 'Cohabitation in Western Europe', *Population Trends,* 96, Office for National Statistics, 1999.

41 In their sample of 694 'women/year' observations, John Ermisch and Marco Francesconi, observed how women in employment, like those with a partner in a job, were less likely to dissolve their union. Similarly, if a couple received income support, the main means-tested benefit, they had a higher rate of dissolution. Ermisch and Francesconi, *Cohabitation in Great Britain: Not for Long, but Here to Stay,* 1998.

42 Qvirtrup, J., A childhood perspective applied to Wolfgang Lutz's paper, *Family Issues Between Gender and Generations,* Vienna: European Commission Directorate-General for Employment and Social Affairs, 2000, p. 71.

43 Gallagher, M., *The Abolition of Marriage,* Washington DC: Regnery Publishing Inc., 1996.

44 Cherlin, A.J., *Marriage, Divorce, Remarriage,* Cambridge, Mass: Harvard University Press, 1992, pp. 98-99.

45 *Survey of Consumer Finance,* Federal Reserve Board (1995), quoted in Fagan, P.F. and Rector, R., *The Effects of Divorce on America,* Backgrounder No. 1373, Heritage Foundation, 2000.

46 *Maori,* Wellington: Statistics New Zealand, 1998.

47 *Demographic Trends 1996,* Wellington: Statistics New Zealand, 1996.

48 *Young New Zealanders,* Wellington: Statistics New Zealand, 1998.

49 Maley, B., *Wedlock and Well-Being,* Policy Monographs 33, Sidney: The Centre for Independent Studies, 1996, p. 23.

50 Maley, *Wedlock and Well-Being,*1996, p. 23.

2: Dancing on the Grave of the Family

1 'Traditional Family is Heading into History', *The New Zealand Herald,* 16 May 2000.

2 Ryan, A., 'From Moralism to Sexual Democracy', in Jesson, B. *et al., Revival of the Right,* Auckland: Heinemann Reed, 1988, p. 123.

3 Armstrong, N., 'State', in Spoonley, P., Pearson, D. and Shipley, I. (eds), *New Zealand Society,* Palmerston North: The Dunmore Press Ltd, 1994, p. 127.

4 Ryan, A., 'Remoralising Politics', in Jesson, *et al., Revival of the Right,* 1988, p. 82.

5 Upton, S., 'What Sort of Nation is New Zealand and Who Does It Belong To?', *Cutting Edge,* No. 51, Feb-March 2001.

6 Dugdale, D.F., 'Legislating for Quasi-Connubiality', *New Zealand Law Journal,* April 1998, p. 125.

7 Atkin, B., '*De factos* Down Under and Their Property', *Child and Family Law Quarterly,* Vol. 11, No. 1, 1999, p. 45.

8 'Succession Law Testamentary Claims', Law Commission Preliminary Paper 24, 1996, p. 3.

9 'Succession Law Testamentary Claims', Law Commission Preliminary Paper 24, 1996, p. 41.

10 Maley, B., *Wedlock and Well-Being,* Policy Monographs 33, Sydney: Centre for Independent Studies, 1996, pp. 24-25.

11   Maley, *Wedlock and Well-Being*, 1996, p. 25.

12   See Phillips, M., 'Death Blow to Marriage', in Whelan, R. (ed.), *Just a Piece of Paper?*, London: IEA Health and Welfare Unit, 1995.

13   Maley, *Wedlock and Well-Being*, 1996, p. 27.

14   Maley, *Wedlock and Well-Being*, 1996, p. 25.

15   See, Atkin, *'De factos* Down Under and Their Property', 1999.

16   See, typically Jackson, N. and Pool, I., *Fertility and Family Formation in the 'Second Demographic Transition': New Zealand Patterns and Trends*, Family and Social Change: Research Report No. 2, Christchurch: New Zealand Institute for Social Research & Development Ltd, 1994.

17   Berger, B. and Berger, P.L., *The War Over the Family*, London: Hutchinson, 1983, p. 60.

18   *New Zealand Now: Families and Households*, 1998 edn, p. 17.

19   Swain, D., 'Family', in Spoonley, P., Pearson, D. and Shipley, I. (eds), *New Zealand Society*, Palmerston North: Dunmore Press Ltd, 1994, pp. 18-19.

20   Swain, D.A., 'Children, Families, Law and Social Policy', *Journal of Comparative Family Studies*, 1987, p. 180.

21   Swain, D., 'Alternative Families', in Koopman Boyden, P.G., *Families in New Zealand Society*, NZ: Methuen, 1978, p. 87.

22   Centrepoint in North Auckland was an exception in that it has continued in some form or another to the present day.

23   Bumpass, L., 'The Declining Significance of Marriage: Changing Family Life in the United States', keynote address, *Changing Britain*, Issue One, Economic and Social Research Council, November 1994, p. 6.

24   Carlson, A., 'A Problem of Definition', *The Human Life Review*, VI, 4, 1980, p. 46.

25   Jackson and Pool, *Fertility and Family Formation in the 'Second Demographic Transition': New Zealand Patterns and Trends*, 1994, p. 182.

26   *New Zealand Now: Families and Households*, Wellington: Statistics New Zealand, p. 9.

27   Smith, A.B., 'Research on the Effect of Marital Transitions on Children', in Smith, A.B. and Taylor, N.J., *Supporting Children and Parents Through Family Changes*, Dunedin: University of Otago, 1996, p. 37.

28   Swain, 'Family', 1994, p. 12.

29   Fortes, M., *Rules and the Emergence of Human Society*, Royal Anthropological Institute of Great Britain, Occasional Paper No. 39, 1983.

30   Swain, 'Alternative Families', 1978, p. 88.

31 Davidson, C., 'The "Family" in New Zealand', *New Zealand Population Review*, 17 (2) 1990, p. 11. This recycling of mindless anti-family clichés current since the 1960s purports to be a 'student essay competition winner'.

32 Swain, 'Family',1994, p. 12.

33 Swain, D. A., 'Children, Families, Law and Social Policy', *Journal of Comparative Family Studies,* 1987, p. 180.

34 Gilling, M., 'Family', *New Zealand Today*, Vol. IV, Social Perspectives Report of The Royal Commission on Social Policy, Wellington, 1988, p. 598.

35 Berger and Berger, *The War Over the Family*, 1983.

36 Brown, H., 'Are Old Family Values So Good Anyway?', *New Zealand Herald*, 6 February 1997.

37 Davidson, 'The "Family" in New Zealand', 1990, p. 10.

38 Davidson, 'The "Family" in New Zealand', 1990, p. 7.

39 Statistics New Zealand, *Children Now*, 1999, pp. 37 and 39.

40 Edgar, D., 'How the Baby Boom Backfired', in *The Bulletin*, Jan 29/Feb 5 1991, pp. 148-50.

41 Cameron, J., 'Conceptualising "Family": An Epistemological Concern for Fertility Researchers', *New Zealand Population Review*, 11(1): 1985, pp. 7-18.

42 Maharey, S., 'For families let's look at what matters', the *New Zealand Herald*, 3 December 2003.

43 McPherson, M.J., *Divorce in New Zealand*, Palmerston North: Social Policy Research Centre, Massey University, 1995, p. 1.

44 Swain, 'Children, Families, Law and Social Policy', 1987, pp. 180-81.

45 Stathern, M., *After Nature: Kinship in the Late Twentieth Century*, Cambridge: Cambridge University Press, 1992, p. 24.

46 Swain, 'Children, Families, Law and Social Policy', 1987, pp. 180-81.

47 Murray, D.W., 'Poor Suffering Bastards: An Anthropologist Looks at Illegitimacy', *Policy Review*, No. 68, Spring 1994, p. 9.

48 Biggs, B., *Maori Marriage*, A.H. & A.W. Reed for the Polynesian Society 1960, reprinted 1970, pp. 24-25.

49 Macfarlane, A., *Marriage and Love in England 1300-1840*, Oxford: Basil Blackwell, 1986.

50 Jackson and Pool, *Fertility and Family Formation in the 'Second Demographic Transition': New Zealand Patterns and Trends*, 1994, p. 4.

51   Houston, S., 'The New Zealand Family: Its Antecedents and Origins', in
     Houston, S., *Marriage and the Family in New Zealand*, Wellington: Sweet
     & Maxwell NZ Ltd, 1970.

52   McPherson, *Divorce in New Zealand*, 1995, p. 2.

53   Lloyd, J., 'Marital Breakdown', in Koopman Boyden, *Families in New
     Zealand Society,* 1978, p. 153.

54   McPherson, *Divorce in New Zealand*, 1995, p. 2.

55   McPherson, *Divorce in New Zealand*, 1995, p. 1.

56   McPherson, *Divorce in New Zealand*, 1995.

57   *Demographic Trends 1998*, Wellington: Statistics New Zealand, 1999.

58   Pool, I. and Hillcoat-Nalletamby, S., 'Fathers, Families, Futures: A
     Population Perspective', in Birks, S. and Callister, P. (eds), *Perspectives
     on Fathering,* Centre for Public Policy Evaluation, Massey University,
     1999, p. 16.

59   Jackson and Pool, *Fertility and Family Formation in the 'Second
     Demographic Transition': New Zealand Patterns and Trends*, 1994,
     p. 192.

60   Parker, S., *Informal Marriage, Cohabitation and the Law, 1750-1989*,
     London: Macmillan, 1990; and see Morgan, P., *Marriage-Lite: The Rise of
     Cohabitation and Its Consequences*, London: Civitas, 2000, for a
     discussion of cohabitation in history.

61   Pool and Hillcoat-Nalletamby, 'Fathers, Families, Futures: A Population
     Perspective',1999, p. 15.

62   Malinowski, B., *Sex and Repression in Savage Society* (1927), reprinted
     Routledge and Kegan Paul, 1960, pp. 212-13.

63   Daly, M. and Wilson, M., *Homicide*, New York: Aldine de Gruyter, 1988,
     p. 187.

64   Wellings, K., Field, J., Johnson, A. and Wadsworth, J., *Sexual Behaviour
     in Britain: The National Survey of Sexual Attitudes and Lifestyles*,
     London: Penguin Books, 1994; and *Living in Britain: Results for the 1995
     General Household Survey*, Office for National Statistics, London: HMSO,
     1997.

65   Rindfuss, R.R. and Vandenheuvel, A., 'Cohabitation: a Precursor to
     Marriage or an Alternative To Being Single?', *Population and
     Development Review*, Vol. 40, 1990, pp. 703-26.

66   Sarantakos, S., *Living Together in Australia*, Melbourne: Longman
     Cheshire, 1984, p. 128.

67   *Demographic Trends 1998*, Wellington: Statistics New Zealand, 1999.

68   Zodgekar, A., 'Population', in Shirley, I., 'Social Policy' in Spoonley,
     Pearson and Shipley, *New Zealand Society*, 1994, p. 318.

69   Ritchie, J. and Ritchie, J., 'Child Rearing and Child Abuse: The Polynesian Context', in Kordin, J.E. (ed.), *Child Abuse and Neglect: Cross Cultural Perspectives*, Berkeley CA: University of California Press, 1981, p. 188.

70   Pool and Hillcoat-Nalletamby, 'Fathers, Families, Futures: A Population Perspective', 1999, p. 17.

71   Ritchie and Ritchie, 'Child Rearing and Child Abuse: The Polynesian Context', 1981, p. 188.

72   Finch, J., *Family Obligations and Social Change*, Routledge & Kegan Paul, 1989, p. 126.

73   Dench, G., *The Place of Men in Changing Family Cultures*, London: Institute of Community Studies, 1996, p. 37.

74   Gluckman, L.K., *Tangiwari: a Medical History of Nineteenth Century New Zealand*, Auckland: Whitcoulls, 1976, pp. 187-88.

75   McPherson, *Divorce in New Zealand*, 1995 p. 53. While it has been given a gloss by modern, European radicalism, claims that Maori lack a family as we might understand it, go back well into the last century. See references in Metze, J., 'The Maori Family', in Houston, *Marriage and the Family in New Zealand*, 1970.

76   In Metze, 'The Maori Family', 1970, pp. 112-13.

77   Biggs, *Maori Marriage*, 1970, pp. 42 and 21. Children of a deserted mother might be subject to slights, where a 'recurring incident in tradition is the child crying to its mother because it has been called fatherless (*poriro)'.

78   Buck, P.H., *The Coming of the Maori*, Wellington: Maori Purposes Fund Board, 1950.

79   Biggs, *Maori Marriage*,1970, p. 42.

80   Orbell, M., 'The Traditional Maori Family', in Koopman Boyden, *Families in New Zealand Society*, 1978.

81   Waite, L.J., 'Does Marriage Matter?', *Demography*, Vol. 32, No. 4, November 1995, pp. 483-507.

82   Biggs, *Maori Marriage*, 1970 p. 83.

83   Murray, 'Poor Suffering Bastards: an Anthropologist Looks at Illegitimacy', 1994, pp. 9-15.

84   Ritchie and Ritchie, 'Child Rearing and Child Abuse: The Polynesian Context', 1981, p. 193.

85   Beaglehole, E. and Beaglehole, P., *Some Modern Maori*, Wellington: New Zealand Council for Educational Research, 1946.

86   Metze, J., *A New Maori Migration*, Athlone and Melbourne University Press, 1964.

87 Hohepa, P.W., *A Northern Maori Community*, Anthropological Department, University of Auckland, 1964.

88 Richie, J., *The Making of a Maori*, Wellington: A.H. & A.W. Reed, 1963, p. 13.

89 Ritchie, J., *Maori Families*, Victoria University of Wellington, Publications in Psychology, 1964.

90 In Metze, 'The Maori Family', 1970, p. 139.

91 Davidson, 'The "Family" in New Zealand', 1990, p. 21.

92 *Maori*, Wellington: Statistics New Zealand, 1998; and *Children*, Statistics New Zealand, 1998.

93 Bunkle, P., *New Zealand Women 1985-1995: Markets and Inequality*, Victoria University of Wellington, undated, p. 61.

94 Dench, G., 'Man's Diminished Role', *Welfare*, Winter 1996/97, pp. 19-23.

95 Hardyment, C., *The Future of the Family*, London: Phoenix, 2000, p. 56.

96 Coleman, M., Ganong, L. and Cable, S., 'Beliefs about Women's Intergenerational Family Obligations to Provide Support Before and After Divorce and Remarriage', *Journal of Marriage and the Family*, Vol. 59, No. 1, 1997.

97 'Children Living in Re-ordered Families', *Social Policy Research Findings*, No. 45, York: Joseph Rowntree Foundation, February 1994; Cockett, M. and Tripp, J., *The Exeter Family Study*, University of Exeter, 1994. See also Pett, M.A., Kang, N. and Gander, A., 'Late-life Divorce: Its Impact on Family Rituals', *Journal of Family Issues*, Vol. 13, No. 4, 1992, pp. 526-52; Dench, G. and Ogg, J., 'The Role of Grandparents', in Thomson, K. and Jowell, R. (eds), *British Social Attitudes: the 16th Report: Who Shares New Labour Values?*, Aldershot: Ashgate, 1999.

98 Murray, 'Poor Suffering Bastards: an Anthropologist Looks at Illegitimacy', 1994, p. 10.

99 'Children Living in Re-ordered Families', *Social Policy Research Findings*, 1994.

100 White, L., 'Growing Up with Single Parents and Stepparents: Long-Term Effects on Family Solidarity', *Journal of Marriage and the Family*, Vol. 56, November 1994, pp. 935-48.

101 McPherson, *Divorce in New Zealand*, 1995, p. 26.

102 Lloyd, J., 'Marital Breakdown', in Koopman Boyden, *Families in New Zealand Society*, 1978, p. 142.

103 Lloyd, 'Marital Breakdown', 1978, p. 151.

104 Lloyd, 'Marital Breakdown', 1978, p. 142.

105 Lloyd, 'Marital Breakdown', 1978, p. 147.

106 Ryan, A., 'Remoralising Politics', in Jesson, B., Ryan, A. and Spoonley, P., *Revival of the Right*, Auckland: Heinemann Reed, 1988.

107 Atkin, B., *'De factos* Down Under and Their Property', 1999, pp. 43-52.

108 Dnes, A.W., 'Cohabitation and Marriage', in Dnes, A.W. and Rowthorn, R., *The Law and Economics of Marriage and Divorce*, Cambridge, 2002, p. 129.

109 Sarontakos, S., *Living Together in Australia*, Melbourne: Longman Cheshire, 1984.

110 Weitzman, L., 'The Divorce Law Revolution and the Transformation of Legal Marriage', in Davies, K., *Contemporary Marriage: Comparative Perspectives on a Changing Institution*, New York: Russell Sage, 1985, pp. 305 and 335.

111 Gallagher, M., *The Abolition of Marriage*, Washington: Regnery Publishing, 1996, p. 171.

112 Ringen, S., *The Family in Question*, London: Demos, 1998.

113 Thornton, A., 'Changing Attitudes Towards Family Issues in the United States', *Journal of Marriage and the Family*, Vol. 51, 1989, pp. 873-95.

114 Swain, 'Family', 1994, p. 23.

115 Family Law in New Zealand, *Families Apart Require Equality*, Wellington, 1994.

116 Giddens, A., *The Third Way: The Renewal of Social Democracy*, Cambridge: Polity Press, 1998.

117 Maclean, M., *Surviving Divorce: Women's Resources After Separation*, London: Macmillan, 1991, p. 130.

118 Dench, G., *The Place of Men in Alternative Family Culture*, London: Institute of Community Studies, 1996, p. 59.

119 Jensen, J.H., 'Family Sociology: A Review of Recent Developments in Theory and Research', in Houston, *Marriage and the Family in New Zealand*, 1970.

120 Report of the Domestic Purposes Benefit Review Committee, 1977, p. 16.

121 Even if the UN Committee on the Rights of the Child expressed 'regrets' over the 'rise in the number of single-parent families and ... the lack of a concerted strategy by the State party to address the needs of children affected by this trend'. Also expressed was 'serious concern at the high rate of youth suicide in New Zealand'. Consideration of Reports Submitted by States Parties Under Article 44 of the Convention. Concluding observations of the Committee on the Rights of the Child: New Zealand, 20 and 21 January 1997, p. 3.

122 Listener/Heylen MONITOR—'Do Children Need a Mum and Dad?', *Listener,* 5 November 1994, p. 13, in Birks, S., 'Fathers-Prejudice and Policy', in Callister, P. and Birks, S. (eds), *Perspectives on Fathering*, Centre for Public Policy Evaluation, Massey University, 1999.

123 Davidson, C., 'The "Family" in New Zealand', *New Zealand Population Review*, 17 (2), 1990, p. 17.

3: The Rise and Fall of Family Policy

1 Bradshaw, J., *Household Budgets and Living Standards*, York: Joseph Rowntree Foundation, September 1993.

2 Sullivan, L., 'Taxation and Family Income', in *Family Matters*, No. 54, Spring/Summer 1999, p. 52.

3 Olson, L., *Costs of Children*, Lexington, Mass: Lexington Books, 1983.

4 Castles, F.G. and Mitchell, D., 'Worlds of Welfare and Families of Nations', in Castles, F.G., *Families of Nations: Patterns of Public Policy in Western Nations*, Aldershot: Dartmouth, 1993, p. 125.

5 New Zealand not only utilised the many forms of maintaining horizontal equity seen elsewhere in the Western and industrialised world, but also developed some curious measures not perhaps found elsewhere. An explanation of how missionaries acquired large land holdings describes how '... the Church Missionary Society, by its policy of providing bonuses for the missionaries with children, unwittingly encouraged exploitation and land aggregation. The society had authorised expenditure of up to £50 for each child. So, where land could be bought for axes and blankets, and where in one district 12 missionaries fathered 84 children between them, profitable annexation was inevitable'. Houston, S., 'The New Zealand Family: Its Antecedents and Origins', in Houston, S., *Marriage and the Family in New Zealand*, Wellington: Sweet & Maxwell NZ Ltd, 1970, p. 29.

6 Thomson, D., *Selfish Generations?*, Wellington: Bridget Williams Books Ltd, 1991, p. 41.

7 Sullivan, L., 'Tax Injustice: Keeping the Family Cap-in-Hand', *Issue Analysis,* No. 3, Centre for Independent Studies, July 1998.

8 Thomson, *Selfish Generations?*, 1991. For those born in 1930, a couple's lifetime income tax contribution would have been around six to seven units of gross average pay (for a man aged 35-44). Those born after 1955, will make more than double that contribution.

9 Sullivan, 'Tax Injustice: Keeping the Family Cap-in-Hand', 1998.

10 At a marginal rate of 15 per cent (for the first $9,500 of annual income) in 1999, 21 per cent (for income in the range from $9,501 to $38,000) or 33 per cent.

11 There is also a modest tax rebate for childcare. It applies where childcare services are bought, the parent is single and the child is under 18 years of age or unable to work because of a disability. The rebate applies where both caregivers (not couples who are separated or divorced) are in receipt of income from which tax is deducted. It also applies where the taxpayer is disabled or physically unable to care for the child or his or her partner or is unable to care for the child. The maximum claim is $940 for which a rebate of one-third is payable.

12 Waldegrave, C. and Frater, P., 'The National Government Budgets of the First Year in Office: A Social Assessment', A Report to Sunday Forum, The Family Centre and Business Economic Research Limited, 1991.

13 It was: '... an impressive exercise in self-deception, not I hasten to add of the Commission itself so much as of the nation the Commission reflected. The Commission's recommendations involved a family benefit at a lower relative level than in 1961. In fact, its attitudes to families was so miserly that the National party parliamentary caucus over-ruled its recommendations and introduced a further supplement of $1.25 a week per child for beneficiaries.' Easton, B., 'Poverty in New Zealand; Estimates and Reflection', *Political Science*, 28(2) 1976, p. 130. Some submissions were concerned with family welfare, and urged a considerable increase in the child allowance based on the costs of typical living standards.

14 Easton, 'Poverty in New Zealand; Estimates and Reflection', 1976, pp. 127-41.

15 Easton, 'Poverty in New Zealand; Estimates and Reflection', 1976, p. 134. Suggested that 29 per cent of children and 24 per cent of their parents were below the PDL (a basic living standard for a pensioner).

16 Thomson, *Selfish Generations?*, 1991, p. 105.

17 The net fiscal cost of direct family assistance fell to 0.8 per cent of GDP in 1993.

18 Stephens, R., 'The Impact of the Changing Economy on Families', *Victoria Economic Commentaries*, March 1995, pp. 17-24.

19 Stephens, R. and Bradshaw, J., 'The Generosity of New Zealand's Assistance to Families with Dependent Children: An Eighteen Country Comparison', *Social Policy Journal of New Zealand*, Issue 4, 1995. Stephens, R., Waldegrave, C. and Frater, P., 'Measuring Poverty in New Zealand', *Social Policy Journal of New Zealand*, Issue 5, December 1995.

20 Thomson, *Selfish Generations?*, 1991, p. 155.

21 Hanan, J.R., 'Domestic Proceedings: A Fresh Approach', Speech on the second reading debate on the Domestic Proceedings Act 1968, Department of Justice Wellington. Quoted in Goodger, K., 'Maintaining Sole Parents in New Zealand: An Historical Review', *Policy Journal of New Zealand*, Issue 10, 1998, pp. 12-153.

22 Goodger, 'Maintaining Sole Parents in New Zealand: An Historical Review', 1998, pp. 143.

23 Royal Commission on Social Security, *Social Security in New Zealand*, Wellington: Report of the Royal Commission of Enquiry, 1972, para. 246.

24 Jean Kahui, quoted in Beaglehole, A., *Benefiting Women: Income Support for Women, 1893-1993,* A Women's Suffrage Centenary Project 1993, Wellington: Social Policy Agency, 1993, p. 31.

25 Burgess, A., 'The Erosion of an Institution: the Place of Marriage in the Law 1850-Today', unpublished manuscript.

26 Mahony, K., 'Gender Bias in Family Law: Deconstructing Husband Privilege', New Zealand Family Law Conference, 1995.

27 Peters, E., 'Marriage and Divorce; Informational Constraints and Private Contracting', *American Economic Review*, Vol. 61, 1986, pp.528-36.

28 Atkin, W.R., 'Child Support in New Zealand Runs into Strife', *Houston Law Review*, Vol. 31, No. 2, Summer 1994, p. 641.

29 McPherson, M.J., *Divorce in New Zealand*, Palmerston North: Social Policy Research Centre, Massey University, 1995, p. 46.

30 Rankin, K., 'Fiscal and Welfare Barriers to Effective Fatherhood', in *Perspectives on Fathering*, Palmerston North: Centre for Public Policy Evaluation, Massey University, 1999, p. 90.

31 Zinsmeister, K., 'Fatherhood is Not for Wimps', *The American Enterprise*, September/October 1999.

32 Shipley, J., *Social Assistance: Welfare that Works*, A Statement of Government Policy on Social Assistance, 1991, p. 23.

33 Thomson, *Selfish Generations?*, 1991, p. 12.

34 Lovering, K., *Cost of Children in Australia*, Institute of Family Studies Working Paper No. 8, 1984.

35 Shirley, I., '"In the Name of the Father": Men, Fatherhood and Public Policy', in Birks, S. and Callister, P., *Perspectives on Fathering II*, Issues Paper No. 6, Palmerston North: Centre for Public Policy Evaluation Massey University, 1999.

36 Beaglehole, *Benefiting Women: Income Support for Women, 1893-1993*, 1993.

37 Castles, F.G., 'Needs Based Strategies of Social Protection in Australia and New Zealand', in Esping-Andersen, G., *Welfare States in Transition*, London: Sage Publications, 1996, p. 93.

38 Introduced to New Zealand in 1908. Castles, F.G., *The Working Class and Welfare*, Wellington: Allen & Unwin, 1985.

39 Castles, *The Working Class and Welfare*, 1985, p. 94.

40 Shirley, '"In the Name of the Father": Men, Fatherhood and Public Policy', 1999, p. 3. Official unemployment was actually around ten per cent in the mid-1930s. Since this figure did not include women or men who did not, or could not, claim relief, the real figure may have been around 20 per cent of the labour force. See also Rosenberg, W., 'Full Employment: the Fulcrum of Social Welfare', in Trlin, A.D. (ed.), *Social Welfare and New Zealand Society*, New Zealand: Macmillan, 1977.

41 Castles, F.G., 'Changing Course in Economic Policy: the English-Speaking Nations in the 1980s', in Castles, F.G., *Families of Nations: Patterns of Public Policy in Western Nations*, Aldershot: Dartmouth, 1993.

42 Castles, *The Working Class and Welfare,* 1985.

43   Castles, *The Working Class and Welfare*, 1985, p. 58.

44   Public employees received state housing loans for a 'civil servant on transfer', as well as allowances for removal expenses, and the Government superannuation scheme gave the 1960 trainee an inflation-proofed pension at about two-thirds average salary before retirement (the 1990 trainee will make larger lifetime contributions, and receive less in return). Thomson, *Selfish Generations?*, 1991.

45   Even as the rationale for all this manipulation was being lost, the 1972 Royal Commission on Social Security might still say in relation to unemployment benefit, that the '"disability" from which it is "designed to safeguard the people of New Zealand" is not, like the disabilities of age, sickness, or widowhood, something which is bound to affect a number of people at any one time ... it is a symptom of internal and external factors affecting the economy as a whole. And it is through the working of the whole economy that the State's primary responsibility in this matter will be carried out ...' Royal Commission on Social Security, *Social Security in New Zealand*, Wellington: Report of the Royal Commission of Enquiry, 1972, p. 291.

46   Thomson, *Selfish Generations?*, 1991.

47   Castles, 'Needs Based Strategies of Social Protection in Australia and New Zealand', 1996.

48   Shirley, '"In the Name of the Father": Men, Fatherhood and Public Policy', 1999, p. 3.

49   Thomson, *Selfish Generations?*, 1991, p. 53.

50   Thomson, *Selfish Generations?*, 1991, p. 44.

51   Castles, 'Changing Course in Economic Policy: The English Speaking Nations in the 1980s', 1993, p. 73.

52   Maley, B., *Wedlock and Well Being*, Policy Monographs, Sidney: Centre for Independent Studies, 1996, p. 3.

53   The young family of median income could have bought their home in the 1960s by putting savings equivalent to one year of total net income into the initial purchase, and handing over about 15 per cent of total net income in mortgage repayments in the first year or two.

54   Thomson, *Selfish Generations?*, 1991, pp. 45 and 129.

55   *New Zealand Now: Women*, Wellington: Statistics New Zealand, 1999. A total of 52.4 per cent of women in one-parent families had incomes in the bottom 20 per cent of all family incomes received by women.

56   *New Zealand Now: Families and Households*, 1998.

57   Burgess, S., Gardiner, K. and Propper, C., *Why Rising Tides Don't Lift All Boats? An Examination of the Relationship Between Poverty and Unemployment in Britain*, CASEpaper 46, Economic and Social Research Council, Centre for the Analysis of Social Exclusion, London School of Economics, 2001.

58 *General Household Survey 1996*, London: Office for National Statistics, 1998.

59 Hobcraft, J. and Kiernan, K., *Childhood Poverty, Early Motherhood and Adult Social Exclusion*, CASEpaper 28, Centre for Analysis of Social Exclusion, London School of Economics, 1999.

60 Hobcraft, J., *Intergenerational and Life-Course Transmission of Social Exclusion: Influences of Childhood Poverty, Family Disruption, and Contact with the Police*, CASEpaper 15, STICERD Centre for Analysis of Social Exclusion, London School of Economics, 1998.

61 Smock, P.J., 'The Economic Costs of Marital Disruption for Young Women over the Past Two Decades', *Demography*, Vol. 30, No. 3, August 1993, pp. 353-71. Other comparisons of white US divorced and married women show a gap in family income of an average 22 per cent. Stroup, A.L. and Pollock, G.E., 'Economic Consequences of Marital Disruption', *Journal of Divorce and Remarriage*, 22, 1994, pp. 37-54. Over a half of British women separating from a partner between 1991 and 1996 saw their (equivalised) income fall by one or more fifths, although the other half either had a stable income or saw this rise. From British Household Panel Study, Institute for Social and Economic Research. Quoted in *Social Trends 29*, London: Office for National Statistics 1999; see also Jarvis, S. and Jenkins, S., *Marital Splits and Income Changes: Evidence for Britain*, ESRC Research Centre on Micro-social Change Working Paper 97-4, Colchester: University of Essex 1997.

62 Bianchi, S. and McArthur, E., *Family Disruption and Economic Hardship: The Short Run Picture for Children*, US Bureau of the Census, Current Population Reports, Series P-70, No. 23, Washington DC: US Government Printing Office, 1991.

63 Richardson, I.L.M., 'Family Courts: Some Questions for Consideration', Australasian Family Courts Conference, 16 October 1999.

64 Maxwell, G., 'Children, Parents and the Family Court: Part II', *Family Law Bulletin* 3(5): 50-53 1992.

65 Bailey-Harris, R. (ed.), *Dividing the Assets on Family Breakdown*, Bristol: Family Law, 1998; and Wasoff, F., *Settling Up: Financial and Property Arrangements When Marriages End*, Report of a seminar organised by FPSC and the Nuffield Foundation, FPSC Working Paper 8, 1999.

66 From 1975 to 1993, the proportion of UK two-adult households where both worked rose from 51 to 60 per cent, but the proportion with no earner increased from three to 11 per cent. Gregg, P., Harkness, S. and Machin, S., *Child Development and Family Income*, York: Joseph Rowntree Foundation, 1999; and Hills, *Inquiry into Income and Wealth*, 1995.

67 *Labour Force Survey 1998*, in *Labour Market Trends*, London: ONS The Stationery Office, 1999. Less than two-thirds of children in workless families were in low-income households in 1979, but by 1995/6, almost all children in workless UK families were in households with less than half average income.

68 Across its member states, the OECD notes that around one-third to one-half of all unemployed are living in households where nobody has a job. *Employment Outlook*, Paris: OECD, 1995.

69 Callister, P., '"Work-rich" and "Work-poor" Individuals, Families, Households and Communities: Changes Between 1986 and 1996', Paper presented at the Institute of Policy Studies, Victoria University, Wellington, 23 October 1997.

70 Couples where both were in the age-group 25-59 and who have a child under five had 8.9 per cent with nobody working in 1996, compared with 2.8 in 1986. Among Maori it was 23.1 in 1996.

71 Even in countries where employment of sole parents is higher, the same distinctions are found. About 50 per cent of Australian sole parents were in employment in the mid-1990s, although 58 per cent of couple-families had both parents in the workforce. More than 87 per cent of couple families had at least one parent employed full-time, compared with under 20 per cent of sole-parent families. *Western Australian Child Health Survey*, TVW Telethon Institute for Child Health Research and the Australian Bureau of Statistics, 1996. About 59 per cent of Australian lone parents received the sole parent pension, and/or Jobs, Education and Training (JET) scheme payment.

72 Comment by Easton, B., 'Approaching Family Economic Issues: Holistically or Pathologically?', in *Rights and Responsibilities'*, Papers from the International Year of the Family Symposium on Rights and Responsibilities of the Family held in Wellington, 14 to 16 October 1994. International Year of the Family Committee in association with the Office of the Commissioner for Children, Wellington 1995, p. 94. See also Dornbusch, S., 'Study of Homeless Families', Seminar presented at the Centre for the Study of Children, Families and Youth, Stanford University, Palo Alto, November 1990.

73 UNICEF: 'A League Table of Child Poverty in Rich Nations', *Innocenti Report Card*, No. 1, Florence: UNICEF Innocenti Research Centre, 2000.

74 Stephens, R., 'Poverty in Aotearoa/ New Zealand', *Social Policy and Administration*, Vol. 34, No. 1, 2000; and Stephens, R., Waldegrave, C. and Frater, P., 'Measuring Poverty in New Zealand', *Social Policy Journal of New Zealand*, Issue 5, December 1995, pp. 88-112.

75 Johnstone, K. and Pool, I., 'New Zealand Families: Size, Income and Labour Force Participation', *Social Policy Journal of New Zealand*, Issue 7, December 1996, pp. 143-73.

76 Hobcraft, J., *Intergenerational and Life-Course Transmission of Social Exclusion: Influences of Childhood Poverty, Family Disruption, and Contact with the Police*, CASEpaper 15, 1998. Kiernan, K. and Mueller, G., *Who are the Divorced and Who Divorces?* CASEpaper 7, STICERD Centre for Analysis of Social Exclusion, London School of Economics, 1998; Bane, M.J., 'Household Composition and Poverty', in Danziger, S.H., and Weinberg, D.H., (eds), *Fighting Poverty: What Works and What Does Not*, Harvard University Press, 1986.

77 Beaglehole, *Benefiting Women: Income Support for Women, 1893-1993*, 1993, p. 43.

78 Burgess, S., Gardiner, K. and Propper, C., *Why Rising Tides Don't Lift All Boats? An Examination of the Relationship Between Poverty and Unemployment in Britain'*, CASEpaper 46, Economic and Social Research Council, Centre for the Analysis of Social Exclusion, London School of Economics, 2001.

79 Hernandez, D.J., 'Poverty Trends', in Duncan, G.J. and Brooks-Gunn, J., *Consequences of Growing Up Poor*, New York: Russell Sage Foundation, 1997.

80 Waldegrave, C., 'Balancing the Three E's, Equality, Efficiency, Employment', *Social Policy Journal of New Zealand*, Issue 10, June 1998, p. 9.

81 Fleming, R. and Easting, S.K., *Couples, Households and Money: The Report of the Pakeha Component*, Intra Family Income Project, in association with the Social Policy Research Centre, Massey University, Palmerston North, 1994.

82 Qvirtrup, a childhood perspective applied to Wolfgang Lutz's paper, *Family Issues Between Gender and Generations,* 2000, p. 71.

83 *New Zealand Now: Families and Households*, Wellington: Statistics New Zealand, 1998.

84 Leibowitz, A. and Klerman, J.A., 'Explaining Changes in Married Mothers' Employment Over Time', *Demography*, Vol. 32, No. 3, 1995, pp. 365-78.

85 Hernandez, 'Poverty Trends', 1997. Among married-couple US families in 1949-1959, the median income of families with the wife in the paid labour force was 26 per cent greater than that of families with a non-working wife. This increased to 31 per cent in 1969, 40 per cent in 1979, 57 per cent in 1989, and to 69 per cent in 1993. By then, 12 per cent of children in two-parent families were either living in subsistence poverty despite the mother's paid employment or would have been if the mother had not been working. For relative poverty (income at half the average) it is 20 per cent.

86 Twenty-one per cent of UK married mothers worked full-time in 1992, compared with 41 per cent part-time, while 31 per cent of New Zealand married mothers worked full-time compared with 27 per cent part-time. Mostly work is part time for New Zealand mothers of pre-school children, except for Maori and Pacific Island mothers, who are more likely to work full-time.

87 Schmidt, M.G., 'Gendered Labour Force Participation', in Castles, *Families of Nations: Patterns of Public Policy in Western Nations*, 1993.

88 *New Zealand Now: Women*, Wellington: Statistics New Zealand, 1999.

89 A similar picture pertained for Australia. From 1973 to 1993, labour force participation of women rose ten percentage points to 52 per cent, while the rate for men fell eight points to 74 per cent. While the overall labour

participation rate rose, this disguised a 3.8 per cent fall in the male participation rate between 1982 and 1993/4 and a 7.6 per cent rise in the female, accompanied by a decline in full time work and rise in part time. With unemployment also reaching 10.5 per cent in 1994, the proportion of Australians over 15 in full time jobs actually fell, particularly for males over 50. Harding, A., 'Emerging Trends in Income Inequality in Australia 1982 to 1993/4', Australian Population Association Eighth National Conference, University of Canberra, 6 December 1996.

90   *New Zealand Now: Incomes*, Wellington: Statistics New Zealand, 1998.

91   Millar, J., 'Lone Mothers', in Glendinning, C. and Millar, J. (eds), *Women and Poverty in Britain*, Harvester, 1987.

92   Morgan, G., 'Career Choice and Cost Come Before Children', *The National Business Review*, 5 May 1995.

93   'Real Babies Programme, Stage One: the Truth About Pregnancy', London: The RED Consultancy for Johnson and Johnson, 2000.

94   Ermisch, J., 'Economic Influences on Birthrates', *National Economic Review*, November 1988; and *Fewer Babies, Longer Lives*, York: Joseph Rowntree Foundation, 1990.

95   McAllister, F. and Clarke, L., *Choosing Childlessness*, London: Family Policy Studies Centre, pp. 52-53.

96   Newman, P. and Smith, A., *Social Focus on Families*, Office for National Statistics, London: HMSO, 1997, p. 94.

97   Hobcraft, J. and Kiernan, K., *Becoming a Parent in Europe*, Welfare State Programme/116, London: Suntory-Toyota International Centre for Economics and Related Disciplines, 1995.

98   Lillard, L. and Waite, L.J., 'Marital Childbearing and Marital Disruption', *Demography*, Vol. 30, No. 4, 1993, pp. 653-81.

99   Brinig, M.F. and Crafton, S.M., 'Marriage and Opportunism', *Journal of Legal Studies*, Vol. XXIII, June 1994, pp. 869-94.

4: War is Declared on the Family

1   Ringen, S., *Citizens, Families and Reform*, Oxford: Clarendon Press, pp. 5-6.

2   Report of the Change Team on Targeting Social Assistance, Wellington: Department of the Prime Minister and Cabinet, 1991, p. 15.

3   Castles, F.G., 'Changing Course in Economic Policy: the English-Speaking Nations in the 1980s', in Castles, F.G., *Families of Nations: Patterns of Public Policy in Western Nations*, Aldershot: Dartmouth, 1993, pp. 19-20.

4   Expenditures up to the mid-1980s in New Zealand, as in other English speaking nations, 'can hardly be regarded as a determinant of the challenge to the state premised on the need to reduce state expenditures', since it began to lag behind most other OECD nations after 1960 in terms of all transfer expenditure (on families or otherwise), falling away at the

highest rate for English speaking nations. Castles, 'Changing Course in Economic Policy: the English-Speaking Nations in the 1980s', 1993, p. 14.

5   Stephens, R. and Bradshaw, J., 'The Generosity of New Zealand's Assistance to Families with Dependent Children: An Eighteen Country Comparison', *Social Policy Journal of New Zealand*, Issue 4, 1995, pp. 53-75.

6   Boston, J., Targeting: Social Assistance for All or Just for the Poor?', in Boston, J. and Dalziel, P. (eds), *The Decent Society? Essays in Response to National's Economic and Social Policies*, Auckland: Oxford University Press, 1992, pp. 79-80.

7   Those over 60 in the 1960s had received about four per cent of GDP in the form of war and age pensions, or health services. See also, Thomson, D., *'Cohort Fortunes and Demographic Change in the Twentieth Century'*, Working Paper Series: No. 6, Cambridge: Cambridge Group for the History of Population and Social Structure, 1998.

8   Preston, S.H., 'Children and the Elderly: Divergent Paths for America's Dependents', *Demography*, Vol. 21, No. 4, 1984, pp. 435-54; and Heclo, H., 'The Political Foundations of Anti-Poverty Policy', in Danziger, S.H. and Weinberg, D.H., *Fighting Poverty: What Works and What Does Not*, Harvard University Press, 1986.

9   Report of Domestic Purposes Benefit Review Committee, 1977, E. 28.

10   Johnstone, K. and Pool, I., 'New Zealand Families: Size, Income and Labour Force Participation', *Social Policy Journal of New Zealand*, Issue 7, December 1996, pp. 143-73.

11   Cox, J., 'The Welfare State and the Good Society', *Agenda*, Vol. 4, No. 1 1997, p. 275.

12   Thomson, *'Cohort Fortunes and Demographic Change in the Twentieth Century'*, 1998.

13   Thomson, D., *Selfish Generations*, Wellington: Bridget Williams Books, 1991, p. 124. Society has turned the current elderly 'with few exceptions, into a generation of welfare dependents, although they were never to think of themselves as such, nor were they asked by their society to do so'. Instead, they tend to see themselves as 'having been poorly treated by unhelpful governments in their earlier adult years. ... [and] wont to contrast their own "self-made" lives with those of their youthful successors who are accused of welfare dependence,' even if they spent little time between entering the workforce and producing children, or in a 'positive' income tax phase in early adult life (p. 54).

14   Thomson, *Selfish Generations*, 1991, p. 215.

15   Castles and Mitchell, 'Worlds of Welfare and Families of Nations', in Castles, *Families of Nations: Patterns of Public Policy in Western Nations*, 1993.

16 Government expenditure on housing claimed about three per cent of GDP through the 1950s and 1960s, as much as all spending on age pensions. The fraction of national income going to housing dropped below one per cent in the 1990s as public housing was sold off.

17 Thomson, D., *A World Without Welfare: New Zealand's Colonial Experiment,* Auckland: Auckland University Press with Bridget Williams Books, 1998.

18 Quoted in Castles, F.G., *The Working Class and Welfare*, Wellington: Allen & Unwin, 1985, p. 14.

19 Lovering, K., *Cost of Children in Australia*, Institute of Family Studies, Working Paper No. 8, 1984.

20 Thomson, *Selfish Generations?*, 1991, p. 40.

21 Quoted in Burgess, A., 'The Erosion of an Institution: the Place of Marriage in the Law 1850-Today', unpublished manuscript.

22 Thomson, *Selfish Generations?*, 1991, p. 26.

23 Carlson, A.C., *Family Questions*, New Jersey: Transaction Inc., 1988, p. xvii.

24 Rich, A., 'The Health of Women Living in the Home and Caring for Young Children', presented at the Women's Health Conference, Massey University, November 1990.

25 Ryan, A., 'From Moralism to Sexual Democracy', in Jesson, B., Ryan, A. and Spoonley, P., *Revival of the Right,* Auckland: Heinemann Reed, 1988, p. 121.

26 Ryan, A., 'Remoralising Politics', in Jesson *et al*, *Revival of the Right,* 1988, p. 65.

27 Particularly if you are middle class, or white, not a teenager or lone parent, or do not live in the developing world, then there is something not quite right about parenthood. Pool, I., 'Family Demographic Changes: Good News or Bad News?', in Smith, A.B. and Taylor, N.J., *Supporting Children and Parents through Family Changes,* Dunedin: University of Otago, 1996.

28 Cameron, J., 'Transition to the No-child "Family": Cultural Constraints in the New Zealand Context', *New Zealand Population Review* 12(1): 1986, pp. 4-17.

29 Cameron, 'Transition to the No-child "Family": Cultural Constraints in the New Zealand Context', 1986, p. 4.

30 Cameron, 'Transition to the No-child "Family": Cultural Constraints in the New Zealand Context', 1986, pp. 15-16.

31 Castles, F.G., 'Needs Based Strategies of Social Protection in Australia and New Zealand', in Esping-Andersen, G., *Welfare States in Transition,* London: Sage Publications, 1996, p. 111.

32   Jesson. B., 'The Libertarian Right' in Jesson *et al, Revival of the Right*, 1988, p. 33.

33   Armstrong, N., 'State', in Spoonley, P., Pearson, D. and Shipley, I. (eds), *New Zealand Society*, Palmerston North: Dunmore Press Ltd, 1994, p. 124.

34   Armstrong, 'State', 1994, p. 127.

35   Sullivan, L. and Sullivan, B., 'Family Incomes: a Matter of Survival', *New Weekly*, 9 January 1999. Background and Working Papers in Labor's Social Security Review tested possible policies against the standard of whether they would make it easier for mothers to stay at home, but they were rejected by the 'femocrats' working with the review.

36   Cook, H.M., 'Towards a Feminist Theoretical Framework for the Politics of Child Care', in Milroy, P. (ed.), *Third Early Childhood Convention 1983*, Hamilton: 3rd Early Childhood Convention Committee, 1984, p. 22.

37   McPherson M.J., *Divorce in New Zealand*, Palmerston North: Social Policy Research Centre Massey University, 1995, p. 57.

38   Saville-Smith, K., Bray, M., Davidson, C. and Field, A., *Bringing Home the Bacon: The Changing Relationship between Family, State, and Market in New Zealand in the 1980s*, Family and Societal Change Report No. 3, Wellington: New Zealand Institute for Social Research and Development Ltd, 1994, p. 1.

39   Shirley, I., 'New Zealand: The Advance of the New Right', in Taylor, I., *The Social Effects of Free Market Policies*, Hemel Hempstead: Harvester Wheatsheaf, 1990, p. 369, referring to the writings of Le Grand.

40   Sullivan and Sullivan, 'Family Incomes: a Matter of Survival', 1999.

41   Fukuyama, F., *The End of Order*, London: The Social Market Foundation, 1997.

42   Gilling, M., 'Family', *New Zealand Today*, Vol. IV, Social Perspectives Report of The Royal Commission on Social Policy, Wellington, 1988, p. 597.

43   Briar, C., 'Problems in the New Zealand Family', in Green, P.F. (ed.), *Studies in New Zealand Social Problems*, Palmerston North: Dunmore Press, 1994, 2nd edn, p. 268.

44   Ryan, 'Remoralising Politics', 1988, pp. 72-73 and 74-75.

45   Davidson, C., 'The "Family" in New Zealand', *New Zealand Population Review*, 17 (2) 1990, p. 23.

46   Briar, 'Problems in the New Zealand Family', 1994, p. 269.

47   Chappe, S., 'Fatherhood and the New Zealand Population "Problem": An Economist's View', in Shirley, I., '"In the Name of the Father": Men, Fatherhood and Public Policy', in Birks, S. and Callister, P., *Perspectives on Fathering II*, Issues Paper No. 6, Palmerston North: Centre for Public Policy Evaluation Massey University, 1999, p. 85.

48 Scruton, R., *The Meaning of Conservatism*, Penguin, 1980.

49 Chappe, 'Fatherhood and the New Zealand Population "Problem"', in Shirley, '"In the Name of the Father": Men, Fatherhood and Public Policy', 1999, p. 86.

50 *Making Provision for Retirement: Findings of the Survey of Retirement Provision*, Department of Statistics, 1992. Moreover, people may then return in later age, having spent a significant portion of their adult life elsewhere. Their future welfare demands will be substantial, boosting the population while consuming its resources.

51 Popenoe, D., 'The National Family Wars', *Journal of Marriage and the Family*, Vol. 55, August 1993, pp. 553-55.

52 Parsons, T., *The Social System*, Free Press, 1951.

53 Fergusson D., 'Family Formation, Dissolution and Reformation', in *Proceedings of the SSRFC Symposium: New Zealand Families in the Eighties and Nineties*, Canterbury University, No. 20, November 1987, pp. 15-30, p. 28.

54 Buckingham, A., 'Is There an Underclass in Britain?', *British Journal of Sociology*, Vol. 50, Issue 1, 1999, pp. 49-75.

55 Levinger, G., 'A Social Psychological Perspective on Marital Dissolution', in Levinger, G. and Moles, O.C. (eds), *Divorce and Separation*, New York: Basic Books, 1979; Levinger, G., 'Marital Cohesiveness and Dissolution: Integrative Review', *Journal of Marriage and the Family*, Vol. 27, 1965, pp. 19-28. Booth, A., Johnson, D. and Edwards, J., 'Measuring Marital Stability', *Journal of Marriage and the Family*, Vol. 45, pp. 387-94; Booth, A., Johnson, D., White, L. and Edwards, J., 'Predicting Divorce and Permanent Separation', *Journal of Family Issues*, Vol. 7, pp. 421-42; and Becker, G.S., *A Treatise on the Family*, Cambridge, Mass: Harvard University Press, 1981.

5: When Men Don't Bring Home the Bacon

1 Warin, J., *et al.*, *Fathers, Work and Family Life*, London: Family Policy Studies Centre, 1999.

2 Warin, *Fathers, Work and Family Life*, 1999, p. 13.

3 Haller, M., 'Family and Gender Roles in Macrosocial Constraints and Cultural Contradictions: a Comparative Analysis of Attitudes and Their Recent Changes in 20 Countries', in Nave-Herz, R. and Richter, R. (eds), *New Qualities in Family Life*, Wurzburg: Ergon Verlag, 1999.

4 Hakim, C., Models of the Family, Women's Role and Social Policy: a New Perspective from Preference Theory', *European Societies* 1(1) 1999 p. 43; see also De Vaus, D., 'Values Nineties, Gap or Generation Gap?', *Family Matters*, Spring/ Summer 1997. Although only a minority of Australian women in their 20s and 30s believe that a husband's job is to earn money and the wife's to look after the family, at least two-thirds believe that a woman should stay at home, or at least not work full-time when young children are in the household.

5   Wilson, W.J. and Neckerman, K.M., 'Poverty and Family Structure', in
     Danziger, S.H. and Weinberg, D.H. (eds), *Fighting Poverty: What Works
     and What Does Not*, Cambridge, Mass: Harvard University Press, 1986;
     and Wilson, W.J., 'Research and the Truly Disadvantaged', in Jencks, C.
     and Peterson, P.E. (eds), *The Urban Underclass*, Washington DC: The
     Brookings Institution, 1991. Slack, P., *Poverty and Policy in Tudor and
     Stuart England*, Longmans, 1988.

6   Rowlingson, K. and McKay, S., *The Growth of Lone Parenthood*, London:
     Policy Studies Institute, 1998, p. 82.

7   Rodgers, H. Jr, *Poor Women, Poor Children: American Poverty in the
     Nineties*, New York: M.E. Sharpe, 1996.

8   Warin, *Fathers, Work and Family Life*, 1999, p. 18.

9   Duncan, G.J. and Hoffman, S.D., 'Teenage Underclass Behaviour and
     Subsequent Poverty: Have the Rules Changed?', in Jencks and Peterson,
     The Urban Underclass, 1991.

10   Mare, R.D. and Winship, C., 'Socioeconomic Change and the Decline of
     Marriage for Blacks and Whites', in Jencks and Peterson, *The Urban
     Underclass*, 1991.

11   Ahlburg, D.A. and De Vita, C.J., 'New Realities of the American Family',
     Population Bulletin, 47, No. 2, 1992, p. 15.

12   Mare and Winship, 'Socioeconomic Change and the Decline of Marriage
     for Blacks and Whites', 1991.

13   Quoted in Marano, H.E., 'A New Focus on Family Values', *Psychology
     Today*, November 1997.

14   Sassler, S. and Schoen, R., 'The Effect of Attitudes and Economic Activity
     on Marriage', *Journal of Marriage and the Family*, Vol. 61, 1999,
     pp. 147-59.

15   Garfinkel, I. and McLanahan, S., *Single Mothers and Their Children: a
     New American Dilemma*, Washington DC: The Urban Institute Press,
     1986.

16   Hernandez, D.J., *America's Children: Resources from Family,
     Government, and the Economy*, New York: Russell Sage Foundation,
     1993.

17   *Census of Population and Dwellings*, Statistics New Zealand, 1998; and
     Birrell, B. and Rapson, V., *A Not So Perfect Match: the Growing
     Male/Female Divide 1986-1996*, Centre for Population and Urban
     Research, Monash University, 1998. In Australia, the proportion of men
     aged 25-44 not working full-time, and either out of the labour force or
     working part-time, rose from 24 per cent in 1986 to 31 per cent by 1996.
        Increasing income inequality in New Zealand meant that between 1981
     and 1994, the real disposable income for earners at the bottom end of the
     income scale declined by 7.5 per cent for the lowest 20 per cent, as the top
     increased by much the same. The top 20 per cent increased 8.6 per cent.
     In Australia, the decline in men with earnings close to the median for full

time employees (between 75 and 125 per cent), is accompanied by increases in those earning between 50 to 75 per cent, and over 125 per cent of the median. As earnings at the bottom declined with increasing inequality (mainly in market incomes), these trends are another aspect of the 'hollowing of the middle'. Harding, A., *Emerging Trends in Income Inequality in Australia 1982 to 1993/4*, Australian Population Association Eighth National Conference, University of Canberra, 6 December 1996. Between 1973 and 1993, the real hourly wage of Americans without a high school diploma fell by almost a third. Since 1979, average weekly earnings of college graduates in America have risen by more than 30 per cent relative to those of high school graduates. The gap between college graduates and high-school drop-outs has grown by twice as much. In the UK, between a third and a half of the growth in earnings dispersion over the 1980s can be explained by higher wage premiums commanded by greater levels of experience and/or educational qualifications. Kapstein, E.B., 'Workers and the World Economy', *Foreign Affairs*, May/June 1996, pp. 16-351. See also Gregory, R.G., *Competing with Dad: Changes in the Intergenerational Distribution of Male-Labour Force Market Income*, Discussion paper No. 400, Centre for Economic Policy Research, Australian National University, May 1999.

18   In the UK, the proportion of men aged 18-24 in work similarly fell from 86 to 73 per cent between 1979 and 1992 and is only partly explained by longer education. In the mid-1970s, 7.5 per cent of males aged 20-24 were unemployed, but more than double, or over 16 per cent, from the mid-1980s. The unemployment rate for female 20-24-year-olds had, meanwhile, fallen back to its mid-1970s level, or around nine per cent in 1996. The proportion of all non-student men of working age with no qualifications who were entirely economically inactive (neither in nor actively seeking work) rose from nearly five per cent to nearly 29 per cent between 1977 and 1997. Labour Force Survey, 1975-77, 1986 and 1996. Hills, J., *Inquiry into Income and Wealth: a Summary of the Evidence*, Vol. 2, York: Joseph Rowntree Foundation, 1995.

19   Dixon, S., 'Labour Force Participation Over the Last Ten Years', *Labour Market Bulletin*, 2, 1996, pp. 71-88.

20   Connell, R.W., 'Live Fast and Die Young: the Construction of Masculinity Among Young Working-class Men on the Margin of the Labour Market', *Australian and New Zealand Journal of Sociology*, Vol. 27, No. 2, 1991, p. 142.

21   Testa, M., 'Joblessness and Absent Fatherhood in the Inner City', Paper presented at the annual meeting of the American Sociological Association, 1990, p. 22, quoted in Wilson, W.J., 'Research and the Truly Disadvantaged', in Jencks and Peterson, *The Urban Underclass*, 1991, p. 468.

22   Busfield, J. and Paddon, M., *Thinking About Children*, Cambridge, UK, 1977.

23   Dennis, N. and Erdos, G., *Families without Fatherhood*, London: IEA Health and Welfare Unit, 1992, p. 70.

24 Wilson, W.J., *When Work Disappears: New Implications for Race and Urban Poverty in the Global Economy*, CASEpaper 17, Centre for Analysis of Social Exclusion, 1998, p. 11.

25 Dex, S. (ed.), *Families and the Labour Market*, London: Family Policy Study Centre for the Joseph Rowntree Foundation, 1999, p. 22.

26 For men, there were nearly 3,000 jobs lost in packing and freight handling between 1991 and 1996, while women increased their numbers by over 600. While there was a small decline in labouring work for men, women increased their numbers by over 800. Examples in Callister, P., '"Work-rich" and "Work-poor" Individuals, Families, Households and Communities: Changes Between 1986 and 1996', Paper presented at the Institute of Policy Studies, Victoria University, Wellington, 23 October 1997.

27 Birrell and Rapson, *A Not So Perfect Match*, 1998.

28 Lichter, D.T. *et al.*, 'Race and the Retreat from Marriage: a Shortage of Marriageable Men?', *American Sociological Review*, 57, 1992, pp. 781-99.

29 Grossbard-Shechtman, S., *On the Economics of Marriage: a Theory of Marriage, Labor and Divorce*, Boulder, Colorado: Westview Press, 1993.

30 Trent, K. and South, S.J., 'Structural Determinants of the Divorce Rate: a Cross-societal Analysis', *Journal of Marriage and the Family*, Vol. 51, pp. 391-404, 1989; and Trent, K. and South, S.J., 'Sex Ratios and Women's Roles: a Cross National Analysis, *American Journal of Sociology*, Vol. 93, 1998, pp. 1096-115. As the first large babyboom cohort reached reproductive age, this not only put pressure on labour markets, but—due to a decrease in the ratio of males to females at the appropriate ages (as a smaller, older male cohort is followed by a larger female cohort), women are short of prospective partners slightly older than themselves. Jackson, N. and Pool, I., *Fertility and Family Formation in the 'Second Demographic Transition': New Zealand Patterns and Trends*, Family and Social Change: Research Report No. 2, Christchurch: New Zealand Institute for Social Research & Development Ltd, 1994.

31 Employment Audit 1998.

32 Haskey, J., 'Social Class and Socio-economic Differentials in Divorce in England and Wales', *Population Studies*, Vol. 38, No. 3, 1984, pp. 419-38; Lampard, R., 'An Examination of the Relationship Between Marital Dissolution and Unemployment', Social Change and Economic Life Institute, Working Paper 17, 1990; Murphy, M.J., 'Demographic and Socio-economic Influence on Recent British Marital Breakdown Patterns', *Population Studies*, Vol. 39, No. 3, 1985. See also Cameron, S., 'A Review of Economic Research into Determinants of Divorce', *British Review of Economic Issues*, Vol. 17, No. 41, 1995, pp. 1-22.

33 Rowlingson, K. and McKay, S., *The Growth of Lone Parenthood*, London: Policy Studies Institute, 1998.

34 Böheim, R. and Ermisch, J., 'Breaking Up: Financial Surprises and Partnership', paper presented at the Royal Economic Society Conference, 1999, Nottingham; and Boheim, R. and Ermisch, J., *Analysis of the Dynamics of Lone-Parent Families,* Institute for Social and Economic Research, Working Paper 98-8, University of Essex, 1998.

35 Wertheimer, A. and McRae, S., 'Family and Household Change in Britain; a Summary of Findings from Projects in the ESRC Population and Household Change Programme', Centre for Family and Household Research, Oxford Brookes University, 1999.

36 See, for example, Hoffman, S.D. and Duncan, G.J., 'The Effect of Incomes, Wages and AFDC Benefits on Marital Disruption', *The Journal of Human Resources*, Vol. 30, 1995, pp.19-41.

37 Birrell and Rapson, *A Not So Perfect Match*, 1998.

38 Levinger, 'Cohesiveness at the Brink', in Levinger, G. and Moles, O.C. (eds), *Divorce and Separation*, New York: Basic Books, 1979.

39 See Fustenberg, Jr, F.F., 'Premarital Pregnancy and Marital Stability', in Levinger, and Moles, *Divorce and Separation*, 1979; and Kiernan, K.E., 'Teenage Marriage and Marital Breakdown: a Longitudinal Study', *Population Studies*, Vol. 40, No. 1, 1986, pp. 35-54.

40 Burgoyne, J., *Unemployment and Married Life*, London: Unemployment Unit Bulletin, 1985.

41 Patterson, S.M., *Divorce in New Zealand*, Wellington: Department of Justice, 1976.

42 Booth, A., Johnson, D.R. and White, L.K., 'Divorce and Marital Instability Over the Life Course', *Journal of Family Issues*, Vol. 7, No. 4, December 1986, pp. 421-42.

43 Collard, J. and Thornes, B., *Who Divorces?*, London: Routledge and Kegan Paul, 1979. The duration of marriages of wives who worked because they needed the money was much shorter than for those who did not work, or did so from personal choice for an outside interest. See also Lewis, S.N.C. and Cooper C.L., 'Stress in Two-earner Couples and Stage in the Life Cycle', *Journal of Occupational Psychology*, Vol. 60, 1987, pp. 289-303; also Goldberg, W.A. and Easterbrooks, M.A., 'Maternal Employment When Children are Toddlers and Kindergartners', in Gottfried, A.E. *et al.* (eds), *Maternal Employment, Family Environment, and Children's Development: Infancy Through the School Years,* Plenum Press, 1988; also Tzeng, M., 'The Effects of Socio-economic Heterogamy and Changes on Marital Dissolution for First Marriages', *Journal of Marriage and the Family*, Vol. 54, 1992, pp. 609-19. The British Women and Employment Survey showed how mothers who had been employed 80 per cent of the time since giving birth had roughly double the probability of divorce compared with mothers who did not work. Ermisch, J., *Lone Parenthood*, Cambridge University Press, 1991.

44   One study showed how 'marrying out' of welfare occurred for only 13 per
      cent of American lone parents on public assistance over a three-year
      period in the 1980s. Rank, M.R., 'The Formation and Dissolution of
      Marriages in the Welfare Population', *Journal of Marriage and the
      Family*, Vol. 49, 1987, pp. 15-20.

45   With just 11 per cent of cohabitees in the top quintile, compared with 21
      per cent of married-couple families. Thirteen per cent of cohabiting
      fathers and 46 per cent of mothers in 1991 were not working compared
      with seven and 36 per cent of married fathers and mothers. Neither was
      working in 9.4 of cases, compared with 4.5 per cent for married couples.
      Twenty-seven per cent of cohabiting fathers received the unemployment
      benefit at some time in the year prior to the 1991 census, compared with
      ten per cent of married fathers. Family support was paid to over a third of
      cohabiting mothers, compared with 18 per cent of married mothers. *New
      Zealand Now: Families*, Wellington: Statistics New Zealand, 1994.

46   See, for example: *Fiscal Year Department of Social Welfare Statistics
      Report*, Wellington: Department of Social Welfare, 1996.

47   In Australian data, 20 per cent of cohabiting couples with children
      received unemployment benefits in the year before study compared with
      three per cent of married couples with children. Quoted in *To Have and
      To Hold: a Report of the Inquiry into Aspects of Family Services*,
      Canberra: House of Representatives Standing Committee on Legal and
      Constitutional Affairs, June 1998.

48   Manning, W.D. and Lichter, D.T., 'Parental Cohabitation and Children's
      Economic Well-being', *Journal of Marriage and the Family*, Vol. 58, 1996,
      pp. 998-1010.

49   British studies report almost identical results. In the Family Resources
      Survey, average weekly income for younger cohabiting men with children
      was almost a third lower than for married fathers, and 32 per cent of the
      younger male cohabitees with children were on income support compared
      with 13 per cent of married fathers. In the older group it was 22 compared
      with eight per cent. Average weekly income for younger cohabiting men
      under 39 with children was almost a third lower than for married fathers,
      who also had significantly higher hourly wage rates. Over a half of cohab-
      iting mothers in another study of 1992 had household incomes in the
      lowest ranges; a quarter lived in households where nobody was employed
      and one-fifth had a partner who had been unemployed for over two years.
      Kiernan, K. and Mueller, G., *The Divorced and Who Divorces?*
      CASEpaper, CASE/7, Centre for Analysis of Social Exclusion, May 1998.
      See also McRae, S., *Cohabiting Mothers*, London: Policy Studies Institute,
      1993. Similar results were obtained from General Household Survey data
      of 1989. While 93 per cent of men in married-couple families were
      working, this applied to only 77 per cent of male cohabitees with children.
      Kiernan, K.E. and Estaugh, V., *Cohabitation: Extra Marital Childbearing
      and Social Policy*, London: Family Policy Studies Centre, 1993.

50 Lingxin, H., 'Family Structure, Private Transfers, and the Economic Well-being of Families with Children', *Social Forces*, Vol. 75, September 1996, pp. 269-92.

51 Amato, P.R. and Booth, A., *A Generation at Risk*, Cambridge, Mass: Harvard University Press, 1997.

52 Ermisch, J. and Francesconi, M., *Cohabitation in Great Britain: Not for Long, but Here to Stay*, Institute for Social and Economic Research, University of Essex, 1998.

53 Santow, G. and Bracher, M., 'Change and Continuity in the Formation of First Marital Unions in Australia', *Population Studies*, Vol. 48, No. 3, 1994, pp. 475-96.

54 Smart, C. and Stevens, P., *Cohabitation Breakdown*, London: Family Policy Studies Centre, 2000. Many women in this study had kept their tenancies in their own names, not only to preserve their housing security in the eventuality of a break-up, but because they did not wish it to appear to Social Security that they were cohabiting. They ensured that the male 'partner' had a different address.

55 Maclean, M. and Eekelaar, J., *The Parental Obligation*, Oxford: Hart Publishing, 1997. Many more of the formerly married fathers in this UK study were employed before separation than the former cohabitees (or 77 per cent in full-time work as against only 55 per cent of the former cohabitees). This is lower than the 93 per cent for all married fathers with dependent children given for 1989, and lower than in other samples of cohabitees, but consistent with the evidence that both marital and cohabitation breakdowns rise as men's employment falls.

56 Maclean and Eekelaar, *The Parental Obligation*, 1997, p. 143.

57 See also, Maclean and Eekelaar, *The Parental Obligation*, 1997, p. 143.

58 Speak, S., Cameron, S. and Gilroy, R., *Young Single Fathers: Participation in Fatherhood*, Family Policy Studies Centre, 1997, p. 6.

59 Moynihan, D.P., *The Negro Family: the Case for National Action*, Washington DC: US Department of Labor, 1965; Wilson, W.J., *The Truly Disadvantaged*, Chicago: University of Chicago Press, 1987.

60 Hernandez, D.J., 'Poverty Trends', in Duncan, G.J. and Brooks-Gunn, J., *Consequences of Growing Up Poor*, New York: Russell Sage Foundation, 1997.

61 Sampson, R.J., 'Urban Black Violence: the Effect of Male Joblessness and Family Disruption', *American Journal of Sociology*, Vol. 93, No. 2, 1987, pp. 348-82.

62 'Strategy Paper on Crime Prevention', Crime Prevention Action Group, Department of Prime Minister and Cabinet, Wellington, 1992.

63 *Maori in the New Zealand Economy*, Wellington: Ministry of Maori Development, 1999.

64 *Statistics New Zealand, Household Labour Force Statistics: December 2002 Quarter*, Wellington: Statistics New Zealand.

65 *Maori*, Wellington: Statistics New Zealand, 1998.

66 Overall, Maori men's real median income fell from $21,200 in 1986 to $16,100 in 1996 (at 1996 levels), as the real median income of non-Maori men also fell from $26,200 to $22,900. Maori real median income was 88.7 per cent of the median income of non-Maori in 1986, falling to 75.5 per cent in 1991, and improving to only 79.3 per cent in 1996. The differences were affected by factors such as occupation, sex, age and benefit receipt. The median income for full-time employed men was $27,461 in 1996, but for Maori men it was $22,750. *Incomes*, Statistics New Zealand, 1998.

67 The proportion of Maori in the lowest income quartile increased from 28.4 per cent in 1986 to 33.8 per cent in 1991, in parallel with the increase in unemployment, before dropping back to 30.9 per cent in 1996. *Maori*, Wellington: Statistics New Zealand, 1998.

68 *Maori*, Statistics New Zealand, 1998.

69 'Strategy Paper on Crime Prevention', Department of Prime Minister and Cabinet, 1992.

70 McLanahan, S. and Sandefur, G., *Growing Up With a Single Parent*, Cambridge, Mass: Harvard University Press, 1994.

71 Shackleton, J.R. and Urwin, P., 'Men and the Labour Market', in *Women or Men: Who are the Victims?*, Civitas, 2001, p. 17.

72 Buckingham, A., 'Is there an underclass in Britain?', *Journal of Sociology*, No. 50, Issue 1, 1999, p. 65.

73 Warin, J., *et al.*, *Fathers, Work and Family Life* London: Family Policy Studies Centre, 1999, p. 40.

74 Warin, *Fathers, Work and Family Life*, 1999, p. 17.

75 Warin, *Fathers, Work and Family Life*, 1999, p. 9. See also Lloyd, T., *Young Men, the Job Market and Gendered Work*, Work and Opportunity Series No. 8, York: Joseph Rowntree Foundation, 1999.

76 Dench, G., *The Place of Men in Changing Family Cultures*, London: Institute of Community Studies, 1996, p. 2.

77 Callister, P., 'Iron John or Ironing John? The Changing Lives of New Zealand Fathers', in Birks, S. and Callister, P., *Perspectives on Fathering*, Issues Paper No. 4, Palmerston North: Massy University, 1999.

78 Lloyd, *Young Men, the Job Market and Gendered Work*, 1999, p. 26.

79 Edgar, D. 'How the Baby Boom Backfired' in *The Bulletin*, 29 January/5 February 1991, pp. 148-50.

80 Black, M.M., Dubowitz, H. and Starr, R.H., 'African American Fathers in Low Income, Urban Families: Development, Behaviour, and Home Environment of Their Three-Year Old Children', *Child Development*, Vol. 70, No. 4, pp. 978-79.

226 FAMILY MATTERS

81 Bayler, N. and Brooks-Gunn, J., 'Effects of Maternal Employment and Child-Care Arrangements on Preschoolers' Cognitive and Behavioural Outcomes: Evidence from the Children of the National Longitudinal Survey of Youth', *Developmental Psychology*, Vol. 27, No. 6, 1991, pp. 932-45.

82 Speak, Cameron and Gilroy, *Young Single Fathers: Participation in Fatherhood*, 1997, p. 23.

83 Speak, Cameron and Gilroy, *Young Single Fathers: Participation in Fatherhood*, 1997, p. 22.

84 Dench, *The Place of Men in Changing Family Cultures*, 1996 p. 36.

85 Berthoud, R., *Young Caribbean Men and the Labour Market: a Comparison With Other Groups*, Work and Opportunity Series No. 16, York: Joseph Rowntree Foundation, 1999.

86 Warin, *Fathers, Work and Family Life*, 1999, p. 15.

87 Ritchie, J.E., *The Making of a Maori*, Wellington: A.H & A.W. Reed, 1963, p. 78.

88 Simms, M. and Smith, C., 'Young Fathers: Attitudes to Marriage and Family Life', in McKee, L. and O'Brien, M. (eds), *The Father Figure*, Tavistock, 1982, pp. 147-48.

89 Mansfield, P. and Collard, J., *The Beginning of the Rest of Your Life*, London: Macmillan, pp. 141-42.

90 Ritchie, *The Making of a Maori*, 1963, p. 77.

91 Dixon, S., 'Labour Force Participation Over the Last Ten Years', *Labour Market Bulletin*, 2, New Zealand: Department of Labour, 1996, pp. 71-88.

92 Berthoud, *Young Caribbean Men and the Labour Market*, 1999.

93 Meadows, P., *Young Men on the Margins of Work: an Overview Report'*, York Publishing Services: Joseph Rowntree Foundation, 2001.

94 Berthoud, R., *Family Formation in Multi-cultural Britain: Three Patterns of Diversity*, Institute for Social and Economic Research, Essex University, 1999.

95 Rosenberg, W., 'Full Employment: The Fulcrum of Social Welfare', in Trlin, A.D. (ed.), *Social Welfare and New Zealand Society*, 1977. In 1981, nearly a third of men becoming unemployed were divorced or separated. Daniel, W., *The Unemployed Flow*, London: Policy Studies Institute, 1981.

96 Teachman, J., Call, D., Vaughn, R.A. and Carver, K.P., 'Marital Status and the Duration of Joblessness Among White Men', *Journal of Marriage and the Family*, Vol. 56, 1994, pp. 415-28.

97 Of all prime age men employed full time, 77 per cent are in a couple (of which 65 per cent were legally married for the first time), compared with 51 per cent of non-participants (and only 58 per cent of these are in couples where both partners are legally married for the first time). In 1987, around 97 per cent of married males aged 25-54 were labour-

market participants, compared with over 91 per cent of never-married men, and 68 compared with 58 per cent for those aged 55-65. Ten years on, nearly 95 per cent of married men were labour-force participants in the younger age group, compared with nearly 85 per cent for the never-married (this likely understates participation rates for married men, since the category includes cohabitees). In the older 55- to 65-year-old group, the fall is from over 70 per cent to nearly 52 per cent for the previously married down to nearly 39 per cent for the never-married. Dixon, 'Labour Force Participation Over the Last Ten Years', 1996, pp. 71-88. Harris, R., 'Ethnicity, Gender and Labour Supply in New Zealand in 1986', *New Zealand Economic Papers*, 26 (2) pp. 199-218, 1992.

98   Callister, P., 'The "Meet" Market: Education and Assortative Mating Patterns in New Zealand', *The New Zealand Population Review*, 24, 1998, pp. 43-70.

99   Dixon, 'Labour Force Participation Over the Last Ten Years', 1996, pp. 71-88.

100 Callister, P., 'No Job, No Wife?: Fathers, Paid Work and Changes in Living Arrangements in New Zealand', Callister, P. and Birks, S. (eds), *Perspectives on Fathering*, Issue Paper No. 6, Palmerston North: Centre for Public Policy Evaluation, Massey University, 1999; also Kiernan, K. and Mueller, G., *The Divorced and Who Divorces?*, CASEpaper, CASE/7, Centre for Analysis of Social Exclusion, May 1998.

101 As well as being less educated and low wage workers, only 44 per cent of 19-54-year-old nonparticipants (as opposed to 70 per cent of the overall group), were married and living with a spouse in samples from the 1980s. Welch, F., 'The Employment of Black Men', *Journal of Labor Economics*, VIII, 1990, S26-S74. In turn, single men aged 20-24, with just 12 years of education, were more than three times as likely to be out of work than married men of the same educational status in the early 1990s. The proportion of such men working a full year was almost 40 per cent greater if married, while a single man was 50 per cent more likely to be unemployed because he had quit his last job—and twice as likely if he was over 25. Akerlof, G., 'Men Without Children', *The Economic Journal*, Vol. 108, 1998, pp. 287-309.

102 Kiernan and Mueller, *The Divorced and Who Divorces?*, 1998. Evidence from the British Household Panel Study showed how 27 per cent of single men aged 25-39 were out of the labour force, together with 30 per cent of the childless divorced, compared with seven per cent of married childless men.

103 Ferri, E. (ed.), *Life at 33*, National Childrens' Bureau, 1993.

104 Research into non-resident fathers in Britain revealed how only two-thirds were in employment compared with over 80 per cent of resident fathers, and only about a half of those unemployed were looking for any work. Only about 15 per cent of fathers not paying child support had any clear paying potential. In Australia, nearly a half of sole-parent pensioners with children aged 0-15 years receive no maintenance at all, mainly because of the low income of the fathers, who are often benefit

recipients. 'Non-resident Fathers in Britain Research Results', No. 14, Oxford: Economic and Social Research Council, 1999.

105 Dench, G., *The Place of Men in Changing Family Cultures*, London: Institute of Community Studies, 1996, p. 24. See also, Bradshaw, J. and Stimson, C., 'Non-resident Fathers in Britain', in Werthheimer, A. and McRae, S., *Research Results*, Economic and Social Research Council Centre for Family and Household Research, Oxford Brookes University, 1999.

106 Dench, *The Place of Men in Changing Family Cultures*, 1996, p. 74. Dixon, S., 'Prime-Aged Males Who Are Not in the Labour Force', Department of Labour Occasional Paper Series, Labour Market Policy Group, 1991; see also Harris, R., 'Ethnicity, Gender and Labour Supply in New Zealand in 1986', *New Zealand Economic Papers* 26 (2) 1992, pp. 199-218. US evidence on non-working men, shows substantial support from other household members, who contributed a greater proportion of household income than when men were employed, and more than government transfers. Juhn, C., 'Decline of Male Labour Market Participation: The Role of Declining Market Opportunities', *The Quarterly Journal of Economics*, February 1992, pp. 81-121.

107 Scott, G., 'Active Labour Market Policies: Let's be Careful Out There', *Social Policy Journal of New Zealand*, Issue 5, December 1995, pp. 43-52.

108 Akerlof 'Men Without Children', 1998, pp. 287-309. Korenman, S. and Neumark, D., 'Does Marriage Really make Men More Productive?', *Journal of Human Resources*, Vol. 26, 1991, pp. 282-307; and Loh, E.S., 'Productivity Differences and the Marriage Wage Premium for White Males', *Journal of Human Resources*, Vol. 31, 1996, pp. 566-89.

109 Polachek, S.W. and Siebert, W.S., *The Economics of Earnings*, Cambridge: Cambridge University Press, 1993; and *New Zealand Now: Women*, Statistics New Zealand, 1999.

110 *New Zealand Now: Families and Households*, 1998 edition.

111 Waite, L.J., 'Does Marriage Matter?', *Demography*, Vol. 32, No. 4, November 1995, pp. 483-507; and Daniel, K., 'The Marriage Premium', in Tommasi, M. and Ierulli, K. (eds), *The New Economics of Human Behaviour*, Cambridge University Press, 1996.

112 Korenman, S. and Neumark, D., *Does Marriage Really Make Men More Productive?* Finance and Economics Discussion Series, No. 29, Washington, DC: Division of Research and Statistics, Federal Reserve Board, May 1988.

113 Mansfield, P. and Collard, J., *The Beginning of the Rest of Your Life*, Macmillan, 1988; Arulanpalam, W. and Booth, A.L., 'Labour Market Flexibility and Skills Acquisition: is there a Trade-Off', in Atkinson, A.B. and Hills, J., *Exclusion, Employment and Opportunity*, CASEpaper 4, STICERD Centre for Analysis of Social Exclusion, London School of Economics 1998.

114 See discussion in Christiansen, G.B. and Williams, W.R., 'Welfare, Family Cohesiveness and Out-of-Wedlock Births', in Peden, J.R. and Glahe, F.R. (eds), *The American Family and the State*, San Francisco: Pacific Research Institute, 1986; Garfinkel, I. and Haveman, R., *Earnings Capacity and Inequality*, New York: Academic Press, 1977.

115 See, for example, Gray, J.S., 'The Fall in Men's Return to Marriage: Declining Productivity Effects or Changing Selection?', *Journal of Human Resources*, Vol. 32, 1997, pp. 481-504; Daniel, 'The Marriage Premium', 1996.

116 Lundberg, S. and Elaina, R., 'The Effects of Sons and Daughters on Men's Labor Supply and Wages', Department of Economics, University of Washington, Seattle, 2000.

117 Daniel, 'The Marriage Premium', 1996.

118 Rowthorn, R., 'Marriage and Trust: Some Lessons from Economics', *Cambridge Journal of Economics*, Vol. 23, 1999, pp. 661-91.

119 Waite, L.J., 'Does Marriage Matter?', *Demography*, Vol. 32, No. 4, November 1995, pp. 483-507; and Daniel, 'The Marriage Premium', 1996.

120 Kiernan and Mueller, *The Divorced and Who Divorces?*, 1998.

121 Akerlof, 'Men Without Children', 1998 p. 303; see also Willis, R.J. and Michael, R.T., 'Innovation in Family Formation: Evidence on Cohabitation in the United States', in Ermisch, J. and Ogawa, N. (eds), *The Family, the Market, and the State in Ageing Societies*, Oxford University Press, 1994.

122 Korenman and Neumark, *Does Marriage Really Make Men More Productive?*, 1988. According to UK data, divorced men are up to eight times more likely to enter psychiatric hospitals, and single men nearly three times more likely, than their married counterparts. Divorced individuals of both sexes make five-fold use of outpatient psychiatric services compared with the married, and over one in five divorced and separated men fall into the heaviest drinking category, compared with only seven per cent of married men. Dominian, J. *et al.*, *Marital Breakdown and the Health of the Nation*, London: One Plus One, 1991, pp. 13, 16-17.

123 Clarkberg, M., Stolzenberg, R.M. and Waite, L.J., 'Attitudes, Values, and Entrance into Cohabitational versus Marital Unions', *Social Forces*, 74 (2), p. 610.

124 Carlson, A. 'Liberty, Order and the Family', in Davies, J. (ed.), *The Family: Is It Just Another Lifestyle Choice?* IEA Health and Welfare Unit, 1993, p. 53.

125 A substantial minority of cohabiting couples disagree about the future of their relationship. Such a lack of concordance may affect the quality of the relationship as much as its stability. In the US National Survey of Families and Households a fifth of cohabiting persons did not expect to marry anyone, let alone their current partner, and there was disagreement over whether marriage might occur in about one-fifth of the couples

in which at least one partner expected this. This was higher for cohabitees from previous relationships. These were more inclined to report
trouble in the relationship and decreased plans to marry where their
partner had children by someone else, while cohabitees with their own
children were prone to 'wishful thinking', and had a markedly increased
expectation of marriage to their partner! A sizeable proportion of women
(but not men) fancied that their economic and emotional security would
improve if they married, as would their overall happiness. Bumpass, L.L.,
Sweet, J.A. and Cherlin, A.J., 'The Role of Cohabitation in Declining
Rates of Marriage', *Journal of Marriage and the Family*, Vol. 53, 1991, pp.
913-27.

126 Bernstam, M.S. and Swan P.L., 'Malthus and the Evolution of the
Welfare State: an Essay on the Second Invisible Hand', Working Paper
89-012, Australian Graduate School of Management, University of New
South Wales, 1989.

127 Slack, P., *Poverty and Policy in Tudor and Stuart England*, New York:
Longmans, 1988.

6: Targeting the Needy—and Creating More of Them

1   Bernstam, M.S. and Swan, P.L., 'Brides of the State', *IPA Review*, 41,
May-July 1987, pp. 22-79; Tapper, A., *The Family in the Welfare State*,
Perth: Australian Institute for Public Policy, 1990; Bernstam, M.S. and
Swan, P.L., 'The State as Marriage Partner of Last Resort: a Labour
Market Approach to Illegitimacy in the United States, 1960-1980',
Kensington: Australian Graduate School of Management Working Paper
86-029, 1986.

2   Maley, B., *Marriage, Divorce and Family Justice*, Monograph 25, Sidney:
The Centre for Independent Studies, 1992.

3   Preston, D.A., 'Welfare Benefit Reform', *Social Policy Journal of New
Zealand*, Issue 8, March 1997, pp. 29-36.

4   'Economic Management', Wellington: The Treasury, July 1984, p. 261;
and see Prebble, M. and Rebstock, P. (eds), *Incentives and the Labour
Supply Modelling Taxes and Benefits*, Wellington: Institute of Policy
Studies, 1992.

5   *Government Management I: Brief to the Incoming Government*,
Wellington: Treasury, 1987, p. 445.

6   Shipley, J., *Social Assistance: Welfare that Works*, a Statement of
Government Policy on Social Assistance, 1991, p. 17.

7   Sullivan, L., 'Tax Injustice: Keeping the Family Cap-in-Hand', *Issue
Analysis*, No. 3, Centre for Independent Studies, July 1998, p. 54. It is
calculated that, for example, Australian families of five on 120 per cent of
average earnings, were made hardly better off than those at 50 per cent of
AWE, due to the way that benefits taper off as income rises. Even
equivalent unemployed families received a comparable income. Middle
income earners (75-120 per cent AWE) take in the majority of primary
earners where, as elsewhere, the range of family incomes is not very wide.

Since 'family welfare payments provide incomes equivalent to those
retained after tax by *average* families ... so we must conclude that, if
indeed families at the lower end of the income scale are living in poverty,
then average-income employed families are equally poor. They would
serve their families just as well, in terms of income, if they worked half
time, or not at all.' *Ibid*, p. 7.

8   Preston, D.A., 'Welfare Benefit Reform', *Social Policy Journal of New
    Zealand*, Issue 8, March 1997, p. 33.

9   Pearson, N., 'Positive and Negative Welfare and Australian Indigenous
    Communities', *Family Matters*, Issue No. 54, Spring/Summer 1999, p. 33.

10 Pearson, 'Positive and Negative Welfare and Australia's Indigenous
    Communities', 1999, p. 32.

11 Briar, C., 'Problems in the New Zealand Family', in Green, P.F. (ed.),
    Studies in New Zealand Social Problems, Palmerston North: Dunmore
    Press 1994, 2nd edn, p. 261.

12 Unsurprisingly, 47 per cent of participants in 'Return to Work'
    programmes run in Britain by the National Council for One Parent
    Families in the early 1990s said they would be worse off at work and 27
    per cent complained of the lack of 'well-paid jobs'. *Lone Parents: Their
    Potential in the Workforce, NCOPF National Return to Work Programme:
    A Detailed Report*, London: National Council for One Parent Families,
    1993.

13 Brooks, R., *Male and Female Labour Force Participation in New Zealand
    1978-88*, Reserve Bank Discussion Paper G60/3, Wellington Reserve Bank
    of New Zealand, 1990; see also Maani, S., 'The Unemployment Benefit,
    Unemployment Duration and Wage Requirements of Job Seekers in New
    Zealand', *New Zealand Economic Papers*, 23, 1989, pp. 12-28; and Maani,
    S., 'Post-Unemployment Wages, the Probability of Re-employment and
    the Unemployment Benefit', *New Zealand Economic Papers*, 27, 1992,
    pp. 35-55.

14 Report of the Change Team on Targeting Social Assistance, Wellington:
    Department of the Prime Minister and Cabinet, 1991, p. 6.

15 *Government Management I: Brief to the Incoming Government*, Treasury,
    1987, p. 110.

16 Mackay, R., *Welfare to Work: New Directions in New Zealand*, Social
    Policy Agency, Department of Social Welfare, 1999, p. 33.

17 *Government Management I: Brief to the Incoming Government*, Treasury,
    1987, p. 445.

18 In Britain, with a mixed system of 'targeting', combined with some
    universal reliefs, the majority of gross receipts were self-financed over the
    lifetime by the third income decile. This does not happen until the sixth in
    Australia, which had a primarily social assistance based system.
    Australia had a greater degree of interpersonal distribution, compared
    with intrapersonal distribution, but the British system actually reduced
    the inequality of the original income distribution by more than the

Australian system did. Cash transfers amounted to about 35 per cent of
the gross income of the bottom decile in Britain and 23 per cent in
Australia, even if, for the top decile, the figures were 9 per cent in Britain
and less than 1 per cent in Australia. Health and education were not
included. Falkingham, J. and Harding, A., 'Poverty Alleviation Versus
Social Insurance Systems: a Comparison of Lifetime Redistribution',
Discussion Paper No. 2, National Centre for Social and Economic
Modelling, University of Canberra, 1996.

19   Cox, J., *Middle Class Welfare*, New Zealand Business Roundtable, 2001,
     table 6.7, p. 174.

20   *Government Management I: Brief to the Incoming Government*, Treasury,
     1987, p. 446.

21   Shipley, *Social Assistance: Welfare that Works*, 1991.

22   Shipley, *Social Assistance: Welfare that Works*, 1991, p. 48.

23   *From Welfare to Well-being*, Wellington: Department of Social Welfare,
     1997, pp. 16 & 22; also *Government Management: Brief to the Incoming
     Government*, Treasury, 1987.

24   Easton, B., 'Approaching Family Economic Issues: Holistically or
     Pathologically?', in *Rights and Responsibilities*, Papers from the
     International Year of the Family Symposium on Rights and
     Responsibilities of the Family held in Wellington, 14-16 October
     1994,Wellington: International Year of the Family Committee in
     association with the Office of the Commissioner for Children, 1995, p. 94.

25   Rankin, K., 'Fiscal and Welfare Barriers to Effective Fatherhood', in
     Callister, P. and Birks, S. (eds), *Perspectives on Fathering,* Palmerston
     North: Centre for Public Policy Evaluation, Massey University, 1999, p. 6.

26   Report of the Domestic Purposes Benefit Review Committee, 1977, pp. 14
     & 16. The 'prompt grant of the benefit may in some cases actually cause a
     separation (though this may be rare) and enable minor disputes or even
     mere disenchantment with marriage to push couples apart.' Once in the
     'solo parent situation ... the parent finds the financial security provided
     by the benefit too attractive for him or her to contemplate marriage, re-
     marriage, or adoption, with subsequent loss of the benefit.' Often: 'while
     maintenance proceedings are grinding their way along, the wife is
     becoming accustomed to regular receipt of an amount of money she has
     probably never had before, the situation between husband and wife has
     become completely polarised, he may have lost interest in the child(ren) ...
     and he may have entered into a *de facto* relationship with someone else
     —in short any hope, however remote, of reconciliation there might have
     been at the beginning has been lost forever.' While the DPB 'undoubtedly
     facilitates the termination of marriages which ought to be terminated',
     the Committee did not 'believe that this advantage offsets the damage it
     may cause in some other cases'. It proposed that full benefit would only be
     granted if the case came into the violent or drunken husband category.
     Otherwise, a reduced benefit should be given until, after a time of
     investigation, the impossibility of reconciliation was evident.

27   Rankin, 'Fiscal and Welfare Barriers to Effective Fatherhood', 1999, p. 82.

28   Maley, B., *Family and Marriage in Australia,* Sidney: The Centre for
     Independent Studies, 2001, p. 88.

29   Ringen, S., *The Family in Question,* London: Demos, 1998, p. 16.

30   Maley, *Family and Marriage in Australia,* 2001, p. 88.

31   Rochford, M., *A Profile of Sole Parents from the 1991 Census,* Research
     Report Series No. 15, Wellington: Research Unit, Department of Social
     Welfare, 1993.

32   Declining by nearly 6,000 between 1986 and 1991. However, trends in the
     non-beneficiary population are not necessarily identical to trends in the
     full-time employed population, because not all non-beneficiary sole
     parents are or have been employed full-time.

33   *From Welfare to Well-being,* Department of Social Welfare Statistics
     Report, 1996.

34   Rochford, *A Profile of Sole Parents from the 1991 Census,* 1993.

35   This was 72 per cent of children living with sole mothers, and nearly 78
     per cent of those with Maori sole mothers, although over 80 per cent of
     sole-parent children had a parent who received income support payments.
     New Zealand Now: Children, 1998 edition, Wellington: Statistics New
     Zealand 1999. In later estimates, 82 per cent of sole parents received
     DPB. 'Towards a Code of Social and Family Responsibility', Fact Sheets,
     1998.

36   Quarterly Review of Benefit Trends, December 1996.

37   See, *New Zealand Now: Families,* Wellington: Statistics New Zealand,
     1994; Rochford, *A Profile of Sole Parents from the 1991 Census,* 1993; *New
     Zealand Now: Children,* Wellington: Statistics New Zealand, 1995;
     Demographic Trends, Wellington: Statistics New Zealand, 1996; also
     Johnstone, K. and Pool, I., 'New Zealand Families: Size, Income and
     Labour Force Participation', *Social Policy Journal of New Zealand,*
     Issue 7, December 1996, pp. 143-73.

38   The number—in contrast to the proportion—of lone parents working full-
     time expanded from 15,440 in 1976 to 21,981 in 1986 to 23,109 in 1991.
     Over two-thirds of Maori sole parents, or 69 per cent, were not in the
     labour force and not seeking work in 1991, similar to Pacific Island people
     at 70 per cent (compared with whites at 51 per cent). However, the
     proportion of those who were not employed but actively seeking work (14
     per cent) was greater than the proportion seeking work among sole
     parents in any other ethnic groups.

39   While the proportion of children with sole fathers in the workforce (full- or
     part-time) fell from 74 per cent to 49 per cent between 1981 and 1991,
     this was still only 54 per cent in 1996. Davey, J.A., 'Children Living in
     Sole Father Homes in New Zealand' in Callister and Birks, *Perspectives
     on Fathering,* 1999.

40   Or 47.3 per cent of sole fathers and 22.5 per cent of sole mothers. For
     Maori lone fathers, it was about 64 per cent not working. Harris, R.,
     'Ethnicity, Gender and Labour Supply in New Zealand in 1986', *New
     Zealand Economic Papers*, 26, 2, 1992, pp. 199-218.

41   About 36 per cent of divorced sole mothers and 55 per cent of divorced sole
     fathers were employed full-time or part-time, followed by widowed sole
     parents (at 27 per cent and 46 per cent, with never-married parents at 16
     per cent and 40 per cent. Johnstone and Pool, 'New Zealand Families:
     Size, Income and Labour Force Participation', 1995 pp. 143-73.

42   Rochford, *A Profile of Sole Parents from the 1991 Census*, 1993.

43   Dixon, 'Labour Force Participation Over the Last Ten Years', *Labour
     Market Bulletin*, 2, 1996, pp. 71-88.

44   *From Welfare to Well-being*, Department of Social Welfare, 1997.

45   With unemployment and sickness benefit cuts in 1991, beneficiaries 'tried
     out their eligibility for invalids' benefit, which was unaffected by the cuts.
     The upward trend in disability allowance numbers abated somewhat in
     1994/5 as attempts were made to improve the definition of valid reasons
     for claiming. The next year, the underlying trend returned. Beaglehole,
     A., *Benefiting Women: Income Support for Women, 1893-1993,* A Women's
     Suffrage Centenary Project 1993, Wellington: Social Policy Agency, 1993;
     From Welfare to Well-being, Department of Social Welfare Statistics
     Report, 1996.

46   Finch, H. *et al., New Deal for Lone Parents: Learning from the Prototype
     Areas*, DSS Research Report, 92, London: HMSO, 1999.

47   *Social Trends*, 30, Office for National Statistics, Stationery Office, 2000.

48   'Analysis of the Cross Benefit Data Base' Analytical Services Division,
     Department of Social Security, quoted in *Child Well-being in Rich and
     Transition Countries*, Luxembourg Conference, 30 September - 2 October
     1999.

49   Nearly two-thirds of the recipients became lone parents. Buckingham, A.,
     'Welfare Reform in Britain, Australia and the United States', in
     Saunders, P. (ed.), *Reforming the Australian Welfare State*, Melbourne:
     Australian Institute of Welfare Studies, 2000.

50   From 77 per cent in 1982 to 72 per cent in 1993.

51   In the period 1982 to 1986, households from deciles one to three of
     household market income deciles gained more transfer income on average
     than they paid in tax. In 1991 to 1996, households in market income
     decile four also gained on average from transfer income. Government
     expenditure on transfers in March 1996 dollars, increased from $6.8 bn in
     1982 to $9.1 bn in 1996. While those receiving New Zealand Superan-
     nuation account for the bulk of spending, the increases also represent the
     numbers receiving income tested benefits. *New Zealand Now: Incomes*,
     Wellington: Statistics New Zealand, 1998.

52   Murray, C., *Losing Ground: American Social Policy, 1950-1980*, New
      York: Basic Books, 1984, p. 212.

53   *Government Management I Brief to the Incoming Government*, Treasury,
      1987, p. 445.

54   Easton, 'Approaching Family Economic Issues: Holistically or Path-
      ologically?, 1995, p. 97.

55   Garfinkel, I. and McLanahan, S., *Single Mothers and Their Children: A
      New American Dilemma*, Washington DC: Urban Institute Press, 1986.
      See also Dench, G., *From Extended Family to State Dependency*, Centre
      for Community Studies, Middlesex University, 1993.

56   Castles, F.G., 'Changing Course in Economic Policy: The English
      Speaking Nations in the 1980s', in Castles, F.G. (ed.), *Families of Nations*,
      Aldershot: Dartmouth, 1993.

57   Rochford, 'A Profile of Sole Parents from the 1991 Census', 1993. Benefit
      control programmes returned about $80 million from conjugal-status
      related benefit abuse alone in 1990/91. Indeed, $60 million was conserv-
      atively estimated as lost to 'client error' in Unemployment Benefit and
      Domestic Purposes Benefit in 1989/90 due to undeclared work and
      relationships. Shipley, *Social Assistance: Welfare that Works*, 1991. Back
      in 1977, the Review Committee were in no doubt that 'in many cases the
      domestic purposes benefit is subject to abuse. ... One educated guess we
      were given was 25 per cent of domestic purposes benefits and related
      emergency unemployment benefits in the Auckland area', 'Report to the
      Domestic Purposes Benefit Review Committee', 1977, p. 30.

58   Plotnick, R.J., 'Welfare and Out-of-Wedlock Childbearing: evidence from
      the 1980s', *Journal of Marriage and the Family*, Vol. 52, 1990, pp. 735-46;
      Duncan, C.J. and Hoffman, S.D., 'Teenage Behaviour and Subsequent
      Poverty', in Jencks, C. and Peterson, P.E. (eds), *The Urban Underclass*,
      Washington DC: The Brookings Institution, 1991.

59   Kempson, E., *et al., Hard Times?*, London: Policy Studies Institute, 1994;
      Marsh, A. and McKay, S., *Families, Work and Benefits*, London: Policy
      Studies Institute, 1993; McLaughlin, E., *Flexibility in Work and Benefits*,
      Council on Social Justice, London: Institute for Public Policy Research,
      1994.

60   Duncan, P., Kerekere, E. and Malaulau, D., *Women on Low Incomes*, The
      Young Women's Christian Association of Aotearoa-New Zealand and the
      New Zealand Council of Christian Social Services, 1998.

61   McLanahan, S., 'Family Structure and the Reproduction of Poverty',
      American Journal of Sociology, 90, 1985, p. 873.

62   Pech, J. and McCoull, F., 'Transgenerational Welfare Dependence: Myth
      or Reality?', Paper presented to the National Social Policy Conference,
      Social Policy for the Twenty-First Century: Justice and Responsibility,
      University of NSW, Sydney, 21-23 July 1999.

63	Dex, S. and Taylor, M., 'Household Employment in 1991', *Employment Gazette*, 102 (10), 1994, pp. 353-57; see also Johnson, P. and Reed, H., 'Intergenerational Mobility Among the Rich and the Poor: Results from the National Child Development Study', *Oxford Review of Economic Policy*, 7, 1996, pp. 127-42. Sons with fathers out of employment when they were 16, were twice as likely to experience at least a year of unemployment themselves.

64	Freeman, R.B. and Holzer, H.J., 'Young Blacks and Jobs–What We Now Know', *The Public Interest,* No. 78, Winter 1985; Freeman, R.B., 'Who Escapes', NBER Working Paper, 1986. Unemployed British 16-19-year-olds picked up by the General Household Survey were three times more likely to live in a family with another unemployed member, and figures for Youth Training Scheme 'non-participants' show two-thirds as living in households with at least one other unemployed adult. Craig, R., *The YTS: A Study of Non-Participants and Early Leavers*, MSC Research and Development No. 34, 1986; and Roll, J., *Young People at the Crossroads*, London: Family Policy Studies Centre, 1988; Main, B. and Shelly, M.E., 'The Economic Effects of YTS', *Employment Gazette*, October 1987; Department of Employment, London, Labour Force Surveys 1984 and 1991.

65	Spruijt, E. and De Goede, M., 'Changing Family Structures and Adolescent Well-being in the Netherlands', *International Journal of Law, Policy and the Family*, Vol. 10, 1996, pp. 1-16.

66	Gregg, P., Harkness, S. and Machin, S., *Child Development and Family Income*, York: Joseph Rowntree Foundation, 1999.

67	*Maori*, Wellington: Statistics New Zealand, 1998.

68	Strategic Directions Post Election Briefing Paper, Wellington: Department of Social Welfare, 1996, p. 6.

69	Murray, *Losing Ground*, 1984, p. 130.

70	Murray, *Losing Ground*, 1984, p. 163.

71	By the time a child reached 17, benefits exceeded costs by $3,000. AFDC, food stamps and Medicaid equalled 73 per cent of real weekly full-time earnings of women in 1975 and 57 per cent in 1987. Moffitt, R., 'Incentive Effects of the US Welfare System', *Journal of Economic Literature*, 30, 1992, pp. 1-61; and Gallaway, L. and Vedder, R., *Poverty, Income Distribution, the Family and Public Policy*, Washington DC: Joint Economic Committee, US Congress, 1986.

72	More than half of welfare spells in a sample of 5,000 families followed between 1968 and 1988 lasted less than two years and only 14 per cent ten years or more. However, 48 per cent of recipients of AFDC at any one time would be there for ten years or more. In turn, 61 per cent of those who had been under the poverty line for ten years or more in the Michigan Panel Study of Income Dynamics were in female headed families by the mid-1980s. For American poverty income and demographic trends and statistics, see Ellwood, D.T., *Poor Support: Poverty and the American Family*, New York: Basic Books, 1988; Danziger, S.H. and Weinberg,

D.H., (eds), *Fighting Poverty: What Works and What Does Not,* Harvard University Press, 1986; Cottingham, P.H. and Ellwood, D.T., (eds), *Welfare Policy for the 1990s,* Harvard University Press, 1989; Hewlitt, S.A., *When the Bough Breaks,* Basic Books, 1991; *Child Neglect in Rich Nations,* UNICEF, 1993; and Jencks and Peterson, *The Urban Underclass,* 1991; Bane, M.J. and Ellwood, D.T., *Welfare Realities: from Rhetoric to Reform,* Cambridge, Mass: Harvard University Press, 1994.

73   Murray, *Losing Ground,* 1984, p. 176.

74   UNICEF, 'A League Table of Child Poverty in Rich Nations', Issue 1, UN Children's Fund, Florence: Innocenti Research Centre, 2000.

75   Podder, N. and Chatterjee, S., *Sharing the National Cake in Post Reform New Zealand: Income Inequality Trends in Terms of Income Sources,* Paper presented at the Annual Conference of the New Zealand Association of Economists, Wellington, 2-4 September 1998, p. 19.

76   'High' levels of benefit have been identified by the Treasury as a major factor preventing a more 'realistic' abatement system, fiscal savings, a reduction in the size of government expenditure, and a disincentive to moving into work—particularly since the Employment Contracts Act put downward pressure on wages. Report of the Change Team on Targeting Social Assistance, Wellington: Department of the Prime Minister and Cabinet, 1991, p. 6. Targeted relief has three main parameters: the benefit amount, the rate at which benefit is withdrawn (the effective marginal tax rate, or EMTR), and the break even level at which it is completely withdrawn (which determines the number of claimants).The value of any two determine the value of the third. If, for example, the amount for someone with no income at all is $100, and benefit is withdrawn at 50c in the $ with earnings, then the break even point is $200. If the withdrawal rate is 25 per cent in the $, then the break even point is $400. Parker, H. and Rhys Williams, B., *Stepping Stones to Independence,* Aberdeen: Aberdeen University Press, 1989.

77   The age limit for youth rates of unemployment benefit was raised to 25; stand down periods were extended and eligibility rules tightened. Under 18s did not qualify for DPB or unemployment benefit. Although real benefits declined by 9.5 per cent on average between 1990 and 1995, the average replacement rate fell by only 5.5 per cent over the same period. The reasons were that real gross labour market earnings fell, the personal income tax increased and partial benefits associated with work also declined slightly. Maloney, T., *Benefit Reform and Labour Market Behaviour in New Zealand,* Wellington: Institute of Policy Studies, 1997.

78   Maloney, *Benefit Reforms and Labour Market Behaviour,* 1997.

79   In 1990, a study of income adequacy was commissioned by the New Zealand Treasury (Brashares, E. and Aynsley, M., *Income Adequacy Standards for New Zealand,* Wellington: The Treasury, 1990) which, among other recommendations, suggested an absolute poverty measure based on minimal food costs (or low-cost food plan times four). Although no official statement has been made, in practice a 'covert move to a minimal absolute view has taken place'. Waldegrave, C., Frater, P. and

Stephens, R., 'An Overview of Research on Poverty in New Zealand', *New Zealand Sociology,* 12 (2) November 1997, p. 228.

80   Waldegrave, C., 'Balancing the Three E's, Equality, Efficiency, Employment', *Social Policy Journal of New Zealand,* Issue 10, June 1998, p. 8.

81   Easton, 'Approaching Family Economic Issues: Holistically or Pathologically?', 1994; International Year of the Family Committee in association with the Office of the Commissioner for Children, Wellington, 1995, p. 97, referring to claims of Charles Waldegrave in Waldegrave, 'Balancing the Three E's, Equality, Efficiency, Employment', 1998.

82   Cox, J., 'Beyond Dependency: Income Support for Persons of Working Age in New Zealand', unpublished paper, 1997.

83   Lerman, R.I., 'Child Support Policies', in Cottingham, P.H. and Ellwood, D.T., (eds), *Welfare Policy for the 1990s,* Harvard University Press, 1989, p. 233.

84   Greenburgh, D. and Wolfe, D.W., 'The Economic Consequences of Experiencing Parental Marital Disruption', *Children and Youth Services Review,* 4, 1982, pp. 141-62.

85   Iacovou, M. and Berthoud, R., *Parents and Employment,* Department of Social Security, quoted in *The Modernisation of Britain's Tax and Benefit System Number Five Supporting Children Through the Tax and Benefit System,* HM Treasury, 1999. If couples with children made up 37 per cent of the bottom 30 per cent in 1991, they were 30 per cent of the persistent poor up to 1996, while lone parents were respectively 14 per cent and 20 per cent. *Households Below Average Income, 1979-1996/7,* DSS Government Statistical Service, 1998. See also Jenkins, S.P. and Jarvis, S., 'Low Income Dynamics in 1990s Britain', *Fiscal Studies,* Vol. 18, No. 2, 1998, pp. 123-42.

86   Wilson, A.G., Houghton, R.M. and Piper, R.K., *Budgeting Assistance and Low-Income Families,* Research Report No.17, Social Policy Agency, 1996.

87   Stevens, A.H., 'Climbing Out of Poverty, Falling Back In', National Bureau of Economic Research,Working Paper 5390, 1996.

88   Burgess, S.M. and Propper, C., *An Economic Model of Household Income Dynamics, with an Application to Poverty Dynamics among American Women,* CASEpaper 9, Economic and Social Research Council, 1998.

89   There is a strong correlation between women's presence in the labour force, household incomes over $42,000 (in 1991) and having an employed partner. O'Reilly, D., 'Family, Work and Social Cohesion', in *Rights and Responsibilities,* Papers from the International Year of the Family Symposium on Rights and Responsibilities of the Family, Wellington, 14-16 October 1994. International Year of the Family Committee in association with the Office of the Commissioner for Children, Wellington, 1995.

90   Ford, R., Marsh, A. and Finlayson, L., *What Happens to Lone Parents: A Cohort Study 1991-1995,* DSS Research Report No. 77, 1998, p. 106.

91   Funder, K. (ed.) *et al.*, *Settling Down: Pathways of Parents after Divorce*, Melbourne: Australian Institute of Family, Studies, No. 13, 1993.

92   Murray, *Losing Ground*, 1984, p. 176.

93   Universal child endowment for two or more children was introduced by the Commonwealth government in Australia in 1941 as part of a wartime package of wage restraint and taxation measures (New South Wales had limited child allowances in 1927). Lovering, K., *Cost of Children in Australia*, Melbourne: Institute of Family Studies, Working Paper No. 8, 1984.

94   Peters, The Hon. W., *The Budget Policy Statement 1998*, Wellington: GP Print, p. 13.

95   Submission on the Public Discussion Document, *Towards a Code of Social and Family Responsibility*, New Zealand Business Roundtable, 1998, pp. 5-6.

96   Cox, J., *Middle Class Welfare*, Wellington: New Zealand Business Roundtable, 2001, p. 193.

97   Cox, *Middle Class Welfare*, 2001, p. 210.

98   A Family Tax Payment was introduced in 2000 for all but the top 10-15 per cent in the income distribution. This gave an effective tax free threshold to families double the general threshold. About a half of these get the top payment and the supplement is higher for children under five. This replaces a complex array of 12 types of assistance. Where the caregiving parent in two-parent families has some earnings, the family does not lose all benefit, or relinquish a sum corresponding to their earnings until a threshold is reached. The costs of children are recognised for incomes up to $37,000 per year, plus $3,000 for each extra child. With Family Tax Benefit part B, the second parent will retain some benefit until income is over $10,500 a year. Childless people continued 'to enjoy a large financial advantage over families with children' and lone parents 'on welfare had the greatest improvement', see Maley, B., *Family and Marriage in Australia*, Sidney: Centre for Independent Studies, 2001, p. 87; Newman, J., 'The Commonwealth Government's Approach to Family Policy', *Family Matters*, Issue No. 54, Spring/Summer 1999. After the election of 1996, a parliamentary inquiry was set up to report on the consequences of marriage breakdown and family disintegration, resulting in *To Have and To Hold : A Report of the Enquiry into Aspects of Family Services*, Canberra: House of Representatives Standing Committee on Legal and Constitutional Affairs, 1998. This proposed a pro-marriage educational programme.

99   Hardy, J.B. and Zabin, L.S., *Adolescent Pregnancy in an Urban Environment: Issues, Programs, and Evaluation*, Washington DC: The Urban Institute Press, 1991; Plotnick, R.D., 'The Effect of Social Policies on Teenage Pregnancy and Childbearing', *Families in Society: the Journal of Contemporary Human Services*, 1993, pp. 324-29; Duncan, C.J. and Hoffman, S.D., 'Teenage Behaviour and Subsequent Poverty', in Jencks and Peterson, *The Urban Underclass*, 1991.

100 Report of the Domestic Purposes Benefit Review Committee, 1977, E.28, Wellington: Department of Social Welfare, p. 18.

101 Ermisch, J., *Lone Parenthood*, Cambridge University Press, 1991. See also *Teenage Pregnancy*, Social Exclusion Unit, London: The Stationery Office, 1999; Wilson, W.J. and Neckerman, K.M., 'Poverty and Family Structure', in Danziger Bane, M.J., 'Household Composition and Poverty', in Danziger, S.H., and Weinberg, D.H., (eds), *Fighting Poverty: What Works and What Does Not,* Harvard University Press, 1986, p. 243; see also Ellwood, D.T. and Lerman, R., *Understanding Dependency: Choices, Confidence or Culture?*, Division of Income Security Policy (ISP), US Department of Health and Human Services, 1987; and Dash, L., *When Children Want Children: An Inside Look at the Crisis of Teenage Pregnancy*, Penguin Books, 1990. Also see Berthoud, R., Mckay, S. and Rowlingson, K., *Explaining the Growth of Lone Parenthood in Britain*, in Wertheimer, A. and McRae, S., *Research Results*, Economic and Social Research Council Centre for Family and Household Research, Oxford Brookes University, 1999.

102 Unsurprisingly, about a half of UK non-working lone parents have no qualifications, compared with 29 per cent of the unemployed and 14 per cent of those in employment. *Welfare Reform Focus File*, No. 3, Department of Social Security, 1997. Over half are in the bottom 20 per cent of the US population distribution and the average aptitude and achievement scores are significantly below the mean of the lowest occupational groups. Zill, N., Moore, K., Ward, C. and Steif, T., *Welfare Mothers as Potential Employees: A Statistical Profile Based on National Data*, Washington DC: Child Trends Inc., 1991; Besharov, D.J., *US Welfare Reform*, paper prepared for the Institute of Economic Affairs by the American Enterprise Institute for Public Policy and Research, May 1994.

103 *New Zealand Now: Children*, Statistics New Zealand, 1998.

104 Birrell, B. and Rapson, V., *A Not So Perfect Match: the Growing Male / Female Divide 1986-1996*, Centre for Population and Urban Research, Monash University, 1998.

105 Dench, G., *The Place of Men in Changing Family Culture*, London: Institute of Community Studies, p. 59.

106 Dench, G., 'Man's Diminished Role', *Welfare,* Winter 1996/97.

107 Smart, C. and Stevens, P., *Cohabitation Breakdown*, London: Family Policy Studies Centre, 2000, p. 82.

108 Rowlingson, K. and McKay, S., *The Growth of Lone Parenthood*, London: Policy Studies Institute, 1998, p. 199.

109 Bernstam, M.S. and Swan, P.L., 'Malthus and the Evolution of the Welfare State: an Essay on the Second Invisible Hand', Working Paper 89-012, Australian Graduate School of Management, University of New South Wales, 1989.

110 Sullivan, L., 'Tax Injustice: Keeping the Family Cap-in-Hand', *Issue Analysis*, No. 3, Sidney: Centre for Independent Studies, July 1998, p. 10.

111 Report of the Change Team on Targeting Social Assistance, Wellington: Department of the Prime Minister and Cabinet, 1991, p. 38.

112 Briefing to the incoming Government Ministry of Women's Affairs, 1996, p. 3.

113 Those with a youngest child aged seven or above were required to attend an annual interview to identify the steps needed to prepare for work readiness. A year later, those with a child aged between six and 13 were required to seek part-time work, while those with a youngest child aged 14 or older were to seek full-time work. For a failure to accept a suitable job, the benefit could have been cut to 50 per cent for the minimum of a week and until such time as the person complied with the requirement. Failure to participate in a mandatory interview could have attracted a 20 per cent reduction in the amount payable for the week in which this occurred.

114 The legislation making sole parents receiving the DPB or the widow's benefit subject to a work capacity test was repealed with effect from 10 March 2003. Instead beneficiaries are required to work with their case manager to develop and implement a personal development and employment plan. Such plans are required to outline personal development, training and employment goals and the action points required to reach those goals.

115 Mead, L.M., *The New Paternalism: Supervisory Approaches to Poverty*, Washington DC: Brookings Institute, 1997.

116 Mead, L.M., 'Welfare Reform and the Family', *Family Matters*, No. 54, Spring/Summer 1999.

117 Shipley, S.M., *Women's Employment and Unemployment: a Research Report*, Palmerston North: Massey University Department of Sociology and the Society for the Research on Women in New Zealand Inc., 1982.

118 In the UK, a government study found that 87 per cent of mothers of pre-school children preferred to look after their own children and that indeed, 'in an ideal world ... the vast majority of women with children would prefer to care for their child themselves, irrespective of their child's age'. *Family and Working Lives Survey*, Department of Education and Employment 1996, Data Source Book Volume 2. The British Social Attitudes Survey found that if women could have the 'childcare arrangement of their choice', only 17 per cent of part-time workers would work full-time and nine per cent would work more hours whilst still being part-time. Only seven per cent of full-time working women would work more hours, whereas 31 per cent would work fewer hours. Ashford, S., 'Family Matters', in Jowell, R. *et al.* (eds), *British Social Attitudes 12th Report*, Social and Community Planning Research Dartmouth, 1995; see also Scott, J., Braun. M. and Alwin D., 'The Family Way', in Jowell, R. *et al.* (eds), *International Social Attitudes: the 10th BSA Report*, SCPR, Dartmouth Publishing Co. Ltd, 1993.

119 Ford, R., 'The Role of Child Care in Lone Mothers' Decisions about
     Whether or Not to Work', in *DSS Research Yearbook 1996/97*, London:
     HMSO; and Hakim, C., 'Five Feminist Myths about Women's
     Employment', *British Journal of Sociology*, Vol. 46, 1995, pp. 429-47.

120 'Income Support Post-Election Briefing Paper', Department of Social
     Welfare, 1996. In the UK, out of all the lone parents invited to take part
     in the New Deal, only 3.8 per cent got jobs. A fifth who got jobs left them
     after six months. After 18 months the number of lone parents on income
     support was only 3.3 per cent lower than it would have been in the
     absence of the programme. Lone parents were also more likely to find
     work outside the areas where the New Deal was operating than they were
     within the scheme. The working families tax credit is expected to increase
     lone-parent labour market participation rates by 2.2 percentage points.
     'Family Poverty and Social Exclusion', Family Briefing Paper 15, London:
     Family Policy Studies Centre, 2000.

121 *Household Labour Force Survey for the Year Ended March 1995*,
     Statistics New Zealand, 1995.

122 The rate was calculated on the difference between previous benefit income
     and employment income. A ceiling, representing the maximum amount
     payable, was set at $40 per week.

123 Murray, *Losing Ground,* 1984, p. 212.

124 St John, S., *The Welfare Mess Revisited*, Department of Economics,
     University of Auckland, 1996, p. 2.

125 Millar, J., Webb, S. and Kemp, M., *Combining Work and Welfare* Joseph
     Rowntree Foundation: York, 1997; and Marsh, A. and McKay, S.,
     Families, Work and Benefits, London: Policy Studies Institute, 1993.

126 The US equivalent, or the Earned Income Tax Credit (EITC) of 1975, was
     originally intended to offset the burden of payroll taxes on low-income
     families, but became one of the fastest growing programmes in the federal
     budget. Between 1975 and 1995, the proportion of recipients grew from
     8.7 per cent to 20.7 per cent of the population and the cost reached $30.8
     billion in 2000. In 1995, approximately 19.3 million households, or 55
     million people, received EITC at a cost of $25.8 billion . In 1996, if two
     $14,500 earners were to marry, or stay married, they would lose their
     benefits, since these terminated at $28,524. But if they stayed single, they
     would gain about $5,000.

127 As these were reduced from 90 to around a 50 per cent withdrawal, in the
     income band around 15 to 60 per cent of average ordinary time earnings
     by the late 1990s, beneficiaries faced high EMTRs between 30 to 75 per
     cent of average ordinary time earnings instead.

128 Strategic Directions Post Election Briefing Paper, Wellington:
     Department of Social Welfare, 1996, p. 76.

129 Mackay, R., *Welfare to Work: New Directions in New Zealand*, Social
     Policy Agency, Department of Social Welfare, 1999.

130 In Ireland, a generous allowance for lone parents allows them to earn a lot a week without losing benefit. Consequently, the community employment programme is disproportionately taken up by lone parents, as the work disregard makes it a more favourable option for them than unemployed couples, who have increased incentives to separate. 'The report of the working group examining the treatment of married, cohabiting and one-parent families under the tax and social welfare codes', Dublin: The Stationery Office, 1999.

131 Mackay, *Welfare to Work: New Directions in New Zealand,* 1999, p. 33.

132 *The Battle Against Exclusion,* Paris: OECD Publications, 1998. The Working Nation scheme in Australia was also premised on the need to help the jobless overcome barriers. Training and educating the unemployed resulted in as few as 22 per cent of Job Compact participants being in unsubsidised employment three months after leaving their placements. The unemployed tended to go through the system and then go back onto benefits. Many of the employers who offered temporary job placements were negative about the work attitudes of the unemployed. Finn, D., 'Job Guarantees for the Unemployed: Lessons from Australian Welfare Reform', *Journal of Social Policy,* Vol. 28, 1999, pp.53-71.

133 'It is odd that training has become the mom and apple pie of economists and public officials across the political spectrum when it could at best provide only a partial answer to the problems of dislocated workers, at least given the knowledge base about what works at current spending levels.' Kapstein, E.B., 'Workers and the World Economy', *Foreign Affairs,* May/June 1996, pp. 27 & 28.

134 Strategic Directions Post Election Briefing Paper, Wellington: Department of Social Welfare, 1996, p. 77.

135 See, for example, US Department of Labor, Employment and Training Administration, *The National JTPA Study: Title II-A Impacts on Earnings and Employment at 18 Months,* Research and Evaluation Report 93-C, Washington DC: US Department of Labor, 1993.

136 Callister, P., '"Work-rich" and "Work-poor" Individuals, Families, Households and Communities: Changes Between 1986 and 1996', Working Paper for the Institute of Policy Studies, Victoria University, 1997. Between 1960 and 1980, the numbers in Swedish public employment tripled, much of it in the welfare sector, just as the number of employees in the Danish public sector grew by about as much as homemakers declined, with most of the growth in daycare, elderly care, hospitals and schools. By 1980, 70 per cent of the 17.3 million social service jobs at all levels of American government were held by women and could account for much of the female job gains since 1960. Carlson, A.C., 'The Family and the Welfare State', *The St Croix Review,* Vol. XXVIII, No. 4, 1995, pp. 21-30.

137 McPherson M.J., *Divorce in New Zealand,* Palmerston North: Social Policy Research Centre Massey University, 1995, p. 51.

138 Mayer, S.M., *What Money Can't Buy*, Cambridge, Mass: Harvard University Press, 1997; Graham, J. *et al.*, 'The Effects of Child Support on Educational Attainment', in Garfinkel, I. and McLanahan, S. (eds), *Child Support and Child Well Being*, Washington DC: Urban Institute Press 1994; and Knox, V. and Bane, M.J., 'Child Support and Schooling', in Garfinkel and McLanahan, *Child Support and Child Well Being*, 1994.

139 Hobcraft, J. and Kiernan, K., *Childhood Poverty, Early Motherhood and Adult Social Exclusion*, CASEpaper 28, London: Centre for Analysis of Social Exclusion, 1999.

7: The Consequences for Children

1 Briar, C., 'Problems in the New Zealand Family', in Green, P.F., *Studies in New Zealand Social Problems*, Palmerston North: The Dunmore Press Ltd, 1994, pp. 253 & 273.

2 Strategic Directions Post Election Briefing Paper, Wellington: Department of Social Welfare, 1996, p. 41.

3 'Inquiry into Children in Education at Risk through Truancy and Behavioural Problems', The Report of the Education and Social Science Committee, Wellington: Ministry of Education, 1995.

4 'Social Welfare in New Zealand Children, Young Persons and their Families', Service Ministerial Briefing Paper, 1996, pp. 4 &16.

5 Strategic Directions Post Election Briefing Paper, 1996, p. 39.

6 Hess, L.E., 'Changing Family Patterns in Western Europe', in Rutter, M. and Smith, D.J. (eds), *Psycho-social Disorders in Young People*, Chichester: John Wiley & Sons, 1995, pp. 173-74.

7 See, for example, Joshi, H. *et al.*, 'Children 5-16', Research Briefing No. 6, Economic and Social Research Council, University of Hull, January 2000.

8 McLanahan, S. and Sandefur, G., *Growing Up With a Single Parent*, Cambridge, Mass: Harvard University Press, 1994, p. 1.

9 McLanahan, S. and Booth, K., 'Mother-Only Families: Problems, Prospects, and Politics', *Journal of Marriage and the Family,* Vol. 51, 1989, p. 565.

10 Rodgers, B. and Pryor, J., *Divorce and Separation: The Outcomes for Children*, York: Joseph Rowntree Foundation, 1998, p. 44.

11 Zubrick, S.R., Silburn, S.R., Gurrin, L., Teoh, H., Shepherd, C., Carlton, J. and Lawrence, D., *Western Australian Child Health Survey: Education, Health and Competence*, Perth, Western Australia: Australian Bureau of Statistics and the TVW Institute for Child Health Research, 1995.

12 Meltzer, H. *et al.*, *Mental Health of Children and Adolescents in Great Britain*, Office for National Statistics, London: The Stationery Office, 2000.

13 Schuman, J., 'Childhood, Infant and Perinatal Mortality, 1996; Social and Biological Factors in Deaths of Children Aged Under 3', *Population Trends*, 92, Summer 1998. Mortality rates for babies registered by the mother alone, or by both parents from different addresses, are between 45 and 68 per cent higher than those for babies born inside marriage in England and Wales between 1993 and 1995, and 25 to 35 per cent higher for infants whose births were registered by the unwed parents from the same address.

14 Wright, R.E., *Sexual Union Status and Infant Mortality in Jamaica*, unpublished manuscript, Dept of Political Economy, Glasgow University, 1994. A clear gradient is revealed for the impact of sexual status on infant mortality, where the risk was highest for women with no relationship to any particular man and lowest for the married, being intermediate for cohabiting women and those with a regular 'visiting' man. When other variables known to affect infant mortality, e.g. years of schooling, education and mother's age, or the birth order of the child, were taken into account, the risk of infant death set marriage even more sharply apart from the other types of union.

15 Manderbacka, K. *et al.*, 'Marital Status as a Predictor of Perinatal Outcome in Finland', *Journal of Marriage and the Family*, Vol. 54, 1992, pp. 508-15.

16 Dubow, E.F. and Luster, T., 'Adjustment of Children Born to Teenage Mothers: The Contribution of Risk and Protective Factors', *Journal of Marriage and the Family*, Vol. 52, 1990, pp. 393-404; Lummis, T., 'The Historical Dimension of Fatherhood: A Case Study 1890-1914', in McKee, L. and O'Brian, M., *The Father Figure*, Tavistock, 1982.

17 Singh, G.K. and Yu, S.M., 'US Childhood Mortality, 1950 through 1993: Trends and Socioeconomic Differentials', *American Journal of Public Health*, Vol. 85, 1995, pp. 1237-245; and Mauldon, J., 'The Effect of Marital Disruption on Children's Health', *Demography*, Vol. 27, 1990, p. 439; Crellin, E., Kellmer-Pringle M.L. and West, P., *Born Illegitimate: Social and Economic Implications*, Windsor, England: NFER, 1971; Eberstadt, M., 'Is Illegitimacy a Public Health Hazard?', *National Review*, 30 December 1988; Judge, K. and Benzeval, M., 'Health Inequalities: New Concerns about the Children of Single Mothers', *British Medical Journal*, Vol. 306, 13 March 1993; Roberts, I. and Pless, B., 'Social Policy as a Cause of Childhood Accidents: the Children of Lone Mothers', *British Medical Journal*, Vol. 311, 7 October 1995.

18 'Health and Selected Socioeconomic Characteristics of the Family: United States, 1988-90', National Centre of Health Statistics (PHS) 97-1523, Washington DC: General Printing Office, 1997.

19 Fergusson, D.M., Horwood, L.J. and Shannon, J.M., 'The Christchurch Child Development Study: A Review of Epidemiological Findings, *Paediatric and Perinatal Epidemiology*, 1989, pp. 302-25; Beautrais, A.L., Fergusson, D.M. and Shannon, F.T., 'Life Events and Childhood Morbidity: a Prospective Study', *Pediatrics*, 70, 1982, pp. 935-40; Fergusson, D.M., Shannon, F.T. and Horwood, L.J., 'Social and Family

Factors in Childhood Hospital Admission', *Journal of Epidemiology and Community Health*, 40, 1986, pp. 50-58.

20 Annual Report for the year ended 30 June 1996, Office for the Commissioner for Children, Ministry for Social Welfare.

21 Gartner, R., 'Family Structure, Welfare Spending, and Child Homicide in Developed Democracies', *Journal of Marriage and The Family*, Vol. 53, 1991, pp. 231-40.

22 Egami, Y., 'Psychiatric Profile and Sociodemographic Characteristics of Adults who Report Physically Abusing or Neglecting Children', *American Journal of Psychiatry*, Vol. 153, 1996, pp. 921-28.

23 Daly, M. and Wilson, M., *The Truth About Cinderella*, London: Weidenfeld and Nicolson, 1998; and Wilson, M.I., Daly, M. and Weghorst, S.J., 'Household Composition and Child Abuse and Neglect', *Journal of Biosocial Sciences*, Vol. 12, 1980, pp. 333-40.

24 Malkin, C.M. and Lamb, M.E., 'Child Maltreatment: A Test of Sociobiological Theory', *Journal of Comparative Family Studies*, Vol. 25, 1994, pp. 121-30. Moreover, toddlers living in Canadian step-households in 1983 were about 40 times more likely to become registered victims of intermediate physical abuse than their two-genetic-parent counterparts, with a step-parent 70 times more likely to kill a child under two than a co-residing genetic parent and 15 times more likely to kill a teenager.

25 Fergusson, D.M., Fleming, J. and O'Neill, D.P., *Child Abuse in New Zealand*, Wellington: Government Printer, 1972.

26 Angus, G. and Hall, G., *Child Abuse and Neglect Australia 1994-5*, Child Welfare Series No. 16, Australian Institute of Child Health and Welfare, Canberra: Australian Government Publishing Service, 1996.

27 Buckingham, J., *Boy Troubles: Understanding Rising Suicide, Rising Crime and Educational Failure*, Sidney: Centre for Independent Studies, Policy Monograph No. 46, 2000.

28 Wilson, Daly and Weghorst, 'Household Composition and Child Abuse and Neglect', 1980, pp. 333-40.

29 Gordon, M. and Creighton, S.J., 'Natal and Non-natal Fathers as Sexual Abusers in the United Kingdom: a Comparative Analysis', *Journal of Marriage and the Family*, Vol. 50, 1988, pp. 99-105. Examination of English court records between 1982 and 1988 found that children living with their mother and her cohabiting boyfriend were 33 times more likely to be abused than those living with their married, biological parents. In turn, the risk of abuse for children whose mothers were cohabiting was five-and-a-half times greater than for children with remarried parents. Whelan, R., *Broken Homes and Battered Children*, Oxford: Family Education Trust, 1994.

30 Mangolin, L., 'Child Abuse by Mothers' Boyfriends: Why the Over-representation?', *Child Abuse and Neglect*, Vol. 16, No. 4, 1992, p. 545.

31 *Sex and America's Teenagers,* Alan Guttmacher Institute, New York, 1994.

32 Saville Smith, K., *Familial Caregivers' Physical Abuse and Neglect of Children: a Literature Review,* Wellington: Ministry of Social Policy, Department of Child, Youth and Family Services, 2001, pp. 20, 32.

33 Amato, P.R., 'Children's adjustment to Divorce; Theories, Hypotheses and Empirical Support', *Journal of Marriage and the Family,* Vol. 55, 1993, pp. 23-38; Fergusson, D.M., Lynskey, M. and Horwood, L.J., 'The Effects of Parental Separation, the Timing of Separation and Gender on Children's Performance in Cognitive Tests', *Journal of Child Psychology and Psychiatry,* 35, 1994, pp. 1077-92; and Fergusson, D.M., Horwood, J. and Lynsky, M.T., 'Parental Separation, Adolescent Psychopathology and Problem Behaviours', *Journal of the American Academy of Child and Adolescent Psychiatry,* Vol. 33, 1994, pp. 1122-31.

34 Dawson, D.A., *Family Structure and Children's Health: United States 1988,* Series 10: 178, Vital and Health Statistics, Maryland: US Department of Health and Human Services, 1991.

35 Bosworth, D., 'Truancy and Pupil Performance', *Education Economics,* 2 (3), 1994, pp. 243-63; Casey, B. and Smith, D., *Truancy and Youth Transitions,* London: Policy Studies Institute, 1995.

36 Evans, M.D.R., Kelley, J. and Wanner, R.A., 'Educational Attainment of the Children of Divorce: Australia, 1940-90', *Journal of Sociology,* Vol. 37, No. 3, 2001, pp. 275-97.

37 Stevenson, J. and Fredman, G., 'The Social Correlates of Reading Ability', *Journal of Child Psychology and Psychiatry,* Vol. 31, 1990, pp. 689-90.

38 Hobcraft, J., 'Intergenerational and Life-Course Transmission of Social Exclusion: Influences of Childhood Poverty, Family Disruption, and Contact with the Police', CASEpaper 15, STICERD Centre for Analyais of Social Exclusion, London: London School of Economics, 1998; also Powell, M.A. and Parcel, T.L., 'Effects of Family Structure on the Earnings Attainment Process: Differences by Gender', *Journal of Marriage and the Family,* Vol. 59, 1997, p. 419. It is speculated that noncustodial fathers may be more likely to stay in contact with sons than daughters and, not only for fathers, but parents generally, tend to put boys education before girls where money is short (this might have reversed with the recent emphasis on girls being more educable than boys). See Amato, P.R. and Keith, B., 'Parental Divorce and Adult Well-being: a Meta-analysis', *Journal of Marriage and the Family,* Vol. 53, 1991, pp. 43-58.

39 Burghes, L., *Lone Parenthood and Family Disruption,* London: Family Policy Studies Centre, 1994, p. 15.

40 Ely, M., Richards, M.P.M., Wadsworth, M.E.J., and Elliot, B.J 'Secular changes in the association of parental divorce and children's educational attainment—evidence from three British cohorts', *Journal of Social Policy,* Vol. 28, No. 3, June 1999, pp. 437-55.

41   Rodgers, B. and Pryor, J., *Divorce and Separation: The Outcomes for Children*, York: Joseph Rowntree Foundation, 1998.

42   Evans, M.D.R., Kelly, J. and Warner, R.A., 'Educational Attainment of the Children of Divorce: Australia 1940-1990, *Journal of Sociology*, Vol. 37, No. 3, 2001, pp. 275-97.

43   Fergusson, D.M., Lynskey, M. and Horwood, L.J., 'The Adolescent Outcomes of Adoption: a 16-Year Longitudinal Study', *Journal of Child Psychology and Psychiatry*, 36, No. 4, 1995, pp. 597-615; Crellin, E., Kellmer-Pringle and West, *Born Illegitimate: Social and Economic Implications*, 1971; and Seglow, J., Kellmer-Pringle, M.L. and Wedge, P., *Growing Up Adopted*, National Foundation for Educational Research in England and Wales, 1972.

44   Fergusson, D.M., Horwood, L.J. and Shannon, F.T., 'Birth Placement and Childhood Disadvantage', *Social Science and Medicine*, 15, 1981, pp. 315-26.

45   Lambert, L. and Streather, J., *Children in Changing Families*, Macmillan, 1980. The sample now included 294 children who had been born out of wedlock and not adopted and 115 adopted children. A problem with longitudinal studies are the losses over time, due to death, emigration, refusals and inability to trace earlier respondents. While a third of the adopted children were lost to the study, analysis showed that the results were unlikely to be biased through non-response.

46   Fergusson, D.M., Horwood, L.J. and Lloyd, M. 'The Outcomes of Adoption: A 12-year Longitudinal Study', Report prepared for the Adoption Practices Review Committee, Christchurch Health and Development Study, June 1990; Fergusson, Lynskey and Horwood, 'The Adolescent Outcomes of Adoption: A 16-Year Longitudinal Study', 1995.

47   Maughan, B. and Pickles, A., 'Adopted and Illegitimate Children Growing-Up', in Robins, L.N. and Rutter, M., *Straight and Devious Pathways from Childhood to Adolescence*, Cambridge University Press, 1990.

48   Zill, N., Coiro, M.J. and Bloom, B., 'Health of Our Nation's Children', *Vital and Health Statistics*, Series 10, No. 191, Public Health Service, 1994; and Zill, N., 'Adopted Children in the United States: a Profile Based on a National Survey of Child Health', testimony before the House Ways and Means Subcommittee on Human Resources, May 1995.

49   Lovell, R. and Norris, M., *One in Four: Offending from Age 10 to 24 in a Cohort of New Zealand Males*, Research Report No. 8, Wellington: Department of Social Welfare, undated.

50   Amato, P.R. and Keith, B., 'Parental Divorce and the Well Being of Children: a Meta-analysis', *Psychological Bulletin*, 110, 1991, pp. 26-46.

51   Hetherington M.E. and Clingempeel, W.G., 'Coping with Marital Transitions', *Monographs of the Society for Research in Child Development*, Series 227, Vol. 47, No. 2-3, 1992.

52   Fergusson, D.M., Horwood, L.J. and Lynskey, M., 'The Childhoods of
      Multiple-Problem Adolescents: a 15-Year Longitudinal Study', *Journal of
      Child Psychology and Psychiatry*, Vol. 35, 1994, pp. 1123-139.

53   Farrington, D.P., 'The Development of Offending and Antisocial
      Behaviour from Childhood: Key Findings from the Cambridge Study in
      Delinquent Development', The Twelfth Jack Tizard Memorial Lecture,
      Journal of Child Psychology and Psychiatry, 1995, pp. 929-59.

54   Henry, B. *et al.*, 'Early Family Predictors of Child and Adolescent
      Antisocial Behaviour: Who Are the Mothers of Delinquents?', *Criminal
      Behaviour and Mental Health*, 3, 1993, pp. 97-100; Campbell, S.B.,
      'Behaviour Problems in Preschool Children: a Review of Recent Evidence',
      Journal of Child Psychology and Psychiatry, 36, No. 1, 1995, pp. 113-49.

55   Maxwell, G.M. and Robertson, J.P., *Child Offenders*, Wellington: Office of
      the Commissioner for Children, 1995.

56   Australian Institute for Community Services, quoted in *Youth Recidivist
      Offending*, Wellington: Project Report New Zealand Police National
      Headquarters, 1995.

57   Koller, K.M. and Williams, W.T., 'Early Parental Deprivation and Later
      Behavioural Outcomes: Cluster Analysis of Normal and Abnormal
      Groups', *Australian and New Zealand Journal of Psychiatry*, 8, 1974,
      pp. 89-96.

58   Hagell, A. and Newburn, T., *Persistent Young Offenders*, London: Policy
      Studies Institute, 1994.

59   Reid, M., *Kids In Trouble*, Christchurch: New Zealand Education
      Development Foundation, 2000.

60   Fergusson, D.M., Lynskey, M. and Horwood, L.J., 'Family Change,
      Parental Discord and Early Offending', *Journal of Child Psychology and
      Psychiatry*, 33, No. 6, 1992, pp. 1059-75; and Fergusson, D.M., Horwood,
      L.J. and Lynskey, M., 'Parental Separation, Adolescent Psychopathology
      and Problem Behaviours', *Journal of the American Academy of Child and
      Adolescent Psychology*, 33, 1994, pp. 1122-33.

61   West, D.J., *Delinquency: Its Roots, Careers and Prospects*, Heinemann,
      1982.

62   West, D.J. and Farrington, D.P., *Who Becomes Delinquent?*, Heinemann,
      1973; and *The Delinquent Way of Life,* Heinemann, 1977.

63   Capaldi, D.M. and Patterson, G.R., 'Relation of Parental Transitions to
      Boys' Adjustment Problems: (i) a Linear Hypothesis, (ii) Mothers at Risk
      for Transitions and Unskilled Parenting', *Developmental Psychology*,
      Vol. 27, No. 3, 1991, pp. 489-504.

64   Rickel, A.U. and Langer, T.S., 'Short-term and Long-term Effects of
      Marital Disruption on Children', *American Journal of Community
      Psychology*, Vol. 13, 1985, pp. 599-661.

65   Ferri, E., *Step Children*, Windsor: NFER-Nelson, 1984.

66   Wadsworth, M., *The Roots of Delinquency*, Martin Robertson, 1979.

67   McLanahan, S. and Harper, C., *Father Absence and Youth Incarceration*, paper presented at the 1998 annual meeting of the American Sociological Association, San Francisco, CA, August 1998.

68   Campbell, S.B. and Ewing, L.J., 'Follow-up of Hard-to-Manage Preschoolers: Adjustment at Age 9 and Predictors of Continuing Symptoms', *Journal of Child Psychology and Psychiatry*, Vol. 31, No. 6, 1990, pp. 871-89.

69   McGee, R., Silva, P.A. and Williams, S., 'Perinatal, Neurological, Environmental, and Developmental Characteristics of Seven-year-old Children with Stable Behaviour Problems', *Journal of Child Psychology and Psychiatry*, 25, 1984, pp. 573-86.

70   Walker, B. and Rochford, M., 'A Research Investigation into the Benefit Status of Caregivers of Children and Young People Who Come to the Notice of NZCYPS Research Unit', NZCYPS, April 1996.

71   Zill, N., Morrison, D.R. and Coiro, M.J., *Long-Term Effects of Parental Divorce on Parent-Child Relationships, Adjustment and Achievement in Young Adulthood*, Washington DC: Child Trends Inc., 2000; see also Needle, R.H., Su, S.S. and Doherty, W.J., 'Divorce, Remarriage and Adolescent Substance Use: a Prospective Longitudinal Study', *Journal of Marriage and the Family*, Vol. 52, 1990, pp. 157-69.

72   Cherlin, A.J., Chase-Lansdale, P.L. and McRae, C., 'Effects of Parental Divorce on Mental Health Throughout the Life Course', *American Sociological Review*, Vol. 63, 1998, pp. 245-46.

73   Buchanan, A. and Ten Brinke, J., *What Happened When They Were Grown Up*, York: Joseph Rowntree Foundation, 1997.

74   McLeod, J.D., 'Childhood Parental Loss and Adult Depression', *Journal of Health and Social Behaviour*, 32, 1991, pp. 205-20.

75   Rodgers, B., 'Pathways between Parental Divorce and Adult Depression', *Journal of Child Psychology and Psychiatry*, 35 (7) 1994, pp. 1289-1308. Originally 5,362, the sample dropped down to 3,262, as people died, lived abroad or refused. It seems that such attrition has caused little bias, apart from the under-representation of those with literacy problems and schizophrenics.

76   Rodgers, 'Pathways between Parental Divorce and Adult Depression', 1994, pp. 1304-05.

77   Maclean, M. and Wadsworth, M.E.J., *The Interests of Children after Parental Divorce: a Long-Term Perspective*, Centre for Socio-Legal Studies, Wolfson College, Oxford: Oxford University Press, 1988; and abstract in *The International Journal of Law and the Family*, Vol. 2, 1988, pp. 155-66; Elliott, B.J. and Richards, M.P.M., 'Children and Divorce: Educational Performance and Behaviour Before and After Parental Separation', *International Journal of Law and the Family*, 1991, pp. 258-76; Elliott, B.J. and Richards, M.P.M., 'Parental Divorce and the Life Chances of Children', *Family Law*, November 1991.

78 MacLean and Wadsworth, *The Interests of Children after Parental Divorce*, 1998; and Kuh, D. and Wadsworth, M., 'Childhood Influences on Adult Male Earnings in a Longitudinal Study', *British Journal of Sociology*, 42, 1991, pp. 537-55.

79 Hobcraft, J., 'Intergenerational and Life-Course Transmission of Social Exclusion: Influences of Childhood Poverty, Family Disruption, and Contact with the Police', CASEpaper 15, STICERD Centre for Analysis of Social Exclusion, London: London School of Economics, 1998.

80 Biblarz, T.J. and Raftery, A.E., 'The Effects of Family Disruption on Social Mobility,' *American Sociological Review*, 58, 1993, pp. 97-109.

81 Dornbusch, S.M. *et al.*, 'Single Parents, Extended Households, and the Control of Adolescents', *Child Development*, Vol. 56, 1985, pp. 326-41; see also Aquilino, W.S., 'Family Structure and Home Leaving: a Further Specification of the Relationship', *Journal of Marriage and the Family*, Vol. 53, 1991, pp. 999-1010.

82 Krein, S.F. and Beller, A.H., 'Educational Attainment of Children from Single-parent Families: Differences by Exposure, Gender and Race', *Demography*, Vol. 25, No. 2, 1988, pp. 221-33.

83 *Western Australian Child Health Survey*, TVW Telethon, Institute for Child Health Research and the Australian Bureau of Statistics, 1996.

84 Wadsworth, M.E.J. and Maclean, M., 'Parents' Divorce and Children's Life Chances', *Children and Youth Services Review*, 8, 1986, pp. 145-59.

85 Elliott, B.J. and Richards, M.P.M., 'Children and Divorce: Educational Performance and Behaviour Before and After Parental Separation,' *International Journal of Law and the Family*, 5,1991, pp. 258-76; Kiernan, K., *The Legacy of Parental Divorce: Social, Economic and Demographic Experiences in Adulthood*, London: Centre for Analysis of Social Exclusion, 1997; Maclean, M. and Kuh, D., 'The Long-Term Effects for Girls of Parental Divorce,' in Maclean, M. and Groves, D. (eds), *Women's Issues in Social Policy*, London: Routledge, 1991.

86 Jonsson, J.O. and Gahler, M., 'Family Dissolution, Family Reconstruction, and Children's Educational Careers: Recent Evidence from Sweden', *Demography*, Vol. 34, No. 2. 1997, pp. 277-93.

87 Hetherington, M.E. and Clingempeel, W.G., 'Coping with Marital Transitions', *Monographs of the Society for Research in Child Development*, Series 227, Vol. 47, No. 2-3, Chicago: University of Chicago Press, 1992.

88 Dawson, D.A., *Family Structure and Children's Health: United States 1988*, Series 10, Vital and Health Statistics, Maryland: US Dept of Health and Human Services, 1991; Pilling, D., *Escape from Disadvantage*, London: The Falmer Press, 1990.

89 Walker, B. and Rochford, M., 'A Research Investigation into the Benefit Status of Caregivers of Children and Young People Who Come to the Notice of NZCYPS Research Unit', NZCYPS, April 1996.

90   McLanahan, S. and Sandefur, G., *Growing Up With a Single Parent*,
     Cambridge, Mass: Harvard University Press, 1994, p. 10.

91   McLanahan, S., 'The Reproduction of Poverty', *American Journal of
     Sociology*, Vol. 90, 1985, pp. 873-901.

92   McLanahan, S. and Booth, K., 'Mother-Only Families: Problems,
     Prospects, and Politics', *Journal of Marriage and the Family*, Vol. 51,
     1989, pp. 557-80.

93   McLanahan, S., 'Family Structure and Dependency: Early Transitions to
     Female Household Headship', *Demography*, Vol. 25, No. 1, 1988, pp. 1-15.
     Those who wish to maintain, in the face of evidence to the contrary, that
     the disadvantages experienced by children from broken or lone-parent
     family backgrounds can be explained in terms of economic variables, and
     therefore have nothing to do with the absence of a parent, have sometimes
     widened the use of the term 'economic' to cover virtually every aspect of a
     child's environment or upbringing. See, for example, Fogelman, K. (ed.),
     Growing Up in Great Britain, Macmillan for the National Children's
     Bureau, 1983. Adjustment is simultaneously made for factors which
     include not only social class and income, but household tenure, mother's
     education and employment, the number of schools attended, amenities
     and maintenance at home, parental aspirations, whether home had a
     room for homework, the child's sex and whether the child had been in
     care—as a significant proportion of lone-parent children had been.
     Outcomes enhanced by parental absenteeism (e.g. going into care) are
     used as causes of others (e.g. lower school scores).

94   Osborn, A.F., Butler, N.R. and Morris, A.C., *The Social Life of Britain's
     Five Year Olds*, Routledge & Kegan Paul, 1984.

95   Mayer, S.E., *What Money Can't Buy*, Cambridge: Harvard University
     Press, 1997.

96   DeGarmo, D.S., Forgatch, M.S. and Martinez, C.R., 'Parenting of Divorced
     Mothers as a Link between Social Status and Boys' Academic Outcomes:
     Unpacking the Effects of Socioeconomic Status', *Child Development*, Vol.
     70, No. 5, 1999, pp. 1231-245.

8: Why Children Don't Do So Well in 'Alternative Family Structures'

1   Patterson, C.J., 'Children of Lesbian and Gay Parents', *Child
     Development*, 63, 1992, pp. 1036 & 1037.

2   Utting, D., Bright, J. and Henricson, C., *Crime and the Family: Improving
     Childrearing and Preventing Delinquency*, London: Family Policy Studies
     Centre, 1993, p. 22.

3   Kim, J.E., Hetherington, E.M. and Reiss, D., 'Associations among Family
     Relationships, Anti-social Peers, and Adolescents' Externalising
     Behaviours: Gender and Family Type Differences', *Child Development*,
     Vol. 70, No. 5, 1999, pp. 1209-30.

4   Stolnick, A.S., *The Intimate Environment: Exploring Marriage and the
     Family*, New York: Harper Collins, 1996, pp. 343-44.

5   In their longitudinal study of 700 Nottingham children, the Newsons and
    Charlie Lewis found that father participation in middle childhood
    encouraged educational achievement and career plans, as well as
    preventing later lawlessness, as measured by criminal records, and
    surpassed any relationship with disciplinary styles or temperament.
    Newson, E., Newson, J. and Lewis, C., 'Father Participation Through
    Childhood and Its Relationship with Career Aspirations and
    Delinquency', in Beail, N. and McGuire, J. (eds), *Fathers: Psychological
    Perspectives*, Junction Books, 1982.

6   Lambert, L. and Hart, S., 'Who Needs a Father?', *New Society*, Vol. 37,
    No. 718, 1976, p. 80.

7   Katz, A., *Leading Lads*, University of Oxford, Department of Applied
    Social Studies and Research in association with TOPMAN.

8   Mosley, J., and Thomson, E., 'Fathering Behaviour and Child Outcomes:
    the Role of Race and Poverty', in Marsiglio, W. (ed.), *Fatherhood: Contem-
    porary Theory, Research, and Social Policy*, Thousand Oaks, CA: Sage,
    1995; see also discussion in Pleck, J.H., 'Paternal Involvement: Levels,
    Sources, and Consequences', in Lamb, M.E. (ed.), *The Role of the Father in
    Child Development*, 3rd edn, New York: John Wiley & Sons, 1997.

9   Furstenberg, F.F., Brooks-Gunn, J. and Morgan, S.P., *Adolescent Mothers
    in Later Life*, Cambridge University Press, 1987. However, as elsewhere,
    it had few effects on adjustment at the pre-school age. Data from the
    National Longitudinal Survey of Youth, the father's presence in the first
    three years of life on cognitive ability and behavioural adjustment at age
    four to six, indicated that children who experienced father co-residence
    fared best. Crockett, L.J., Eggebeen, D.J. and Hawkins, A.J., 'Father's
    Presence and Young Children's Behavioural and Cognitive Adjustment',
    Journal of Family Issues, Vol. 14, No. 3, 1993, pp. 355-77. However, with
    controls for mother's characteristics like her age at birth, IQ and
    education, and family resources, the effects disappeared. Of course, more
    intelligent, older mothers may choose men with more skills, resources and
    interest to contribute to the well-being of families. Moreover the role of
    attachments in early life for paternal involvement and children's later
    adjustment need to be remembered.

10 Franz, C.E., McClelland, D.C. and Weinberger, J., 'Childhood Antecedents
    of Conventional Social Accomplishments in Midlife Adults: A Thirty-Six
    Year Prospective Study', *Journal of Personality and Social Psychology*,
    Vol. 60, 1991, pp. 586-95.

11 Snarey, J., *How Fathers Care for the Next Generation*, Cambridge, Mass:
    Harvard University Press, 1993.

12 Weiss, Y. and Willis, R.J., 'Children as Collective Goods and Divorce
    Settlements', *Journal of Labor Economics*, Vol. 3, 1985, pp. 268-92.

13 Acquilino, W.S., 'Impact of Childhood Family Disruption on Young Adults'
    Relationships with Parents', *Journal of Marriage and the Family*, Vol. 56,
    1994, pp. 295-313.

14   Cockett, M. and Tripp, J., *The Exeter Family Study*, Exeter: University of Exeter, 1994.

15   Furstenberg, F.F. and Nord, C.W., 'Parenting Apart: Patterns of Childrearing after Marital Disruption', *Journal of Marriage and the Family*, Vol. 47, 1985, p. 902. See also Zill, N., Morrison, D. and Coiro, M.J., 'Long-Term Effects of Parental Divorce on Parent-Child Relationships, Adjustment, and Achievement in Young Adulthood', *Journal of Family Psychology*, Vol. 7, 1993, pp. 91-103.

16   McLanahan, S. and Sandefur, G., *Growing Up With a Single Parent*, Cambridge, Mass: Harvard University Press, 1994.

17   Dawson, D.A., *Family Structure and Children's Health: United States 1988*, Series 10,Vital and Health Statistics, Maryland: US Department of Health and Human Services, 1991.

18   Kim, J.E., Hetherington, E.M. and Reiss, D., 'Associations Among Family Relationships, Anti-social Peers, and Adolescents' Externalising Behaviours: Gender and Family Type Differences', *Child Development*, Vol. 70, No. 5, 1999, p. 1225.

19   Glenn, N., *Closed Hearts, Closed Minds: The Textbook Story of Marriage*, New York: Institute for American Values, 1997, p. 22.

20   McLanahan, S., 'The Consequences of Single Parenthood for Subsequent Generations', *Focus*, Institute for Research on Poverty, University of Wisconsin-Madison, 1988.

21   Warr, M., 'Parents, Peers and Delinquency', *Social Forces*, 72, 1993.

22   Matsueda, R.L. and Heimer, K., 'Race, Family Structure, and Delinquency: a Test of Differential Association and Social Control Theories', *American Sociological Review*, Vol. 52, 1987, pp. 826-40. Exploring one of the long-term implications of poor parent/child relationships, Matsueda's and Heimer's work on race, family structure, and delinquency, treats variables like parental supervision, attachment to peers and attitudes to delinquency as aspects of social control and association. Living in a troubled neighbourhood or a broken home is likely to weaken parental supervision, and low supervision increases delinquent peer relations, pro-delinquent attitudes and, ultimately, delinquent behaviour. As such, troubled neighbourhoods and broken homes both dilute the ties to parents, reduce the strength of conventional beliefs and increase the number of delinquent friends, compared with situations in which youths have warm relationships in intact families. As older children from disrupted or fragmented families often combine disengagement from the home situation with establishing supportive relationships with friends, such 'overinvestment' in peer relationships with an absence of monitoring by parents leads to problem behaviour.

23   It has been long observed how cold, unaffectionate fathers actually have fewer psychopathic children. This may be related to the fact that such fathers are usually strict disciplinarians and, as found elsewhere, strict discipline reduces the incidence of adult psychopathy. Robins, L.N., *Deviant Children Grown Up*, Baltimore: Williams and Wilkins, 1966; and

discussion in Hare, R.D., *Psychopathy*, New York: John Wiley & Sons Inc., 1970.

24 Astone, N.M. and McLanahan, S.S., 'Family Structure, Parenting Practices, and High School Completion', *American Sociological Review*, 56, 1991, pp. 309-20; and Hetherington, E.M., Cox, M. and Cox, R., 'Effects of Divorce on Parents and Children', in Lamb, M.E., *Nontraditional Families: Parenting and Child Development*, Hillsdale, NJ: Erlbaum, 1982.

25 *Western Australian Child Health Survey*, TVW Telethon, Institute for Child Health Research and the Australian Bureau of Statistics, 1996.

26 Dornbusch, S.M. *et al*, 'Single Parents, Extended Households, and the Control of Adolescents', *Child Development,* Vol. 56, 1985, p. 340.

27 Steinberg, L., 'Single Parents, Step-parents, and the Susceptibility of Adolescents to Anti-social Peer Pressure', *Child Development*, Vol. 58, 1987, pp. 269-75.

28 Offord, D.R., 'Family Backgrounds of Male and Female Delinquents', in Gunn, J. and Farrington, D.P. (eds), *Abnormal Offenders, Delinquency, and the Criminal Justice System*, Chichester: John Wiley & Sons, 1982.

29 McCord, J., 'A Longitudinal View of the Relationship Between Paternal Absence and Crime', in Gunn and Farrington, *Abnormal Offenders, Delinquency, and the Criminal Justice System*, 1982.

30 McCord, 'A Longitudinal View of the Relationship Between Paternal Absence and Crime', 1982, p. 125.

31 Richters, J.E. and Martinez, P.E., 'Violent Communities, Family Choices, and Children's Chances: An Algorithm for Improving the Odds', *Development and Psychopathology*, Vol. 5, 1993, pp. 609-27.

32 Dornbusch, 'Single Parents, Extended Households, and the Control of Adolescents', 1985, p. 340.

33 Hetherington, M.E. and Clingempeel, W.G., 'Coping with Marital Transitions', *Monographs of the Society for Research in Child Development*, Series 227, Vol. 47, No. 2-3, 1992; see Scarr, S. *et al.*, 'Developmental Status and School Achievements of Minority and Non-minority Children from Birth to 18 Years in a British Midlands Town', *British Journal of Development Psychology*, No. 1, 1983, pp. 31-48.

34 Amato, P.R., 'Children's Adjustment to Divorce; Theories, Hypotheses, and Empirical Support', *Journal of Marriage and the Family*, Vol. 55, 1993, pp. 23-38.

35 Furstenberg Jr, F.F., and Cherlin, A.J., *Divided Families: What Happens to Children When Parents Part?*, Cambridge, Mass: Harvard University Press, p. 118.

36 Amato, P.R and Booth, A., *A Generation at Risk* Cambridge, Mass: Harvard University Press, 1997.

37 Wallerstein, J.S. and Blakeslee, S., *Second Chances*, New York: Ticknor and Fields, 1989, pp. 52-53.

38 McLanahan and Sandefur, *Growing Up With a Single Parent*, 1994, p. 28.

39 Ritchie, J. and Ritchie, J., 'Child Rearing and Child Abuse: The Polynesian Context', in Korbin, J.E. (ed.), *Child Abuse and Neglect: Cross Cultural Perspectives*, Berkeley: University of California Press, 1981, p. 193.

40 Korbin, *Child Abuse and Neglect,* 1981, pp. 7-8.

41 Korbin, *Child Abuse and Neglect*, 1981, p. 19.

42 Bumpass, L.L., 'What's Happening to the Family? Interaction Between Demographic and Institutional Change', *Demography*, 27, 1990, pp. 483-98.

43 Rutter, M. and Quinton, D., 'Long-term Follow-up of Women Institutionalised in Childhood: Factors Promoting Good Functioning in Adult Life', *British Journal of Developmental Psychology*, Vol. 2, 1984, pp. 191-204.

44 McPherson, M.J., *Divorce in New Zealand*, Palmerston North: Social Policy Research Centre Massey University, 1995, p. 46

45 Cherlin, A.J., Chase-Lansdale, P.L. and McRae, C., 'Effects of Parental Divorce on Mental Health Throughout the Life Course', *American Sociological Review*, 63, 1998, pp. 239-49.

46 Cherlin, A.J. *et al.*, Longitudinal Studies of the Effects of Divorce on Children in Great Britain and the US', *Science*, 252, 1991, pp. 1486-89.

47 Hobcraft, J., 'Intergenerational and Life-Course Transmission of Social Exclusion: Influences of Childhood Poverty, Family Disruption, and Contact with the Police', CASEpaper 15, London: STICERD Centre for Analysis of Social Exclusion, London School of Economics, 1998, p. 40; see also Kiernan, K., *The Legacy of Parental Divorce: Social, Economic and Demographic Experiences in Adulthood,* London: Centre for Analysis of Social Exclusion, 1997.

48 Excluding anyone from one-parent families formed by death or out-of-wedlock birth. Amato, P.R. and Keith, B., 'Parental Divorce and Adult Well-being: A Meta Analysis', *Journal of Marriage and the Family*, Vol. 53, 1991, pp. 43-58.

49 Amato and Keith, 'Parental Divorce and Adult Well-being: a Meta Analysis', 1991, p. 55; see also Woodward, L., Fergusson, D.M. and Belsky, J., 'Timing of Parental Separation and Attachment to Parents of Adolescents', *Journal of Marriage and the Family*, Vol. 62, 2000, pp. 162-74.

50 Patterson, C.J., 'Children of Lesbian and Gay Parents', *Child Development*, 63, 1992, p. 1027.

51 Fincham, F.D., 'Understanding the Association between Marital Conflict and Child Adjustment: An Overview', *Journal of Family Psychology*, Vol. 8, No. 2, pp. 123-27; and Erel, O. and Burman, B., 'Interrelatedness of Marital Relations and Parent-child Relations: a Meta-analytic Review', *Psychological Bulletin*, Vol. 118, 1995, pp. 108-32.

52 Wallerstein, J.S., and Blakeslee, S., *Second Chances*, New York: Ticknor and Fields, 1989; Quinton, D. and Rutter, M., *Parenting Breakdown: the Making and Breaking of Inter Generational Links*, Aldershot: Avebury, 1988.

53 *Social Policy Research Findings*, No. 45, York: Joseph Rowntree Foundation, February 1994; see also Wallerstein and Blakeslee, *Second Chances*, 1989.

54 Crockett, M. and Tripp, J., *Children Living in Re-ordered Families*, York: Joseph Rowntree Foundation, 1994.

55 Spruijt, E. and De Goede, M., 'Changing Family Structures and Adolescent Well-being in the Netherlands', *International Journal of Law, Policy and the Family*, 10, 1996, pp. 1-16. Adolescents from conflicted intact families were close to those from one-parent families in terms of physical and psychological well-being, but closer to stable intact families with respect to emotional relationships and employment. Those in step-families were closer to the stable intact families for physical, relational and occupational matters, but most resembled the one-parent group on psychological matters.

56 Simons, R.L., Lin, K-H., Gordon, L.C., Conger, R.D. and Lorenz, F.O., 'Explaining the Higher Incidence of Adjustment Problems Among Children of Divorce Compared with Those in Two-Parent Families', *Journal of Marriage and the Family*, Vol. 61, 1999, pp. 1020-33.

57 Zubrick, S.R. *et al.*, *Western Australian Child Health Survey: Education, Health and Competence*, Perth, Western Australia: Australian Bureau of Statistics and the TVW Institute for Child Health Research, 1995.

58 Wallerstein, J.S. and Lewis, J., *The Unexpected Legacy of Divorce: A 25-Year Landmark Study*, Hyperion, 2000.

59 Fincham, F.D., Grych, J.H. and Osborne, L.N., 'Does Marital Conflict Cause Child Malajustment? Directions and Challenges for Longitudinal Research', *Journal of Family Psychology*, Vol. 8, No. 2, 1994, pp. 128-34.

60 O'Brien, M., Margolin, G. and John, R.S., 'Relation Among Marital Conflict, Child Coping, and Child Adjustment', *Journal of Clinical Child Psychology*, Vol. 24, No. 3, 1995, pp. 346-61.

61 Simons, *et al.*,'Explaining the Higher Incidence of Adjustment Problems Among Children of Divorce Compared with Those in Two-Parent Families', 1999.

62 Fergusson, D.M., Lynskey, M and Horwood, L.J., 'Family Change, Parental Discord and Early Offending', *Journal of Child Psychology and Psychiatry*, 33, No. 6, 1992, pp. 1059-75.

63 Fergusson, D.M., Horwood, L.J. and Dimond, M.E., 'A Survival Analysis of Childhood Family History', *Journal of Marriage and the Family*, Vol. 47, 1985, pp. 287-95.

64 Fergusson, Lynskey and Horwood, 'Family Change, Parental Discord and Early Offending', 1992, p. 1071.

65 Amato and Booth, *A Generation at Risk*, 1997. Twenty-eight per cent of parents who divorced during the study reported any sort of spousal physical abuse prior to divorce, 30 per cent reported more than two serious quarrels in the last month, and 23 per cent reported they disagreed 'often' or 'very often'.

66 Amato and Booth, *A Generation at Risk*, 1997, p. 221.

67 *Western Australian Child Health Survey*, TVW Telethon Institute for Child Health Research and the Australian Bureau of Statistics, 1996.

68 Miller, J.E. and Davis, D., 'Poverty History, Marital History, and Quality of Children's Home Environments', *Journal of Marriage and the Family*, Vol. 59, 1997, pp. 996-1007.

69 Dunn, J., Deater-Deckard, K., Pickering, K., O'Connor, T.G. and Golding, J., 'Children's Adjustment and Prosocial Behaviour in Step-, Single-parent and Nonstep-family Settings: Findings from a Community Study', *The Journal of Child Psychology and Psychiatry and Allied Disciplines*, Vol. 39, Issue 8, November 1998, pp. 1083-95.

70 Zill, Morrison and Coiro, 'Long-term Effects of Parental Divorce on Parent-Child Relationships, Adjustment, and Achievement in Young Adulthood', 1993.

71 Amato and Booth, *A Generation at Risk*, 1997.

72 Campbell, S.B. *et al.*, 'Noncompliant Behaviour, Overactivity, and Family Stress as Predictors of Negative Maternal Control with Pre-school Children', *Development and Psychopathology*, 3, 1991, pp. 175-90.

73 O'Brien, Margolin and John, 'Relation Among Marital Conflict, Child Coping, and Child Adjustment', 1995.

74 Richman, N., Stevenson, J. and Graham, P., *Pre-school to School; a Behavioural Study,* London: Academic Press, 1982; also Kellam, S. *et al.*, 'The Long-term Evolution of the Family Structure of Teenage and Older Mothers', *Journal of Marriage and the Family*, Vol. 44, 1982, pp. 539-54.

75 Amato, P.R. and Keith, B., 'Parental Divorce and the Well-being of Children: A Meta-analysis', *Psychological Bulletin*, 110, 1991, pp. 26-46.

76 Fergusson D., 'Family Formation, Dissolution and Reformation', in *Proceedings of the SSRFC Symposium: New Zealand Families in the Eighties and Nineties*, Canterbury University, No. 20, November 1987, pp. 15-30.

77 Cockett, M. and Tripp, J., *The Exeter Family Study*, Exeter: University of Exeter, 1994.

78 Fergusson, 'Family Formation, Dissolution and Reformation', 1987.

79 Hanson, T., McLanahan, S.S. and Thomson, E., 'Double Jeopardy: Parental Conflict and Step-family Outcomes for Children', *Journal of Marriage and the Family*, Vol. 58, 1996, p. 141.

80   Hetherington, M.E. and Clingempeel, W.G., 'Coping with Marital
     Transitions', *Monographs of the Society for Research in Child
     Development*, Series 227, Vol. 47, No. 2-3, 1992.

81   Elliott, J., Richards, M. and Warwick, H., *The Consequences of Divorce for
     the Health and Well-being of Adults and Children*, Final Report for
     Health Promotion Trust No. 2, Cambridge: Centre for Family Research,
     1993; and Sweeting, H. and West, P., 'Family Life and Health in
     Adolescence: a Role for Culture in the Health Equalities Debate?', *Social
     Science and Medicine* 40, 1995, pp. 163-75.

82   See, for example, from the National Child Development Study Ferri, E.,
     Step Children, Windsor: NFER-Nelson, 1984. In the Oregon Youth Study,
     the chances that boys who had been through divorce by the age of 10
     would be more anti-social was especially marked where they had step-
     fathers. Capaldi, D.M. and Patterson, G.R., 'Relation of Parental
     Transitions to Boy's Adjustment Problems: (i) A Linear Hypothesis, (ii)
     Mothers at Risk for Transitions and Unskilled Parenting', *Developmental
     Psychology*, Vol. 27, No. 3, 1991, pp. 489-504; and Haurin, J.R., 'Patterns
     of Childhood Residence and the Relation to Young Adult Outcomes',
     Journal of Marriage and the Family, Vol. 54, 1992, pp. 846-60. Also,
     Steinberg, L., 'Single Parents, Step-parents, and the Susceptibility of
     Adolescents to Anti-social Peer Pressure', *Child Development*, Vol. 58,
     1987, pp. 269-75.

83   Hanson, McLanahan and Thomson, 'Double jeopardy', 1996, pp. 141-54.

84   McLanahan and Sandefur, *Growing Up With a Single Parent*, 1994.

85   McLanahan, S. and Harper, C., *Father Absence and Youth Incarceration*,
     paper presented at the 1998 annual meeting of the American Sociological
     Association, San Francisco, CA, August 1998.

86   Spruijt, E. and De Goede, M., 'Changing Family Structures and
     Adolescent Well-being in the Netherlands', *International Journal of Law,
     Policy and the Family*, Vol. 10, 1996, pp. 1-16.

87   White, L.K. and Booth, A., 'The Quality and Stability of Remarriage: the
     Role of Stepchildren', *American Sociological Review*, Vol. 50, 1985,
     pp. 689-98.

88   Fergusson, 'Family Formation, Dissolution and Reformation', 1987.

89   Thomson, E., McLanahan, S. and Curtin, R.B., 'Family Structure, Gender
     and Parental Socialisation', *Journal of Marriage and the Family*, Vol. 54,
     1992, pp. 368-78.

90   Cockett and Tripp, *The Exeter Family Study*, 1994; Ferri, *Step Children*,
     1984; Honess, T.M. *et al.*, 'Conflict Between Parents and Adolescents:
     Variation by Family Constitution', *British Journal of Developmental
     Psychology*, 15, 1997, pp. 367-85; and Kiernan, K., 'The Impact of Family
     Disruption in Childhood on Transitions Made in Young Adult Life',
     Population Studies, Vol. 46, 1992, pp. 213-34. Dunn, Deater-Deckard,
     Pickering, O'Connor and Golding, 'Children's Adjustment and Prosocial

Behaviour in Step-, Single-parent and Nonstep-family Settings: Findings from a Community Study', 1998.

91 Kim, Hetherington and Reiss, 'Associations among Family Relationships, Anti-social Peers, and Adolescents' Externalising Behaviours: Gender and Family Type Differences', 1999. This followed 720 two-parent families (each with a pair of adolescent siblings of the same sex close in age).

92 See also Hetherington and Clingempeel, 'Coping with Marital Transitions', 1992.

93 West, D.J. and Farrington, D.P., *Who Becomes Delinquent?*, Heinemann, 1973; and *The Delinquent Way of Life*, Heinemann, 1977.

94 White, L., 'Growing Up with Single Parents and Step-parents: Long-term Effects on Family Solidarity', *Journal of Marriage and the Family*, Vol. 56, November 1994, p. 937; also Amato, P., *Children in Australian Families: The Growth of Competence*, New York: Prentice Hall, 1987; and Santrock, J.W., Sitterle, K.A. and Warshak, R.A., 'Parent-child Relationships in Stepfather Families', in Bronstein, P. and Pape-Cowan, C. (eds), *Fatherhood Today: Men's Changing Role in the Family*, New York: Wiley, 1988; and Hetherington, E.M., Stanley-Hagan, M. and Anderson, E.R., 'Marital Transitions: a Child's Perspective', *American Psychologist*, 44, No. 2, February 1989.

95 Ferri, *Step Children*, 1984. Also see, Hobcraft, J., Inter-generational and Life-Course Transmission of Social Exclusion: Influences of Childhood Poverty, Family Disruption, and Contact with the Police, CASEpaper 15, London: STICERD Centre for Analyais of Social Exclusion, LSE, 1998.

96 According to data from the National Survey of Families and Households, see Thomson, E., McLanahan, S. and Curtin, R.B., 'Family Structure, Gender and Parental Socialisation', *Journal of Marriage and the Family*, Vol. 54, 1992, pp. 368-78. See also Zill, N. and Nord, C.W., *Running in Place: How American Families are Faring in a Changing Economy and an Individualistic Society*, Washington, DC: Child Trends, 1994.

97 Kim, Hetherington and Reiss, 'Associations among Family Relationships, Anti-social Peers, and Adolescents' Externalising Behaviours: Gender and Family Type Differences', 1999.

98 According to data from the National Survey of Families and Households, see Thomson, McLanahan and Curtin, 'Family Structure, Gender and Parental Socialisation', 1992. See also Zill and Nord, *Runnning in Place: How American Families are Faring in a Changing Economy and an Individualistic Society*, 1994.

99 Amato, P., *Children in Australian Families: The Growth of Competence*, New York: Prentice Hall, 1987.

100 Amato, P.R. and Booth, A., 'Consequences of Parental Divorce and Marital Unhappiness for Adult Well-being', *Social Forces*, Vol. 69, 1991, pp. 895-914.

101 Aquilino, W.S., 'Family Structure and Home-Leaving: A Further Specification of the Relationship', *Journal of Marriage and the Family*, Vol. 53, 1991, pp. 999-1010.

102 Jones, G., *Leaving Home*, Open University Press, 1995.

103 Burdekin Report: Report of the National Inquiry into Homeless Children, *Our Homeless Children*, Canberra: AGPS, 1989, discussed in Tapper, A., *The Family in the Welfare State*, Allen & Unwin and the Australian Institute for Public Policy, p. 202.

104 The National Inquiry into Youth Homelessness, report in Evans, A., *We Don't Choose to be Homeless*, London: CHAR (now National Homeless Alliance), 1996.

105 Smith, J., Gilford, S. and O'Sullivan, A., *The Family Backgrounds of Homeless Young People*, London: Family Policy Studies Centre, 1998, p. 32; also see Jones, *Leaving Home*, 1995; and Strathdee, R., *No Way Back*, London: Centre Point, 1992.

106 Smith, Gilford and O'Sullivan, *The Family Backgrounds of Homeless Young People*, 1998, pp. 49 & 32.

107 Smith, Gilford and O'Sullivan, *The Family Backgrounds of Homeless Young People*, 1998, p. 31.

108 Smith, Gilford and O'Sullivan, *The Family Backgrounds of Homeless Young People*, 1998, p. 32. People generally took it for granted that when a child is 16 and legally entitled to leave, parents with new partners have a right to remake their lives, and some even felt that a child should leave at 14. Young people themselves may share expectations that they should be self-supporting.

109 Rees, G. and Rutherford, C., *Homerun: Families and Young Runaways*, The Children's Society, Briefing Paper, 2001.

110 The immediate cause of eviction was likely to be stealing from parents, offering them violence or 'trashing' the family home. Smith, Gilford and O'Sullivan, *The Family Backgrounds of Homeless Young People*, 1998, p. 22.

111 Hanson, McLanahan and Thomson, 'Double Jeopardy', 1996.

112 Ferri, *Step Children*, 1984; Ely, M., Richards, M.P.M., Wadsworth, M.E.J., and Elliot, B.J., 'Secular Changes in the Association of Parental Divorce and Children's Educational Attainment—Evidence from Three British Cohorts', *Journal of Social Policy*, Vol. 28, 1999, pp. 464-495; and Kiernan, K., 'The Impact of Family Disruption in Childhood on Transitions Made in Young Adult Life', *Population Studies*, Vol. 46, 1992, pp. 213-34; Rodgers, B. and Pryor, J., *Divorce and Separation: The Outcomes for Children*, York: Joseph Rowntree Foundation, 1998; Cockett and Tripp, *The Exeter Family Study*, 1994; Essen, J., 'Living in One-parent Families; Attainment at School', *Child: Care, Health and Development*, 5, 1979, pp. 189-200.

113 McLanahan, S. and Harper, C., *Father Absence and Youth Incarceration*, paper presented at the 1998 annual meeting of the American Sociological Association, San Francisco, CA, August 1998. See also, Fine, M.A., and Kurdek, L.A., 'Parenting Cognitions in Stepfamilies: Differences Between Parents and Stepparents and the Relations to Parenting Satisfaction', *Journal of Social and Personal Relationships*, 11, 1994, pp. 95-112.

114 Blankenhorn, D., *Fatherless America*, New York: Basic Books, 1995, p. 187.

115 Daly, M. and Wilson, M., *The Truth About Cinderella*, London: Weidenfeld and Nicolson, 1998, p. 48; and Daly, M. and Wilson, M., *Homicide*, New York: Aldine De Gruyter, 1988.

116 Rodgers and Pryor, *Divorce and Separation: The Outcomes for Children*, 1998, p. 36.

117 Ferri, *Step Children*, 1984.

118 Daly and Wilson, *Homicide*, 1988, p. 93.

119 Rodgers and Pryor, *Divorce and Separation: The Outcomes for Children*, 1998, p. 46.

120 Fergusson, D.M., Horwood, L.J. and Lynskey, M., 'The Childhoods of Multiple-problem Adolescents: A 15-Year Longitudinal Study', *Journal of Child Psychology and Psychiatry*, 1994, pp. 1123-139.

121 Walker, B. and Rochford, M., 'A Research Investigation into the Benefit Status of Caregivers of Children and Young People Who Come to the Notice of NZCYPS Research Unit', NZCYPS, April 1996.

122 Zill, N., Morrison, D.R. and Coiro, M.J., *Long-Term Effects of Parental Divorce on Parent-Child Relationships, Adjustment and Achievement in Young Adulthood*, Washington DC: Child Trends Inc., 2000, p. 34.

123 Fergusson, D., 'Family Formation, Dissolution and Reformation', in *Proceedings of the SSRFC Symposium: New Zealand Families in the Eighties and Nineties*, Canterbury University, No. 20, 1987, p. 29.

124 Glenn, N.D., 'A Critique of Twenty Family and Marriage and the Family Textbooks', *Family Relations*, Vol. 46, No. 3, 1997, p. 202.

125 Walters, R., 'Should NZ Introduce Boot Camps?', in *Youth Recidivist Offending Project Report*, New Zealand Police, National HQ, 1995, p. 87.

126 Pool, I., 'Family Demographic Changes: Good News or Bad News', in Smith, A.B. and Taylor, N.J., *Supporting Children and Parents through Family Changes*, Dunedin: University of Otago, 1996, p. 12. This man sees so many 'moral panics' that he must be in the most heightened state of confusion himself.

9: Problems for Adults

1   Ministerial Committee of Inquiry, *Report of the Ministerial Committee of Inquiry into Violence*, Wellington: Department of Justice, 1987.

2   Snively, S., *The New Zealand Economic Cost of Family Violence*,
     Wellington: Family Violence Unit, 1994.

3   Morris, A., *Women's Safety Survey 1996*, Wellington: Victimisation Survey
     Committee, 1996. The response to this survey was high at 79 per cent.
     However, it has to be seen in the context of the response to National
     Survey of Crime Victims, where the response rate was 57 per cent.
     Women who reported to this earlier investigation that they had suffered
     partner abuse were more likely to participate in the later survey,
     although it is not known how many did not admit to being victimised in
     the first place. In the earlier National Survey of Crime Victims (which the
     Women's Safety Survey followed), 16 per cent of non-Maori and 31 per
     cent of Maori women reported abuse by any partner. The difference may
     be due to the focus of the earlier survey on a range of crimes rather than
     specific acts by partners—which might have led to more disclosures in
     face to face interviews.

4   Women may be under-reporting violence from current partners because
     they are still living with them. We know from other research that women
     may also be violent, or initiate violence. Asked whether they had hit first,
     28 per cent with current partners and 15 per cent with recent partners
     admitted to this. Forty-nine per cent of women with current partners and
     more than two-thirds (67 per cent) of women with recent partners hit
     back.

5   Although Maori women reported higher levels of all items. Any act of
     violence towards current partners was reported by 21 per cent (or eight
     per cent non-Maori and 23 per cent for Maori).

6   The Canadian Violence against Women survey reported that respectively
     15 and 48 per cent of Canadian women had experienced at least one
     incidence of physical or sexual assault by their current or previous
     partner, compared with New Zealand's 24 and 73 per cent, with three per
     cent of Canadian women having experienced violence in the last 12
     months, compared with the New Zealand 15 per cent from current
     partners in this time. Johnson, H. and Sacco, V., 'Researching Violence
     Against Women: Statistics Canada National Survey', *Canadian Journal
     of Criminology*, July 1995, pp. 281-304. The National Family Violence
     Surveys indicate that around 16 per cent of American couples experienced
     an assault during the survey year, although there was 'the virtual
     certainty that not every respondent was completely frank in describing
     violent incidents. The true rates could be as much as double ...' And,
     anyway, two-thirds of the couples who experienced an assault reported
     more than one incident during the base year of the study. About one-third
     represent serious assaults. Straus, M.A. and Gelles, R. J., 'How Violent
     are American Families? Estimates from the National Violence Resurvey,
     and Other Studies', in Straus, M.A. and Gelles, R.J., *Physical Violence in
     American Families*, Brunswick, NJ: Transaction Pub., 1990, p. 96. The
     Women's Safety Survey of Australia found that 22.5 per cent of women
     who currently, or who had ever, had a partner had experienced physical
     violence (based on actions that could be considered as offences under state
     criminal law.) Hegarty, K. and Roberts, G., 'How Common is Domestic

Violence Against Women? The Definition of Partner Abuse in Prevalence Studies', *Australia and New Zealand Journal of Public Health*, Vol. 22, No. 1, 1998, pp. 49-54. Australian samples yield lifetime prevalences of between 19.3 to 25 per cent but, like other overseas studies, they often suffer from problems of definitional clarity of the term domestic violence and some have tried to broaden the definitions to include emotional abuse. For New Zealand, also see Mullen, P. *et al*, 'The Impact of Sexual and Physical Abuse on Women's Mental Health', *Lancet*, 1988, pp. 841-45.

7   In the same year that New Zealand women became entitled to vote, The Society for the Protection of Women and Children was set up to press for legislative change to protect women and children from domestic violence. Much of the early legislation on divorce related to the ill treatment of women and children and the failure of husbands to provide for them.

8   Haines, H., 'Women's Mental Health as a Feminist Issue', *Women's Studies Journal*, December 1989, p. 33.

9   Ryan, A., 'Remoralising Politics', in Jesson, B., Ryan, A. and Spoonley, P., *Revival of the Right*, Auckland: Heinemann Reed, 1988, p. 82.

10   Gelles, R.J. and Straus, M.A., *Intimate Violence*, New York: Simon and Schuster, 1988.

11   Dobash, R.P. and Dobash, R.E., *Violence Against Wives: The Case Against the Patriarchy*, New York: Free Press, 1980, p. 24.

12   McPherson M.J., *Divorce in New Zealand*, Palmerston North: Social Policy Research Centre Massey University, 1995, p. 2.

13   Briar, C., 'Problems in the New Zealand Family', in Green, P.F. (ed.), *Studies in New Zealand Social Problems*, 2nd edn, Palmerston North: Dunmore Press, 1994, p. 263.

14   Cartwright, S., 'Violence and Water: Women's Issues and the Law', F.W Guest Memorial Lecture, 1993, *Otago Law Review*, 1994, p. 7.

15   Apparently 'women in particular', condemn the family as '... a site of violent interaction', Saville-Smith, K., Bray, M., Davidson, C. and Field, A., *Bringing Home the Bacon: The Changing Relationship between Family, State, and Market in New Zealand in the 1980s*, Family and Societal Change Report No. 3, Wellington: New Zealand Institute for Social Research and Development Ltd, 1994, p. 2.

16   Haines, 'Women's Mental Health as a Feminist Issue', 1989, p. 33.

17   Renzetti, C., *Violent Betrayal: Partner Abuse in Lesbian Relationships*, Sage, 1992, p. 93.

18   *Western Australian Child Health Survey*, TVW Telethon, Institute for Child Health Research and the Australian Bureau of Statistics, 1996.

19   Brown, S.L. and Booth, A., 'Cohabitation Versus Marriage: a Comparison of Relationship Quality', *Journal of Marriage and the Family*, Vol. 58, No. 3, 1996, pp. 668-78.

20 US Bureau of Justice Statistics, *Highlights from 20 Years of Surveying Crime Victims: The National Crime Victimisation Survey, 1973-92*, Washington DC: US Department of Justice, 1993.

21 Bachman, R., 'Violence Against Women', Washington, DC: Bureau of Justice Statistics, 1994, p. 6. See also, Marks, N.F. and Lambert, J.D., 'Marital Status, Continuity and Change among Young and Midlife Adults: Longitudinal Effects on Psychological Well-being', *Journal of Family Issues*, 19, 1998, pp. 652-86.

22 Centres for Disease Control and Prevention, *Morbidity and Mortality Weekly Report 43,* No. 8, Washington DC: US Government Printing Office, 4 March 1994.

23 Roberts, A.R., 'Psychosocial Characteristics of Batterers: a Study of 234 Men Charged with Domestic Violence Offences', *Journal of Family Violence*, Vol. 2, No. 1, 1987, pp. 85-95.

24 *The 1998 British Crime Survey*, Home Office Statistical Bulletin Issue 21/98, Government Statistical Service, 1998.

25 Brown, G.W. and Moran, P.M., 'Single Mothers, Poverty and Depression', *Psychological Medicine*, 27, 1997, pp. 21-33.

26 Morris, *Women's Safety Survey 1996*, 1997.

27 'Strategy Paper on Crime Prevention', Crime Prevention Action Group, Department of Prime Minister and Cabinet, 1992, pp. 6 & 30.

28 'Strategy Paper on Crime Prevention', 1992, p. 42.

29 Maxwell, G.M., 'Children and Family Violence: The Unnoticed Victims', *Social Policy Journal of New Zealand*, 2, 1994, pp. 81-96.

30 Atkin, B., 'The Domestic Violence Act', *The New Zealand Law Journal*, Jan 1998, pp. 24-31.

31 Smart, C. and Stevens, P., *Cohabitation Breakdown*, London: Family Policy Studies Centre, 2000.

32 Smart, C. and Stevens, P., *Cohabitation Breakdown*, London: Family Policy Studies Centre, 2000, pp. 23 & 33.

33 The discrepancy applies to all forms of abuse, whether being pushed or grabbed in a way that hurt (Maori with current partners 29 per cent, compared with 14 per cent for non-Maori, and for recent partners, it was 77 per cent with 55 per cent), or hit with fist (16 per cent current with four per cent, and 48 per cent with 22 per cent), or being choked (11 per cent with one per cent and 40 per cent with 14 per cent). Maori women also experienced violence from non-Maori partners—in a third of cases. Morris, *Women's Safety Survey 1996*, 1997.

34 For example: while three per cent of all women with current partners and 24 per cent with recent partners reported that they had been afraid their partner might kill them, for Maori it was five and 44 per cent. Violence experienced by Maori women was both rated more serious by the women themselves as well as having more serious consequences than for non-

Maori women. While one per cent of women with current partners and eight per cent of the women with recent partners reported that they had been treated or admitted to hospital as a result of their partner's violence, the figures were two and 19 per cent for Maori. In turn, while one per cent of the women with current partners and seven per cent with recent partners also reported that they had received medical treatment from a doctor as a result of violence, for Maori this was three and 24 per cent. Similar distributions are shown for more broadly defined partner abuse and controlling behaviour. Thus, 14 per cent of Maori women with current partners reported being frightened by them, compared with seven per cent of non-Maori women, and the figures were 94 with 54 per cent for recent partners. For being prevented from knowing about the family income, even if asking, the figures are 11 with four per cent and 64 with 30 per cent. Morris, *Women's Safety Survey 1996*, 1997.

35   Maxwell, G.M., *Physical Punishment in the Home in New Zealand*, Occasional Paper No. 2, Wellington: Office of the Commissioner for Children, 1993. By the early 1970s it was already reported as six-fold (and for children of other Pacific Island people, it was nine-fold), with Maori females the most abused group. Ritchie, J. and Ritchie, J., 'Child Rearing and Child Abuse: The Polynesian Context', in Korbin, J.E. (ed.), *Child Abuse and Neglect: Cross-Cultural Perspectives*, Berkeley: University of California Press, 1981.

36   Walker, B. and Rochford, M., 'A Research Investigation into the Benefit Status of Caregivers of Children and Young People Who Come to the Notice of NZCYPS Research Unit', NZCYPS, April 1996. Previous unpublished statistics showed how 51 per cent of neglect complaints referred to Maori, 41 per cent of 'detrimental environment', 54 per cent of not being under proper control, and 46 per cent of children committed to the care of the state. Maxwell, *Physical Punishment in the Home in New Zealand*, 1993.

37   The actual population over 65 was 91 per cent European, Maori 3.7 per cent and 1.4 per cent Pacific Island, compared with 76 per cent European, nine per cent Maori and two per cent Pacific Island for abuse referrals in 1998/9. Nineteen per cent of alleged abusers showed evidence of drug or alcohol abuse. *Age Concern Elder Abuse and Neglect Services*, Age Concern New Zealand Incorporated, Wellington 1999.

38   Cazenave, N.A. and Straus, M.A., 'Race, Class, Network Embeddedness, and Family Violence: A Search for Potent Support Systems', in Straus, M.A. and Gelles, R.J., *Physical Violence in American Families*, Brunswick, N. Jersey: Transaction Pub., 1990.

39   Straus, M.A., Gelles, R.J. and Steinmetz, S.K., *Behind Closed Doors: Violence in the American Family*, New York: Doubleday/Anchor, 1980.

40   Moreover, while men's occupational status is more highly associated with child abuse, sibling abuse and parent abuse for blacks than whites, higher black rates of hitting a spouse occur in all groups. Higher black rates for severe wife-to- husband violence disappear for white collar respondents.

41 Counts, D.Y., 'Domestic Violence in Oceania: Conclusions', *Pacific Studies*, Vol. 13, No. 3, 1990, pp. 225-54.

42 Straus, M.A. and Smith, C., 'Family Patterns and Primary Prevention of Family Violence', in Straus and Gelles, *Physical Violence in American Families*, 1990; see also Orbell, M., 'The Traditional Maori Family', in Koopman Boyden, P.G., *Families in New Zealand Society*, NZ: Methuen, 1978.

43 Farrington, D.P., 'The Development of Offending and Antisocial Behaviour from Childhood: Key Findings from the Cambridge Study in Delinquent Development', The Twelfth Jack Tizard Memorial Lecture, *Journal of Child Psychology and Psychiatry*, 1995, pp. 929-59.

44 Hotaling, G.T., Straus, M.A. and Lincoln, A.J., 'Intrafamily Violence and Crime and Violence Outside the Family', in Straus and Gelles, *Physical Violence in American Families*, 1990.

45 Maxwell, G.M., 'Children and Family Violence: The Unnoticed Victims', *Social Policy Journal of New Zealand*, 2, 1994, pp. 81-96; see also Maxwell, G.M. and Robertson, J., 'Children and Family Violence: The Unnoticed Victims Revisited', in *Children*, a newsletter from the Office of the Commissioner for Children, No. 21, 1996.

46 Stets, J.E. and Straus, M.A., 'The Marriage License as a Hitting License: A Comparison of Assaults in Dating, Cohabiting, and Married Couples', in Straus and Gelles, *Physical Violence in American Families*, 1995, p. 227. See Yllo, K. and Straus, M.A., 'Interpersonal Violence Among Married and Cohabiting Couples', *Family Relations*, 30, 1981, pp. 339-347.

47 Sarantakos, S., 'Trial Cohabitation on Trial', *Australian Social Work*, Vol. 47, No. 3, 1994.

48 Stets, J.E., 'Cohabiting and Marital Aggression: the Role of Social Isolation', *Journal of Marriage and the Family*, Vol. 53, 1991, pp. 669-80.

49 Sarantakos, S., *Living Together in Australia*, Melbourne: Longman Cheshire, 1984, p. 138; and Huffman, T., *et al.*, 'Gender Differences and Factors Related to the Disposition Toward Cohabitation', *Family Therapy*, Vol. 21, 1994, pp. 171-84.

50 Morris, *Women's Safety Survey 1996*, 1997; Kantor, G.K. and Straus M.A., 'The "Drunken Bum" Theory of Wife Beating', in Straus and Gelles, *Physical Violence in American Families*, 1990, p. 203.

51 Counts, D.Y., 'Domestic Violence in Oceania: Conclusions', *Pacific Studies*, Vol. 13, No. 3, 1990, pp. 225-54.

52 Horwitz, A.V. and White, H.R., 'The Relationship of Cohabitation and Mental Health: a Study of a Young Adult Cohort', *Journal of Marriage and the Family*, Vol. 60, 1998, p. 512.

53 Nock, S.L., 'A Comparison of Marriages and Cohabiting Relationships', *Journal of Family Issues*, 16, 1995, pp. 53-76. Those who married after cohabiting were closer to those who married without cohabiting than

those who were currently cohabiting. As cohabitations do not endure, the analysis was limited to relationships of no more than ten years duration, and, even then, the average length of the marriages picked up in the sample was almost twice that of cohabitations.

54 Smart, C. and Stevens, P., *Cohabitation Breakdown*, London: Family Policy Studies Centre, 2000, pp. 23 & 33.

55 Blankenhorn, D., *Fatherless America,* New York: Basic Books, 1995, p. 36.

56 Ritchie, 'Child Rearing and Child Abuse: The Polynesian Context', 1981.

57 Nock, 'A Comparison of Marriages and Cohabiting Relationships', 1995.

58 'Strategy Paper on Crime Prevention', Crime Prevention Action Group, Department of Prime Minister and Cabinet, 1992, p. 61.

59 There is evidence, for example, that networks are more important in reducing family violence for US Blacks as compared with Whites at similar socio-economic levels.

60 Pilott, B., 'Stopping Family Violence', in *Rights and Responsibilities*, Papers from the International Year of the Family Symposium on 'Rights and Responsibilities of the Family' held in Wellington, 14 to 16 October 1994, Wellington: International Year of the Family Committee in association with the Office of the Commissioner for Children, 1995, p. 172.

61 Brinig, M.F. and Crafton, S.M., 'Marriage and Opportunism', *Journal of Legal Studies*, Vol. XXIII, June 1994, pp. 869-94.

62 Kantor, G.K. and Straus, M.A., 'Response of Victims and the Police to Assaults on Wives', in Straus and Gelles, *Physical Violence in American Families*, 1995. This quotes findings from US data that, while arrest is viewed as a severe sanction, 'the subjectively experienced deterrence of this sanction may be almost zero because batterers believe that arrest is very unlikely. Our finding of a police intervention rate of only 6.7 per cent and an arrest rate of about one per cent indicates that batterers are correct in this belief'. However, it is objected that claims about police tolerating domestic violence 'misses the more basic point: the criminal justice system's indifferent response to most violence in general. Virtually every police agency under-reinforces the law to a great extent, and not just for domestic violence.' Sherman, L.W., *Policing Domestic Violence*, New York: The Free Press, 1992, p. 25.

63 In two-fifths of 'call outs' in 1995-6 partners were arrested, the usual action was to get the man to calm down.

64 The comparisons were either ordering the suspect out of the home for eight hours, or the police leaving the home after advising the couple to 'calm down'.

65 This recommendation was adopted by Maryland and a dozen more states. Sherman, L.W *Policing Domestic Violence* New York: The Free Press, 1992. It is claimed that, after mandated arrest, calls to police fell sharply. It may have been that women were afraid to call the police if their partner was going to be arrested.

66   Initially, it seemed that this depended upon racial composition, which might suggest that white suspects more often see arrest as a legitimate response to their conduct, while other groups construe it as harassment.

67   The 26-week counselling program is mandated in lieu of a 30-day jail term, which is imposed if the batterer misses three successive counselling sessions. L.W. Sherman argues that if using mandatory arrest policies, states should mandate that each police agency develop its own list of approved options to be exercised at the discretion of the officer. The options should include allowing the victims to decide whether a suspect should be arrested, transporting victims to shelters, or taking the suspect to an alcohol detoxification centre. Of course, there are two other arguments to justify the arrest policy. (i) Moral argument that arrest should be imposed as the proper punishment for the suspected crime, even if it causes an increase in domestic violence; and (ii) That general deterrence of domestic violence reduces its overall frequency among the potential or current batterers who never come to police attention.

68   Haines, H., 'Women's Mental Health as a Feminist Issue', *Women's Studies Journal,* December 1989, p. 23.

69   Hu, Y. and Goldman, N., 'Mortality Differentials by Marital Status: an International Comparison', *Demography,* Vol. 27, No. 20, 1990, pp. 233-50.

70   This can be, for example, five-fold compared with ten-fold. Bloom, B.L. *et al.,* 'Marital Disruption as a Stressful Life Event', in *Divorce and Separation: Context, Causes, and Consequences,* New York: Basic Books, 1979; and Regier, D.A. *et al.,* 'One-month Prevalence of Mental Disorders in the United States', *Archives of General Psychiatry,* 45, 1988, pp. 977-86.

71   *Surveys of Psychiatric Morbidity in Great Britain: Report 1. The Prevalence of Psychiatric Morbidity Among Adults Living in Private Households,* OPCS, London: HMSO, 1995.

72   *Western Australian Child Health Survey,* TVW Telethon, Institute for Child Health Research and the Australian Bureau of Statistics, 1996.

73   Kurdek, L.A., 'The Relations Between Reported Well-being and Divorce History, Availability of a Proximate Adult, and Gender', *Journal of Marriage and the Family,* Vol. 53, February 1991, pp. 71-78.

74   Briefing to the incoming Government Ministry of Women's Affairs, Wellington, 1996; and *All about Women in New Zealand,* Wellington: Statistics New Zealand, 1993.

75   Brown, G.W. and Moran, P.M., 'Single Mothers, Poverty and Depression', *Psychological Medicine,* 27, 1997, pp. 21-33. Mothers in couples had partners in manual occupations, while lone mothers were selected regardless of social class. Financial hardship among single mothers was 62 per cent at first contact and the same percentage had received public assistance for at least six of the previous 12 months, compared with 32 per cent and 11 per cent of couple women. For married women, the husband's unemployment, and irritable, hostile behaviour played a large

part in mediating economic pressures, resulting in depression. However, rates of humiliation/entrapment events for lone mothers were more than double those of married mothers, just as they experienced more loss and danger (usually involving a partner, lover, or a child and almost always criminal or troublesome behaviour), and had fewer or no close others. This largely explained their greater risk. Full-time work was also an important risk factor, despite this reducing financial hardship.

76 Blanchflower, D.G., Oswald, A.J., *Well-being Over Time in Britain and the USA*, Eurobarometer Series, 1999.

77 Wood, W. *et al.*, 'Sex Differences in Positive Well-Being: a Consideration of Emotional Style and Marital Status', *Psychological Bulletin*, Vol. 106, No. 2, 1989, pp. 249-64.

78 The proportion of the sample who are married changes from 72 per cent in the early 1970s to 55 per cent by the late 1990s in Britain and from 67 per cent to 48 per cent in the United States. Blanchflower and Oswald, *Well-being Over Time in Britain and the USA*, 1999.

79 The female age-standardised rate has been high compared with other countries, but relatively stable over time, being 5.6 in 1974 to 5.8 and 1993-98. *Human Development Report 2000*, United Nations Development Programme, Oxford: Oxford University Press, 2000, pp. 251-52.

80 *Suicide Trends in New Zealand 1974-94*, New Zealand Health Information Service, Wellington: Ministry of Health, 1997.

81 *Young New Zealanders*, Wellington: Statistics New Zealand, 1998.

82 *Young New Zealanders*, 1998.

83 *Maori in the New Zealand Economy*, Wellington: Ministry of Maori Development, 1999.

84 'The Suicide Index', reported in *Children*, No. 21, Office of the Commissioner for Children, June 1996.

85 Beautrais, A.L. Joyce, P.R. and Mulder, R.T., 'Risk Factors for Serious Suicide Attempts Among Youths Aged 13 Through 24 Years', *Journal American Academy of Child and Adolescent Psychiatry*, Vol. 35, No. 9, September 1996.

86 Eastman, M., 'Family Variables, Health Outcomes and National Strategies', *Threshold*, 56, 1997, pp. 14-25; and Ladbrook, D., 'Why Marriage Matters: an Australian Perspective', *Threshold*, 57, 1997, pp. 9-11. For Australia, the divorced/widowed have suicide rates over three times that of the married, and the never-married rates are almost three times the rate of the married. UK research shows that those who are separated, but not divorced, have suicide rates 20 times that of the married. A recent Australian study (Pierre Baume at Griffith University) of 4,000 suicides found that 70 per cent were related to relationship breakdown, where men were nine times more likely to commit suicide than women. Quoted in *To Have and to Hold*, a Report of the inquiry into aspects of family services, Canberra: House of Representatives Standing Committee on Legal and Constitutional Affairs, June 1998.

Stack, S., 'The Impact of Divorce on Suicide in Norway, 1951-1980',
Journal of Marriage and the Family, Vol. 51, 1989, pp. 229-38; 'The Effect
of Suicide in Denmark, 1961-1980', *The Sociological Quarterly*, Vol. 31,
1990, pp. 361-68; McCall, P.L. and Land, K.C., 'Trends in White Male
Adolescent, Young Adult, and Elderly Suicide: Are There Common
Underlying Factors?', *Social Science Research*, 23, 1994, pp. 57-81.

 See *To Have and to Hold*,1998. See also Buckingham, J., *Boy Troubles:
Understanding Rising Suicide, Rising Crime and Educational Failure*,
Policy Monograph, No. 46, Sydney: Centre for Independent Studies, 2000.

89 Breault, K.D., 'Suicide in America: The Test of Durkheim's Theory of
Religious and Family Integration, 1933-1980', *American Journal of
Sociology*, Vol. 92, 1986, pp. 651-52. See also Burr, J.A. *et al.*, 'Catholic
Religion and Suicide; the Mediating Effect of Divorce', *Social Science
Quarterly*, Vol. 75 No. 2, 1984, pp. 300-18. Stack, S., 'The Effect of Marital
Dissolution on Suicide', *Journal of Marriage and the Family*, Vol. 42,
1980, pp. 83-92; Stack, S., 'New Micro-level Data on the Effect of Divorce
on Suicide, 1959-1980: a Test of Two Theories', *Journal of Marriage and
the Family*, Vol. 52, 1990, pp. 119-552; and Smith, J.J, *et al.*, Marital
Status and the Risk of Suicide', *American Journal of Public Health*,
Vol. 78, No. 1, 1988, pp. 78-80.

90 Ladbrook, 'Why Marriage Matters: An Australian Perspective', 1997.

91 Kelly, S. and Bunting, J., 'Trends in Suicide in England and Wales, 1982-
96', *Population Trends*, 92, Office for National Statistics, Summer 1998.
The suicide rate for divorced men and women is respectively five and
three times higher than for married people. See also *The Funding of
Marriage Support: a Review by Sir Graham Hart*, London: Lord
Chancellor's Department, 1999.

92 McCall, P.L. and Land, K.C., 'Trends in White Male Adolescent, Young
Adult, and Elderly Suicide: Are There Common Underlying Factors?',
Social Science Research, 23, 1994, pp. 57-81. Between 1946 and 1988, the
suicide rate for adolescent white males aged 15-19, rose from approximately 3.5 to 19.5 per 100,000 of their population, and the rate for the
20-29-year-old age group rose nearly 200 per cent.

93 Stack, S. and Wasserman, I., 'Marital Status, Alcohol Consumption, and
Suicide: an Analysis of National Data', *Journal of Marriage and the
Family*, Vol. 55, 1993, pp. 1018-024.

94 Crum, R.M. *et al.*, 'Level of Education and Alcohol Abuse and Dependence
in Adulthood: a Further Inquiry', *American Journal of Public Health*, 83,
1993, pp. 830-37.

10: There Goes the Neighbourhood

1 Smith, D.J., 'Youth Crime and Conduct Disorders', in Rutter, M. and
Smith, D.J. (eds), *Psycho-social Disorders in Young People*, John Wiley &
Sons, 1996, p. 479.

2   Sampson, R. J., 'Crime in Cities: The Effects of Formal and Informal Social Control', in Reiss Jr, A.J. and Tonry, M. (eds), *Communities and Crime*, Vol. 8 in *Crime and Justice*, University of Chicago Press, 1987.

3   Smith, D. and Jarjoura, G.R., 'Social Structure and Criminal Victimisation', *Journal of Research in Crime and Delinquency*, Vol. 25, February 1988, pp. 27-52.

4   Wilson, W.J., *The Truly Disadvantaged*, University of Chicago, 1987.

5   Yang, B. and Lester, D., 'Crime and Unemployment', *The Journal of Economics*, Vol. 23, No. 1/2, pp. 215-22.

6   Sampson, R.J., 'Does an Intact Family Reduce Burglary Risks for Its Neighbours?', *Sociology and Social Research*, Vol. 71, 1987, pp. 404-07; Sampson, R.J., 'Crime in Cities: The Effects of Formal and Informal Social Control', in Tonry, M. and Morris, N., *Crime and Justice*, Chicago: University of Chicago Press, 1992.

7   Sampson, 'Does an Intact Family Reduce Burglary Risks for Neighbours?', 1987; Sampson, R.J. and Wooldredge, J.D., 'Linking the Micro- and Macro-level Dimensions of Lifestyle: Routine Activity and Opportunity Models of Predatory Victimisation', *Journal of Quantitative Criminology*, 3, pp. 371-93.

8   *Western Australian Child Health Survey*, TVW Telethon, Institute for Child Health Research and the Australian Bureau of Statistics, 1996.

9   Hill, M.A. and O'Neill, J., *Underclass Behaviors in the United States: Measurement and Analysis of Determinants*, City University of New York, Baruch College, 1993.

10   Glaeser, E.L., Sacerdote, B. and Schheinkman, J.A., 'Crime and Social Interaction', *The Quarterly Journal of Economics*, May 1996, pp. 507-48.

11   Knight, B.J. and West, D.J., 'Temporary and Continuing Delinquency', *British Journal of Criminology*, 15, 1975, pp. 43-50.

12   Reiss, A.J., 'Co-offending and Criminal Careers', in Tonry, M. and Morris, N., *Crime and Justice; A Review of Research*, Vol. 10, University of Chicago Press, 1988.

13   Page, D.,*Communities in the Balance*, York: Joseph Rowntree Foundation, 2000.

14   Sampson, R.J. and Laub, J.H., *Crime in the Making: Pathways and Turning Points through Life*, Cambridge, Mass: Harvard University Press, 1993.

15   Sampson and Laub, *Crime in the Making*, 1993.

16   Ritchie, J. and Ritchie, J., 'Child Rearing and Child Abuse: The Polynesian Context', in Kordin, J.E. (ed.), *Child Abuse and Neglect: Cross Cultural Perspectives*, Berkeley: University of California Press, 1981, pp. 197-98.

17 Steinberg, L., 'Single Parents, Step-parents, and the Susceptibility of Adolescents to Antisocial Peer Pressure', *Child Development*, 58, 1987, pp. 269-75.

18 Case, A.C. and Katz, L.F., *The Company You Keep: The Effects of Family and Neighbourhood on Disadvantaged Youths*, Cambridge, Mass: National Bureau of Economic Research Working Paper No. 3705, 1999; Brooks-Gunn, J. et al., *Neighbourhood Poverty: Context and Consequences for Children*, Vol. I, and *Policy Implications in Studying Neighbourhoods*, Vol. II, New York: Russell Sage, 1997.

19 Examination of the neighbourhood effects on US small subgroups, using microdata samples, strongly supports the hypothesis in relation to dropping out of school and teenage pregnancy. Crane, J., 'The Epidemic Theory of Ghettos and Neighbourhood Effects on Dropping Out and Teenage Childbearing', *American Journal of Sociology*, Vol. 96, No. 5, 1991, pp. 1226-59. See also Hogan, D.P. and Kitagawa, E.M., 'The Impact of Social Status, Family Structure, and Neighbourhood on the Fertility of Black Adolescents', *American Journal of Sociology*, 90, 1985, pp. 825-55.

20 Where, for example, only about four per cent of workers held high-status jobs, the probability of black males dropping out of school explodes upwards. The neighbourhood effects are almost 38 times greater below the key point than above it, and the effect among the worst neighbourhoods is more than 50 times greater than the effect in the middle. The few white females who live in the worst neighbourhoods are more like black females in terms of teenage child-bearing than whites. Both the sharpness of the increases in school drop-out and teenage child-bearing occur at virtually the same place in each distribution. Crane, 'The Epidemic Theory of Ghettos and Neighbourhood Effects on Dropping Out and Teenage Childbearing', 1991; Case and Katz, *The Company You Keep*, 1991.

21 Grogger, J., *Local Violence, Educational Attainment and Teacher Pay*, Working Paper, Cambridge Mass: National Bureau of Economic Research, 1997.

22 Corcoran, M., et al., 'Intergenerational Transmission of Education, Income and Earnings', unpublished manuscript, University of Michigan, 1987. In Case and Katz, *The Company You Keep*, 1991, peer influences were significant for criminality and drug use, but less significant in affecting the propensity of youths to have children out of wedlock or in idleness, where family effects were paramount. However, there is a discrepancy here between this study and others using tightly defined neighbourhoods when it comes to neighbourhood effects on out-of-wedlock child-bearing. Crane, 'The Epidemic Theory of Ghettos and Neighbourhood Effects on Dropping Out and Teenage Childbearing', *American Journal of Sociology*, 1991, finds strong neighbourhood influences on dropping-out behaviour and teenage pregnancy in a national sample using geographic neighbourhoods of similar size to the one's used in Case and Katz's analysis. Brooks-Gunn et al., 1991, also find evidence that a geographic neighbourhood's socioecomic mix is significantly related to adolescent behaviours (out-of-wedlock child-bearing and dropping out of school).

FAMILY MATTERS

23 Dench, G., *From Extended Family to State Dependency*, Centre for
Community Studies, Middlesex University, 1993, p. 7. See also Field, S.
and Southgate, P., *Public Disorder: A Review of Research and a Study in
one Inner City Area*, Study No. 72, London: HMSO, 1982; Moens, F.G.G. *et
al.*, 'Epidemiological Aspects of Suicide Among the Young in Selected
European Countries', *Journal of Epidemiology and Community Health*,
Vol. 42, 1988, pp. 431-47.

24 Akerlof, G., 'Men Without Children', *The Economic Journal*, Vol. 108,
1998, pp. 287-309.

25 Dench, *From Extended Family to State Dependency*, 1993, p. 61.

26 Matza, D., *Delinquency and Drift*, Chichester: John Wiley & Sons, 1964,
p. 55.

27 Reiss, A.J., 'Co-offending and Criminal Careers', in Tonry and Morris,
Crime and Justice: A Review of Research, 1988.

28 West, W.G., 'The Short-Term Careers of Serious Thieves', *Canadian
Journal of Criminology*, 20, 1978, pp. 169-90.

29 Farrington, D.P., 'The Development of Offending and Antisocial
Behaviour from Childhood: Key Findings from the Cambridge Study in
Delinquent Development', The Twelfth Jack Tizard Memorial Lecture,
Journal of Child Psychology and Psychiatry, 1995, p. 936.

30 Farrington, 'The Development of Offending and Antisocial Behaviour
from Childhood', 1995, p. 943.

31 Laub, J.H., Nagin, D.S. and Sampson, R.J., 'Trajectories of Change in
Criminal Offending: Good Marriages and the Desistence Process',
American Sociological Review, Vol. 63, 1998, pp. 225-38.

32 Akerlof, 'Men Without Children', 1998, p. 289.

33 Akerlof, 'Men Without Children', 1998, p. 289.

34 Graham, J. and Bowling, B., *Young People and Crime*, Home Office
Research Study 145, London: Home Office, 1995.

35 Akerlof, 'Men Without Children', 1998, p. 289. In the UK, there is a
relatively large group of young Caribbean men with so few bonds or
formal commitments that they are alienated from conventional standards,
resentful, in trouble with the law and a problem for race relations.
Berthoud, R., *Family Formation in Multi-Cultural Britain: Three Patterns
of Diversity*, ISER, University of Essex (undated).

36 Sherman, L.W., *Policing Domestic Violence*, New York: The Free Press,
1992, p. 248.

37 Zinsmeister, K., 'Fatherhood is Not for Wimps', *The American Enterprise*,
Sept/Oct 1999.

38 Will, G.F., 'Nature and the Male Sex', *Newsweek*, 7 June 1991.

39   James, B. and Saville-Smith, K., *Gender, Culture and Power—Critical Issues in New Zealand Society*, Auckland: Oxford University Press, 1989, p. 33.

40   Dench, *From Extended Family to State Dependency*, 1993, p. 74; Snarey, J. *et al.*, 'The Role of Parenting in Men's Psychosocial Development: a Longitudinal Study of Early Adulthood, Infertility and Mid-life Generativity', *Developmental Psychology*, Vol. 23, No. 4, 1987, pp. 593-603; and Sundeen, R.A., 'Family Life Course Status and Volunteer Behaviour', *Sociological Perspectives*, Vol. 33, No. 4, 1990, pp. 483-500.

41   Sampson, R.J., 'Urban Black Violence: The Effect of Male Joblessness and Family Disruption', *American Journal of Sociology*, Vol. 93, No. 2, 1987, pp. 348-82.

42   Suttles, G., *The Social Order of the Slum*, University of Chicago Press, 1968; and *The Social Construction of Communities*, University of Chicago Press, 1972.

43   Mead, L.M., 'Welfare Reform and the Family', *Family Matters*, Issue No. 54, Australian Institute of Family Studies, Spring/Summer 1999.

44   Jargowsky, P., *Poverty and Place: Ghettos, Barrios, and the American City*, New York: Russell Sage Foundation, 1997.

45   Smith, G., *Area-based Initiative: the Rationale and Options for Area Targeting*, CASE paper 25, London School of Economics, 1999.

46   Social Exclusion Unit, *Bringing Britain Together: a National Strategy for Neighbourhood Renewal*, Cm 4045, London: The Stationery Office, 1999.

47   Callister, P., 'Iron John or Ironing John?: The Changing Lives of New Zealand Fathers', in Birks, S. and Callister, P. (eds), *Perspectives on Fathering*, Palmerston North: Centre of Public Policy Evaluation, 1999.

48   The steep upturn in the early 1990s, has been related to the reduction in benefit rates and, particularly, the move from 'income related' rents to 'market related' rents in the public housing sector. Waldegrave, C. and Stuart, S., 'Out of the Rat Race: The Migration of Low-Income Urban Families to Small Town Wairarapa', *New Zealand Geographer*, 53, 1, 1997, pp. 22-29. See also Smiley, L. *et al.*, *Primary Needs Assessment*, Community Services Unit, Department of Social Welfare, Masterton, 1989; also Callister, P., '"Work-rich" and "Work-poor" Individuals, Families, Households and Communities: Changes Between 1986 and 1996', Working Paper for the Institute of Policy Studies, Victoria University, 1997.

49   Smith, J., Gilford, S. and O'Sullivan, A., *The Family Backgrounds of Homeless Young People*, London: Family Policy Studies Centre, 1998, p. 45.

50   Smith, Gilford and O'Sullivan, *The Family Backgrounds of Homeless Young People*, 1998, p. 23.

11: Feedback Loops and the Spiral of Decline

1   Patterson, S.M., *Divorce in New Zealand: A Statistical Study*, Wellington: Department of Justice, 1976.

2   Such social decay is not limited to present Anglo-Saxon democracies. In the old Soviet Union. '... the semi-serf intergenerational underclass of the so-called "limited people" (rural immigrant workers without permanent residence rights) and their children (many of whom are out-of-wedlock and placed in orphanages) constituted about 15 per cent of the Soviet urban population. The production of children became an instrument for single mothers to claim the most precious Soviet asset, public housing, and for establishing permanent urban residence. By some official Soviet estimates, this new Soviet underclass had a 78 per cent rate of intergenerational immobility.' Bernstam, M.S. and Swan, P.L., 'Malthus and the Evolution of the Welfare State: An Essay on the Second Invisible Hand', Working Paper 89-012, Australian Graduate School of Management, University of New South Wales, 1989, pp. 3-4.

3   Power, A., 'Area Problems and Multiple Deprivation', in *Persistent Poverty and Lifelong Inequality: the Evidence*, London: CASE and Her Majesty's Treasury, 1999.

4   Gregg, P. Harkness, S. and Machin, S., *Child Development and Family Income*, York: Joseph Rowntree Foundation, 1999. Also connected to later unemployment, low earnings, single parenthood and imprisonment are being in trouble with the law when young, playing truant or being in local authority care. Hobcraft, J. and Kiernan, K., *Childhood Poverty, Early Motherhood and Adult Social Exclusion*, CASEpaper 28, London: Centre for Analysis of Social Exclusion, 1999.

5   Third generation effects are apparent from the 1958 British cohort of the National Child Development Study. Gregg, P. and Machin, S., 'Child Development and Success or Failure in the Youth Labour Market', Centre for Economic Performance, London School of Economics and Political Science, 1998. See also Hill, M.A. and O'Neill, J., 'Family Endowments and the Achievement of Young Children with Special Reference to the Underclass', *The Journal of Human Resources*, XXIX, No. 4, pp. 1065-1100.

6   McLanahan, S., 'The Consequences of Single Parenthood for Subsequent Generations', *Focus*, Institute for Research on Poverty, University of Wisconsin-Madison, 1988.

7   Case, A.C. and Katz, L.F., *The Company You Keep: The Effects of Family and Neighbourhood on Disadvantaged Youths*, Working paper No. 3705, Cambridge, Mass: National Bureau of Economic Research, 1991.

8   Wallerstein, J.S. and Lewis, J., *The Unexpected Legacy of Divorce: A 25 Year Landmark Study*, Hyperion, 2000.

9   Fergusson, D., 'Family Formation, Dissolution and Reformation', in *Proceedings of the SSRFC Symposium: New Zealand Families in the Eighties and Nineties*, Canterbury University, No. 20, November 1987, pp. 15-30.

10 Kiernan, K., *The Legacy of Parental Divorce: Social, Economic and Demographic Experiences in Adulthood*, Casepaper 1, Centre for Analysis of Social Exclusion, London School of Economics, 1997; see also *Population and Household Change Research Results*, No. 4, Economic and Social Research Council, June 1997; Bradshaw, J. and Stimson, C., 'Nonresident Fathers in Britain' in Wertheimer, A. and McRae, S., *Research Results*, Economic and Social Research Council, Centre for Family and Household Research, Oxford, Brookes University, 1999.

11 Hobcraft, J., 'Intergenerational and Life-Course Transmission of Social Exclusion: Influences of Childhood Poverty, Family Disruption, and Contact with the Police', CASEpaper 15, London: STICERD Centre for Analysis of Social Exclusion, London School of Economics, 1998.

12 And by nearly a half—from 51 per cent more down to 27 per cent—for women.

13 Wertheimer, A. and McRae, S., 'Family and Household Change in Britain; A Summary of Findings from Projects in the ESRC Population and Household Change Programme', Centre for Family and Household Research, Oxford, 1999.

14 Bumpass, L.L., Martin, T.C. and Sweet, J.A., 'The Impact of Family Background and Early Marital Factors on Marital Disruption', *Journal of Family Issues*, 12, 1991, pp. 22-42.

15 Amato, P.R., 'Explaining the Intergenerational Transmission of Divorce', *Journal of Marriage and the Family*, Vol. 58, 1996, pp. 628-40.

16 Axinn, W.G. and Thornton, A., 'Premarital Cohabitation and Divorce: Selectivity or Causal Influence?', *Demography*, 29, 1992, pp. 357-74.

17 *Population and Household Change Research Results*, No. 4, ESRC, June 1997.

18 Hobcraft, J., 'Intergenerational and Life-Course Transmission of Social Exclusion: Influences of Childhood Poverty, Family Disruption, and Contact with the Police', CASEpaper 15, London: STICERD Centre for Analysis of Social Exclusion, London School of Economics, 1998.

19 Wertheimer and McRae, 'Family and Household Change in Britain: a Summary of Findings from Projects in the ESRC Population and Household Change Programme', 1999; also seen in National Child Development Study data Kiernan, K., *Transition to Parenthood: Young Mothers, Young Fathers—Associated Factors and Later Life Experiences*, STICERD Welfare State Programme, Discussion Paper WSP/113, London: London School of Economics, 1995.

20 From the American PSID (Panel Study of Income Dynamics) sample, Sara McLanahan calculated that living with a lone mother at age 16 increases a daughter's risk of becoming a female head of household during the next year by 72 per cent for whites and 100 per cent for blacks. Exposure at any time during adolescence increases the risk to 137 per cent for whites. Differences in the incomes of one- and two-parent families only seem to be related to a quarter of the difference. McLanahan, S.,

'Family Structure and Dependency: Early Transitions to Female
Household Headship', *Demography*, 25, No.1, 1988, pp.1-17. The National
Survey of Family Growth (involving 7,969 women aged 15-44 years),
found that women who spent time with a lone parent were 111 per cent
more likely to have teenage births, 164 per cent more likely to have premarital births and 92 per cent more likely to have failed marriages than
daughters who grow up in two-parent homes. This study could not control
directly for parental income, but very little of these effects could be
attributed to differences in family socio-economic status and they were
not affected by parental remarriage. The educational attainment of the
youngster had some effect only on the likelihood of teenage birth.
McLanahan, S. and Bumpass, L., 'Intergenerational Consequences of
Family Disruption', *American Journal of Sociology*, Vol. 94, No. 1, 1988,
p. 147.

21   Dornbusch, S.M. *et al.*, 'Single Parents, Extended Households, and the
      Control of Adolescents', *Child Development*, 56, 1985, pp. 326-41;
      Flewelling, R.L. and Bauman, K.E., 'Family Structure as a Predictor of
      Initial Substance Use and Sexual Intercourse in Early Adolescence',
      Journal of Marriage and the Family, Vol. 52, 1990, pp. 171-81; and
      Day, R.D., 'The Transition to First Intercourse among Racially and
      Culturally Diverse Youth', *Journal of Marriage and the Family*, Vol. 53,
      1991, pp. 573-84.

22   Hill, C., *Sex Under Sixteen?*, London: Family Education Trust, 2000.

23   Seidman, S.N., Mosher, W.D. and Aral, S.O., 'Predictors of High Risk
      Behaviour in Unmarried American Women: Adolescent Environment as a
      Risk Factor', *Journal of Adolescent Health*, 15, 1994, pp. 126-132.

24   Thornton, A., 'Influence of the Marital History of Parents on the Marital
      and Cohabitational Experience of Children', *American Journal of
      Sociology*, Vol. 96, No. 4, pp. 868-94.

25   Keith, V.M. and Kiernan, K.E., 'The Impact of Family Disruption in
      Childhood on Transitions made in Young Adult Life', *Population Studies*,
      46, 1992, pp. 213-34; Finlay, B., 'The Impact of Parental Divorce on
      Children's Educational Attainment, Marital Timing, and Likelihood of
      Divorce', *Journal of Marriage and the Family*, Vol. 50, 1988, pp. 797-809;
      and Miller, B.C. and Moore, K.A., 'Adolescent Sexual Behaviour, Preg-
      nancy and Parenting: Research Through the 1980s', *Journal of Marriage
      and the Family*, Vol. 53, 1991, p. 1,028; Brohlchain, M.N., Chappell, R.
      and Diamond, I., 'Educational and Socio-demographic Outcomes Among
      Children of Disrupted and Intact Marriages', *Population*, 49, 6, 1994, pp.
      1585-1612. Recently, Kiernan, K., 'Partnership Behaviour Across Nations
      and Generations: Continuities and Discontinuities and Inter-relations',
      Conference on 'Well-being and Dysfunction Across the Generations',
      Change and Continuity Centre for Analysis of Social Exclusion, London
      School of Economics, 25-27 October 2001.

26   Glezer, H, Edgar, D. and Prolisko, A., 'The Importance of Family
      Background and Early Life Experiences on Premarital Cohabitation and
      Marital Dissolution', Paper presented 'Family Formation and Dissolution:

East and West Perspectives', Taipei, May 1991, ISSP and Sun Yat Sen
Institute for Social Science, Academica Sinica, 1992.

27 Spruijt, E. and De Goede, M., 'Changing Family Structures and
Adolescent Well-being in the Netherlands', *International Journal of Law,
Policy and the Family*, 10, 1996, pp. 1-16.

28 Kiernan, K.E., 'Teenage Marriage and Marital Breakdown: A
Longitudinal Study', *Population Studies*, 40, 1986.

29 Glezer, Edgar and Prolisko, 'The Importance of Family Background and
Early Life Experiences on Premarital Cohabitation and Marital
Dissolution', 1992.

30 Keith and Kiernan, 'The Impact of Family Disruption in Childhood on
Transitions Made in Young Adult Life', *Population Studies*, 46, 1992.
Kinnaird, K. and Gerrard, M., 'Premarital Sexual Behaviour and
Attitudes Toward Marriage and Divorce Among Young Women as a
Function of Their Mother's Marital Status', *Journal of Marriage and the
Family*, Vol. 48, 1986, pp. 757-65; Nock, S.L., *The Sociology of the Family*,
Englewood Cliffs, NJ: Prentice Hill, 1987; and Michael, R. and Tuma, N.,
'Entry into Marriage and Parenthood by Young Men and Women:
Influence of Family Background', *Demography*, Vol. 22, 1985 pp. 515-44.

31 Hogan, D.P. and Kitagawa, E.M., 'The Impact of Social Status, Family
Structure, and Neighbourhood on the Fertility of Black Adolescents',
American Journal of Sociology, Vol. 90, 1985, pp. 825-55.

32 Mueller, C.W. and Pope, H., 'Marital Stability: a Study of Its Transitions
between Generations', *Journal of Marriage and the Family*, Vol. 39, 1977,
pp. 83-93.

33 Thornton, A. and Camburn, D., 'The Influence of the Family on
Premarital Sexual Attitudes and Behaviour', *Demography*, 24, 1987,
pp. 323-40.

34 Whitbeck, L.B., Simons, R.L. and Kao, M., 'The Effects of Divorced
Mothers' Dating Behaviours and Sexual Attitudes on the Sexual
Attitudes and Behaviours of Their Adolescent Children', *Journal of
Marriage and the Family*, Vol. 56, 1994, pp. 615-21.

35 Axinn, W.G. and Barber, J.S., 'Living Arrangements and Family
Formation Attitudes in Early Adulthood', *Journal of Marriage and the
Family*, Vol. 59, 1997, pp. 595-611.

36 Phillips, R., *Putting Asunder: A History of Divorce in Western Society*,
New York: Cambridge University Press, 1988; Cherlin, A.J., *Marriage,
Divorce, Remarriage*, Cambridge, Mass: Harvard University Press, 1981;
and Thornton, A., 'Changing Attitudes Towards Separation and Divorce:
Causes and Consequences', *American Journal of Sociology*, Vol. 90, No. 4,
1985, pp. 856-72; White, L.K., 'Determinants of Divorce: a Review of
Research in the Eighties', *Journal of Marriage and the Family*, Vol. 52,
1990, pp. 904-12.

37 Axinn, W.G. and Thornton, A., 'Premarital Cohabitation and Divorce: Selectivity or Causal Influence?', *Demography*, 29, 1992, pp. 357-74; Newcomer, S. and Urdry, J.R., 'Parental Marital Status Effects on Adolescent Sexual Behaviour', *Journal of Marriage and the Family*, Vol. 49, 1987, pp. 235-40.

38 Axinn and Thornton 'Premarital Cohabitation and Divorce: Selectivity or Causal Influence?', 1992; Masur, E., 'Developmental Differences in Children's Understanding of Marriage, Divorce, and Remarriage', *Journal of Applied Developmental Psychology*, 14, 1993, pp.191-212. In the analysis of the Study of Marital Instability over the Life Course, parents' 'nontraditional' attitudes and behaviour increased the chances that offspring cohabited either prior to, or instead of, marriage. Moreover, offspring who begin cohabiting relationships are more likely to end these without marrying if parents were reported as 'nontraditional'. Whitbeck, L.B., Simons, R.L. and Kao, M., 'The Effects of Divorced Mothers' Dating Behaviours and Sexual Attitudes on the Sexual Attitudes and Behaviours of Their Adolescent Children', *Journal of Marriage and the Family*, Vol. 56, 1994, pp. 615-21; also, see Thornton, A. and Camburn, D., 'The Influence of Family on Premarital Sexual Attitudes and Behaviour', *Demography*, 24, 3, 1987, pp. 323-40.

39 Glezer, Edgar and Prolisko, 'The Importance of Family Background and Early Life Experiences on Premarital Cohabitation and Marital Dissolution', 1992.

40 Axinn and Thornton 'Premarital Cohabitation and Divorce: Selectivity or Causal Influence?', 1992.

41 Axinn and Barber, 'Living Arrangements and Family Formation Attitudes in Early Adulthood', 1997.

42 Amato, P.R. and Booth, A., *A Generation at Risk*, Cambridge, Mass: Harvard University Press, 1997, pp. 118-19.

43 Goldscheider, F.K. and Kaufman, G., 'Fertility and commitment: bringing men back in', presented at the Workshop on Expanding Frameworks for Fertility Research in Industrialised Countries, National Research Council, Woods Hole, MA, 1994, p. 3. See also Jones, G.W., 'Review of William J. Goode, *World Changes in Divorce Patterns*', *Population and Development Review*, 20, 1994, pp. 899-901.

44 Dench, G., *The Place of Men in Changing Family Cultures*, London: Institute of Community Studies, 1996, p. 60.

12: Conclusion

1 National Science Foundation, *Investing in Human Resources: A Strategic Plan for the Human Capital Initiative*, Washington DC: National Science Foundation, 1994, p. 1.

2 Peden, J.R. and Glahe, F.R., *The American Family and the State*, Pacific Research Institute for Public Policy, reviewing work of Gabriel Marcel, 1986 p. 23; Fortes, M., *Rules and the Emergence of Human Society*,

Occasional Paper No. 39, Royal Anthropological Institute of Great Britain, 1983; and Sacks, J., *Faith in the Future*, London: Darton, Longman and Todd, 1995.

3   Ringen, S., *The Family in Question*, London: Demos, 1998, p. 16.

4   Strategic Directions Post-Election Briefing Paper 1996, Department of Social Welfare, 1996, p. 35.

5   'Traditional Family is Heading Into History', *The New Zealand Herald*, 16 May 2000.

6   With 'dysfunctional family relationships' held likely to significantly increase the likelihood of criminal offending and recidivism, the indicators for those at 'high risk' of entering cycles of disadvantage are children variously sole parented, highly mobile, in poor neighbourhoods, with low parental education and having parents who are long-term unemployed or benefit dependent. Strategic Directions Post-Election Briefing Paper 1996, Department of Social Welfare, 1996, p. 39.

7   Post-Election Briefing Paper New Zealand Community Funding Agency, Department of Social Welfare, 1996, p. 4.

8   Strategic Directions Post-Election Briefing Paper 1996, Department of Social Welfare, 1996, p. 35.

9   *Inquiry into Children in Education at Risk through Truancy and Behavioural Problems*, The Report of the Education and Science Committee, Wellington: Ministry of Education, 1995, p. 21.

10 McGeorge, P., *Report on Child, Adolescent and Family Health Services*, Ministry of Health, 1995.

11 Mead, L.M., 'Welfare Reform and the Family', *Family Matters*, Issue No. 54, Australian Institute of Family Studies, Spring/Summer 1999.

12 See Hardie Boys, Sir M., 3rd National Marriage Education Conference, the Catholic Diocese of Auckland, Auckland, 15 August 1997.

13 McPherson M.J., *Divorce in New Zealand*, Palmerston North: Social Policy Research Centre Massey University, 1995, p. 57.

14 *Inquiry into Children in Education at Risk Through Truancy and Behavioural Problems*, 1995, p. 21.

15 'The Social Development Approach', Ministry of Social Policy, Part 2, 2001, p. 10.

16 'The Social Development Approach', 2001, p. 8.

17 Saville-Smith, K., *Familial Caregivers' Physical Abuse and Neglect of Children: a Literature Review*, Child, Youth and Family Service and the Ministry of Social Policy, 2000, p. 32.

18 'The Social Development Approach', 2001, p. 2.

19 Dench, G., *The Place of Men in Changing Family Cultures*, London: Institute of Community Studies, 1996, p. 69.

20 Burgess, A., *The Erosion of Marriage: The Effect of Law on New Zealand's Foundational Institution,* Auckland: Maxim Institute, 2002, p. 61.

21 Burgess, *The Erosion of Marriage,* 2002, pp. 68-73.

22 Maley, *Family and Marriage in Australia,* 2001, p. 206.

23 A bill to establish the Families Commission is before parliament. The Commission is expected to start its work in July 2004. It is to be responsible for advocating for families and promoting a better understanding of family issues; promoting, funding and disseminating research into family issues; and contributing to policy development on family-related issues.

    The Commission is unlikely to focus on the erosion of the institution of marriage. In commenting on the intention to establish the Commission, Steve Maharey, the minister for social services and employment, said he 'welcomed the Families Commission's inclusive approach to New Zealand families. Questions of family ... structure are for people to decide for themselves. The Families Commission will concern itself with the issues faced by all New Zealand families, and by specific types of families'.

24 Maley, *Family and Marriage in Australia,* 2001, p. 207.

25 Maley, *Family and Marriage in Australia,* 2001, p. 208.

26 Maley, *Family and Marriage in Australia,* 2001, pp. 209-10.

27 Maley, B., *Wedlock and Well-Being,* Policy Monographs 33, Sydney: Centre for Independent Studies, 1996, p. 32.

28 White, L.K, 'Determinants of Divorce: A Review of Research in the Eighties', *Journal of Marriage and the Family,* Vol. 52, 1990, pp. 904-12.

29 Scott, E.S., 'Marital commitment and regulation of divorce' in Rowthorn, R. and Dnes, A.W. (eds), *The Law and Economics of Marriage and Divorce,* Cambridge University Press, 2002.

30 Gallagher, M., *The Abolition of Marriage: How We Destroy Lasting Love,* Washington DC: Regnery Publishing, 1996, p. 171.

31 Allen. D.W., 'The impact of legal reforms on marriage and divorce' in *The Law and Economics of Marriage and Divorce,* 2002, p. 196.

32 Johnson, W. and Skinner, J., 'Labor Supply and Marital Separation', *American Economic Review,* 76, 1986, pp. 455-69; and Parkman, A.M. 'Why Are Married Women Working So Hard?', *International Review of Law and Economics,* 18, 1998, pp. 41-49.

33 Maley, B., *Divorce Law and the Future of Marriage* CIS Policy Monograph 58, St Leonards, NSW: Centre for Independent Studies, 2003.

34 Rawls. J., *A Theory of Justice,* Cambridge, Mass: Harvard University Press, 1971, pp. 55-56.

35 See Phillips M., in Davis, E. and Phillips, M., *A Fruitless Marriage?,* London: Social Market Foundation 1999.

36 Mawson, P. and Scobie, G., 'Climbing the OECD Ladder: What Does New Zealand Have to Do? ', Wellington: The Treasury, 2001.

37 Green, D., *Poverty and Benefit Dependency*, New Zealand Business Roundtable, 2001, p. 77.

38 A voluntary agreement for the support of the custodial parents may be brought within the Child Support Scheme. Beneficiaries are required to apply for Child Support.

39 Inland Revenue Department, *Help You to Understand Child Support*, Wellington: Inland Revenue Department, 2002 and Inland Revenue Department, *Child Support: Calculating Child Support*, Wellington: Inland Revenue Department, 2003.

40 Inland Revenue Department, Briefing For Incoming Minister of Revenue, Wellington: Inland Revenue Department, 2002, pp. 40 and 51.

41 Maharey, S., 'Sole parents to receive more help to lift capacity', press release, New Zealand government, 6 March 2003.

42 Ringen, *The Family in Question*, 1998, p. 16.

Index